PATTERSON SMITH SERIES IN
CRIMINOLOGY, LAW ENFORCEMENT, AND SOCIAL PROBLEMS
A listing of publications in the SERIES *will be found at rear of volume*

THE LIFE AND WORK

OF

MARY CARPENTER.

Mary Carpenter.

Engraved by C.H. Jeens from a Photograph

PUBLICATION No. 145: PATTERSON SMITH SERIES IN
CRIMINOLOGY, LAW ENFORCEMENT & SOCIAL PROBLEMS

THE LIFE AND WORK

OF

MARY CARPENTER

BY

J. ESTLIN CARPENTER

SECOND EDITION

Reprinted with Index Added

MONTCLAIR, NEW JERSEY

PATTERSON SMITH

1974

First published 1879 by Macmillan & Company, London
Second edition 1881
Reprinted 1974 by Patterson Smith Publishing Corporation
Montclair, New Jersey 07042
New material copyright © 1974 by
Patterson Smith Publishing Corporation

Library of Congress Cataloging in Publication Data

Carpenter, Joseph Estlin, 1844–1927.
    The life and work of Mary Carpenter.

    (Patterson Smith series in criminology, law enforcement &
social problems. Publication no. 145)
    Reprint of the 2d ed., 1881, with index added.
    1. Carpenter, Mary, 1807–1877. I. Title.

HV28.C3C3   1974   361'.92'4 [B]   77–172564
                ISBN 0–87585–145–2

This book is printed on
permanent/durable paper

PREFACE TO THE FIRST EDITION.

THIS book is chiefly written as a record of work for workers. Its main object is to tell the story of a life of singular activity and far-reaching usefulness, in the hope that some who are engaged in the same or in like duties, may be helped by beholding the persistence of a woman's devotion. To them, perhaps, it will not seem amiss that her inmost springs of thought and feeling, her difficulties and discouragements, her cares and griefs, her self-appreciations and self-condemnations, as well as her achievements and successes, should be unsparingly revealed.

If others should read this book, and should deem that the reserve which befits a noble memory has been unduly violated, they are entreated to believe that the writer has sought only after truthfulness of presentment, being persuaded that no one would have demanded a loving fidelity more urgently than Mary Carpenter herself.

The trials which beset the way of those who labour in great causes, must needs be of many kinds. Over one grave obstacle this book relates a triumph,

gradual but sure. The members of small and misunderstood communions had frequently, at one time,
to encounter coldness and mistrust from without,
which tended to confine their friendships and restrain
their efforts. These limitations have for many years
been slowly breaking down beneath the influence of
a true sympathy with every sincere desire to realise
the Christian life. If this narrative shall add any
further evidence to the experience of the faithful,
that, beneath many varieties of form, the deepest
things are often essentially the same ; if it shall open
to any earnest heart the way to fruitful toil, or warn
it against inward danger, or cheer it in hours of
weariness,—its purpose will be fulfilled.

J. E. C.

November, 1879.

PREFACE TO THE SECOND EDITION.

THE kindly interest which this book has awakened in many quarters may warrant the writer in adding a few words of explanation concerning the materials available for the Biography of Mary Carpenter.

The records of her inner life were kept during the earlier years of womanhood with some copiousness ; but as her philanthropic labours became more and more engrossing, they were reduced to two or three entries annually, sometimes only of a few lines each. A single copybook held the memoranda of her last seven years, and was still unfilled at her death. Of her correspondence not much could be recovered. Various circumstances had led to the destruction of large numbers of valuable family letters. The incessant occupations in which the second half of her life was engaged, left her scarcely any time for communication of thought or feeling, except such as was directly concerned with her actual work; and her strong natural reserve prevented her from finding an outlet through this channel for the deeper emotions of her heart. To those, however, of her fellow-workers and friends who freely placed the letters in their possession at the author's disposal, his warmest thanks are due.

The events of Mary Carpenter's career were really chronicled in her books, her papers, and her institutions. Strong as was her personality, she concentrated it wholly on her immediate tasks, and some of the many elements in her nature, her intellectual and artistic culture, her social powers, her friendships, were sacrificed to the high demands which she had in part created for herself. Hence the story of her life must needs lack variety; the exaltation of a few interests to the greatest intensity necessarily contracts their range; at home or abroad—in England, in India, in America—there is one monotone of toil. Moreover, she was obliged to live much alone. The most cherished companion of all her joys and sorrows passed away before her; and some of her characteristic traits, though they left strong impressions on her fellow-workers, inevitably escaped record, and could not be reproduced in any memoir.

In spite, however, of defects of which none is more conscious than the writer, he is not without hope that the aim with which this book was first prepared will not be wholly unrealised.

J. E. C.

May, 1881.

CONTENTS.

CHAPTER I.
THE HOME.
1807–1833.

CHAPTER II.
THE SEED TIME OF PURPOSE.
1833–1840.

CHAPTER III.
THE WORK FOUND.
1841–1846.

CONTENTS.

CHAPTER IV.

THE RAGGED SCHOOL.

1846–1850.

CHAPTER V.

THE WIDENING AIM.

1850–1852.

CHAPTER VI.

REFORMATORY WORK.

1853–1857.

CHAPTER VII.

FROM RAGGED SCHOOLS TO CONVICTS.

1856–1866.

CHAPTER VIII.

INDIA.

1866–1870.

CHAPTER IX.

PRISON REFORM IN ENGLAND AND AMERICA.

1870–1873.

CHAPTER X.

THE WORK CROWNED.

1874–1877.

APPENDIX.

INDEX.

CHAPTER I.

THE HOME.

1807—1833.

'Our object throughout, in our endeavours to bring up our children religiously, must be to give the affections which we cultivate in their minds towards God, as much power as possible as *actuating motives*; to give them as much influence as possible over the other dispositions and the conduct. We are not to leave this till the affections, by frequent impressions, acquire great firmness and vividness; but to aim to give them their proportional influence in every stage of their progress.

'It cannot be doubted that religious *obedience* is the best means of cultivating, supporting, and confirming the religious *affections*: that habitual regard to the will of God, where ideas respecting Him are tolerably correct, will always cherish the love of God where it exists, and will gradually produce it where before it did not exist.'

From 'Principles of Education,' by Lant Carpenter.

THE

LIFE AND WORK OF MARY CARPENTER.

CHAPTER I.

THE HOME.

1807—1833.

MARY CARPENTER was born at Exeter on April 3rd, 1807. Two sisters and three brothers afterwards made up the home circle ; but she never lost the consciousness that she was the eldest, and clung with a tender tenacity to her place in the family group as the 'first-born.' Her father, Dr. Lant Carpenter, had recently settled in Exeter as one of the ministers of the congregation worshipping in George's Meeting. His Nonconformist ancestry had for a century been connected, nearly or remotely, with the ministry ; and the peculiarly earnest spirit of devotion which marked his life and thought, descended in the fullest measure to his daughter Mary. Her mother possessed a like deeply religious nature. The Penn family to which she belonged were, like her husband's, originally Nonconformists. Most of them had been orthodox; but, in passing out of the old traditional lines of faith, Anna Penn had not lost the fervour or intensity of spiritual feeling nurtured within them, though she often thought it needful in the busy hours of family and school life to repress their outward manifestation, and confided to none the touching records of her inner struggles.[1] No one who saw only the calm and well-ordered home, the

---

[1] These were preserved in a diary irregularly kept, but carried down to her last years.

school in which Dr. Carpenter's learning and character impressed themselves with uncommon force and beauty, the active pastorate filled with public and private labours of philanthropy, would have suspected what bitter confessions of unfulfilled duty, what mournful utterances of unrealised aspiration, were poured forth in the solitary hours of the wife and mother who took so large a share of the burden. If in after days similar confessions were wrung from Mary Carpenter, it was because a nature of extreme sensitiveness had been early trained to measure itself by the highest standards, and to exact from itself the most scrupulous performance.

But the spirit of the home-life in which the child was reared, was never that of stiff and formal piety, or of gloom and unrest; its earnestness was not oppressive, only healthful and bracing, and abundant room was given for the free play of every activity. The mother, who had much penetration, and also a keen sense of humour, noted already the first signs of character in the baby of thirteen months old; 'she had her father's love of order, and busied herself 'a good deal in putting things in their places.' At another time the childish self-importance burst into harmless display, to the amusement of the elders, for her mother wrote, in November, 1808 : 'The little sweet lamb' (Anna, the second child, born September 17th, 1808) 'would engage almost all 'my attention, did not the young doctor, with her funny 'ways and curious speeches, make me attend to her whether 'I will or not. You will wonder at my giving her that 'name, but she gave it herself. Some time ago she was 'very pleased with being called Mary; afterwards she 'insisted on being called Miss Mary; next, that would not 'do, she must be called Miss Carpenter, and lately she said 'to the nurse : "No Miss Mary." "What am I to call '"you then?" said nurse. "Dr. Carpenter," was the young 'lass's reply.' A ready grasp of facts, an exceedingly tenacious memory, and quick sensibility, rendered the ordinary process of education easy, and her earliest impressions were never obliterated. 'I took the little dear with me up David's 'Hill,' reported Mrs. Carpenter to her sisters, in August, 1809. 'I told her I believed she had never been there 'before. "Yes, mamma, I believe I have." I asked her 'who brought her. "You did, mamma." I told her I

'thought she was mistaken. "No, mamma, I believe not ;
' " you did bring me here in a chaise," which was the
' matter of fact. The beginning of last July twelvemonth,
' when she was just a year and a quarter old, we went up
' David's Hill in a chaise on our way to Crediton.' Amid
her lightest hours, however, some larger interests often sought
to enter, and the ordinary pursuits were constantly abandoned for an unexpected sobriety of thought. Her father
one day took the two sisters for a walk, and led them into a
field of new-mown hay. To roll in the sunshine like the
little Anna was not enough for the elder Mary, who saw the
haymakers busily at work. 'I want to be ooseful, I want
' to be ooseful,' she cried, and would not be satisfied till her
father cut a stick from the hedge, with which she might rake
together what her sister scattered. So early did she sound
the key-note of the after time.

At three years old she had already begun to receive from
her father that quickening of her moral and religious affections which made him ever afterwards the guide and inspirer
of her life, the interpreter to her of divine things. The first
notions of religion were solemn, but with a simple gladness,
and they found their way to her heart through the love and
gentleness which surrounded her. To this she responded at
once, comprehending with ready sympathy the essence alike
of Christian trust and sacrifice. In the summer of 1810 the
parents and children were at the sea-side, where they were
joined by a friend, with whom the conversation one day
turned on the character of Jesus. Dr. Carpenter dwelt on
it, as his manner was, with overflowing devotion, and ended
by saying how strange it was that he who felt its beauty so
vividly should be so far from following its example. 'But
' you are very like the good Jesus, indeed,' said Mary,
looking up from her dinner, on which she had appeared
intent. Her father checked her, but when the child
earnestly persisted, his friend asked her why she thought so.
Taking heart with this encouragement, she related several
acts of self-denial which she had observed in her father,
ending each by saying, 'And that was very like the good
' Jesus,' and finally added : 'Last night papa took me a
' walk, and when we were coming back, the sea was come
' up under the rocks, and papa thought mamma would
' be frightened if we went all the way back again, so he

'took off his shoes and stockings and carried me through
'the sea, and that was very like the good Jesus.'

A little later she has caught the missionary enthusiasm which
mingles with her studies and her home dramas. 'Mary's
'mind is constantly occupied by some magnificent scheme
'or other; she may have difficulty in getting her sum done
'or her multiplication table learnt, but she does not go to
'sleep over it; her attention is occupied by some plan for
'converting the heathen, or turning her doll's frocks into
'pelisses.' The dolls indeed exercised a tranquillising
influence on an intellect to which the world was constantly
presenting new problems. Now she was eagerly following
the fate of the parts of a sea-anemone when divided into
two; or boldly plunged into the metaphysical labyrinth of
necessity and free-will; but from these excursions she con-
tentedly returned to 'the grand affairs of her dolls.' The
buoyant energy of her nature had as yet encountered no care,
and poured itself forth in 'an unceasing flow of animal
'spirits,' to which experience and observation had already
added 'a never-failing stock of good sense.' 'I never saw
'such a little animal as Mary,' wrote her mother, in 1815.
'She is now as intent upon dressing wax dolls and making
'wax candles as if she never had an idea beyond, and yet
'her little mind is capable of more than most of our lads
'are capable of.' To these traits may be added a large
generosity and disinterestedness, which found abundant
scope towards her two younger sisters and the circle of her
companions; and a delight in being the object of affection,
which, if it exposed her afterwards to bitter trials, nevertheless kept her heart fresh for seventy years. Already at the
age of three, she had said that 'the good God had given her
'a great deal of love;' and this was the chief happiness
which bound her afterwards to the neglected, who found
their friend in her. Her mother, indeed, predicted that she
would often feel too much to act with energy; but she then
hardly knew how strongly she was herself to impress upon
her daughter the necessity of controlling excess of feeling
beneath a resolute purpose of duty.

The removal of her father from Exeter to Bristol in 1817,
to become one of the ministers of the congregation of the
Lewin's Mead Meeting, laid the first young sorrow upon
Mary Carpenter. The fibres of her life were too deeply

rooted in the familiar scenes to bear transplanting without injury; and she never again felt the same perfect and unclouded happiness which had sprung from the freedom and joyousness of her first decade. To return to her old friends from time to time was one of her greatest pleasures; there no anxiety gathered round the story of her father's work, and no shadow of death hung over the much-loved home. Not even half a century dulled the vividness of remembrance. After attending the meeting of the British Association at Exeter in 1869, she wrote : ' It was so ' pleasant, a joy unmixed with any painful feeling, to see ' the places familiar to us in childhood, the very house ' where we lived, the dear old chapel. And so delightful ' also to find his memory cherished, and the institutions he ' planted flourishing.'

The life at Bristol proved far more stimulating than the quieter circle of duties and interests now left behind; and Dr. Carpenter's activity led him into wide and far-reaching plans, with which his eldest daughter early learned to sympathise. A lecture-room was built adjoining the chapel, where tender associations gathered about the familiar instruction which he gave to the young, and the courses of lectures, explanatory of the Scriptures, which he delivered to the more advanced. A Sunday school was established, in which ere long Mary Carpenter was permitted to teach a class of boys, the management of the girls' branch of it afterwards devolving largely upon her. When the Literary and Philosophical Institution was founded, Dr. Carpenter was an active coadjutor of the little band, which included Conybeare, De la Beche, Prichard, names well known in the history of English science; and his house was long a centre of intelligent culture, which had a most quickening effect upon its inmates. Of this Mary was the most fitted, alike by position and powers, to feel the advantage. Her place, however, was fixed first of all in the home and in the school, where she was associated in some classes with the youths under her father's care. Her studies were carried considerably beyond the range at that time usually open to girls, and included Latin, Greek, and Mathematics, with some of the elements of physical science and natural history. Homer and Sophocles early roused her enthusiasm together with

Shakespeare and Scott; and the familiarity which she gained with the mysteries of the air-pump and the contents of the geological cabinet, gave variety and illustration to her teaching, long years after all opportunity of acquiring new knowledge had ceased. The exactness which her father demanded in all learning, and the independence of judgment which he strove to foster, became part of her mental habits. In later life, indeed, her interest in intellectual pursuits was merged in the labours of philanthropy; yet her capacity for apprehending the underlying principles on which well-considered schemes of social reform must be based, without neglecting minute accuracy of detail in their development, indicated abilities of no common order. These found their object, indeed, under the mingled inspiration of duty and affection, among the poor and outcast of society; but first received their training on the ground of literature and history, of science and philosophy. She had not long been in the school before her quiet stedfastness made itself felt with not less power than her attainments. 'Mary and Anna,' wrote her mother in the summer of 1820, 'have for some time 'past been two complete schoolboys, and it is to their 'honour that though each has been the head of their respec-'tive classes, they are very much beloved by their school-'fellows. Mary has very great influence among the boys, 'and with her gentle voice and mild but firm expostulation 'can maintain an astonishing degree of order among them.' Indeed a tradition was long current of a time when the empty desk of the father, whom illness kept away, was filled as a matter of course by the girl, under whose supervision, assisted by her schoolfellow James Martineau,[1] the lessons went on without disturbance of their usual course. To the picture which that schoolfellow once drew of the teacher and his work,[2] he now adds a sketch of the occasional companion of his studies.

London, December 20, 1878.

MY DEAR MR. CARPENTER,

Thirty-seven years ago I put on record, at the request of his biographer, a few recollections of your grandfather's

---

[1] The Rev. James Martineau, D.D., LL.D.
[2] *Memoir of Lant Carpenter, LL.D.*, by R. L. Carpenter, B.A., 1842, p. 342.

household during my school years. The chief figure in the
picture which I had then to call up naturally stood out in very
strong lights of memory, which rendered it easy to reproduce
it with some minuteness of detail. A man must be without
head or heart who, by mid-life, could forget such a master as
Dr. Lant Carpenter, or remember him without affectionate
veneration. But it is not easy, at double that age, to recover
distinct vision of a figure then quite secondary, and moving
only in the shadowy background of the scene; and in yielding
to your request for some contemporary impressions of your
Aunt Mary's childhood, I am led rather by a veteran's impulse
of friendship than by any hope of adding a single lineament to
the portrait you will have to draw.

It was in the summer of 1819 that I became a pupil of your
grandfather's—a sallow stripling of fourteen, of shy and
sensitive temperament, but superficially hardened by the rude
discipline of a public school. Of the twelve pupils, nearly half
were my superiors or equals in age: and we formed together
an upper class with studies distinct from the juniors. This
association, however, did not extend to all our pursuits. While
we had the same lessons in science, in history, in geography,
and in the Greek Testament, a regard for our unequal proficiency and different destinations threw us into smaller
groups for classics and mathematics; and in the latter especially, from their importance to my intended profession of
civil engineer, I had to work alone. At two or three points,
this round of studies brought us into contact with Mary
Carpenter.

A boy's impressions of new companions is necessarily
relative to his own family experience. And I well remember
the kind of respectful wonder with which, coming from free
and easy ways with my sisters, I was inspired towards the
sedate little girl of twelve, who looked at you so steadily and
always spoke like a book; so that, in talking to her, what you
meant for sense seemed to turn into nonsense on the way. In
her exterior, as in her mental characteristics, she seemed to be
no longer the child. With a somewhat columnar figure and no
springiness of movement, she glided quietly about and was
seldom seen to run, and a certain want of suppleness and
natural grace interfered with her proficiency in the usual
feminine accomplishments with the needle, at the piano, and
in the dance, and occasioned a pleasant surprise when, taking
her pencil and colour-box in hand, she revealed the direction
in which her sense of beauty could conquer difficulties and
enable her really to excel. The early maturity which is so
often reached by the eldest in a family was strongly marked
in her countenance; not by any look of forwardness or careless
ease, still less by any seeming hardness against sympathetic

impressions from others, but by a certain fixity of thoughtful
attention, and the clear self-possession which arises from self-
forgetfulness. There were traces upon that grave young face
if my memory does not mislead me, of an inward conflict for
ascendency between the anxious vigilance of a scrupulous
conscience and the trustful reverence of a filial heart, tender
alike to the father on earth and the Father in heaven.

In the public grammar-schools sixty years ago the really
efficient teaching was almost limited to Greek and Latin, with
the subsidiary mythology and history ; and I never can forget
the shame I felt on discovering at Bristol the depths of my
ignorance of the natural world and of modern times. Mrs.
Carpenter had an extraordinary knowledge of geography, and
taught it to her children and the pupils with admirable fulness
of both physical description and historical incident ; and, in
comparison particularly with Mary Carpenter, I soon found
myself a simpleton in this field, and looked up to her as an
oracle. She appeared to me to have the world, and all that
had happened in it, at her fingers' end, as if she had been
always and everywhere in it ; whilst I could only blunder
through the counties and the kings of England, and could
make a better map of Greece than of Great Britain. This
feeling of humiliation was not abated by Mrs. Carpenter's
willingness (doubtless with a view to stimulate emulation) to
play upon it with ridicule, or with compassionate excuses that
were very like contempt; but at all events it had its compensations in the sincere respect with which it filled me for
the well-informed and unassuming girl who picked up my
dropped answers and corrected my mistakes.

It was not, I think, till the second of my Bristol years that
Mary Carpenter joined the older pupils in certain special
lessons. Successive courses of instruction were given on
geology, on natural philosophy, and chemistry, with illustra-
tive specimens, diagrams, and experiments; but interesting
as they were to us, I recall nothing memorable with regard to
her personal share in the work. Her Latin reading, which I
seem to associate most with the *Agricola* of Tacitus, was
marked by the same conscientious care which she evinced in
everything; securing accuracy, but not escaping stiffness,
unless, at the appeal of some pathetic passage which softened
more than the outer voice, it assumed for the moment a higher
character, and admitted a gleam of poetic light. Of these
exceptional touches I retain the most lively impression,
because through some difference of temperament I was not in
general much moved by the things which most satisfied her
taste in literature, poetry, and art : so that where a real chord
of sympathy was struck the tones have naturally vibrated
long.

Every Monday morning we had a Greek Testament reading with Dr. Carpenter, intended not less as a religious lesson than as an exercise in the language and criticism of Scripture. That hour was always one of deep interest, and left, I am persuaded, lasting traces on the character of many a boy previously averse to serious thought. The influences of Sunday were still fresh. Upon the dear master they were visible in a certain toning down of his usual restless energy, and a serenity and tenderness of spirit which removed all fears and all reserves, and often made the lesson an exchange of confidences among us all. To his daughter he was prophet as well as parent, and her whole mood and demeanour reflected his. While translating her verses with precision, and prepared with answers to questions of history and archæology, she unconsciously betrayed, by voice, by eye, by the very mode of holding her book, that she treated the text as sacred, and in following its story felt a touch from which a divine virtue went out. The Gospels were certainly read with critical care and faithful comparison; and if the hopelessness of the harmonist's problem was unfelt, and the plain anachronisms of thought were unobserved, and its hills and valleys were levelled to one highway of sanctity, it was because an absorbing veneration for the person of Christ as supernatural filled the teacher's whole mind, and excluded the finer perceptions of the historical sense, and even obscured the gradations of spiritual character. I suspect that this early set of her religious affections, carried out as it was through her whole inner and outer life, rendered the newer lights of biblical criticism always unwelcome to Mary Carpenter, and made her glad to seek her reforming inspirations in purely practical directions.

Similar in its nature and influence was the Sunday lesson, in which also she was our companion. We had not, indeed, always the same subjects; at one time Paley's *Natural Theology*, at another his *Evidences of Christianity*, formed our text-book. But my most considerable memory is of certain Notes and Observations on the Gospels, which Dr. Carpenter wrote for us, and sent to press as they were produced. They remained a fragment; but, as far as they went, they supplied all that was necessary to render the study of the Evangelical History intelligible and interesting. In this class, too, it was a matter of course that Mary's answers were exact and complete, and rendered so less by superior intelligence than by deeper interest, being subsidiary to a picture on which her inner eye was reverently fixed. The remainder of the day was so distributed as to leave no room for listless idleness, and yet to infuse into it a bright though serious repose; and her profound entrance into its spirit,

manifest in a certain air of quickened yet calmer life, has left
with me an indelible image still prominent among the contents
of those delightful days.   Even her figure, in listening to her
father's services at Lewin's Mead Meeting-house, rises distinctly before me as I write.   For, instead of having my place
with the other pupils in the long line of the family pew, I
usually sat with an aunt in a seat at right-angles to the other,
and with a near front-view of it.   And as I now range in
thought over its series of vanished forms, not one of them is
clearer than that intent young daughter, lost to herself and
all around, and surrendered to the sweet pieties that flowed
upon that winning voice.   And at the end of the day, when
evening prayers and supper were over and the juniors had
gone to bed, and the rest of us lingered for a precious half-
hour of serious talk, she was privileged to sit with her arm in
her father's—sometimes as a silent listener, at others helping
us to draw from him his thoughts on some problems that
perplexed us; or, in lighter moods, tempting him to tell the
stories of his college days.   From these Sunday evenings we
seemed to go to rest with better-ordered minds and warmer
hearts.

    Sometime during my two years at Bristol (I think it was
shortly after your uncle Philip's birth) Mary Carpenter was
laid up with a long and painful affection of the eyes, requiring
her to live for many weeks in a darkened room, and abstain
from all attempt to use her sight.   The illness involved not
only privation, but anxiety; for there was serious danger of
its ending in blindness.   To few natures could the passiveness
to which she was then reduced be more trying than to her.
But her patience and sweetness of disposition remained perfect
throughout; and her ingenuity was never at fault in saving
trouble to others by acting as general memory and time-
keeper with regard to all household arrangements as they
came due.   These characteristics would naturally go to the
hearts of her parents, and appear to them in the brightest
light.   But I believe that my impression of them is due rather
to the testimony of her medical attendant, Mr. Estlin, whose
experience and temperament protected him from enthusiasm,
and who spoke of her spirit through this illness with an
unwonted warmth.[1]

---

[1] From an early age she had found much pleasure in composing
verses, and this illness, and the devoted care of her sister Anna, she
thus shortly after described :

        Two sisters were together in a room
        Cheerless and dark.   The elder mourning sat,
        Suffering, dejected, for no more she hailed

On looking back at these slight notes, I think it possible that they give too solemn an air to the young figure which they attempt to sketch. Two causes may have contributed to this. Of the two sisters nearest in age, Mary and Anna, whom one always remembers together, the latter was so gleeful and kindling that, beside her, many a bright nature would look grave. And then, the eldest daughter of the family could not have been the companion of our studies without some habitual exercise of discretion and reserve; nor was she our associate except at times of serious interest or pursuit. If I have dwelt too exclusively on the more earnest aspects of her early life, it is simply that the lighter play of her character was reserved for other witnesses, few of whom, I fear, survive to tell the pleasant tale.

Believe me always,

Yours very faithfully,

JAMES MARTINEAU.

The young girl was, in truth, as so often happens with the eldest of a large family, the centre on which the equipoise of various interests was maintained; so that when she was away, there seemed to be less ease in harmonising conflicting claims and reconciling opposite interests. 'Mary and 'Russell,' wrote her mother in 1823, 'were absent from 'home a little more than three weeks, and I felt her 'increased judgment and usefulness by the evils which

> The bright return of morn; the sun's blest rays
> To her were agony. With hanging head
> She sat where most the gloom o'ershadowed her.
> The other seemed the very soul of youth
> And girlish beauty. She had left her play,
> And, full of tenderness and sympathy,
> Was reading to her sister. In her voice
> Was mixed such kind solicitude and love
> As touched the sufferer's heart; she raised her eyes
> To snatch one painful hasty glance, and saw
> A countenance so lovely! On it fell
> The only beams that stole into the room,
> And brightened that sweet face, so full of love!
> One look sufficed; and often as she lay
> Suffering the tedious nights, and when she mourned
> The long and darksome day, she mused upon
> That dear and beauteous vision; when her eyes
> Refused her wonted office, then she saw
> Rise in imagination that sweet form,
> Cheering her solitude.

'arose from her absence. She seemed to be the bond of
'union to the whole family.'

Beneath all her outward gravity, however, she had a
strong sense of the humorous, which, indeed, she never lost ;
and among her closest intimates this often expressed itself in
innocent fun. But it was not long before advancing years
brought with them anxieties, beneath the pressure of which
the sportiveness of her childhood quite passed away. The
affection of her eyes, which had twice threatened her sight,
withdrew her for long periods from her customary occupations, and in the visits to South Devon, to Wales, to
Malvern, on which she was frequently sent to restore her
strength, she had leisure to reflect at once on her family
circumstances and her own character. She saw her father
bearing a burden of work, domestic and educational, pastoral
and literary, plainly too much for his strength, and she
eagerly rushed to the rescue with plans by which he might
be relieved of his school, and part of the toil transferred to
her mother, to her sister Anna, and to herself. For this she
steadily began to prepare herself from the age of seventeen,
letting no opportunity slip by for securing some fresh qualifi-
cation, and already even taking a share in the teaching of the
younger pupils. Meanwhile she scrutinised her conduct with
unflinching keenness, and recorded, sometimes from week to
week, sometimes at longer intervals, the results of her intro-
spection. The daily faults of the home life, the irritability
born of frequent suffering, the conceit fostered by the atten-
tions she received in illness, the mortification of her desire to
be thought agreeable, her inattention to the thoughts and
wishes of those around her, her disappointment when those
for whom she had made little sacrifices failed to display the
expected gratitude, her unwillingness to own herself in the
wrong, or to allow herself to be considered in the wrong
when she had actually been in the right; all these, and
many another incident of temper, are unsparingly set down ;
every failure is confessed, but again the bitter avowal is
repeated—'the evil that I would not, that I do.' Her
consciousness of power early brought with it a peculiar
desire to excel. 'I used to fancy,' she wrote in 1826, 'that
'I could not pass through life with any tolerable comfort
'unless I became distinguished in some way ;' but she found
quiet of heart in the saying that 'the highest and most

' difficult attainment of any is a resignation to be as mean
' an agent and as unsuccessful a one as God pleases to make
' us.' She would have been content indeed with the reflected
distinction of being her father's child ; but the illness which
had been long dreaded, now compelled him to abandon all
his work, and robbed her of even this source of self-satisfac-
tion. ' I *have* gloried in being the daughter of one who
' has justly gained the esteem and love of all by his endea-
' vours to promote the happiness and well-being of others.
' Now he is suffering and cast down; let me make his affliction
' useful to myself by lowering my pride of heart.' It was
with poignant regret that she saw, or thought she saw, others
more able to meet the crisis than herself. ' I see almost
' everyone around me,' she wrote in November, 1826, ' excel-
' ling me in something. My mother possesses a firm and
' lively faith which I shall be very long before I attain ; my
' Anna shows a far greater firmness and presence of mind in
' trial than I do ; one shames me by a sweet obliging dis-
' position, another by a readiness to amend, and gentleness
' when censured.' One of the greatest trials attending her
father's illness and consequent absence, was the loss of his
daily guidance and support ; the confidence and help which
he gave her were for a time withdrawn ; and she who
desired in her turn to sustain others, found that she was
unable to stand alone. But the discovery of her weakness
brought her new strength ; and in the spring of 1827 she
accepted the charge of some young girls in the Isle of Wight,
and left home with a spirit already matured by no ordinary
experience.

Her sojourn in the Isle of Wight, though it restored
her to occasional intercourse with her father, who stayed
for some time at Newport, brought at first its own difficulties, but helped by degrees to tranquillise her mind.
With her strong literary tastes, she felt acutely her isolation
from the accustomed sources of interest : ' You cannot think,'
she wrote, ' what a change I find this in an intellectual
' point of view ; here the subjects which at home are the
' most common topics of conversation are scarcely noticed,
' and I have been so long now with those who are well
' acquainted with our best poets, that it seems quite strange
' to find them here scarcely known at all.' She was not,
however, altogether without compensations. She had always

been profoundly susceptible to the influence of natural scenery, and the numerous excursions and visits of her girlhood had given her unusual opportunities of enjoying it; and this, together with her strong religious feeling, easily led her to an earnest admiration of Wordsworth, which had been largely stimulated by her former schoolfellow Mr. Martineau, now once more in Bristol, taking the chief part in the management of her father's school. In the Isle of Wight she found much to harmonise with the teachings of the Excursion and Tintern Abbey; and she had occasionally the solace of communion with a disciple like herself: 'Mrs. R. is of course a great Wordsworthian, and admires 'Peter Bell, which, by the way, I have never read; but as 'I wish to continue a Wordsworthian, I do not mean to read 'his trash. (It is well Mr. Martineau is not by.)'

With the completion of her twenty-first year, she was welcomed in lively strains by her aunt Bache, to whom, in after years, she looked back as one of her early helpers, into the venerable band of 'female majoritans,' who had the privilege of remaining at the age of 'one-and-twenty and 'upwards.' But Mary Carpenter was too much oppressed with the solemnity of existence to reply to this raillery, and she left the Isle of Wight, a few weeks later, feeling that she had made her first great experiment in the work of life with undetermined success.

After a brief sojourn at home she again set forth to Odsey,[1] near Royston; and in her new circumstances and fresh and more congenial companionship, found with alarm that serious injury had been wrought in her by her seclusion in the Isle of Wight, where everything she said had been received as an oracle. In an agony of self-abasement she felt herself wholly unworthy of the divine favour, and poured out her misery to her mother, whose firm grasp at last restored her calm without need of the doctrine of the Atonement, on which she was at one time ready to fling herself in despair. 'I am not sorry,' she wrote at last, 'that my attention has been turned to the doctrine of 'Atonement, for now when reading the Scriptures I find so

---

[1] The house of J. G. Fordham, Esq., with whose family Mary Carpenter maintained to the last affectionate intercourse.

'many texts strongly against it, that I do not think I can
' ever again embrace such a doctrine while I keep to the
' Scriptures.'

In the meantime she was assiduously keeping up her own
mental culture, poetry being still her predominant interest,
though biography began already to fascinate her; and the
attention which she had early been trained by her father
to bestow on passing events, now enabled her to form
independent judgments on the policy of the Government.
At one time she is busy with the *Epicurean* of Moore,
' respecting which you know that Mr. Martineau and I had
' a grand discussion. I read it rather as a penance. My
' opinion of it remains much the same. I do not like a
' garden filled with nothing but gaudy flowers.' Next it
is *Zeluco:* 'I never so much repented undertaking to get
' through a book. Whenever I read of wicked people I
' always dream of them; and thus I have had a double
' portion of *Zeluco.*' Then it is Virgil's turn : 'F. has
' begun the *Eclogues.* I am quite astonished to find them
' so beautiful; they are certainly far superior to any English
' pastorals I have ever read. I could not help laughing when
' I read Tityrus' opinion that Rome would resemble the
' villages he had seen in the same manner that goats resem-
' bled their youngsters.' The following extracts may serve
as samples of her home correspondence with her brothers and
sisters :

TO HER SISTER SUSAN (AFTER A VISIT TO LONDON).

Odsey, January 13th, 1829.

One of the greatest events of my stay there was going to
the theatre, but, as is usual where we have anticipated much,
I was disappointed in it. I had expected to be quite absorbed
in it, and to have images which before were faint in my mind
brought vividly before me; but this was not the case; for
seeing ' Othello ' acted as I did was just like seeing a picture
on any subject unequal to the idea you had previously formed.
Kean did not make me feel interested for Othello even at
first, and he did not at all make my blood either freeze or
boil.

March 5th, 1829.

What do you think of the Duke of Wellington?[1] I confess
I do not feel much faith in him; but he is a good strong stick,
that will perhaps cudgel the asses along the road he has chosen
to travel. I do earnestly hope that nothing will induce him to
resign; I do not much fear it, for he is not a man to make a
mistake of that kind. It is generally said that the sense of
the country is against the Catholics; but from the accounts of
the manner in which the Anti-Catholic petitions have been got
up, I really think that the sense of those who have a sense
about the matter is for them.

Odsey, March 12th, 1829.

Though you may be sure that I have not much time to read
the newspapers, yet I contrive to pick up enough to make me
much interested in the proceedings of Parliament; but I shall
not call this a glorious victory if it is gained, for it is very
evident that most of those who have changed their opinions
have done so, not from conviction, but merely from seeing 'the
'time come,' that is, the king's mind turned. Most of the
common people about here are very much afraid of being burnt
in Smithfield; but the clergyman at A—— is so much disliked
that his parishioners think they could not be much worse
off; and when he desired them to sign the anti-petition they
refused, for, as they justly observed, they should not have to
pay more tithes even if the Pope did come over. . . . I have
lately been reading Leigh Hunt's *Feast of the Poets*, which is
most entertaining. Poor Wordsworth comes rather badly off;
he is not admitted to the feast because he had 'changed his
'harp for a whistle;' but Apollo sent him home enveloped in a
purple cloud which had been a garment of his own. I think
too much honour is given to Moore; I wish some capable
person would let Apollo give another entertainment at which
Lord Byron would be introduced, and I think the poetesses
should be allowed at least to be in the gallery.

March 25th, 1829.

I am now much enjoying reading Gibbon's life of himself. . . . I do not like his letters nearly as well as Cowper's,

---

[1] The measure for Catholic Emancipation had been just introduced by the Duke of Wellington and Sir Robert Peel.

but they are two men who certainly cannot be compared together. Cowper's letters breathe a spirit of grateful disinterested friendship; Gibbon's rather show a solicitude to be so kind to his friends as to give them every particular about so interesting a personage as himself. He is certainly very conceited; notwithstanding he tells us that when he heard recited some verses of Mr. Hayley's, in praise of himself, he 'seemed (!) to blush!'

In the spring of 1829, Dr. Carpenter, who had shortly before returned to part of his duties in Bristol, finally relinquished his school, intending to devote himself wholly to his ministry; and the project which his daughters had so long entertained took definite shape. They decided to open a school for girls under the superintendence of their mother; and, by way of further qualifying themselves for this fresh enterprise, Mary and Anna resolved to spend the summer months in Paris. In the stedfastness of their devotion to study they had no time to throw themselves into the new life around them. They saw the Louvre with eyes already trained to appreciation by exhibitions of the works of the Old Masters, gathered at the Institution of their own city. But it was characteristic that of all the sights they witnessed, their presence at the annual Séance of the Institut Royal, where they beheld Cuvier in the flesh, and heard a eulogium on Laplace, who had died the year before, afforded them the greatest pleasure; the enthusiasm of hero-worship was already a sustaining power. To Mary Carpenter, however, the dearest interest was that of her faith, which was soon brought into contact with modes of thought—or perhaps thoughtlessness—from which it had hitherto been carefully shielded. In a letter written soon after her return, she describes an encounter with a young *avocat*, which proves that she could at least keep her temper on the most exciting of all subjects.

TO MRS. WRIGHT.
Bristol, September 19th, 1829.

M. George, Madame B.'s son, is the pride of the family; he is an *avocat*, and very clever, of which he is fully aware. Anna and I sometimes had an argument with him, which we much liked. One Sunday evening he said, in the course of conversation, that he thought the doctrine of the transmigration of souls a very delightful one; he liked to think that our souls would not be annihilated with death, but would again exist in another form. I said that I thought it much more interesting to believe, what we were certain would take place, that we should be raised *in propriâ personâ*; besides, why should we rest on empty theories when a more glorious *certainty* is offered to us? 'Yes,' he replied, 'if we are sure of a resur-'rection from the dead, it is indeed glorious!' Anna and I then found that he was an unbeliever in revelation. Though we knew that there were such persons in the world, yet we had never met with any, or realised to ourselves their existence, and felt much shocked when we discovered that he rejected the sacred writings, and thought it impossible that anyone should believe them without the previous preparation of faith. He said that he thought religion a very good thing for women and children (he generally classes these two together), but it was quite unnecessary for men who study philosophy. We were glad to have another opportunity of conversing on the subject, when I pointed out to him some passages in Channing's sermon on the Evidences, which he liked very much, and promised to read the whole. I was not a little pleased when he told me that he thought it *très bien raisonné*. I do not suppose he will pay any more attention to the subject, as he is engaged in a course of severer study, but still I think a little good has been done, if Dr. Channing has led him to see that religion can be supported by *reason*. . . . You will perhaps be surprised to hear that I am almost a believer in animal magnetism, which at present excites considerable attention in Paris. M. de F. is a firm believer in it, and was kind enough to procure Anna and me an opportunity of witnessing it. We were certainly much astonished, and I cannot but think that the effects we saw must be caused by some laws of nature at present quite unknown. It is, I believe, at present introduced in London under the name of mesmerism; and I do hope that the physicians there will not be deterred by a fear of ridicule from investigating the subject—to expose it if it is all an imposition, or to make an important use of it if true.

August found Mrs. Carpenter and her daughter Mary ready for their new work, in which the other two sisters joined by degrees, as the school grew and demanded further help. The labour was hard, but in the completeness of their family union, in the education of the brothers, who already gave promise of future distinction, in the hope that one or other of these might one day follow in the father's steps, and in the consciousness that they were themselves ministering to that father's usefulness, they found ample sources of happiness. With the usual energy of her nature, Mary Carpenter threw herself into fresh studies, wherewith to win her pupils' interest. 'You will perhaps be rather amused,' she wrote, ' at the idea of my teaching a class of conchology ' when I know nothing of it myself ; but you remember the ' motto, *Dum doceo, disco*. . . . School-keeping is certainly ' difficult work, but we have been so long accustomed to ' have something to do, that I do not think we should be ' happy without some regular employment which is useful.' Summer excursions enriched her geological cabinet, and she wrote with ardour from the Isle of Wight, after climbing Headen Hill : 'It was truly delightful to find, halfway up ' the rock, unbroken beds of fossil shells lying as com- ' fortably as if they had been placed there.' Lyell's *Geology* was carefully read and analysed : and her note-books were filled with reports of the courses of lectures on Natural History, Chemistry, and similar subjects delivered at the adjoining Institution, to which her neat pencil added accurate reproductions of the principal diagrams. Meanwhile, in works of romance such as Cooper's *Bravo*, and of religious biography like the *Life of Oberlin*, she found stimulus for her imagination and social affections. No sooner did Macaulay's article on Milton appear, than it was eagerly mastered, and as eagerly discussed, in the little circle of critics around her. It was hardly surprising that the girls under her care looked upon her as a sort of prodigy, and felt a respectful awe for her attainments, compared with the imperfect learning and inexact habits of mind of which they soon became painfully conscious. Those who had the capacity to share her enthusiasm, and the zeal to follow where she led the way, found by degrees every barrier of reserve broken down, and were gradually drawn, they hardly knew how, into the confidence of a peculiarly ardent and tender friendship. ' Miss Carpenter is quite delightful,' wrote one, a few weeks after her arrival in 1833 ; ' she ' understands Greek, Latin, Italian, French, and every other ' language for anything I know to the contrary, for I only ' know of these, hearing her teach them. She is fond of ' poetry, geology, and conchology, which two latter she ' seems to understand very well. In short, she seems to be ' universal. She possesses the quality of great kindness, ' as do all the family.'

The strenuous activities which her school engagements thus demanded of her, left her little time for the meditation in which she had been wont .to pass many a sacred hour in her earlier years. She looked back to the heights of ecstasy which she had from time to time ascended, with trembling and doubt whether 'those delectable mountains' had fitted her for the common walk of life. A suggestion of one of her aunts[1] had sent her to the writings of Law, and his *Letters*, with Hartley's *Rule of Life*, formed her chief books of devotion and ethical counsel; while the preaching of Robert Hall, of whom she was a frequent hearer, had further stimulated a sensitiveness already almost too keen. From time to time her self-reproach broke forth with almost unendurable bitterness, and the new accusations rise out of a riper experience than in her earlier years. The irritability which occasionally flamed out against even the dearest of the home circle, the pride which led her to regard the infringement of her rules as personal disrespect, her inability to suppress a desire of admiration, her want of control over wandering thoughts, her unreadiness to make sacrifices for others while she knew herself to be peculiarly dependent on their love and sympathy for her, her longing for great intellectual attainments,—these are all set down with a stern resolve to drag every hidden weakness to the light, and leave no guilty secret unconfessed.

'If I have performed any service well,' she wrote at the close of 1830, 'I profess not to think myself deserving of 'praise, but I have a secret consciousness of having per-'formed it better than others would have done. I also 'feel a very unchristian satisfaction in imagining my own 'feelings of a superior cast to those of others : this I hope I 'am correcting. Besides this, I am not careful enough to 'avoid irritating the weak side of others, particularly when I 'imagine myself strong in that very point. These things seem 'very bad when distinctly expressed : are they not equally 'so when imperceptibly mingling with the constant habit 'of the mind ?'

---

[1] Mrs. Fisher, her mother's sister, a woman of much accomplishment. She published a little volume of poetry : *A Legend of the Puritans, or the Influence of Poetry and Religion on the Female Character, with other Poems.* London, 1837.

In moods such as these, the sense of unworthiness and inefficiency to work the work assigned her could not help stripping life of much of its joyousness, and burdening it with a load which she would willingly lay down; and she found it needful to brace herself resolutely for the common tasks of daily duty.

A DREAM.

I had a dream.   Methought I passed away
Into the land of spirits, and I knew
To-morrow's sun would not behold me here.
Around me were no horrors of the tomb ;
Gently the messenger of Death had come,
And I was summoned ; so I bade adieu
To those I loved on earth, with peaceful trust
That shortly we should meet to part no more.
Oh then what precious thoughts were mine !   To heaven
I turned my longing eyes, and knew that soon
I there should ever *rest*, to *sin* no more ;
Should see those friends with whom my spirit here
Had oft held sweet communion, and with them
Dwell in th' eternal glory of my God !
Oh blest such hopes !   Upward I longed to soar,
And peacefully I bade the world farewell.
    My dream was o'er.   I started yet to feel
The glow of health and strength ; yet joyed I not
To wake from holy rest, to toil and sin ;
To find no port at hand, but the long voyage
Of life before me ; I would fain have sunk
Back to the gentle sleep which led to heaven.
But then a voice aroused and startled me :
' Forgetful one !   Thou *hop'st* to see thy God ;
Hast thou no *fears ?*   Oh bless the Gracious Power
Which lengthens still thy little span of life,
And gives thee time to learn to serve Him more.'
I owned the heavenly counsel, checked my haste,
And sad forgetfulness of all my sins,
And with fresh ardour trod the vale of life.

From the weariness of inward conflict, suspected by few around her, she was recalled by the birth of new purposes, which seemed to promise a means of transcending the limits then restraining her, and offered a possible expansion to a nature that constantly fretted against restraints which were not self-imposed.   In 1831 she had become the

Superintendent of the afternoon Sunday School; and the
visits she paid to the homes of the scholars first stirred her
into consciousness of the hapless lot of the poor and ignorant
in large cities. In the Reform struggle of that year she
took an eager interest, and the riots which broke out in
Bristol on the last Sunday of October produced a profound
impression upon her. The contrast between the peaceful
sunshine of the autumn morning, with its inspiring worship,
and the dreadful glare of the fire-lit sky at night, fixed
itself ineffaceably in her remembrance; and her heart was
filled with a deep pity for those whose mad passions had
brought on the innocent such calamity and disgrace. The
impression deepened as day after day brought tidings of
fresh crime and misery. She began to ponder on the causes
of the outbreak, and to find their place in the general
circumstances of the time ; and the desire was already
stirring within her to devote herself to the service of the
degraded around her. 'How awful the state of public
'affairs,' she wrote on January 1st, 1832, 'in which we
'have entered this new year ! I feel deeply moved that I
'can do no more towards alleviating the distress of the
'poor, but I hope that I shall be enabled to do so.' Two
months' further reflection developed the hope into a solemn
and consecrated purpose ; and the following entry on the
Fast day, appointed in view of the first advent of cholera,
registers her self-dedication.

Wednesday, March 21*st.*—I wish on this day appointed for
public humiliation before God to record my earnest desire to
become more useful to my fellow-creatures, and my prayer to
our Heavenly Father to guide me by His light into the way of
discovering the means and of rightly employing them. The
first and most obvious way is by myself giving to others such
an example as may lead them to glorify their Father in
heaven; and I must do this by simply and humbly, but
zealously and constantly, working the work of Him who placed
us here. I must be careful never to neglect any certain duties
for others which only appear to me useful and desirable; but
when the hand of Providence does point out any way of doing
good more extensively, I must engage in it with thankfulness
and ardour, but with humility, caring not at all for my own
comfort or labour. These things I have written to be a witness
against me, if ever I should forget what ought to be the object
of all my *active* exertions in this life.

A purpose once formed by Mary Carpenter was not to be lightly laid aside or speedily forgotten. She did not speak of it, but kept it in reserve, as her manner was; willing to wait for years if necessary, but never relaxing her hold. From time to time she renewed her vow in private meditation; sometimes with hesitation, as though she feared to seek great things, sometimes with a consciousness of power which would not be repressed. Now the purpose rises with fresh enthusiasm from the perusal of some record of heroism, and now from a thankfulness for divine mercy; and though it is only dimly feeling after its true scope, it is already rich in affection and earnestness.

Sunday, October 6th.—I have been reading this morning a noble example of self-devotedness in the inhabitants of a small village; they were led on by their self-sacrificing pastor and his wife; she sank beneath the scourge; it was appointed for him to be separated from her for a season, in order still to lead his flock on the road of their pilgrimage. I feel again stimulated with a great desire to imitate them and the holy Howard (to use merely human examples) in the blessed employment of devoting themselves to their fellow-creatures. *I think that I have strength to do so;* may these words be recalled to my recollection if ever I desert the sacred cause; it is possible that some great duty is reserved for me.

Tuesday, November 27th.—This day has been set apart for public thanksgiving to our Heavenly Preserver during the dreadful scourge. And I have felt it a day of cheerful gratitude. . . . But this day has been one of renewed resolutions of benefiting my fellow-creatures. I have never forgotten the determination I made on the day of public humiliation, nor has it at all weakened, but I have not yet had the means of putting it into action. God grant that I soon may have them!

The prayer was to be fulfilled in ways far other and more varied than she could have dreamed. The very next year (1833) brought to her the two great impulses to which the rest of her life was slowly to give effect. The Rajah Rammohun Roy came to Bristol and died there, but not before he had filled Mary Carpenter with an ardent interest in the regeneration of India; and Dr. Joseph Tuckerman, of Boston, U.S., as the guest of Dr. Carpenter, first specifically directed her earnest attention to the condition of destitute children. What preparation her past life had made for these twofold influences may best be presented in her own words, written on a plan of self-scrutiny which in a later time she abandoned.

Wednesday, April 3rd, 1833.—It has long been my intention, on this birthday, when I complete my twenty-sixth year, to write a brief sketch of my character, that I may in future years be able to observe whether I have made progress in self-knowledge, and whether any material change has taken place in the tree or in the fruit. What I write is not the result of a moment's thought, but of long reflection; yet the more I think about it the more difficult I find it to begin.

In my intellectual qualities the most striking feature is perhaps quickness of perception; this is an advantage and a disadvantage to me; I readily catch ideas and make them my own, but I think I have ground for forming them before I have observed carefully everything that was necessary; this frequently gives rise to inaccuracy and errors of judgment. My associative power is strong. My memory is moderately good for facts and ideas, but not for words unconnected with ideas; it is tolerably retentive, for I seldom find anything quite forgotten which has been once accurately fixed in my mind. My favourite pursuits are those which are connected with analogy and generalisation; I therefore take great pleasure in the proceedings of nature and in language. I also am very fond of order and arrangement. According to my own ideas of poetry I have much poetical taste, and have written some things which I think good ; my object in writing is generally to unfold some idea which is interesting to me from appearing elevated, or from its being the simple emotion of the mind. My poetry is generally deficient in suitable ornament and in elegance of expression. I am very fond of music and of painting, when expressing beauty and poetry. My acquirements are nearly as follows : I am well acquainted with French, I understand the construction of Greek, Latin, and Italian, and can read the two latter with facility. I have just begun German. I have enough knowledge of the different branches of natural philosophy, and of conchology, mineralogy, and geology, to enable me to take great pleasure in gaining knowledge on any of these subjects. I know a little of geometry and algebra, and desire much to study them. I am fond of history, but am not very well acquainted with it. I draw pretty well, but have not sufficient accuracy and neatness. I have learnt music and studied the principles of it, but have quite neglected it the last five years.

The more I think of the last part of my subject the more difficult I find it. Indeed it begins to seem almost impossible to dive into the recesses of my heart, and, having first removed the veil of self-love, to assign to each passion and emotion, as well as to each power of the mind, its appropriate place. The most striking trait in my character is perhaps warmth and quickness of feeling. In my earlier years this was greatly checked, or rather the expression of it was, and I had a humiliating sense of great want of attractive manner, so that I had a general feeling of being disliked. I have been lately more called, of course, to take a station in society, and to feel that I can make my company agreeable; this has in some degree lessened the curb on my affections—at times, I fear, injudiciously. The affections are sometimes a source of overwhelming delight to me, while at other times they fill every leisure thought with sorrow, and make me almost wish that mine were a heart of stone; this shows want of due regulation. At some periods I have been made very uncomfortable by another branch of the affections. I try to guard against them; they are a source of nothing but sorrow to me. I pray to God to help me to subdue them. I fear that my affections have a greater tendency to gratify themselves than to lead to any *real* sacrifice on my part for the object of them. In my memoranda I observe that from the commencement pride is spoken of as my great enemy. I hope in humility that late years have gradually led me to feel more how essential humility is to the Christian character; if we compare ourselves with ourselves how very little ground there is of self-gratulation; and if with others, how impossible it is to form a correct judgment. My occupations render it necessary for me continually to bring forward my own opinions and wishes; this is a dangerous tendency. I think that I possess courage when I know that I am in the path of duty, and perseverance—or rather a desire of completing everything. I think that I am thankful to be told of my faults, and think that I could bear for a friend to tell me any one of them. I trust that I have a sincere and ardent desire to come to God, and I think much about the things of another world; the subject is always delightful to me, but it does not sufficiently influence my life. I desire to close this earthly career, for I have full confidence that my Father will, in another life, only inflict such punishment on His children as is necessary to bring them to Him. But I endeavour to be patient, and am on the whole happy. Amidst all my mournings for sins of omission and neglect, or of actual disobedience, of unrestrained will, of irregularity and lukewarmness in coming to God, when otherwise the heart might sink, how delightful it is certainly to know that a time will come when, though it may have been by the refining of the fiery furnace, our dross will be completely purged away, when we shall be white as wool. The time *will* come—but how long it may be first is awful to think—when every power and emotion of the mind, every disposition implanted in us by our Maker, shall be elevated and purified; and when this holy spark of heavenly flame, however dimmed now by earthly mists, shall burn *for ever* bright and pure in the presence of its Maker. Amen.

CHAPTER II.

THE SEED TIME OF PURPOSE.
1833—1840.

'There is a day in Spring
When under all the earth the secret germs
Begin to stir and glow before they bud:
The wealth and festal pomps of midsummer
Lie in the heart of that inglorious day,
Which no man names with blessing, though its work
Is blest by all the world.'

Gerald Massey.

'We are prone to imagine that our temptations are peculiar;
that other hearts are free from secret burthens that oppress
our energies, and cast a cloud upon our joy; that life has for
others a freer movement and a less embarrassed way. But
the more we know of what passes in the minds of others, the
more our friends disclose to us their secret consciousness, the
more do we learn that no man is peculiar in his moral experience, that beneath the smoothest surface of outward life lie
deep cares of the heart, and that if we fall under our burthens
we fall beneath the temptations that are common to man, the
existence of which others as little suspect in us as we do in
them.'

J. Hamilton Thom.

CHAPTER II.

1833—1840.

EARLY in the present century a little work was published at
Moorshedabad, *Against the Idolatry of all Religions.* It
was written in Persian, with an Arabic preface. The
author was a young Brahman of high caste, whose grandfather had filled some important offices under the Moguls.
He had himself been trained at Patna and Benares, where
he had been instructed in the Hindu learning which
gathered round the sacred books of his ancestors, and had
been introduced to some important elements of Western
thought through Arabic translations from Euclid and
Aristotle. To an unusually large and varied culture he
added great tenacity of purpose, and a singular breadth of
sympathy and openness of mind, so that he was enabled to
become to some extent the interpreter, at once to his countrymen and to his English fellow-subjects, of monotheistic
principles which he regarded as the original inheritance of
his race, and even to act as a mediator between Oriental and
Christian faith. This was the justly famous and venerated
Rajah Rammohun Roy.

The hostility which his first publication excited against
him on the part of his co-religionists led him, in 1814, to
settle in Calcutta, where he devoted himself to the study
of English, Latin, and mathematics, in the intervals of the
preparation of a series of translations into English, Bengali,
and Hindustani, from the Upanishads and other works of

Hindu theology, in which he believed 'the unity and sole
'omnipotence of the Supreme Being' to be set forth. The
bitter opposition of some of his own family, as well as
of the members of his caste, threw him more and more on
the sympathy of his European friends. His attention was
strongly directed to Christianity ; and, in order that he
might form an independent judgment of its various doctrines,
he counted it well worth while to master sufficient Hebrew
and Greek to enable him to read its Scriptures in their
original languages. The results of his inquiry he published
in 1820, in English, Sanskrit, and Bengali, in the form of
selections, chiefly from the first three gospels, entitled *The
Precepts of Jesus, the Guide to Peace and Happiness.* A
First and a *Second Appeal* followed, in defence of the
positions which he had maintained in the preface, against
the animadversions of an orthodox critic. These works
were printed at a Baptist missionary press ; but its managers
felt themselves unable to lend him further aid in bringing
out works with which they were not in accord, and he
therefore set up an independent press of his own, from
which a *Final Appeal* was soon issued. The press served as
a centre round which other agencies—a chapel, a school, a
library—were instituted ; and in these he found compensation for the ill-will of some of his countrymen, and the
coolness of some of his English friends. 'Whatever may be
'the opinion of the world,' he wrote, 'my own conscience
'fully approves of my past endeavours to defend what I
'esteem the cause of truth.'

The controversy in which Rammohun Roy had been
engaged in Calcutta speedily excited attention in England,
where his eminent attainments and his earnest renunciation
of idolatry had already become known. The principal works
of both disputants were republished, and the interest of the
Unitarians was powerfully roused by the discovery of so
able and so unexpected an ally. Letters were quickly
interchanged, and the correspondence, in which Dr. Carpenter
and his valued friend, Mr. J. B. Estlin, of Bristol, took a
share, stimulated the Rajah's desire to visit Europe. In the
spring of 1831 he landed at Liverpool, and, after making
the acquaintance of the historian Roscoe, then in his seventy-
eighth year, and enjoying the hospitalities of Mr. and Mrs.
Rathbone, at Greenbank, he hastened to London. An

invitation to Bristol soon followed and was at once accepted;
but the eagerness with which he watched the Reform
struggle, and the press of Indian business in which he
became involved, prevented him from making his way to
the West until the autumn of 1833. Dr. Carpenter had
already seen him frequently, and the enthusiasm of his
daughter Mary had been likewise quickened by an interview,
when his arrival at Stapleton Grove,[1] near Bristol, early in
September, and the almost daily intercourse which followed,
raised her ardour to its highest point. 'It would be vain
'to attempt to describe our emotions,' she wrote in after life,
'on finding that this champion of truth had burst through
'all the fetters of prejudice and conventionality, had crossed
'the ocean, had come to our England, had desired above all
'to embrace my father, to whom he had long felt united in
'the bonds of Christianity, had seen him, had come to our
'city to be in daily intercourse with him. At the distance
'of thirty long years all this rises before me in its early
'freshness.' The meeting-house in Lewin's Mead appeared
to win a new consecration in her eyes because the Rajah
worshipped there; it was just after the death of Wilberforce,
and her father, in speaking of the progress of the cause of
negro emancipation, became to her the prophet of a still
more glorious liberty, of which Rammohun Roy was already
the splendid forerunner. The climax was reached when the
Rajah declared his belief in the resurrection of Christ, which
she supposed must involve in his mind the conviction of the
Saviour's supernatural endowment and divine mission;
India and England seemed already to share in one common
faith.

But the great hopes which had thus sprung up in many
hearts, and in none with more fervour than in that of Mary
Carpenter, were doomed to a sudden disappointment. The
Rajah had scarcely been a fortnight at Stapleton, when
symptoms of indisposition appeared. The disease developed
with alarming rapidity into fever, which seized with fatal
power on a constitution already subjected to the strain of
long and severe labour. Early on the morning of the 27th
of September, Rammohun Roy passed away. The progress

---

[1] The residence of Miss Castle, who had been committed by her
parents to Dr. Carpenter's guardianship.

of his illness had been watched with the utmost anxiety by
his friends in Great George Street, but the tidings of his
death came with a shock of grief and consternation. In the
anguish of perplexity, the whole future of India seemed
plunged in darkness. 'This is to all of us a most awful
'and affecting event,' wrote Mary Carpenter to a friend in
Exeter immediately after; 'to have seen the person in
'whom we had long felt an interest, as perhaps more likely
'than any other to promote the diffusion of Christian prin-
'ciples in India; to have heard him declare, in the most
'manly and unequivocal manner, his belief in the unity of
'God and in the divine mission of our Saviour; to have
'admired his noble bearing, his interesting and intelligent
'countenance, and his courteous manners, all the while
'looking forward to long years of continued usefulness and
'happiness—and then to hear that he is no more!' In the
death-chamber, to which she was admitted, and beside the
open grave, she meditated profoundly on the work which the
Rajah had already accomplished; and her childish desires
were quickened into some more definite shape, as the enthusiasm of discipleship pointed to untrodden fields in India.
Some of her thoughts found utterance in Sonnets, which she
confided to her father, who read them aloud, to her surprise,
to the mourners at Stapleton Grove, on the morning when
the remains of the Rajah had been laid in a quiet spot within
the grounds. Of these the following may serve to record
the feelings which she could never recall without profound
emotion.

Thy nation sat in darkness, for the night
Of pagan gloom was o'er it. Thou wast born
'Midst superstition's ignorance forlorn;
Yet in thy breast there glowed a heavenly light
Of purest truth and love; and to thy sight
Appeared the day-star of approaching morn.
What ardent zeal did then thy life adorn,
From deep degrading guilt to lead aright
Thy fallen people; to direct their view
To that bless'd Sun of Righteousness, whence beams
Guidance to all that seek it—faithful—true;
To call them to the Saviour's living streams.
The cities of the East have heard thy voice:
'Nations, behold your God! Rejoice, rejoice!'

Far from thy native clime a sea-girt land
Sits thron'd among the nations; in the breasts
Of all her sons immortal freedom rests;
And of her patriots many a holy band
Have sought to rouse the world from the command
Of that debasing Tyrant who detests
The reign of truth and love.   At their behests
The slave is free! and Superstition's hand
Sinks powerless.   Hitherward thy steps were bent
To seek free commune with each kindred soul,
Whose highest powers are ever willing lent
To free their race from Folly's dark control.
To our blest isle thou didst with transport come;
Here thou hast found thy last, thy silent home.

Bright hopes of immortality were given
To guide thy dubious footsteps, and to cheer
Thine earthly pilgrimage.   How firm and clear
Arose thy faith—that as the Lord hath risen,
So all His followers shall meet in heaven!
Thou art gone from us; but thy memory, dear
To all that knew thee, fades not: still we hear
And see thee yet as with us; ne'er are riven
The bands of Christian love!   Thy mortal frame
With us is laid in holy silent rest;
Thy spirit is immortal, and thy name
Shall by thy countrymen be ever blest.
E'en from the tomb thy words with power shall rise,
Shall touch their hearts and bear them to the skies.

Not even to her father, however, did Mary Carpenter
venture to utter all the visions that rose within her heart.
The longing to fling herself into the work which there
seemed few or none to undertake, could not be wholly
repressed.   The way of duty clearly lay for her in the home
and the school, in the management of which she bore so
large a share; but though she was ready to tread it cheerfully, she could not close her eyes to the larger task without
regret.   'On the 18th of last month,' she wrote on the first
Sunday in November, 'I saw laid in the silent tomb the
'mortal remains of one who seemed a light to lighten the
'Gentiles.   Yet his death, which seemed at first an extinc-
'tion of many glowing hopes, may serve to kindle renewed
'endeavour in the hearts of many.   For myself I fear there
'is nothing to do but to endeavour to cherish in myself and

'those around me pure religion, but more than ever do I
' feel the line,

> ' Spread Thy great name through every land.'

Not thus was the resolution of the fast-day to win its
accomplishment. The preparation and the toil of thirty
years had to be fulfilled, before India would again come into
her view.

Meanwhile a fresh stimulus, and one of more immediate
operation, entered her life from a new and very different
quarter. The eminent attainments and the literary activity
of Dr. Carpenter had long secured for him the friendship of
leading Unitarian clergy in the United States; and his
house in Bristol had already been the happy resting-place of
Transatlantic visitors. With Dr. Channing an active correspondence and interchange of publications had been maintained,
which made all the best writings of the New England divines
familiar to the circle in Great George Street, and there every
fresh arrival from Boston was expected almost as a matter
of course. Henry Ware had already laid the foundation of
a friendship afterwards cherished by his family for more
than forty years ; and now, in the last days of 1833, a year
already so eventful to Mary Carpenter, came Dr. Joseph
Tuckerman, who had spent his strength with untiring devotion in the Ministry to the Poor,[1] in Boston. Failing health
brought him to England, and in no long time he became the
guest of Dr. Carpenter. He found himself at once in the
midst of sympathies which responded eagerly to his enthusiasm. A well-ordered home, where every duty was punctually
discharged under the inspiration of a pervading affection,
was exactly the place in which to pour out his most earnest
appeals on behalf of the destitute, for whom there seemed
no one to care. To spread that home life, drawing into it
those who had never known any true parental care, was
afterwards one of Mary Carpenter's leading aims. Meanwhile, the impression which Dr. Tuckerman produced upon
her, was thus communicated to her brother Russell.

---

[1] Otherwise called the ' Ministry at Large.'

Bristol, December 31st, 1833.

As to Dr. Tuckerman himself, I cannot make you *feel* how very full he is of love to man—the child of God—and how very low is his estimate of himself. His devotededness to his labour of love is unbounded, and he says that his self-denial consists in being in his study and partaking in the pleasures of life. He began to preach soon after he was twenty; then he settled in a small village (Chelsea) much in the same state as the Ban de la Roche; indeed, Dr. Tuckerman is quite an Oberlin. In this village he remained till he was called to the Ministry of the Poor, ten years ago; he had been there *twenty-five* years. He says that his views on entering the ministry have been much matured since, for he was at first filled with visionary ideas of God; but he was never at all ambitious, nor did he ever seek the applause of the world; indeed, he says that nothing is more painful to him than to receive the expressions of approbation for what is the highest happiness of his life.

In spite of his feeble health, Dr. Tuckerman could not rest without exploring the narrow streets around the chapel in Lewin's Mead, already known to Mary Carpenter as the neighbourhood from which many of her Sunday scholars were drawn. On these walks it was her privilege to accompany the guest, who was never weary of relating the events of his rich experience. One day as they passed along beneath the shadow of abodes of vice, a miserable ragged boy darted out of a dark entry, and rushed wildly across their path. 'That child,' remarked Dr. Tuckerman, 'should ' be followed to his home and seen after.' Nothing further occurred, but the observation was not lost. Six-and-thirty years afterwards she still recalled the incident as one of the quickening moments of her life. 'His words sank into my ' mind with a painful feeling that a duty was being neglected.' The beginning of compunction was of necessity with her the beginning of fresh resolve; her purpose of devotion was now clearer than ever; her quick insight had gathered up every detail of method which she thought might be available; but the opportunity was yet wanting. The home-ties which made India little more to her than a country on the map, seemed to stop even the way to Lewin's Mead. On her and her sisters fell the cherishing of parents, the care of the school, and the education of her brothers; and amid claims

so tender and engrossing there seemed no room for fresh
responsibilities. With habitual self-restraint she waited,
wisely cultivating such graces as the daily work allowed.
She could not bear, however, to shut out the hope altogether,
and the private talk of the sisters ran on the far-off prospect
of giving up the school. Then they would spend a year or
two in Boston ' observing the excellent plans there adopted,'
and after that settle quietly in Exeter or Bristol (Mary voted
for Bristol), and devote themselves to visiting the poor. A
second visit from Dr. Tuckerman, in 1834, brought the fulfilment of her desires nearer; and early in the following year the
plan was ripening. What one could not undertake alone,
several might attempt in joint enterprise; and in 1835 a
society was accordingly formed under the name of the Working
and Visiting Society, for visiting the homes of the poor of
the congregation and of the Sunday School. Districts were
allotted to the visitors, who were expected to keep regular
records of the cases under their charge. To prevent the
demoralisation of indiscriminate almsgiving, the visitor was
forbidden to give relief without the sanction of the Committee, to whom every case was at once reported; but ample
provision was made by the monthly working party and other
means for supplying efficient aid. Into this organisation
Mary Carpenter threw herself with fresh enthusiasm. For
more than twenty years she was its secretary. When the
districts were first apportioned, she unhesitatingly chose the
poorest and the worst; and there it was that she first gained
her insight into the condition of what she afterwards described as the ' perishing and dangerous classes.' Nevertheless
the new work must be strictly subordinated to other claims.

Thursday, May 21*st*, 1835.—In the year 1832, on occasion
of the public fast and also of the public thanksgiving, I made
a solemn determination to devote myself in any way that lay
in my power to the good of my fellow-creatures. A means
appears to be now open to me to do this more efficiently than
heretofore, and I feel much gratitude to my Father for it. I
pray to Him to enable me to discharge these happy duties to
His glory; never to allow them to interfere with my other
duties, but only with my hours of relaxation; and to remember
that, though I give my goods to feed the poor and have not
charity towards all men, I am nothing.

The tasks thus ardently undertaken were not, however, by any means easy. The concentration of mind which their effective discharge required, constantly withdrew her thought as well as her time from studies which she had hitherto pursued with the utmost zest. From the geological cabinet, the drawing-board, the well-stocked library of history and poetry, and all the bright and cheerful associations of refined family life, she had to plunge into the midst of squalor and misery such as few cities in the kingdom, perhaps, could have presented. The narrow courts reeking with filth, the dark alleys, the wretched tenements where every room had its own degraded inmates, filled her at times with unutterable loathing and disgust. The scenes which she witnessed fastened on an imagination peculiarly sensitive, rose in her nightly visions, and at times caused her painful excitement well-nigh intolerable. But she would not forsake the cause she had espoused. Again and again she had to force herself into contact with the foul air and fouler life that lay so near the peace and sweetness of her own home; but once there, the springs of pity were immediately unloosed, and what was begun with stern and almost desperate resolve was continued with free and spontaneous love. From a mind thus occupied, the missionary impulse naturally faded away; and a visit from Mr. Williams, the well-known missionary in the South Pacific, only excited a little friendly interest. 'He seems exactly cut out for such a life,' she observed, 'having, as far as we could judge, deep and enlarged 'religious convictions, great benevolence, a gift of tongues, 'handicraft skill, and some of brother Martin's way-wisdom 'and simplicity. He breakfasted with us and made all the 'young ladies wish to go out to the Society Islands; if I had 'no tie to England, I should like it very much; now, I 'think that we have enough to do at home, and am very 'thankful that there are some to do the good work.' The labour around her was, indeed, becoming more engrossing; before its importance all ordinary occupations lost their significance; at times it seemed as though it were the one thing worth living for, to which all personal interests should be gladly sacrificed. Into the abundant openings now before her, when day after day revealed some fresh scope, she would have flung herself at once with entire self-surrender; but cir-

cumstance still laid its restraints upon her, and she compelled
herself to abide in patience.

December 31*st*, 1836.—It is my earnest and greatest desire,
if God sees it well in His own good time that it should be so,
to devote my life entirely to the blessed employment of aiding
the poor and destitute. I feel sure that I should most cheerfully give up for this *all other* employments and pursuits; but
as in all things so in this, I must wait for the pointing of
His Providence.

The work, so far as it went, was faithfully done, and
met with a fair share of visible success. ' It has been
' a half year of much anxiety and occupation,' wrote
Mrs. Carpenter one Christmas Day a year or two later,
' but the labour has not been without its reward. Our
' pupils have improved. Our poor have been well cared
' for; and Mary can look up to the gallery and see families
' decently clad, with their fathers whom she has rescued
' from the lowest state of misery by reclaiming them from
' intemperance, and bringing them to the house of prayer.
' Our girls' daily School, too, under Anna's care and that of
' the good mistresses, is becoming more and more a place
' of valuable instruction.' It early became clear, however,
to Mary Carpenter, that the Working and Visiting Society
could not possibly achieve all that she desired. Not all the
visitors were as courageous and resolute as herself; they
soon came across families whose moral condition was such
that they shrank from endeavouring to cope with them. It
seemed as if, after all, the plan would be frustrated, or at
any rate would fail of its full usefulness. Without delay
she communicated her difficulties to Dr. Tuckerman. ' You
' say,' he wrote from Boston, ' that your Working Society
' does not extend its visits to "the very lowest of the poor."
' I suppose, indeed, that with propriety they cannot. And
' yet, does not every circumstance which makes it improper
' that ladies should visit these destitute and degraded fellow
' beings, cry out for the visitation of them by those who
' might not only safely, but most profitably visit them? Is
' not every circumstance of their moral necessities a demand
' of God's Providence for the moral aid without which they
' must be perpetually sinking deeper in moral abasement?'

To this appeal Mary Carpenter and her fellow workers could not remain indifferent. They resolved that the next step should be the establishment of a Ministry to the Poor, or a Domestic Mission, on the New England model. The stimulus came again from America. The visit of Dr. Ezra Stiles Gannett, then the ardent colleague of Dr. Channing, brought the occasion. None was fitter than he to expound the needs of the poor, or to tell the tale of how they could be met. It was in the summer of 1838. Mary Carpenter was at Ilfracombe with her mother, who was recovering from a long illness; but as soon as she heard that Dr. Gannett was expected in Bristol, she wrote at once to her father. 'There should be a meeting in one of 'the school-rooms (for our people to see him and he 'them), expressly to communicate to our people the work 'and effect of the Ministry to the Poor in Boston. It 'seems to me that this is an opportunity which should not 'be lost to stimulate the minds of some and encourage 'others to attend to this important subject. You perhaps 'know that several among us are earnestly looking for an 'opportunity to bring the subject forward, and this is one 'that will not recur.' Further action was soon taken. A committee of members of the congregation was appointed to devise a plan; and the visitors set themselves to work to obtain subscriptions. It was a satisfactory testimony to the hold they had acquired, that above one hundred of the families under their care cheerfully promised each to contribute a penny a week. Into this new scheme Mary Carpenter threw all her hopes.

The years which thus witnessed the beginning of what was afterwards to be her life-work, were fraught with an unusual number of agitating experiences. The daily toil brought ample occupation of thought and feeling; and when to these were added the burden of outward sorrow and the secret of inward strife, there seemed at times almost more than could be borne. The home circle remained unbroken save by the departure of the brothers to their professional studies; but in the years 1834 and 1835 one after another among relatives and friends passed away; the shocks of grief followed in quick succession, and the heart of Mary Carpenter was wounded again and again, as the companions of her girlhood were laid beside the more venerable friends whose departure her parents mourned. She had been accustomed so much to meditate on another life, and had already at times longed for it herself so ardently, that it was not surprising that this desire should recur with renewed force. She found some relief in fusing into verse the thoughts that had arisen by many a death-bed; and the following Ode, completed in 1836, and constantly cited in her later memoranda, records some of her deepest feelings.

ODE.

'Mourn not, therefore, child of immortality! for the spoiler, the cruel spoiler, that laid waste the works of God, is subdued; Jesus hath conquered Death. Child of immortality, mourn no longer!'

FIRST VOICE.

Strike, strike, my lyre, the solemn notes of woe,
For all that's fair is fleeting, here below.
Swifter than April gleams they pass away—
The joys, the hopes, that rise but to decay.
They seem our own,
We know no fear,
But they are gone
For ever here—
Our life's long hopes, our purest joys, all withered in a day!

SECOND VOICE.

Yet there is gladness round;
Why list we only to the voice of sorrow?
Hark! that full joyous sound!
Sweet child, so gay, so thoughtless of the morrow;
Oh turn on me thy smile—
The sunny promise of a day so bright—
Let it my soul beguile,
And shed on me its hope, its love, its light;
Yes! let it banish dismal care and sorrow's gloomy night.

And hark! the voice of Spring!
It sounds full cheerily;
The blithe young greenwoods sing
Merrily, merrily!
And see the buds all opening fair and bright,
Promise of loveliest flowers;
And see the trees all decked in virgin white,
Gladdening the bridal bowers;
Oh 'tis a world of life and love! a joyous world is ours!

And there is many a fair young form
  Too bright to die;
  And strong and high
Beats many a heart with feelings warm;
And there are heads round which the laurels twine
  In earliest youth;
There are blest spirits hallowed at the shrine
  Of holy truth;
Oh these are lovelier far than Spring, these cannot fade and fly!

FIRST VOICE.

Thus may'st thou sing, whose springtide hour is bright,
  On whom no wintry storms as yet have burst—
Who hast not seen cold Autumn shed his blight
  On beauties Spring and Summer hours had nurst.
    Now hope is round thee,
      Soon she'll fly;
    Sorrow hath found me,
      Let me sigh;
Stay not my dirge of grief for joys that quickly fade and fly.

Once, too, for me the laughing day
  Shed sweets around;
Life was in all most bright and gay;
  Too soon I found
That Death is in the world; his gloomy pall
  Once seen is ever near;
And coldly sheds its ghastly shade on all,
  Filling the soul with fear,
And telling us our dearest joys, our highest hopes, must fall.

Why does that mother always mourn, nor raise her drooping
  eye?
Why does a cloud o'ershadow all, and never pass her by?
    Her morning star is hid in gloom,
    Her daughter sunk into the tomb.
Why does that matron grieving sit within her palace gate,
Nor heed, while years roll tedious on, her noble mansion's state?
Her thoughts are ever in the grave, her only hope and trust,
Soon with her husband and her son to mingle dust with dust.
Oh gloomy is this narrow vale! sad, sad is mortal fate!

Yes! there hath been a gladness in my soul,
  Like that of infancy;
Now naught but gloomy sorrows round me roll—
  I've lost its buoyancy!

Once in my heart young hopes were gay and fair,
    Like bright leaves springing,
    Like sweet bells ringing;
But never more shall happiness be there;
Deep sorrow ever o'er me broods, and dark corroding care.

THIRD VOICE.

Thou sorrowing child of dust, why grieves thy heart
    That earthly charms depart ?
When the green earth its choicest treasures brings
    It tells of heavenly springs;
The dying year touches with brightest hues
    The drooping trees and flowers,
Which in our souls the blessed thoughts infuse,
    Of ever sunny hours,
Where the blest Tree of Life shall bloom, and be for ever ours.

E'en when Death circles in his icy arms
    All that thou hast most dear,
And from our hope vanish all earthly charms,
    A heavenly hope is near.
Faith gilds the mists of human feeling,
    Love glows more brightly near the tomb;
Peace in the sorrowing bosom stealing,
    Sheds light amidst the thickest gloom,
All to the prayerful soul a glimpse of brighter worlds revealing.

Such was the voice that cheered the dying bed,
    As o'er her son the mother bent,
And soothed with tender love his drooping head,
    On whom her fondest hopes were lent.
    ' These sufferings of a day
    Soon, soon shall pass away,
And I shall see my dear Redeemer's face.
My mother, follow me to that blest place,
And let us all together share our Heavenly Father's grace ! '

And would that mother call to earth her son,
    To share the toils of life's perplexing way ?
No !   Though in grief her course she now must run,
    And o'er his vacant place her tears will stray,
    Religion's soft control
    Illumes her inmost soul.
In hopeful trust she says, ' Thy will is best,
    My Father !   Be Thy name for ever blest;
I would not take my son again from his eternal rest.'

Death blights not, chills not, but awakes
　The heart's immortal pure desires ;
O'er the dark vale a glory breaks
　From heaven, to which the soul aspires.
I've seen the wife and mother dying,
All her fair earthly visions flying ;
Yet as her life was ebbing fast,
These accents were her last—
' My Father, 'tis a glorious morn ; all, all is bright within ! '

' Live in the power of an eternal life ! '
　'Twas thus the Saviour, dwelling still on earth,
O'ercame its cares and sorrows, toil and strife ;
　And thus his followers of the second birth,
To whom immortal hopes and joys are given,
　　Fear not to die ;
The holy ties of earth can ne'er be riven ;
　　For soon on high
The ransomed shall with Christ partake their purer bliss in
　heaven.

Let hope and joy kindle their fairest rays
　In all that's lovely here,
Faint earnest of a brighter blaze
　In the celestial sphere.
Let pain and sorrow shade the dazzled sight,
　Unused to such excess of light ;
　　Death draws the veils aside
　　Which endless glories hide,
And opens to the faithful soul its high eternal home !

There were other griefs, however, which could not seek
this expression or receive this consolation. The irritability
which had in former years caused her from time to time
such poignant anguish, could not be wholly suppressed, even
under the force of new and larger aims. The strain of
continued responsibility, operating on a nature acutely
sensitive, was sometimes too great for her strength ; her
mental vigour qualified her to take the lead, but the
administration of the home and the school belonged of right
to the mother, and the slightest semblance of collision of
purposes or interests awoke the keenest self-reproach. Each
fresh occasion of conflict added a new sting to memories
already bitter, and she could only probe instead of healing
her wounds ; again she would gladly have sought peace in

the doctrine of the Atonement, could she have satisfied
herself of its scriptural basis; or at another time she would
have readily embraced the severest penance, if she could
thereby have tamed the offending temper and wiped out the
intolerable past. The history of these years wrote itself in
her heart in lines that were never erased, and left deep
traces in her after life. Few could have suspected by
what inner conflicts she was torn; those who have themselves fought the same fight will most readily understand
the frequent confessions in which she recorded her short-
comings.

Sunday, March 26th, 1836.—I am continually sinning against
the light which is in me, by allowing in myself wayward expressions which may hurt the feelings of others, and pursuing
my own will instead of humbling myself and becoming as a
little child. The great temptation and trial is this, I magnify
to myself the importance of the object before me; I think that
I ought to use every effort to accomplish it, and then, if this is
not possible, I feel irritated. I also feel in danger of allowing
religious emotion to take the place of what is to me far more
difficult—the active cheerful discharge of the duty of the
hour. Again another temptation—I cannot accuse myself of
neglecting or leaving half-performed any of the duties of our
school; on the contrary, I believe that I conscientiously prevent
anything from interfering with my discharge of them, and at
once check my thoughts if ever I find them wandering, which
is not often; but yet I fear that I neither love these duties,
which I ought to do as the appointments of my Father, nor do
I feel that vivid interest in them which I do in others to which
I am sometimes tempted to wish that my Father had destined
me—a wish that I check at its first rising, for He knoweth what
is best. My mind is also much too full of thoughts which keep
me in a constant state of excitement which I know to be very
injurious to me. I know that it is useless to consult any human
being on these subjects, for no one save Him who gave it can
truly know the spirit that is in us. To Him do I go with
'strong crying and tears,' many tears and deep sighs; He is
not far from me, yet I do not feel His presence as I ought.
This shows that I do not pray with *full* purpose of heart, and
that I am not truly contrite. Cleanse me, O my God, from
secret faults. However deep the anguish of my soul, oh may
I never be separated from Thee! Be Thou with me, my Father,
in the fiery furnace! I *have* felt Thee with me in my deepest
sorrow, and no mortal can tell what that has been.

Weariness and dejection were the inevitable issues of these self-dissections. She felt her relish for intellectual pursuits declining, her grasp of mind growing weaker, her love of life becoming fainter and fainter. She could scarcely bear even the affection of those around her; in her exceeding unprofitableness she could have no right (she thought) to instruct others; she forgot herself only in the public services of religion, and in visiting the poor and suffering; yet even this source of happiness seemed poisoned to her by her own unworthiness. The depression, which had been in part produced by physical causes, reacted again upon her health; and she went through her daily tasks with increasing difficulty. It was the darkest period of her life. Sorrows beset her again and again in later years, but the bitter sense of sin was past. Failure in her plans could in part be remedied by fresh labours; bereavement could be borne with trust; even the guilty relapses of the half-reformed could be overcome with new endeavours, or at least could be committed to the mercy of a Father of infinite pity; but in none of these ways could the anguish of personal unfaithfulness be assuaged. That load must be carried in silence till the end should come, or till the burden, she knew not how, should melt away.

Little by little, however, the gloom that hung over her lightened. Increase of vigour without brought more composure within. Moreover, the eye which had been trained to search out the dark secrets of storm and struggle was unexpectedly opened on the light of divine peace and love. In some verses, dated December, 1837, Mary Carpenter strove to embody one of the rare experiences of intense religious communion, the reality of which the souls that have passed through them can never afterwards question.

WHETHER IN THE BODY OR OUT OF THE BODY I KNOW NOT.

Sorrow and darkness fled away,
And I beheld eternal day,
    No night was ever there;
None feebly drew the parting breath,
Gained *was* the victory over death,
    And life was ever there.

I felt as ne'er I had before,
I knew that I should sin no more;
    And straight within my soul
There was a calm and holy peace,
A joy so true it ne'er *could* cease,
    A gentle sweet control.

I knew that I was with my God,
Yet feared I not His chastening rod,
    Fear dwelleth not with love;
I felt his presence ever nigh,
'Twas bliss to live beneath his eye,
    It was in heaven above.

I was so filled with holy awe,
I nothing heard, and nothing saw;
    Yet every power and thought
Was bent on that excess of light,
Absorbed in fulness of delight,
    In him whose face I sought.

But then a mortal veil was thrown
Upon me, and I was alone !
    My course was still to run,
I came from realms of endless day,
To see the dim and troubled ray
    Of the earth's midday sun.

Yet now, methought, a fairer glow
Was shed on all things here below;
    Light from above was given;
My Father's love dispelled the gloom,
And made the valley of the tomb
    Appear the gate of heaven.

The way of restoration was now open. It was, indeed,
impossible at once to cast all weakness away, yet the path
of duty was trodden with firmer steps, and the interest of
life awoke once more. Self-reproach was less frequent, and
a healthful activity of mind revived. The routine of school
tasks was broken in the spring of 1838 by the long and
severe illness of Mrs. Carpenter; and the fresh and varied
efforts which this called forth from her eldest daughter
helped further to disperse the sadness of recent remembrance. Together they sojourned at Ilfracombe during the
long summer days; and there the restraints which the home

life had imposed were broken down. The freedom from anxiety, the 'tender ministrations' of the Nature which she loved, and the interchange of affectionate confidences between the two sufferers, all brought new strength of mind to the younger patient, who returned home with a heart of hope to enter on larger undertakings.

She found the scheme for the Domestic Mission slowly making way. Without delay she commenced correspondence with the promoters of such institutions elsewhere, to gather information and counsel. She was more earnest than ever now, for she had sounded depths unknown to her before. 'Yesterday,' she wrote to her brother Russell in October, 'when reading Dr. Tuckerman's work on the Ministry at 'Large, there occurred to me as a good subject for a sermon 'the individuality of man in his moral and intellectual 'existence. The Gospel, while addressing *Mankind*, 'addresses *Man*: Christ, when delivering the Sermon on 'the Mount to multitudes, concludes (as often elsewhere) 'with " whosoever . . . him." Hence individual respon- 'sibility, and our efforts to benefit mankind must be so 'directed as to affect individuals. I fancy that I could 'write a long sermon on this subject if I had time and 'words; it appears at first sight trite, but has not been 'sufficiently realised to many minds.' The sermon was never written, but it was not the less earnestly preached; it was, as she anticipated, a long one, for it lasted through all but forty years of toil, in which the most comprehensive aims never lost sight of single souls.

It would, however, be a very imperfect picture of Mary Carpenter's life at thirty years of age, which should exhibit it as completely shrouded in sorrows or self-abasement. To the affection of her family, unmerited as it sometimes seemed to her, she responded with the keenest delight; no anniversary passed unmarked by her, but for each the generous gift must be prepared. Nor did she by any means abandon the pursuits in which her interest had for a time apparently declined. She followed successive lectures at the Philosophical Institution with a diligence in which no slovenliness betrayed a wandering attention. Her father's courses on Mental and Moral Philosophy had ere this supplied her with a method of thought; her brother William's on

Physiology revealed to her new operations in Nature, from which she derived a high intellectual satisfaction; the geologist, the historian, the critic, and the poet each found in her a willing listener. She had not yet ceased to take pleasure in works of fiction; and though she could not make her way through *Pelham*, she admired the *Last Days of Pompeii*. The social relaxation which she most enjoyed was a literary discussion with Dr. Symonds, afterwards the leading physician of Clifton and the neighbourhood, to whose constant kindness both her mother and herself were greatly indebted. He was a frequent visitor; and, whether by opposition or sympathy, compelled her to justify her preferences, or assisted her to solve difficulties which were scarcely grave enough to be obtruded on her father's busy hours.

Her geological cabinet steadily gathered new treasures from her summer excursions as well as from the friendly offices of her correspondents. When the British Association, after meeting in four of the University cities in the United Kingdom, selected Bristol for the place of its next assembly, in 1836, she entered with alacrity into all the preparations. The regret with which she found herself excluded by the rule which then prohibited the attendance of ladies at its sections, received its compensation in part in the intercourse with many distinguished men who gathered at her father's table, where she was well able to take a share in the conversation. The acquaintance then begun was occasionally renewed afterwards. ' In the afternoon ' (in the following October) ' Professor Buckland called on his way back to ' Oxford. He stayed half-an-hour conversing in a most ' agreeable and sensible manner about his book, and the ' contested point of the Creation; he very wisely determines ' not to attempt to reason with those who shut their eyes ' and say that the geologists invent facts. With regard to ' the progressiveness of the Creation, proved by geologists, ' he remarked : " Let man be placed in the early periods ' "of the earth; deprive him of oxen, horses, and all ' " domestic animals " (you know that none are to be found ' in the limestone) ; "put him to live among the crocodiles ' " and mammoths, and he would die." ' The next summer she was at Birmingham, and there alighted on an un-expected pleasure. ' A delightful lecture,' she reported,

'from Mr. Phillips, and a still more delightful evening with
'him at Mr. Bache's. We talked of nothing but geology;
'you may imagine how much I was pleased.' Yet a year
later and Mr. Phillips was in Bristol again, and the
enthusiasm which his lectures excited was sustained by his
personal kindness. 'He breakfasted with us one morning;
'and what I enjoyed more than all was his spending an
'hour in my geological cabinet, making remarks, and
'throwing much light on many specimens.'

Poetry and criticism also occupied much of her attention.
But her tastes were confined in their range by the moral
and religious earnestness of her nature, which found no
sustenance in works of passion or imagination uncontrolled
by the high aims she demanded. Among contemporary
poets, Wordsworth was the only one who fully satisfied her;
and his influence is obvious in her own choice of themes,
as well as in her treatment of them. Admiration of
Wordsworth became one of the passports to her goodwill,
and was a test immediately applied to any new literary
acquaintance. In the autumn of 1838 James Montgomery,
well known as a religious poet, delivered a course of lectures
at the Philosophical Institution on English poetry. He was
often at Dr. Carpenter's house, where he encountered in
Mary Carpenter an independent though a friendly critic.
'I have been more busy than usual,' she wrote, 'in con-
'sequence of Mr. Montgomery's lectures, of which the Y.L.[1]
'write unmercifully long recollections. Last afternoon he
'spent two hours with us before the lecture, which I
'enjoyed very much though I had not intended to do so,
'for though I think his poetry pleasing and good, yet it
'does not appear to me of the high style which I most
'like. He delights in Wordsworth to my heart's content,
'and admires Leonardo da Vinci's *Logos* as much as I do.'
Her feeling indeed transcended her powers of expression.
Twice she boldly planned vast poetical projects. The
second poem, sketched out in 1838, aspired to nothing less
than to relate the story of the earth, of man's entry on it,
the vicissitudes of his progress, the triumph of the kingdom
of God, and the final abode of the soul with Him in whose
presence is fulness of joy. The longing of girlhood for

---

[1] A favourite abbreviation for the 'young ladies.'

intellectual distinction reappeared in a higher ambition in the memorandum which she attached to her plan. ' It has ' long and often been my desire to embody in a permanent ' form the thoughts in which my soul delights when it is ' free, when it is not weighed down by care or sorrow ;— ' to give them a local habitation and a shape. Occasionally, ' too, I have longed to leave behind me something "which ' "men should not willingly let die," something which ' should enable my thoughts to mingle with those of my ' fellow beings, when my mortal frame is sleeping in death. ' But this last is a hope little suited to my power.' The desire is fulfilled, for her name will be remembered ; but the poetry in which she will live is written on the hearts of those for whom she toiled.

One more source of interest may be noted, for it remained with her long after her geological cabinet had ceased to receive new specimens and her last verses had been composed, and only ended with her life. This was her drawing. Into this she poured the love of Nature which had early filled her, and by this she delighted to win and to convey impressions of localities which she had perhaps never seen, yet which roused her to the most vivid interest. Exhibitions of pictures (some of which she had copied) from the great houses of the adjoining counties had trained her taste, which was further cultivated by some of the group of artists who then found a home in Clifton. Her studies under Messrs. S. Jackson, sen., Müller, and G. Fripp opened to her a way of beauty which she could at all times enter from the most distracting scenes of misery and degradation ; and again and again, when the composition of poetry proved too great an excitement, she found relief at the drawing-board. What capacity of judgment she acquired may be inferred from the following criticism after a visit to the Academy in 1839.

TO HER SISTER ANNA.

Odsey, July 10th, 1839.

I admired all Wilkins' and Landseer's very much. . . . Scarcely any of the portraits showed any soul either in the subject or the artist. . . . But I must not omit Turner, whom I had never seen before. Leaving entirely out of view that Nature has anything to do with the art of painting, and that

she has any charms which should be copied, or should inspire
the artist with her spirit, Turner is certainly a wonderful
painter. His pictures consist of beautiful arrangements of
the prismatic colours, particularly of the three principal ones ;
for he seems to have a peculiar horror of his pictures being a
' leetle, leetle green,' and does not like to torment the lovers of
yellow and red with brown and grey. There is doubtless
much poetry and feeling, and the engravings from his pictures
show his power of composition ; but the unpractised eye has
difficulty in discerning these elements in the midst of his
gorgeous display of glaring and unnatural colours.

The Turner pictures this year included 'Ancient and
' Modern Rome,' ' Pluto carrying off Proserpine,' and ' The
' Fighting Téméraire tugged to her last Berth.' Further study
led the critic to abate her severity, and converted her at last
into an enthusiastic admirer ; and nothing delighted her
more in later years than to steal away between appointments
with Ministers at Whitehall or the India Office, and sit for
half an hour before one of the great landscapes in the National
Gallery, or linger almost lovingly over the sketches and
drawings which afforded her ample demonstration of that
very fidelity to Nature which she had at first been unable to
discern.

It was well for Mary Carpenter that her vigour had of
late increased, for the great bereavement of her life was fast
approaching. Long continued pressure of work of many
kinds brought on her father a renewal of his former illness.
The fears of his family during the summer of 1839 were at
last realised in the imperative need of his complete withdrawal from his usual labours ; and arrangements were made
for a long journey abroad, on which he was accompanied by
a medical friend. The year closed in much anxiety over the
wife and daughters now left alone in Bristol, though cheerful
letters from the travellers were full of hopeful promise.
When the anniversary of her birthday came round in the
spring, it was a grief to Mary Carpenter to miss the father's
cherished greeting; all personal interests were absorbed in
the one yearning for his restoration; but she wrote, ' I formed
' a resolution on the first Sunday in the year to give up all
' my desires and hopes to God. I feel from experience that
' the more I can do this, the more my mind will be at peace.'

Within a few days came the life-long test of this resolve. On the day before Good Friday the news reached Bristol that, while on the way from Leghorn to Marseilles, Dr. Carpenter had been drowned.

In the sudden anguish of the shock, the first thought of all the children was for the widowed mother. The solemn hours of the first days of bereavement went by, unrelieved by any offices of love for him whom they had lost, and tempered only by the deep trusts of religion and the abounding sympathy of friends. To the very last Mary Carpenter treasured the expressions of affectionate condolence, public and private, which flowed in upon them. The long separation had already taught them how to maintain the home tasks without him; but to her who had peculiarly shared her father's confidence and participated in his work, who had at every step felt his support, and by his guidance ruled her daily life, the blank was the most appalling. In quiet retreat during the summer holidays she and her mother sought to comfort and strengthen each other. As the year wore away and the usual duties had been resumed, she strove to regain the calm which she had before so hardly won out of her struggles. Nor did she strive in vain. On the last day of the year she thus summed up its deep experiences, in words with which many hearts that have sorrowed will know how to sympathise.

December 31*st*, 1840.—In outward sorrow, but in inward peace; having lost him whom most we loved on earth, yet possessing him in purer love, in (I trust) increased filial obedience, in hallowed memory, and in heavenly hope; having been sorely smitten of the Lord, yet kissing in a closer union of love the Fatherly Hand which pours in balm while it wounds; in much weakness of spirit, yet with renewed confidence in that love which cannot err; in thankfulness for His chastenings, and for His very many mercies,—would I close a year for ever to be loved and hallowed, because that which exchanged for my beloved father the weariness of mortality for the everlasting rest and peace of immortality; which saw him for the last time a child of earth and welcomed him to the bliss of heaven; which knew his last thoughts of love for us here, and set an eternal seal on his love for us in the Father's home.

CHAPTER III.

THE WORK FOUND.

1841—1846.

'Then, in such hour of need,
Of your fainting, dispirited race,
Ye, like angels appear,
Radiant with ardour divine.
Beacons of hope ye appear!
Languor is not in your heart,
Weakness is not in your word,
Weariness not on your brow.
Ye alight in our van!   At your voice
Panic, despair, flee away.
Ye move through the ranks, recall
The stragglers, refresh the outworn,
Praise, re-inspire the brave.
Order, courage, return ;
Eyes rekindling, and prayers
Follow your steps as ye go.
Ye fill up the gaps in our files,
Strengthen the wavering line,
Stablish, continue our march,
On, to the bound of the waste,
On, to the City of God.'

Matthew Arnold.

CHAPTER III.

THE WORK FOUND.
1841—1846.

THE death of her father threw over all the after years of
Mary Carpenter a peculiar solemnity and consecration. She
was hardly herself aware of the extent to which her thoughts
and purposes had been guided by his, until his outward presence was withdrawn. But when he was no longer by her
side as the inspirer and stay of her life, she sought and found
a peace of heart in an ideal communion with him. He seemed
to her to be yet close at hand, whispering encouragement at
each fresh step of her course. The circumstances of his
death at first oppressed her with the desolate sense that no
hand of affection had rendered him the last offices of love ;
but soon she gained comfort in the thought that no memories
of suffering and dissolution interrupted the realisation of his
living influence. For her, he had passed from life to life ;
and the unseen world became infinitely more real to her
because he was in it. Others of her kindred and her friends
—the venerated relative, the cherished intimate—had departed
before ; but none had ever so infused an invisible presence
into the scenes that beheld them no more ; none had ever so
carried away into the silence a trust and love which could not
die. The companionship of study, of philanthropic interest,
of worship and affection, was thus exchanged for an inward
fellowship, transcending the conditions of her daily work,
and mingling with every higher aspiration. Not only in the
pursuits with which he had been associated, but in each new

enterprise, he led the way for her; even amid the sickening moments of failure and defeat, or the weary details of administrative economy, a spiritual sympathy gave strength and light; and wherever she moved, with slow and steady steps among the haunts of shame in her own city, or with rapid passage from the Indus to the Ganges, it mattered not, the heaven in which he dwelt was near her still.

With the thought of her father there was also linked the memory of her revered friend Dr. Tuckerman, whose death took place within a few weeks of the loss of Dr. Carpenter. Brief as had been her intercourse with him, it had given a stimulus which never faded, opening to her new modes of usefulness, and providing for vague though ardent sympathies a method of practical effect. For six years he had been 'a guide and a rest to her soul.' The tenderness and the strength of his nature had produced on her an ineffaceable impression; and he, too, was enshrined in undying communion by her father's side. ' He will live in my thoughts ' as long as I am here,' she had written when she was awaiting the tidings of his departure; and her words were fulfilled with richer and richer meaning, as one institution after another arose to testify to the devotedness of her self-surrender to his call. Not all the labour of six times six years could weaken the tenacity of her affection; and she regarded the final recognition of the ' Feeding Industrial Schools ' in 1876, as the completion of the scheme developed in accordance with principles of action first unfolded to her by him.

How these two were henceforth to mingle with her thoughts of devotion, may be inferred from the following record :

Sunday, January 3rd, 1841.—On this first sabbath, seven years ago, I had the happiness of receiving the memorials of the dying love of my Lord from the hands of my beloved father, in company with my own dear family and my venerated aunt—that old disciple whom doubtless Jesus loveth, and one who, more than anyone I ever met with, realised that beautiful delineation of love, in its effects and nature, given by St. John. That was an hour which, though soon overshadowed by clouds, and succeeded by trial and temptation, has left an enduring and blessed memory in my soul, and seemed a foretaste of the bliss of heaven. Now it is doubly hallowed. Those two beloved friends who were suffering—the one darkness of mind,

the other weakness of body—on the last anniversary of this
day, now sleep in Jesus and are blest.

Nevertheless, it was long before Mary Carpenter recovered
from the shock of her double bereavement. She had been
in so many ways identified with her father, that she strove as
far as she could to take his place in the home circle, and the
work among the poor. But she could not conceal her depression. Her mother, who had learned by much self-
discipline to bear anxiety and sorrow in secret, saw with
apprehension the twofold effect of her grief and her exertions.
'I am continually fearing for her,' she wrote, 'for all the
'poor think of her as her father's representative, and she,
'like him, has all their troubles and sorrows to share.' She
resumed some of her wonted pursuits, but without interest;
her scientific tastes ceased to stimulate her mind ; she relinquished her drawing, for Nature could not give her back what
she had lost. As spring came round, year after year, she felt
all the more keenly the contrast of its brightness with the
shadow upon her life.

TO THE REV. R. L. CARPENTER.

Bristol, April 28th, 1842.

I am very glad that you are feeling so delightfully the
soothing and elevating influence of this most lovely season.
To me the bright opening leaves will perhaps always be
associated with our irreparable loss; and yet perhaps that
very association makes me feel more vividly that

> When the green earth its choicest treasures brings
> It tells of heavenly springs;

so that the fugitive brightness here gives me a certain hope
of enduring brightness hereafter. . . . Yet do I feel very
grateful for all this beauty. Perhaps there is nothing which
excites in me such pure, unmixed, and ardent gratitude as the
exquisite loveliness of Nature ; for nothing strikes me so
forcibly as the effect of pure spontaneous love, intended to
excite in us some of that sense of beauty which will be perfect
in another world, and which can hardly be distinguished from
love.

The visits to friends, in which the vacations were usually
spent, failed to give sufficient variety to her mind, and her

mother accordingly, in the summer of 1842, planned for her a little journey on the Continent. Travelling companions were soon found for her in a former and well-beloved pupil, Miss Lucy Sanford, and her brother Langton ; [1] the latter of whom, deriving much amusement from the assumption of a Coblentz waiter that they were her children, loved to describe himself playfully as her 'undutiful son.' The journey served its purpose in effecting a diversion in her usual trains of thought and feeling. A mind peculiarly susceptible to natural beauty was stored with fresh memories of loveliness ; historic and literary interests were quickened by inspiring contact with the very soil out of which they sprang, though it was the religious and social sympathies which responded most readily to new suggestions ; and last, but by no means least, fresh companionship awakened the sportiveness which had been long suppressed, and gave free play to a humour or a tenderness which was sometimes circumscribed by the labours and cares of the home. Some traces of her journey, gathered from the remains of her letters, may be here presented.

TO MRS. CARPENTER.

Schaffhausen, Sunday, July 24th, 1842.

At length we are again in a Protestant region, and have quiet on a bright Sunday morning, and have been listening to the sweet and solemn singing from a church near us. There is only German service here, but I shall go with Lucy to hear it, as I like to join in spirit in worshipping with my fellow Christians. . . .

We stayed at Baden till Thursday morning, and took a delightful day's excursion up the valley of the Mourg, into the outskirts of the Black Forest. Thursday morning was very wet, and we did not anticipate a very pleasant journey; but we were agreeably surprised in our fellow-traveller, who was a Captain of Artillery at Strasburg and one of Napoleon's Legion of Honour. With him we had much interesting conversation all the way. The cathedral of Strasburg rose most beautifully before us, like that of Salisbury ; it is a most beautiful building, and quite repaid our journey. I was,

---

[1] Afterwards author of *Studies of the Great Rebellion, Estimates of the English Kings, etc.* Miss Sanford also became known as a translator and a novelist.

perhaps, even more delighted on entering a Protestant church with seeing a monument to Oberlin's brother—the profile is just like his—and with hearing the sexton say that he had heard Oberlin preach there. I went up into the pulpit. Finding no other attractions in Strasburg, we went on the same evening by railroad to Basle, where we spent Friday, interested in the Protestant cathedral, and at the university in portraits of Erasmus, Wetstein, and other celebrated men, and in a collection of Holbein's pictures. We set off at five in the afternoon, and had to travel all night. During the first stage we had a very interesting elderly minister who knew Oberlin and Neff well; both he and the Strasburg sexton were much pleased to hear of the Oberlin Institute. This minister thinks that Strauss has done rather more good than harm to religion ; for he was merely the echo of a party, and the public expression of what had long been received in private led to much beneficial investigation of the subject. Yesterday we saw the glorious falls. The first sight of them disappointed us ; but after we had seen them in various points of view we agreed that they are magnificent and quite worth coming for.

TO MRS. CARPENTER.

Heidelberg, August 2nd, 1842.

We set off [from St. Gallen] early the next morning. It was very bright and beautiful, and wonderful to see clouds, which we think quite high in the sky, just rolling down the sides of the mountains. Then we went in a steamer along the lake [of Wallenstadt] to Wesen, where I found my view. No painter can give any faint idea of the loveliness of the lake and the grandeur of the rocks, but I was rather disappointed to find my snow mountains rocks without snow.[1] We could hardly tear ourselves from that lovely sunset lake—not till Jupiter warned us to depart. We returned the next day, feeling that we had indeed stored up treasures. I love the mountains more than I can tell; no one but Wordsworth can do so.

TO MISS SANFORD.

Bristol, August 14th, 1842.

I was quite grieved, my dear Lucy, to part from *mes enfants*, whom I love not only for themselves, but from being associated with most delightful recollections. Can you fancy that I was

---

[1] Referring to a drawing of Müller's, which she had formerly copied, and frequently reproduced.

even going to indulge in a few quiet tears upstairs, but a summons to dinner obliged me to refrain ? I thought that your luck was going to attend me to the railroad, for the porter, with a most kind and confidential air, almost worthy a Bonn waiter, told me that the Queen was going shortly, and that if I just secured my place in the carriage, he would take me where I should have a good view of her. However, I had only the satisfaction of seeing her carriage, and the carpets being put down for her, and hearing from the porter how she went the last time, for she deferred going till the next hour. I like to receive kindness. Our terminus struck me as very well managed, dignified, and quiet, in comparison with the Belgic ones. Judge of my alarm when I found my next neighbour a black-whiskered and mustachioed gentleman, speaking French ! I thought how Langton would have triumphed over me. But when I had courage to look again, I found him a very pleasant country-looking man, something in the style of our Liègeois. Several in the carriage seemed to know him, and did him civility in speaking French, whether they could or not, and pulling him this way and that to see the lions, which were many and great ; and I felt bound by gratitude·to do my little utmost with him, so that I could hardly fancy myself in an English railroad. But the country ! There ought to be a panorama of it engraved, which would undeceive people about the Bergstrasse ; if Mr. Fallenstein should go that way on a fine afternoon, I am sure that he would allow that it is far, far superior—so varied, so rich, everything in such perfect order, and all the buildings looking good. My Frenchman quite appreciated it.

TO MISS SANFORD.

Bristol, August 26th, 1842.

Your last note made me truly envious of you—first in having a hungry relish for intellectual food, next in having the means of gratifying it with something more than the stale morsels which used to excite Langton's contempt, and lastly in having so calm a spirit that visions of mountains and rocks float by you in the night watches. My head is as yet so perplexed between home affairs, hearing lessons, and intrusive thoughts of the Rhine, that I have as yet no fancy for reading, and until the last two nights have dreamt only of setting off by steamboats and railways. Now I have begun a pleasing review of our journey in Flanders, and at Bonn, with variations, and I hope to continue. I am gradually introducing Anna to my travelling companions. She and F. B. declare that sitting with one's back to the Rhine at sunset, and quoting lines ending with 'slaughter' and 'milk-and-water,' is quite a capital offence, and that, if I *did* annihilate the perpetrator of it (which I still deny), it was quite a praiseworthy action. I could plead my cause *then* without being interrupted by impertinent young gentlemen. I should be quite pleased *now* to see even Mr. B——. Really I ought to be ashamed of writing so much nonsense.

The heaviness of heart which had beset Mary Carpenter for the past two years was now gradually passing away; and she was able to give a fuller attention to her former occupations. Poetical composition, indeed, ceased for a time to be the medium through which she uttered her feelings; but in one sonnet written shortly after her return from abroad, she endeavoured to describe the impression produced upon her by Dannecker's statue of Christ. A suggestion of Lady Byron's had led the travellers to Stuttgart to see it, and the remembrance of it long afterwards mingled with her most devout thoughts. Nor, indeed, did she ever forget it; though her interest in works even of religious art declined, when she found that she had derived from them all that they could contribute to their own aims.

THE REDEEMER.

BY DANNECKER.

'Through me unto the Father!' 'Tis thy voice
Breathes from the stone, my Saviour! I would bend
In reverence before thee, and attend
To all thy words, and make thy way my choice.
Thou wast a man of sorrows, and thy frame
Sank 'neath the cross; but yet a god-like grace
Is with thee; and from forth that hallowed face
Beam wisdom, meekness, and the love that came
To save mankind. Was it a *mortal's* thought
That gave the marble moulding so divine?
Or did a bright celestial vision shine
Upon the sculptor's soul? Surely he caught
From the Redeemer's life a heavenly ray,
Then stamped a living image on the clay.

One of the results that followed from her summer tour was a quickened interest in German literature, into which she boldly plunged soon after her return home. She was soon reading Schiller with ardent admiration, some of which overflowed also on to Wieland and Gellert, while it was specially concentrated on Herder. But her literary judgments were always controlled by her moral instincts; and it was rather on the excellences of character than on any qualities of art that her preferences and her condemnations were based. Hence she felt little attraction for Goethe's writings; and many a lesser name, when tried by the same measure, was found wanting. 'I have been lately reading 'a most delightful book,' she wrote in the winter of 1843, 'the *Life of J. P. Richter.* His must have been a truly 'beautiful mind, and I do not wonder that he excited so 'much enthusiasm. I regret that his genius was not led 'to pursue a track more useful to mankind. Perhaps his 'writings had a useful effect in awakening in his country-'men a sense of their spiritual nature and aspirations after 'the good and beautiful; but yet they had an injurious over-'exciting effect, as was shown in too many instances. Yet 'how pure must have been his mind for him to be able to 'say not only that he had never written anything injurious 'to morals, but that he wished that after his death his 'every thought could be given to the world! He was a 'living poem of exquisite beauty, sublime and yet playful, 'varied as our own Shakespeare.' Where she once felt herself repelled, she made no efforts to overcome dislike; and the same aversion which she felt for Goethe, seems to have been inspired by the passion of some of Tennyson's early poems which fell in her way, though in the *Idylls* she afterwards took great delight.

The following letter relates a curious comparison of opinions with Mr. J. S. Mill.

TO MISS SANFORD.

London, January 18th, 1844.

Your flowers were much admired at Mrs. Mill's; I think that they were the only natural ones in the room. I was pleased to have a little conversation with Mr. Mill, and to hear his opinions on various poets. He is a very superior-looking man, but looks like one whose mental is crushing his bodily strength. He considers Coleridge, Shelley, and Tennyson the

first poets of the present age, and Wordsworth next. I am
inclined to agree with him about Coleridge's poetical *powers*,
but he can never blend with my highest and holiest imaginings
like Wordsworth. With respect to the two others, I feel
myself incompetent to judge, having only seen fragments of
Shelley, and having been so disgusted with most of what I
have read of Tennyson, that I could proceed no further. Mr. Mill
says that Tennyson's poor prosaical pieces are bad imitations
of Wordsworth (I cannot imagine a real genius imitating). He
thinks that Talfourd has failed in giving a true Greek costume
and character to *Ion*, which are indispensable, as he has
founded the piece on Greek ideas; and he does not give him a
high rank as a poet, though admiring him much in many
respects.

Even her interest in art was not wholly independent of
the character of the artist; and while she transported herself
with rapture from the studio of David Roberts to the soli-
tudes of Arabia, she did not fail to gather an added testimony
to the practice of total abstinence on which her experience
among the poor led her to insist with ardour.[1]

TO THE REV. R. L. CARPENTER.

Bristol, January 30th, 1844.

On my return to London I went with Aunt S. and Hodgson
Pratt to see Mr. Roberts' sketches in Egypt and Petra, which
are most beautiful and striking. We seemed quite in another
atmosphere when we turned from the ponderous magnificence
of Egypt, standing in solitary state amidst the desolation of
unbounded sand-plains, to the wild and elegant picturesqueness
of Petra, where nature and art seemed to have been trying
together to form the most fascinating combination of elegance
and grandeur, magnificence and wildness. Mr. R. himself is
a very pleasant person, full of delight in his art, and of
modesty and kind appreciation of others. He said that while
travelling in Syria he could not get a drop of any fermented
liquor for six weeks, and he never was better in his life. . . .
Mrs. S. also took me to see a most beautiful collection of
Turner's watercolours, in possession of Mr. Ruskin, who has
written a work in defence of modern art. I can now understand something about the enthusiasm which the artists feel

---

[1] In May, 1843, after an address by her brother P. P. Carpenter,
then minister of Stand, she had formally taken the pledge.

for Turner. I have not, however, yet arrived at such a point as to admire what I cannot, by a strong effort of imagination, imagine to be like Nature.

The combination in Mary Carpenter of high imagination and strong personal sympathies naturally led her to history for something more than amusement. 'To watch the struggle ' of minds that have actually existed,' she wrote, after reading the first volume of D'Aubigné's *History of the Reformation*, 'to see their influence on society and the progress of great ' events, is far more interesting to me than any novel.' She never, indeed, pursued it with the independent study which she had in earlier years bestowed on her favourite branch of science, geology; but it attracted more and more of her interest, as her share in the lives of others became larger. Here, as elsewhere, her vigour of judgment was guided entirely by moral decisions. A few passages from her letters will suffice to show what power of illustration she possessed, and how she could employ it on works of earnest purpose as well as of high-wrought fancy.

TO MISS SANFORD.

Bristol, June 6th, 1843.

Have you seen an article in *The Quarterly*, on Lord Mahon's *Essai sur le Grand Condé?* It is history fraught with true and awful lessons. Though I did not of course expect to find Condé a Christian, nor what we should now consider a great man, yet I thought that I should find much to admire in Bossuet's Hero of Rocroi. But how is the mighty fallen! He reminds me in many respects of Napoleon; his talents were probably as great, though they had not such a field of action; he had the same unbounded ' selfism,' the same neglect of what ought to be the closest ties, only Condé was even worse than Napoleon, more deliberately cruel and ungrateful; there seems to me much less to admire in Condé, and I cannot imagine anyone speaking of him as our Strasburg captain did of Napoleon. His true appreciation of greatness makes one mourn that he did not better know what greatness is; that is almost the only point in his character one can dwell on with pleasure. He has one advantage over Napoleon. Condé in prison never showed the littleness of Napoleon in exile. But what a scene of wickedness and intrigue the court presents! One can hardly believe that such beings knew that they were born for immortality.

Ivy Lodge, May 13th, 1844.

As I have very little power of hand, and have not ventured to recommence drawing, I have indulged myself in more reading than usual. I am very vigorously studying Arnold's *Rome* at all my spare intervals of sense, and delight in it quite as much as even Langton would desire; indeed, except Sharon Turner's *History of England*, I never read any history which seemed to me to enter so deeply and truly into the true purposes of history; besides, one becomes quite acquainted with the author, with whose mind one seems to be holding delightful intercourse. I do not feel that I have read the book as it ought to be read, and look forward for a future re-perusal of it; but still I hope to have gained several new ideas, especially about the Agrarian law. Poor Cincinnatus and Camillus rather fall from their ancient glory in my estimation. Have you seen a volume of Dr. Arnold's sermons, with an introduction respecting the Oxford theology? Langton would be much interested in it.

I have also been reading your favourite *Undine*, with which I am as much fascinated as even you could desire. Do you not think that the conclusion is rather painful? There should have been a slight intimation that as he had given her a soul, she now opened to him through the gates of death an eternal paradise, where they would be for ever united. . . .

I must not forget to tell you a charming idea of Anna's of which she is very proud. It is that as Dickens's sister was your governess, there can be no doubt that she is Ruth[1], and thus it is evident that you are the young lady ; the similarity between your Papa and the cannon-founder is of course striking. Mamma was quite shocked, and begged me not to tell you; but I thought that you would not forgive me if I withheld from you such a compliment.

After reading Stephens' *Incidents of Travel in Central America :*

Bristol, June 18th, 1844.

There is a strange and mysterious feeling about these remains of forgotten races. When one disinters fossil animals and plants that lived some ages before Adam, they tell their story very clearly to the geologist, and say how they lived and

---

[1] See *Martin Chuzzlewit.*

died, and what sort of climate they had, and how and where
they were buried, and everything one could reasonably wish
to know; and when one gets the hard Greek or German
crust off the thoughts of centuries ago, they come forth so
living and beautiful that you could almost fancy you have
just created them yourself, and you know by intuition all
about them; but in these cities you feel that mortals have
lived, and thoughts have grown, and you can tell scarcely
anything about them.

TO MISS SANFORD.

Bristol, September 13th, 1844.

I am glad you have been reading Tasso; it is certainly
a most beautiful poem, though perhaps too long. I hope you
like Tancred, and that glorious creature Clorinda; the book
containing her death is one of the most pathetic things I
know. Godfrey is more interesting than could be expected
for a pattern hero; I am not as much in love with *il fanciullo*
Rinaldo as Tasso probably meant us to be. The Italian poetry
is very beautiful, though full of imitations of the classics.

The tone and vigour of Mary Carpenter's mind were now
sufficiently restored to enable her to carry out a cherished
project in the preparation of a little book of devotion. She
had been early directed under the influence of one of her
aunts to the writings of Law; and she was well read in
devotional literature far beyond the range of her own communion. She had long realised that the same trusts and
aspirations might coexist with widely different forms of belief;
and she resolved that her work should deal with the universal
elements of religion, and thus have something to say to all
who took upon themselves the Christian name. The spare
time of the autumn of 1844 was spent in the selection and
preparation of meditations and prayers; and the modest little
volume was issued in the spring of the following year. Her
name was not allowed to appear on the title page, and only in
secret did she consecrate this, her first attempt, to her father.
'My father,' she wrote on April 6th, 1845, 'I have this day
' made thee a little offering; perhaps in another world I may
' be permitted to tell thee how I rejoiced to have associated
' with thee my humble efforts to help others in their morning
' and evening thoughts of things spiritual.' The success was
far greater than she had anticipated. The first edition was

sold off in a few months ; and she learned with pleasure that
it had found its way into many homes from which a book
bearing a denominational name might have been excluded.
Before long it was reprinted in the United States ; and the
six editions through which it afterwards ran were an ample
justification of the compiler's design, as well as a sufficient
test of the spirit in which it was carried out.

The completion of this first effort, however, by no means
absorbed all her energies. The labours of benevolence were
becoming more and more engrossing, but room was still to be
found for the newest scientific reading ; and the favourite
occupation of drawing, to which visits to the galleries and
studios of London had of late given fresh impetus, was
resumed with increased activity. Her acquaintance with
Roberts led her to study his drawings of the Holy Land,
which helped to give local form and colour to many a scene
long familiar to her imagination. Opportunity befriended
her, for the summer of 1844 had brought Lady Noel Byron
to Clifton, when the foundation of a cherished friendship
was laid ; and Lady Byron's introduction led a former acquaintance with Mrs. Schimmelpenninck, the gifted authoress
of a history of Port Royal, to ripen into intimacy. These
interests soon brought further variety to her life.

TO MISS SANFORD.

Bristol, February 7th, 1845.

Have you read *The Vestiges of Creation ?* When it first
came out people were very enthusiastic about it, and the
first review Mamma saw made her buy the book, which we
thought a wonderful step on her part. But one soon began
to feel that the author was very superficial, and everyone
found particular fault with the branch of science with
which he or she was most acquainted. Altogether it is an
interesting book as the production of a mind aspiring after
the grand, beautiful, and universal, but not sufficiently
acquainted with the height and depth and breadth of Nature
to subject all her kingdoms to one great law. I have not
much satisfaction in reading the book, not being able to
repose with security on the accuracy of his facts. For
instance, an important theory much depends for support on
the fact that Mr. Crosse's creatures, which made a sensation
at the British Association in 1836, appear in an infusion

containing 'gelatinous silex,' which this author supposes to be silex transformed into gelatine, and thus exhibiting a transition from the mineral to the animal kingdom. Now Mr. Crosse, whom I had the great pleasure of meeting the other day at Mr. Estlin's, told me that this was a complete error, as gelatinous silex was a perfect mineral, deriving its name not from its nature but from its appearance. This was certainly a most careless assumption which ought not to have been made on so important a question.

I quite agree with you in feeling that *The Chimes* gives one a heart-ache, and do not wonder that you feel it often very painful to witness the mass of evil in the metropolis which you can do nothing to alleviate. I do not possess your gaiety of heart to help to remove the painfulness of the feeling; and I believe that it was intended that we should suffer sympathetic pain to stimulate us to make efforts for our fellow-creatures; but I feel the most supporting view to take to be a firm conviction of the parental character of the Deity, and of His infinite wisdom, love, and power. He would not permit all these evils but for His own benevolent purposes.

I am still harassed by drunkenness. The man who gave me so much trouble a few months ago has been quite sober now for more than three months, but his family have been suffering much, as well as himself, from the natural consequences of his conduct; now a little money will be a help which it would not before, and this is an easier remedy to apply. But another father of our children has been in the same state; it will be a great cause for thankfulness if he can be reformed. The mother of one of our late charity girls died a little time since, the father died about two years ago. She confided to me her little savings, twenty-nine pounds, for her two sons and daughters, begging me to watch over them. I feel now as if they were my children. I think that I must have strong natural instincts, for now they seem to have a relationship to me. I quite love them, though before I had only a general interest in them.

TO MISS SANFORD.

Bristol, April 11th, 1845.

Last Saturday fortnight Anna and I breakfasted with Mrs. Schimmelpenninck, a most fascinating woman, full of genius and sentiment and religious feeling, and a keen sense of the ludicrous. She asked me about Dannecker's Christ, and of the effect produced on us by it, and what Mrs. Jameson had said of Dannecker; and then she was quite satisfied, because she had heard a corresponding account from Mrs. ——, a missionary's wife. When she saw this statue in a gallery, she remained for some time quite transfixed with absorbing feeling looking at it: at last she perceived a gentleman attentively observing her, and struck with her admiration, he said: 'That statue converted to Christianity the artist who 'sculptured it—and I am he!' He told her that he had a strong desire to leave something that should immortalise him, and after in vain attempting to satisfy himself, travelled in Italy, but none of the splendid works of art he saw there seemed to reach his ideal. Then he devoted himself to the study of the Gospels; but at first he could see nothing but beautiful and sublime disjointed fragments, until one text seemed a key-note to him, 'God manifested in the flesh.' He became a devout Christian, but the subject he had proposed to himself seemed too great for him; after a time, however, he reflected that as others could preach and write on Christianity, which he could not, he should do something, and consequently determined to make the statue.

Mrs. Schimmelpenninck allowed me to come to her house and draw quietly during the Easter week,[1] and seldom have I enjoyed any view more than the view of Jerusalem from the road to Bethany over the Mount of Olives, where I could better imagine our Saviour walking than in almost any sketch I have ever seen. I made a tolerable copy in colours of that, and of the Desert of the Temptation with the Dead Sea in the distance; but how often did I long for the privilege which I had at your house, of having Mr. Roberts' own touches on my drawing.

In the meantime further scope was given to Mary Carpenter's energy by the visits of American friends who roused her enthusiasm for the cause of Abolition. The interest which her father had taken in the struggle for Emancipation which culminated on August 1st, 1834, gave to the kindred efforts across the Atlantic something of a personal claim upon her. It was one of the questions on which Dr. Tuckerman had spoken, and when he was afterwards charged with luke-warmness concerning it, she had eagerly availed herself of the testimony of a new-comer from Boston to vindicate his ardour in its behalf. She was prepared, therefore, for fresh appeals, and the visitors of 1843 effectually roused her efforts. First came Dr. Howe, 'the instructor and former, one may say, 'of Laura Bridgman.' Mary Carpenter was his guide over the

---

[1] From Roberts' *Views in Egypt and Palestine*, of which Mrs. Schimmelpenninck possessed a copy.

various schools then connected with the Lewin's Mead Congregation ; and was carried away on ' the deep current of philan-' thropy which evidently pervaded his soul.' The same summer brought the Rev. S. May of Leicester, Mass., and the Rev. Dr. Dewey of New York. These gentlemen were then actively enlisted in the Abolition cause. From the position which Dr. Dewey subsequently adopted, Mary Carpenter was one of the strongest dissentients ; but it was his emphatic words '*Do something*,' which first led her to ask what could be done. The immediate need of funds for carrying on what was regarded as a sacred crusade, had led to the establishment of an Abolition Fair, held every Christmas at Boston. To this she at once resolved to send contributions. Without delay she prepared some drawings which proved highly acceptable, and year after year the gifts were renewed. Her sister Anna entered into the same work with great earnestness. The interest of friends and pupils was aroused, and by-and-by the annual box swelled to larger dimensions, till another and another was sent by its side to bear the donations drawn from a score of towns. The rooms in Great George Street were filled for a day or two with the specimens of workmanship which at last amounted to a regular yearly show ; and hundreds of visitors poured in to bring some utterance of goodwill. In after years the labour of collecting and organising these contributions devolved on the beloved sister who was ever at hand to take up the work that the full and sometimes tired hands could no longer grasp; but the chief correspondence was carried on by Mary Carpenter.

The friendships that were thus formed opened to her new sources of information of which she was not slow to avail herself. The letters that sped across the Atlantic rarely went alone. Reports of institutions and elementary school-books were eagerly exchanged, as well as the last important sermon or speech, or the weightier biography. Among the books which thus found their way to Bristol was the *Life of Dr. Follen*, by his widow. It produced a profound impression upon the hearts that had recently lost a like husband and father ; and by the advice of Miss Harriet Martineau, who at that time retained a grateful recollection of Dr. Carpenter's teachings and always cherished warm feelings of regard towards his daughter Mary, communications were addressed to Mrs. Follen. The cordial response which these elicited led to a tender intimacy between those who had not yet ceased to mourn; and the letters to America which often discussed grave questions of social reform, slavery, temperance, the condition of the poor in large cities, of agricultural labourers, and especially of the Irish peasantry, were blended with touching confidences of memory and hope.

TO MRS. FOLLEN.

Bristol, February 25th, 1844.

Can you tell me anything about Confalonieri, Maroncelli, or any of the exiles in whom Silvio Pellico has given us so lively an interest? During a recent indisposition I read Silvio's touching story—probably for the sixth time at least—and though no part was new to me, everything had a fresh beauty. After reading Dickens's inimitable *Christmas Carol*, I had been thinking whether it would be possible for him, after introducing the love of man into a worldly heart, to carry that on to the love of God. 'He prayeth best who 'loveth best.' Silvio has shown in his own case how one leads to the other.

TO THE REV. SAMUEL MAY, LEICESTER, MASS.

Bristol, October 13th, 1844.

Your visit to England has been, I think, of much service to the great cause of Abolition, by leading us to feel that we may strengthen the hands of our Transatlantic brethren by our sympathy and encouragement. The address of our ministers, though perhaps not altogether palatable to some of your clergy, may still lead them to suspect that they have hitherto seen the truth through a mist of prejudice, and that they may perhaps allow the fear of the world's censure to assume the guise of a love of peace. Why should not Christian churches and Christian ministers counsel and exhort each other? It is certainly true that one state cannot understand the real condition in which another is, and therefore cannot point out the true remedy for its disease, but they may point out principles. We can show you that slavery is a crying sin which everyone should bend his energies to renounce; though we cannot advise you in what manner to do so, any more than you can understand the real position of our labouring classes or of Ireland, or form a correct opinion of the mode of relieving them. My father used frequently to point out to us that great principles take a long time to work their way, and that great and important changes require a long course of patient effort to accomplish them. Thus Catholic Emancipation was passed nearly *fifty* years after the Gordon riots, and the abolition of slavery cost nearly forty years of persevering labour. So you must not be discouraged if your efforts seem at present crowned with but little success.

TO THE REV. SAMUEL MAY.

Bristol, January 15th, 1845.

It is delightful to see a man of some property, like Mr. B——, making it his hobby, as he says, to contribute so judiciously to the real comfort of the labouring classes. There is a *very* large amount of individual exertion in our country to do good to others ; and I believe that never more than at the present moment has the public mind been called to direct its energies to the removal of the heavy burdens which oppress our nation, and which, I am fully persuaded, are so inwrought into our social fabric that no Government measure, however good, can produce more than a very partial and inadequate effect. Dickens has done much good, and so has Hood, in presenting pictures which startle by their frightful truth. I hope, however, that our American friends will remember that their object has been to awaken, and that they have presented only one part of one side of the picture. They must not, therefore, found their idea of the state of our nation in general on *The Chimes*, any more than we should of the Americans from *Martin Chuzzlewit*.

TO MRS. FOLLEN.

Bristol, August 16th, 1845.

The slaves *here* for whom I am most concerned, are those enslaved to the use of intoxicating liquors. I feel on this subject somewhat as you do about slavery, and perhaps in some respects more painfully, as here the soul is enslaved as well as the body, and the whole family is ruined by the vice of one. No one who has not come into immediate contact, as I have, with such cases, can realise the horror of them; indeed, I am fully persuaded that no legislation can raise the working classes of England so long as this evil exists amongst them.

Bristol, February 15th, 1846.

It is very cheering to observe how much these great
questions of humanity occupy the public mind at present, and
how much public opinion, calmly but firmly expressed, influences the Government. The proposal to call out the militia
has led to many public meetings all over the country; the
minds of the people have been enlightened respecting the true
nature of the war system; petitions have been sent most
largely signed; clubs have been formed to protect those who
suffer by enrolment, and the result has been a ministerial an-
nouncement that if the militia should be called out, which is
by no means decided, it will not be done on the present compulsory ballot system. The Americans, who do not study
history, and who do not reflect how very difficult it is to change
the whole nature of things, customs, feelings, laws, which have
been the growth of ages, may think us slow in rectifying
abuses; but when I read such works as Taylor's *History of
the Spiritual Life in England*, and any real history of particular
periods of English history (such as the life of Lord Bacon, in
Campbell's *Lives of the Chancellors*) I am astonished at the
amount of progress which has been made, and at the rapid
strides which are now being made for the elevation of the
people and the promotion of their freedom. The day is dawn-
ing. 'Wait a little longer,' says one of the 'Voices from the
Crowd,' in *The Daily News*. We have, it is true, abundance to
do at home; but that need not prevent us from giving our
sympathies to help our brethren abroad, who will, we trust, be
gathered with us into the same fold of Christ. I should often
feel much oppressed by all the misery, wickedness, conten-
tions, and strife in this world, did I not reflect how soon it
would be over, and that a time will soon come when we shall
see and know, and love, and adore, without cloud or hindrance.
In the meantime we must strive to *do* the will of our Father
in Heaven.

TO MRS. FOLLEN.

Bristol, April 1st, 1846.

The present seems a very critical state of affairs. A
charming French friend once wrote to me : *On parle de
guerre avec l'Angleterre, mais lorsque je me rappelle que vous êtes
Anglaise, je ne puis pas le croire!* This is the feeling of a
large proportion of your nation and ours (how strange it
seems to be talking of *yours* and *ours*, when we are united by
so many strong interests); and it is refreshing to the spirit to
observe how many strong and earnest protests in favour of

the peace principle are excited by the bare mention of war.
Charles Sumner's oration was admirable in the circumstances
in which it was delivered; it has been much read and esteemed
here, and I learn has been reprinted in England. If you see
some of our popular papers, you will see a tone of earnest
remonstrance against the war spirit. Even *Punch* does his
part; I wish you could see his satires on the militiaman,
which probably have had more influence than grave argument.

The drawings which Mary Carpenter forwarded to Boston
were soon dispersed among her friends. One of them found
its way into the study of Theodore Parker, who had already
distinguished himself by his earnest and powerful advocacy
of the Antislavery cause, but had at the same time challenged
the older Unitarian party by his *Discourse on Religion*. On
this side of the ocean, however, it was possible to avoid the
controversy in which such hard blows were given on both
sides ; and in spite of wide diversity of view—for her ad-
herence to the position which Mr. Parker had abandoned
remained unchanged—Mary Carpenter felt herself drawn
into strong sympathy with him. 'When you write to
' Theodore Parker,' so she instructed her brother Russell,
' please to tell him, with my respects, how much delighted
' I am that he looks with pleasure at my drawing of Geth-
' semane. Greatly admiring the elevated and truly Christian
' spirit of his writings, while on many points differing from
' him, I am much pleased that my pencil should give him
' any interesting thoughts.' In the meantime she became
otherwise known in New England by the republication in
Boston, through the good offices of her friendly correspondent
Mr. May, of her little volume of *Meditations*, and this led to
further exchange of inquiries. The following letter, addressed to the Rev. A. A. Livermore,[1] and written under the
friendly roof of the Rev. James Martineau, affords a judicious
view of the condition of many of the Unitarian congregations
of this country a generation ago.

TO THE REV. A. A. LIVERMORE.

Liverpool, July 27th, 1846.

In the meantime I may answer such of your questions as
come within my own knowledge. 1st. *No* confessions or

[1] Now President of the Meadville Theological School.

creeds of any kind are used in *any* of the Unitarian churches.
No test is required for admission to any congregation, nor
would it be asked from any minister. 2nd. The Lord's Supper
is generally administered on the first Sunday in every month;
in some congregations once in two months; in a few, I believe,
even less often. An address from the minister usually pre-
cedes the ordinance, together with prayer; in some congregations the minister carries round the bread and wine to
the communicants, in others, as our own in Lewin's Mead,
the deacons. Our ministers encourage the young, or new communicants, to converse with them in private before commencing
to attend, but this is not necessary; no restriction of any kind
is laid on participating in this rite; all are encouraged to
come who desire thus to profess their love to Christ and submission to his authority. 3rd. Our churches and ministry
vary in their use of the rite of baptism. The baptismal form
is still employed by most, without attaching to it any
mysterious importance, but rather as a mark of the parents'
desire that the child should be dedicated to God. Others (as
was the case with my father) employ a dedication service
without sprinkling, conceiving that the ceremony has no
meaning as applied to infants, and is associated with much
baneful superstition. 4th. Unitarians do not as a sect coalesce
with any others, except with General Baptists, many of whose
congregations have become, strictly speaking, Unitarian, and
associate with us freely, only retaining the rite of adult
baptism, and the Lord's Supper being essential to church
membership. The Universalists do not form any distinct sect
in England. 5th. Respecting the ' growth or otherwise of the
Liberal cause,' a different answer would probably be given by
different persons, according to their means of judging, and
the circumstances in which they are placed. From what I
have observed and heard, I do not think that Unitarianism is
rapidly increasing as a sect, but that its principles are
decidedly spreading, though the outbreaks of bigotry certainly
do not diminish. Whether it spreads, and in what direction,
much depends on the character of the minister and congregation in each town. In some towns the congregations
are almost exclusively among the educated classes, in others
among the poorer; our own was, before my father's ministry,
the richest and most aristocratic in Bristol, perhaps in
England; now it presents a happy mixture of all classes, and
continues steadily increasing in number, though many of the
rich and great, those whom one is tempted to call worldly,
have left us. 6th. The church funds and government differ
in almost every congregation. In many there is an endowment, which partly maintains the minister, the rest is made
up by voluntary contributions or seat-rent. The funds are

generally managed by a congregational committee (which with us is chosen annually and meets monthly) or by the trustees to the property.

Bristol, October 30th, 1846.

The part of your letter which most interested me was that in which you speak of slavery. It is a *giant iniquity*, the oppressive tyrant of your *self*-styled free country, and it grieves me much when I hear those whom I esteem as wise and good in your country endeavouring to stifle the voices that are lifted up against it. Wendell Phillips nobly said : ' I do not ' know that God destines me to overthrow slavery, but I do ' know that He expects me to do my duty,' or words to that effect. If *every* American who *professes* to hate slavery would throw his *efforts*, his *influence*, his *voice* in the scale against it, instead of making the injudicious course (as he deems it) of the Abolitionists an excuse for his own inaction, the blessed day of emancipation would soon arrive. I rejoice at your appreciation of W. L. Garrison, and *entirely* unite with it. If you see *The New York A. S. Standard* or *The Liberator* you will perceive how he has been esteemed in Bristol. Though I do not agree with him in many of his opinions on various topics, and wish that he often modified his language a little, yet I most warmly sympathise with him in his noble self-forgetting devotion to the great cause, his Christ-like love to the oppressed, and his uncompromising determination in carrying out important principles, his *oneness* of purpose. I esteem it a high privilege to have had personal intercourse with him, and to be numbered among his friends. If you should visit Boston this Christmas, you will see the fruits of Garrison's and Douglas's visit to England in the number of contributions to the bazaar. Above three hundred have been working for the cause in Bristol only.

The new interest of the Antislavery cause, however, by no means withdrew Mary Carpenter's activities from the lines which she had already laid down for herself. Whatever fresh tasks she undertook, she abandoned nothing once begun. To awaken the love of knowledge in her Sunday scholars, she arranged a small museum of geological and other specimens, which she presented to the school, and was always delighted to exhibit and explain. When the Domestic Mission was opened in 1841, she hailed it as a further agency for dealing with the degraded population among whom she was working; and though its course was somewhat different from that which she had desired, she never failed to give to it all the support in her power.   Her personal efforts were devoted to her visiting, where her quick sympathy exposed her, indeed, to many trials, but opened to her likewise abundant joys.   The painful excitement of former years now passed away; she had more gladness and calm in the discharge of her daily duties, and she could therefore throw herself into each fresh opening for useful action without the bitterness of self-reproach.   That which she had at first imposed upon herself out of a solemn sense of responsibility, became now a cherished source of happiness.   'When I feel how I seem to love a family,' she wrote to her brother Russell, ' in which I hope that I have been ' of some spiritual good, I somewhat enter into St. Paul's ' deep affection for his converts.'   The dying mother, who confided her children to her care, rightly estimated the wealth of love hidden beneath an exterior that often seemed cold and reserved ; and though her keen susceptibilities suffered much even from the mere physical contact with squalor and misery, and her anxieties were at times highly wrought up as she watched the conflict between good and evil going on in scores of homes, yet the same capacity for suffering held an equal freight of thankfulness when she could share in the 'joy over ' one sinner that repenteth.'

In the meantime she was steadily waiting for the opportunity which she had so long desired.   She noted with disappointment that the Domestic Mission failed to gather in the very lowest of the poor ; excellent as was its administration, and promising as was its beginning, it did not touch the class whom most she sought to raise ; and it became clear to her that there was room for yet another agency, which might attempt the difficult task of dealing with the boys and girls who filled the streets and roamed about the quays near Lewin's Mead.   The year 1843 was a marked one in the educational history of the country.   The speech of Lord Ashley [1] in the House of Commons on February 28th, in moving an Address praying 'that her Majesty will be

---

[1] With whom, as Lord Shaftesbury, Mary Carpenter afterwards worked in friendly union.

' graciously pleased to take into her instant and serious
' consideration the best means of diffusing the benefits of a
' moral and religious education among the working classes of
' her people,' drew public attention with unusual force to the
deplorable condition of vast numbers of children, especially
in the manufacturing districts. The Government were awake
to the magnitude of the evil, and, in the course of the discussion on Lord Ashley's motion, Sir J. Graham intimated
that two Bills on the subject were already in preparation.
A week later, on March 7th, he introduced a Bill containing
an elaborate provision for the better education of children in
manufacturing districts, and expressed his hope that the
Government plan, if adopted, ' would go far to establish a
' national scheme of education on a large scale.' The proposed organisation, however, met with severe criticism,
especially from the Nonconformists; the Government were
ultimately obliged to withdraw the education clauses, and the
settlement of the question was indefinitely deferred. The
general excitement was not unfelt in Bristol, but the conditions of the plan seemed to offer Mary Carpenter no aid in
the attainment of her special objects, and she took little
interest in it ; the vigilance with which she afterwards followed Parliamentary proceedings was not yet awakened.
She naturally, therefore, shared the view of those around her,
and acquiesced in the opposition offered to the Bill by the
several bodies of Dissenters.

TO MISS SANFORD.

Bristol, April 21st, 1843.

Do you live in comparative quiet, or are you, like other
people, agitated by educational movements ? Some people
here think that we had better have no Bill at all than such
a one, but all agree that many clauses must be vigorously
protested against by Dissenters. I am obliged to form my
opinions rather second-hand, not having yet read the Bill
itself; it seems to me a great step taken that the Tories
should acknowledge the necessity of a national education,
but it would be wrong for us to submit to see snares laid for
the consciences of our fellow Christians, and an engine of such
power for tyranny placed in the hands of the Church, without
a strong effort to avert the evil. . . .
I am going down to be present at the exhibition of the

air-pump to some of our poor people. I showed it on Easter
Tuesday to eighty delighted children. I rejoice when my
dear father's things are made useful in this way.

The failure of legislation, however, only made private
efforts the more needful ; and institutions were already in
the field which were to do their quiet work for a generation, until a really national system of education could be
established. In the year 1839, there passed away at
Portsmouth the venerable John Pounds, who had for many
years delighted to draw into his shoemaker's workshop the
wild boys and girls whom his singular influence subdued
into peace and order. Little by little the experiment was
tried in London and elsewhere, at first only on Sundays, of
collecting the restless wanderers of the street into a
'Ragged School.' The remarkable success of Sheriff Watson
and his fellow labourers in the Industrial Schools at
Aberdeen, which by degrees nearly cleared the town of
juvenile delinquents, gradually led to similar efforts elsewhere. Schools of this type sprang up in Dundee and at
Huntly, and later on Edinburgh and Glasgow prepared
to adopt like measures. Organisation followed, and the
Ragged School Union was formed ; but the English schools
were essentially different from those in Aberdeen and
Dundee, as the regular distribution of food formed no part
of the plan, and no municipal authorities were found bold
enough to confer power on the police to seek the children
in the highways and byways and ' compel them to come in.'
The Ragged Schools seemed to Mary Carpenter completely to realise her aims, and the establishment of such a
school in Lewin's Mead appeared the readiest means of
reaching the outcast and destitute, whose wants she had
borne in her heart for more than twelve years. But the
effort had to be made with slender resources, and without
the avowed fellowship of those whose names were already
prominently devoted to the cause. Only a year or two
before, a large committee had been formed in Bristol for
the promotion of unsectarian education, on which a number
of the leading clergy and Nonconformist ministers were
jointly appointed. But the senior pastor of the Lewin's
Mead Meeting was coldly excluded on the one side, while
the door was shut on the Catholic priest on the other. In

after years, Mary Carpenter used to look back with wonder
on the isolation in which she was at first compelled to work,
and the cordial sympathy and aid which she then received
from members of all religious denominations filled her with
delight ; but the want of this sustaining power rendered the
first steps all the more laborious. A few friends, however,
were at hand to assist her; and in the summer of 1846 the
plan was ripe. A room was secured in Lewin's Mead, a
master was engaged, and the 1st of August was fixed for
the opening. It was the anniversary of the emancipation
of the slaves in the British dominions ; and with the
peculiar observance of days which characterised her, Mary
Carpenter loved to connect with that earlier liberation the
beginning of her own work for the deliverance of mind and
soul from the bondage of ignorance and sin.

Everything was now ready for the new enterprise ;
but before the school was actually opened, a long desired
excursion to the Lakes was devised, in which her two
sisters and her brothers Russell and Philip joined her.
The tender sense of family union always remained strong
in her heart, through every fresh separation. One Christmas
Day (always additionally sacred to her as her parents'
marriage-day) she noted with regret that the anniversary
was spent by the little circle—no longer united—in six
different towns ; but the greetings to the absent were never
forgotten, nor did the birthdays pass unheeded. One of
her brothers she scarcely ever failed playfully to remind of
the first disappointment he had caused her, and the note of
1845 was often sounded again : ' To-morrow will carry me
' back to the years of childhood, when I used to nurse you,
' and when I wrote a Latin letter describing you, and when
' I took my pet china box with glass in the lid and a picture
' on the outside, to catch your first tears and keep them as a
' relic—and you had none ! ' As the brothers had settled,
one in London, the others in the ministry at Bridgewater
and at Stand near Manchester, she followed their work with
eager and affectionate interest. One sister, too, had gone to
share the northern home, and thus the union at Ambleside
of five out of the scattered group came to have for her a
special delight, for such a season of refreshing never came
again. Moreover at Ambleside they were close to Rydal,
and daily passed over ground made sacred to her by her

study of Wordsworth. Her reserve made her shrink from
asking an introduction to him, but she could not refrain
from offering some act of homage, and 'bribed Miss Martineau,'
as she used afterwards to say, by a little view of the Knoll,
to present to him a drawing of Rydal Water: 'I did not
' put my name, for fear of disgracing the family.' Yet even
more interest was kindled in her at Keswick, by the Southey
monument in Crosthwaite Church, of which she afterwards
wrote :

Liverpool, July 28th, 1846.

I have admired Southey's genius much more since I have
been in his region, and seen him lying so grandly and sweetly
in his own church, turning from the earthly hymns of praise
to unite his spirit with that which Nature raises from her
eternal hills.   His is not like the sleep of the old crusaders in
Westminster Abbey—*duro quiete, ferreo sonno*—but a living
sleep. Do you know that I think with deeper interest of sitting
worshipping with that exquisite countenance of the departed
before me, than of having joined in the service with the living
poet whose genius is still shrined in a mantle of clay.

Not even the sojourn at the Lakes, however, was wholly
without its inward sorrows and anxieties :

Ambleside, July 5th, 1846.—I constantly fear in my exertions for the good of others, lest some vain-glory, self-esteem,
or other unworthy motive, should mingle itself with what I
would fain desire to be zeal for the glory of God. This fear,
and the increasing perception how little we can of ourselves
do, sometimes casts a gloom over my efforts and removes that
brightness of hope which used to animate me. But I will not
despond. My God checks what is wrong in me sometimes by
painful discipline ; but I will thank Him for it, and go on my
way rejoicing ; grateful if He does sometimes allow me to
receive a reward even in this life, but still more grateful if
He is thus preparing me for a better world.

The depression, which arose in part from the overstrain
of the previous half-year, was but temporary, and Mary
Carpenter returned to Bristol to superintend the new
Ragged School with a more cheerful heart. The first
experience may be related in her mother's words.

Bristol, August 7th, 1846.

At home we are beginning to be busy as usual. We had
had it in contemplation to begin a 'Ragged School,' which
waited for Mary's return. She returned on Thursday night;
the master, Mr. Phelps, came on Friday, and on the following
Sunday nearly twenty boys were assembled. The seven which
Mr. Phelps had collected brought a dozen more in the afternoon,
which showed that they liked it; but, beginning to be tired in
the afternoon, one of them said, 'Now let us fight,' and in an
instant they were all fighting. Peace was, however, soon
restored, and they have gone on with increasing numbers and
more order than could have been expected; and to Mary's
astonishment, she did not meet with one group of boys
gambling or fighting on Lewin's Mead yesterday. It is
literally a 'Ragged School;' none have shoes or stockings,
some have no shirt, and no home, sleeping in casks on the
quay, or on steps, and living, I suppose, by petty depreda-
tions; but all appear better fed than the children of the
decent poor are. I have furnished the woman of the house
with towels and soap, and some sort of approach to cleanliness
is insisted upon.

From this time forth the Ragged School naturally occupied the chief place in Mary Carpenter's time and thoughts.
But within a few weeks after it was opened, the visits of
W. Lloyd Garrison and Frederick Douglas, and in the following month of Elihu Burritt, roused her to the highest
enthusiasm for the Abolition cause. 'We are in a state of
'intense Antislavery excitement,' she wrote, and her feeling
poured itself forth in verses accompanying her drawings in
the annual box, and in a poetical address to Garrison, which
found their way, much to her dismay, under her own name,
into the Antislavery journals in the States. Her intercourse
with these distinguished workers naturally stimulated her
efforts and gave added vigour to her correspondence; but the
school in Lewin's Mead was destined to absorb more and
more of her strength and attention. The temporary experiment proved so successful that it soon became evident that a
larger room would be required; and accordingly, the small
band of friends whom she had enlisted resolved to hire for a
year a room in St. James's Back ('a place swarming with raga-
'muffins'), previously fitted up as a chapel. Early in Decem-

ber the school was transferred to the new premises, where it
was to remain in active operation for a quarter of a century.
'Our Tuesday opening of our room was deeply interesting,
'and called forth a purer emotion in my heart than I have
'felt for some time; the boys behaved wonderfully and
'excited much admiration. Altogether, we thank God and
'take courage.'

Thus was the first of the series of institutions in
which Mary Carpenter was to develop her plans for destitute and degraded children, firmly established. Could she
have foreseen the tasks that yet lay before her, she might
perhaps have shrunk from entering on a path of labour from
which she found it impossible to draw back. She perceived
already that if it brought its own reward, it would require
its own sacrifices, and that, in particular, the mental culture
in which she had taken so much delight must be gradually
relinquished. As the autumn passed into the winter, she
found that neither her favourite German authors nor Grote's
Greece could hold her attention. 'Direct intellectual effort,'
she wrote, 'always does me good if without worrying; in-
'deed I wish that I could begin some regular intellectual
'employment in the afternoons, but I cannot now devote
'myself to acquiring knowledge as I used to do for its own
'sake.' But she had received at last the opportunity of full
devotion, which in early womanhood she had desired so
earnestly, and she would not shrink from embracing it wholly,
even though it bore on its front a heavy price. She even
felt new capacities unfolding within her, called into life by
the needs of those among whom she had been labouring;
fresh forces were stirring in her being in response to new
calls; and in the strength of these she prepared to go her
way, if it must be, alone.

London, December 31st, 1846.—This year is a marked one in
my soul's history. The first half of it was marked by much
distress of spirit; then came a season which should have been
one of refreshment, yet it did not seem to be from the presence
of the Lord. I rejoiced in it, but not so much as I hoped or
ought. Yet it was a refreshment, and left food for many
pleasant thoughts afterwards. Then again the daily round of
duties were more cheerfully and hopefully performed, but
rather overburdened by extraneous calls on our time, and
thoughts, and efforts. Yet they were better done, and more

cheerfully and hopefully done, and thus came a stirring and awakening of our spirits; and I felt as if my existence were increased, that I had more powers than I thought, that my individual being was more prized by others than I had thought; this sometimes made me lowly in gratitude, yet sometimes I fear that it made me bear myself with more self-reliance and more thought and consciousness of self than I ought. And then the desire of my heart for these twelve years—since I knew our beloved Dr. Tuckerman—has been brought near its accomplishment; this has given me unspeakable joy. These things have given me greater independence of sympathy, because greater consciousness of my own existence with powers which I trust will be perfected in that world to which I ardently, though not impatiently, aspire. Yet still there seems a want of my nature unsatisfied; if I loved my God and my Saviour enough I should not feel it so. I have of late dwelt with much interest on a character exhibiting a most beautiful combination of rare intellectual powers with wonderful gentleness and benevolence. But if my God knew that it would be good for me to have such a companion in my pilgrimage, to whom I could pour out my inmost thoughts, he would not withhold the blessing. Be still then, my soul, and cast thy care on the Rock of Ages.

CHAPTER IV.

THE RAGGED SCHOOL.
1846—1850.

'How can a man learn to know himself? By observation never, but by action. Endeavour to do thy duty, and thou shalt know what is within thee '—*Goethe*.

' Such lived not in the past alone,
   But thread to-day the unheeding street,
And stairs to sin and sorrow known
   Sing to the welcome of their feet.

The den they enter glows a shrine,
   The grimy sash an oriel burns;
Their cup of water warms like wine,
   Their speech is filled from heavenly urns.

Around their brows to me appears
   An aureole traced in tenderest light—
The rainbow-gleam of smiles through tears,
   In dying eyes to them made bright,

Of souls who shivered on the edge
   Of that chill ford, repassed no more,
And in their mercy felt the pledge
   And sweetness of that farther shore.'

J. G. Whittier.

CHAPTER IV.

THE Ragged School was now fairly established, and soon began to tax to the utmost the resources of its managers. They had boldly fixed it in one of the most crowded, and at the same time one of the lowest neighbourhoods of the city; and the opening of a Night School in connection with it soon brought in a swarm of young men and women, whose habits and character almost caused even the resolute heart of Mary Carpenter to quail. Early in 1847, the numbers one Sunday evening amounted to two hundred; the attempt to conclude the school with prayer was baffled by mockery and disorder, and the court beneath resounded with screams and blows. The neighbours resented the disturbance, and even insulted the friends of the school on their way to and fro. It became plain that some restriction must be imposed; and though several working men did all they could, it was needful for a time to obtain aid from the police. But the officer who came to protect soon remained for another purpose; the control acquired by the master gradually rendered his vigilance needless, and it was not long before he was one day reported to the magistrates for neglect of duty, 'having been 'two hours in the Ragged School setting copies to the boys.'

Thus tranquillised, the school at once took its place as the little centre of affection and enlightenment for the miserable district in which it was situated. The fluctuating character of the population, and the restlessness of the children, in-

evitably interfered with the steadiness of the attendance ; in
1848, though upwards of five hundred children passed through
the school, the average number present daily did not exceed
a hundred and sixty.   Yet even in spite of these difficulties,
a greater impression was produced than the most sanguine had
anticipated ; order was secured and regular teaching was soon
organised ; and at the close of 1848, after two years' hard
work, Mary Carpenter had the satisfaction of hearing H.M.
Inspector, Mr. J. Fletcher, declare that 'he did not know of any
' other ragged school where there was so large an amount of
' intellect and well-directed effort exerted to raise the school,
' to train up self-acting beings.'
    The secret of the success lay in the untiring devotion of
the teachers, who could not fail to catch the enthusiasm with
which Mary Carpenter entered into their labours.   Week by
week and month by month she was ever at hand to lighten
the burden not only by ready counsel and sympathy, but by
taking a large share in the toil.   The morning and evening
of Sunday were consecrated to her scripture-class in St.
James's Back—the afternoon being already pledged to the
Sunday School : two nights every week were regularly given,
at no matter what social sacrifice, to the Evening School;
and day after day found her in the same haunt, ready to take
a class, to preside over the mid-day distribution of the soup
to the most needy, or even bear the sole charge of management if sickness kept the master away.   By this constancy
she soon acquired a complete familiarity with the ways of
the scholars, and also with the habits of the neighbourhood.
Strong in the power of a sacred purpose, she was perfectly
devoid of fear, and would traverse alone and at night courts into
which policemen only went by twos.   The street quarrel was
hushed at her approach, as a guilty lad slunk away to avoid
her look of sorrowful reproof ; and her approving word, with
the gift of a flower, a picture, or a Testament, often made sad
homes cheerful and renewed the courage of the wavering.
    Her long practice in the art of teaching now began to
stand her in good stead ; and it was well that she could
bring a swift and incisive intellect to bear upon the unformed
minds with which she came in contact.   With the boys she
found little or no difficulty in exciting interest—their wits
were active enough, though their ignorance of the commonest
facts frequently amazed her ; but the girls often presented

a stolid and impenetrable front of stupidity which made her
well-nigh desperate. It was from the boys' classes, therefore, that she had most satisfaction. She delighted in the
quick appreciation with which the facts of Natural History
were often received by them, as well as in the ready application to their own circumstances of the principles underlying
the incidents of history. One or two instances from the
journal of her school work which she kept for some years,
may serve to illustrate her methods of teaching.

'I showed them the orrery, which greatly delighted them,
and they seemed quite to understand it, and to enter into the
idea of the inclination of the earth's axis producing a change
of seasons.'

'This class had never seen a map, and had the greatest
difficulty in realising it. T. was delighted to see Bristol,
Keynsham, and Bath. I always begin with the "known,"
carrying them on afterwards to the "unknown."'

'I had taken to my class on the preceding week some
specimens of ferns neatly gummed on white paper; they were
much struck with their beauty, but none knew what they
were, though W. thought he had seen them growing; one
thought they were palm-trees. They seemed interested in the
account of their fructification I gave them. This time I took
a piece of coal-shale with impressions of ferns to show them.
I explained that this had once been in a liquid state, telling
them that some things could be proved to be certain while
others were doubtful; that time did not permit me to explain
the proofs to them, nor would they understand them if I did;
but that I was careful to tell them nothing as certain which
could not be fully proved. I then told each to examine the
specimen and tell me what he thought it was. W. gave so
bright a smile that I saw he knew; none of the others could tell;
he said they were ferns like what I showed them last week, but
he thought they were chiselled on the stone. Their surprise
and pleasure were great when I explained the matter to them.'

'The History of Joseph: They all found a difficulty in
realising that this had actually occurred. One asked if Egypt
existed now, and if people lived in it. When I told them that
buildings now stood which had been erected about the time of
Joseph, one said that it was impossible, as they must have
fallen down ere this. I showed them the form of a pyramid,
and they were satisfied. One asked if *all* books were true.'

The story of Macbeth impressed them much : 'They knew
the name of Shakespeare, having seen his head over a public
house!'

The mental improvement of the scholars was thus watched by Mary Carpenter with eagerness; and every instance of memory, of attention, or of the practical application of the truths which she taught, was carefully treasured up. She even ventured on the experiment of inviting an accomplished blind friend, Mr. S. Worsley, to give a lecture on the air-pump. About two hundred were present, and she noted with deep satisfaction the impression produced upon both boys and girls by the simple demonstrations. 'A year ago,' she wrote, 'I could not have imagined such 'progress,—that they could be brought to so great a power 'of self-control and power of experiencing intellectual 'pleasure so soon.'

It was, however, into the moral and religious training that Mary Carpenter threw herself with the greatest earnestness. She brought to her work a deep faith in the capacities for virtue even of the most depraved, which never deserted her. This trust she had received in part, as it were, by inheritance. It had been further strengthened by education, for her father's school had been founded upon this confidence; and it had been enriched by the glowing utterances of Dr. Channing, and confirmed with ample illustration by the experience of Dr. Tuckerman. To the latent elements of good which she could often discern when they were hidden from every other eye, she never failed to make her appeal; and whatever disappointments awaited her, she renewed her efforts with unwearied hope. At the very outset her resolution was taken. 'We must not attempt,' she wrote in 1847, 'to break the will, but to train it to govern itself 'wisely; and it must be our great aim to call out the good 'which still exists even in the most degraded, and to make 'this conquer the bad.' She noted with delight the influence which by degrees tamed the unruly; which made truthfulness the habit, at least in her class; and suppressed all open manifestations of ill-will. Those who were thieves before they came into the school, did not always abandon their former companions or leave their old ways; when they reappeared in the class after a brief term of imprisonment, she found at first that they entered without shame, and were greeted almost respectfully by their fellows; but this boldness gradually gave way to compunction, and by 1850 she was able to record, 'I am pleased to see how much the 'sympathies of the school are with the good.'[1] To her, indeed, the wonder was not that there was so much tendency to sink, but that there was so much power to rise. As she learned the boys' inner histories, she could estimate better the overwhelming force of their temptations. Even when she saw them through the prison grating in the warder's charge, it was with pity and sympathy rather than anger or alienation. With the first reaching after better things, she was on the watch to give encouragement and support; nor could any number of relapses exhaust her faith. 'It was a 'most touching sight,' so she wrote of a young penitent, 'to see T. between his two brothers, and my other two 'poor prisoners: also little G. who has so young to fight 'with the powers of darkness, and my two poor starved 'Irish boys looking as yet without an idea. I felt in-'describable gratitude to our Heavenly Father, who has 'placed such an instrumentality in our hands and enabled 'us by the power of Christian love to draw to us these 'perishing ones.' Or again : 'It is wonderful what movings 'of the spirit sometimes seem to prompt them to good. I 'felt the deepest pity for these poor boys, feeling sure that, 'if in better circumstances, they might be very different.'

The chief mode of appeal by which Mary Carpenter softened these young hearts was the power of her religious teaching. She had herself struggled long and severely; indeed, the time of conflict was not over yet; but she had found the secret of unseen strength. Into all her work she threw a weight of character which belonged only to few; but her Scripture lessons allowed all the tenderness of her soul to flow freely forth without the checks of scholastic necessity. Morning and evening on Sundays, and on many a week night besides, she was found in the school with the little band of youths around her, to whom she delighted to unfold the truths of the Gospel story. Many of them were Catholics, and had never seen Bibles or Testaments, and even those who occasionally came from other schools seemed to have been but little impressed by any religious influence. The field was altogether new ; and

---

[1] The year before she reported that there was a poor negro in the evening school, who was brought by the boys, and who chiefly subsisted on what they gave him; and her journal contains more than one reference to their kindness and gentleness to him.

she felt herself to possess powers of which she had before hardly been aware, as one after another was led by her to realise in some degree the principles and trusts on which her own life was founded. The New Testament was read with the greatest interest, and the favourite lessons were drawn from the teachings of Jesus; and her early studies under her father were constantly in her mind as she poured forth the conceptions she had largely derived from him. Pictures were freely employed in illustration, and she was sometimes met with unexpected appreciation. 'I showed 'them a large outline from Raphael of the crossing of the 'Red Sea, and was surprised to observe how it fixed their 'attention. They said they preferred it to the coloured 'print. They evidently had a feeling for Raphael's genius.' Her cabinets and the collections of friends were ransacked for specimens of every kind that could make Galilee and Jerusalem something more than 'Bible words;' and, when once this difficulty was overcome, she was better able to awaken the slumbering reverence to which nothing had as yet appealed. At first she contented herself with comparatively small demands upon their attention; yet even of these she could write: 'I never enjoy any lesson more than these 'half-hours, for I seem to touch these poor children's 'hearts with the loveliness and holiness of the Saviour's 'heart.' But by-and-by she found herself often followed with an intensity of desire that eagerly craved more food for mind and soul; the rough boys sat, as she would say, 'transfixed,' and all restlessness was merged in an absorbing interest. She might be long teaching, but no hearer fell asleep. Thus she was able to report, one Good Friday:

A truly happy evening with my class, who were with me for nearly two hours, dwelling on the scenes of the last day of the Saviour's mortal life, without appearing in the least wearied. Indeed I had to make no effort to control them or to keep up their attention. A year and a half ago there was scarcely one of these boys with whom I could have ventured to read this sacred narrative, so wild were they and untouched by religion; yet now they delight to understand every incident, and to realise the whole scene to themselves; by this means the living character of Jesus will, I trust, take hold of their hearts, and his commands and promises be a guide and support to them.

The boys passed out of the school, sometimes, alas! to their old haunts of vice, sometimes into situations which Mary Carpenter or the master obtained for them. Whenever it was possible she corresponded with them, and the illustrated papers that had done duty here were punctually sent to former scholars far away in the Colonies; or those who were near home assembled at the annual Christmas festivals, and there renewed the friendly intercourse which had first helped them to rise to better things. The following spontaneous testimony from one of her first scholars, published in one of the Bristol papers just after her death, will show how deeply the memory of her influence was cherished in after days.

TO THE EDITOR OF *The Bristol Daily Post.*

June 21st, 1877.

Perhaps I am rather intruding by asking you to insert my few lines; but permit me to say that as I know your paper to be a widely-circulated one, I thought it might be interesting to some to drop a few words upon the subject of the late lamented death of Miss M. Carpenter, especially to those who were unable to witness the sad ceremony of Tuesday. I myself was one of those who, although many years ago, received her sympathy and love, which words cannot express. I was one of those four who were picked up as careless, neglected, and forsaken boys. When first that dear friend took an interest in me and my companions, we were assembled in a small room in Lewin's Mead. Here our numbers so increased that we were removed to a larger school in St. James's Back, where everything greatly improved. For many years I remained there, and was brought up under her watchful care, combined with that of Mr. and Miss Andrews. About twenty-six years ago I was compelled to leave to seek for employment; but I took with me the best of all blessings, which she had so deeply engrafted in me, and which, I trust, has and ever will remain there: it was the love of God.

The new labours in which Mary Carpenter was now engaged withdrew her more and more from her former pursuits. But she could not lay them aside entirely as long as any time could be rescued for them. ' I am ' reading Niebuhr with great interest,' she wrote in March,

1847; 'I could not summon up courage to spend an hour
'with old Romans who have not much in common with us,
'and are particularly unconnected with Ragged Schools,
'were it not that Niebuhr is telling me the tale with his
'own thoughts and feelings intermingled, and I do enjoy
'a little intercourse with *der grosse Mensch.* We are
'fascinated with Zschokke; what a soul he had!' Her
correspondence, however, became more and more occupied
with her growing interest in the work to which she was now
devoting herself; everything that she read was estimated
in its relation to it, and even political and social movements grouped themselves to her view around this centre.
Especially her Antislavery enthusiasm, though by no means
diminished in itself, seemed to pale before the glow of the
new ardour. The bondage of the soul in which she found
the wild youths of Lewin's Mead entangled, appeared to her
not less but rather more terrible than positive slavery; and
though she did not admit the analogy when it was urged by
those who were but lukewarm in the cause of Abolition,
she was not unwilling to use it in justification of her own
devotion to the Ragged School. The visits of American
friends, as in former years, still helped to keep up communication with the leaders of the great crusade for freedom;
and the annual box for the Antislavery Bazaar began to
carry with it contributions made by willing hands in the
upper room at St. James's Back. Many a time did the
girls freely work long hours beyond school-time to finish
their neat patchwork quilts; and barefooted children who
had been taught to knit, brought stockings made in secret to
escape the eyes of drunken parents, and begged to be
allowed to send them to the poor slaves; so quickly were
the springs of sympathy opened in hearts to which it was a
new thing to care for others. How these first years of
daily work among the destitute passed for Mary Carpenter,
some of her letters during this period may in part set
forth.

TO MRS. FOLLEN.

Bristol, December 8th, 1846.

We were much interested in what you say of your sister's
death. I have watched by many dying beds, but never have
witnessed the moment of dissolution, and death has never

entered our house. I do not now think of our beloved father as dead; I think of him as Vittoria Colonna did of her husband, *Il suo sol, benchè gli altri lo riputavan morto, per lei sempre viveva* : it is only sometimes that I feel that there is between us and him a deep gulf fixed. Oh blessed hour to each of us when that shall be passed, and we shall meet to part no more! In the meantime it is happy to labour about what he would have laboured to accomplish. The accompanying paper will tell you a little of what we are doing. It is an indescribable happiness to me to see that being accomplished which has been the one earnest wish of my heart since I took a walk through those wretched streets with our beloved Dr. Tuckerman, more than twelve years ago. and he spoke of the duty of following those unhappy children to their homes, and endeavouring to exert a moral influence over them. This gave a definiteness to the general and vague feeling which already existed in my mind, of desire to do something for these forsaken ones. The first-fruits of Dr. Tuckerman's visit appeared in our Working and Visiting Society. This did not reach the evil, but only made us feel it more painfully. Then the Domestic Mission arose—my father's last effort. Our missionary proved a worthy man, but not one whose forte lay in collecting round him those outcasts of society; he could not reach them, and he had not love enough visible to attract them to him; he is very useful among a higher and different class. A fortunate union of circumstances enabled us to begin our experiment last August; you will form a judgment of our master by his report; and a little paper which Mr. Estlin will, I hope, be able to inclose in this packet, will tell you what an interesting occasion we had last Tuesday and what encouragement it gave us from the very great improvement of the boys. It is a very singular but delightful feeling to us to find ourselves in the stream of popularity; but so it is; we are quite struck with the interest excited in our movement. So we have great hopes, but I have now learnt to rejoice with trembling. Some people blame us for expending our sympathies and efforts on the distant slaves, when we have so much to be done at home. I believe, on the other hand, that the more our benevolent sympathies are called out, the more they expand.

TO MISS SANFORD.

Bristol, after Whit Tuesday, May, 1847.

I wish you could have been with me invisibly at my last visit to the W.'s, where I took you to see how some people exist. The room was rather improved in appearance, being

only covered with ingrimed dirt, without much loose. Mr. W.
came in to hold a discourse with me, he sitting in state, his
wife standing admiring by.   After discussing various topics
of politics, the state of Bristol, Sabbatical observance, etc.,
on which we ended by agreeing very well, at last he asked me
what I thought of the apple with which Eve was tempted.
I was sorely perplexed, having the fear of Mr. Kenrick, whose
Essay on Primeval History we are reading, before my eyes;
so, fortunately, the bright idea occurred to me to tell him that
the whole is a sort of parable, to show that in those early
times, as now, disobedience was punished by God, and that
we can only be happy, now as then, while obedient to God's
commands.   The good man was quite satisfied.

Yesterday I went up to the Zoological Gardens; though
very hot, it was delightful to see so many thousands enjoying
themselves innocently; I hear that there were ten thousand
yesterday at the Gardens.   Seven hundred went a cheap trip
to Chepstow, and the Institution was crowded.   Think of ten
thousand persons enjoying themselves for a whole day without
drinking!   Truly Teetotalism appears to me, when one divests
it of the nonsense and vulgarity which too often accompanies
it, the sublimest institution that exists, next to Christianity.
Think of a body of men, uniting in personal self-denial, laying
aside all prejudices and antipathies about religion and politics,
and all for no personal gain, but to stem a dreadful moral
evil.

TO THE REV. SAMUEL MAY.

Bristol, June 16th, 1847.

Thank you for your kind note, and all the trouble you
have taken about my little volume.[1] I am glad that my
name does not, after all, appear, having a particular dislike to
seeing it in print, much as I rejoice in it, both Christian and
surname.   On another point you have, through your great
kindness, defeated my intention, in declining to receive anything for the book.   I wished that *you* should devote the
proceeds to some good cause; probably the Antislavery, or
the Ministry at Large, if you had none more intimately connected with you; however, the thing cannot be helped now.
What a glorious meeting you must have had at Theodore

---

[1] The *Meditations*, which Mr. 'May had most kindly undertaken
to see through the press.   Mary Carpenter had at this time a peculiar
horror of publicity, and had been sorely troubled at the appearance
in print of some of her Antislavery poems, and passages from her
letters to Mr. Garrison and others, with her signature.

Parker's![1] Truly one must be thankful that so many truth-loving and man-loving spirits still are left amongst us; one sometimes half despairs when one reads of the 'giants' of olden times. I can hardly imagine any meeting more inspiring than that of such beings in free and open intercourse of mind with mind. I do not at all agree with much that Parker, Emerson, Garrison, etc., write, but I *greatly* admire much in the spirit of their writings.

TO MISS SANFORD.

Bristol, September 6th, 1847.

You quite make me long to read Lorenzo de Medici. Now I read such books with a different (but not less earnest) interest from what I used to feel; every piece of history like that I look on as a scrap of the world's life, which has its bearing on every other part. It is wonderful how much living importance great principles give to the most common occurrences. Having dwelt more than before lately on the development of some grand principles, such as the effect of Christianity on the human race, the peace principle, etc., I like to watch their progress in different minds, and among different nations. But for this I should not have read, with the deep interest I have done, the horrid details of the degradation of the Roman nation under the emperors, as given by Niebuhr, though I believe I must confess that *der grosse Mensch* would fascinate me on with him wherever he chose to take me.

To another correspondent, the Rev. A. A. Livermore, she recommended Mr. F. W. Newman's *History of the Hebrew Monarchy*, 'in which the freest principles of 'criticism and historical research are applied to the Bible;' and then in reply to some homethrust about the condition of the Irish peasantry, she thus continued:

Bristol, February 11th, 1848.

In your last letter but one you remark that from our different positions we must entertain different views respecting many subjects. I think that on matters of abstract right we can often best judge from a distance, unswayed by interest;

---

[1] A 'Council of Reformers,' at which there were present, among others, R. W. Emerson, Amos B. Alcott, W. H. Channing, James Freeman Clarke, W. L. Garrison, Wendell Phillips, and Charles Sumner.

though we may not see *how* these principles are to be brought to bear, still we can see that they ought to be so. It therefore seems to me that, however removed from you by the ocean, we can judge, just as well as if we were nearer, of the surpassing wickedness of slavery, and you can see the injustice of many Irish landlords as well as if you were near, and hate it as much as we do. But I cannot admit the cases to be at all parallel. Slavery is unparalleled, both in its intrinsic wickedness and by its collateral evils. It is not satisfied with crushing the body, it crushes the soul as much as any human force *can* do it, and reduces the image of God to a chattel. When this high treason against the Supreme is committed, what wonder that every conceivable and inconceivable crime follows in its train, so that your own Jefferson trembled for his country when he remembered that God is just. No, I cannot admit that anything *can* be brought into comparison with that ' crime above all crime, union of all.' But for argument's sake let us suppose the slaveholder and Irish landlord equally criminal; the victims of their cruelty are very differently circumstanced. The Irish peasants may have the consolation of sharing each other's sufferings, and of the supports of religion ; they may be helped and solaced by their fellow-creatures, who will be blessed for it ; and they are *free*, they may fly in broad daylight and seek a less thickly peopled country, where their fathers have before taken refuge. In *all* these respects the poor slaves must envy their lot; if they have enough food, we know that man liveth not by bread alone ; and though thousands do annually reach our land of freedom, where they are received and treated like men, yet it must be as a thief in the night that they may regain their own. But allow that in even these respects the cases were equal, there would be yet another grand difference. Your Congress does all in its power to stifle any voice that is upraised against the crying sin, and will not *attempt* to put away the iniquity ; our Parliaments, session after session, are *striving* to amend the evil ; individually and collectively the English are trying to benefit that unhappy people. Do not suppose that we shut our eyes to our own faults while opening them to those of our neighbours. You would find generally here that those persons who exert themselves most in the Antislavery cause, are the most earnest in their exertions to rectify home abuses. I can say that of all whom I know; and be assured that much as we ourselves have at heart the great cause for which those whom we love and honour among you are labouring, and in which they ask our sympathy, our own poor degraded children have a deeper place in it, and call forth more constant and zealous exertion, even than our degraded coloured sisters.

You have no need of Ragged Schools; Elihu Burritt told
me that you have not in America so great a field for martyr
enterprise as we have in these schools. Ours is beginning to
give us much hope; it will be a great happiness to have
rescued some few even from the ' dangerous' classes, and to
have called forth their noble powers in a right direction.
The world is beginning to awake to its true life, I firmly
believe it. One true and strong spirit, with the armour of
faith, will destroy a whole army of selfish Goliaths.

TO THE REV. SAMUEL MAY.

Liverpool, July 12th, 1848.

In your country the Chartists are probably sympathised
much with, not so much so by enlightened philanthropists in
general; and when I have had an opportunity of knowing
anything about them, I have found that only the least re-
putable, the most ignorant of the labouring classes join them.
This is particularly the case in Bristol, where attempts to get
up meetings have quite failed. I saw in the papers that one
was mentioned as having been held on Brandon Hill, attended
by five thousand persons; I was on the hill at the time, and
should not suppose there were as many hundreds. There are
great abuses existing in England, but it needs the highest
wisdom and knowledge to rectify them ; the awful example of
Paris shows that a mobocracy is the worst of all governments,
and that it is not sufficient to have the best intentions if one
has not knowledge. I dare not venture to speak of the horrors
that have been, and the horrors that are and will be at Paris.
What can be hoped for that unhappy country where moral
force seems paralysed, and nothing but physical strength can
hold the reins of government? We are reading with the
deepest interest the life of Dr. Channing, and well has his
nephew executed his noble task—thankful are we to him for
having given such a treasure to the world. It will do the
cause of the slave much good, I trust, and will stimulate many
to lift up their voices for him more boldly. How thankful do
I feel that a man of such noble powers as Theodore Parker
has devoted them so gloriously to the service of the oppressed,
as he has done in his letter to the people of the United States.
The whole is written in a tone of such calmness, 'truth and
soberness,' that the most unimpassioned can find no just cause
of complaint with it, and with such attention to statistics that
the most calculating must be satisfied; and yet with all this
he soars into a sublimity in the last chapters that must, one
would think, send a thrill into the most sluggish heart.

TO MRS. FOLLEN.

Bristol, February 17th, 1849.

My mind is now almost as much engrossed by our Ragged School as yours is by the Abolition question. Indeed they are very kindred subjects; you are trying to free the god-like spirit which has been enthralled by the wickedness of man, by external force; we are trying to free that divine nature from the still more than heathenish darkness in which it is growing to become a fiend, a worse than American slave. I feel this work inexpressibly glorious, nor have I ever felt the inextinguishable greatness of the human soul so much as I have at seeing it rise superior to such very degrading circumstances as it does in many of these children. Some of the boys are beginning to be civilised enough to enable me to read the Testament with them on Sunday evenings; it is a most interesting time to me. . . .

The public is more awakened than it has ever been to the duty of man to care for his fellow-men. The dreadful evils existing are doubtless more exposed to view, and consequently more distressing to the benevolent mind, than they were some twenty years ago; but there is more wisely directed effort to remedy them. So I thank God and take courage.

TO THE REV. SAMUEL MAY.

Bristol, April 6th, 1849.

The result of all your labours is clearly showing itself; crime cannot now be perpetrated as it used to be, nor can the slaveholders *rule* Congress and stop the mouths of whom they will. I do not believe, however, that you can go on without a dissolution of the Union. As it is, you have a dead and living body tied up together. I have been lately reading Fowell Buxton's Memoir with extreme interest; the days of struggle are brought most vividly before us, and excite almost intense interest. It is very striking to compare the similarity of the battle on this side of the Atlantic and yours. I clearly see from the conduct of the West Indians, and the strength of their influence in England, that it will be quite in vain to expect the slaveholders voluntarily to abandon their prey, and that the victory can never be achieved but by the most determined courage and perseverance and *faith.* But it must be by purely Christian means; and I have been much struck by perceiving how much influence Buxton had, from never using any language which was inconsistent with Christian courtesy, though it was as firm and uncompromising as the sternest Abolitionist could desire. We had an advantage over you in the contest, that the Church was opposed to slavery, and by the persecutions with which its ministers were treated by the planters, the eyes of the English people were opened.

TO MISS SANFORD.

Bristol, October 14th, 1849.

I often feel very glad that in my early days my mind was provided with so many varied stores, for now I should not be able to fix my attention to acquiring what is fugitive and earthly, and yet I find them all very useful in the work to which I have devoted myself. It is a blessed work, and I am very thankful to my Heavenly Father that he permits me to carry it on, and that it is of such a nature that it does me great good, calling me out of myself, stimulating my intellectual activity, leading me to see and correct my faults, and giving me constantly the most abundant and undeserved rewards, in the bright smiles of the poor children. I have been lately reading Mrs. Schimmelpenninck's *History of Port Royal*. I never read such a book! It fills one with thankfulness that such a testimony to the power of the Gospel was given to the human race ; and those nuns are among the holy ones that I hope to meet in heaven. Without seeking walls of monastic seclusion I only desire to carry their spirit into my intercourse with the world. Do read it. It will not convert you to Catholicism, but rather show you the evils of the system which their spirituality overcame.

The next letter refers to the possibility of true Christian fellowship in the midst of diversity of creed ; its conditions were already clearly foreseen by her.

TO THE REV. A. A. LIVERMORE.

Bristol, November 2nd, 1849.

I do not believe that this union will take place by any formal effort, still less do I believe that our orthodox brethren will ever formally unite with Unitarians on any ground. Yet this union is in many cases taking place insensibly, as men are led to fix their view on some important central moral movement, such as the abolition of slavery, peace, temperance. When they find that they really can work together, the more will they be ready to sink sectarian differences. This is an interesting phase in the present philanthropic movements, which have as yet kept pretty clear from doctrinal differences. I cannot make out whether you are freer than we are from the bane of bigotry ; I fancy not.

Your eyes are doubtless much turned to Europe. I do not attempt to follow all the changes that are going on ; I fear that for a time tyranny will resume its sway over the nations, which as yet are not ripe for liberty. France seems longing again for the leading-strings which she attempted to throw

away before she could do without them. One cannot help
watching with interest the struggle for liberty, but it is a
melancholy interest, for I see that men have suffered much
and will suffer much more because they do not yet comprehend
that the Supreme Ruler will not have his laws broken, to bring
about the best ends. Poor Hungary! I mourn for her, and if
ever there was a just war it was here; but she has fallen by
what must inevitably attend the best wars—the passions which
are necessarily excited by them.

TO THE REV. SAMUEL MAY.

Bristol, October 5th, 1850.

Perhaps the greatest real sacrifice has been made for the
cause by the children of the Ragged School. W. W. Brown[1]
paid a short visit to the school, and the older ones heard him
lecture. Their excellent instructress, Miss Andrews, talked
to them on the subject and excited their sympathy for those
who were deprived of the blessing most precious to them—
liberty. Miss A. has devoted a large amount of time and
trouble to the preparation of the table-cover formed of a
number of tailor's pattern-cards, which had been given to the
school. The girls worked earnestly 'for the poor slaves.'
When it was finished I offered to pay them for their work,
but they all exclaimed that they wished to *give* their work.
Many little girls worked most diligently at knitting edging.
Those who understand these matters will perceive that *many*
long and patient hours have been given. The evening scholars
have devoted one evening in the week to a work to most of
them quite new. One crippled girl, who maintains herself by
such work, made all the purses and dressed the doll, for herself and her friends; each purse *cost* the donor 3s. 6d., and you
may imagine how much self-denial must have been exercised
to procure this money. One girl rose every morning at five
to net a handkerchief; another brought some favourite toys.
These little facts will show the deep interest felt. They cheer
and stimulate us.

TO THE REV. SAMUEL MAY.

[After the passing of the Fugitive Slave Law.]

Bristol, May 29th, 1851.

You have been much and often in my thoughts since the
last atrocious act of your Legislature, and much do I wish that
a small portion of the warm sympathy which I feel for you

---

[1] An escaped slave who was on a lecturing tour in England.

and your fellow workers could have reached you; but I will
not delay any longer to give you a faint and feeble expression
of some of the deep and inexpressible thoughts and feelings
that sometimes nearly overpower me. Indeed I feel obliged to
put a strong curb on myself when speaking on the subject, so
awful an offence does it appear to me is being committed by
your nation against humanity, against itself, against God. By
your *nation!* We need not cross the Atlantic to find crushing
oppression, deadly cruelty, offences against God and man, that
make the blood curdle, and raise even the men of peace to
forget themselves for a moment, and to suppose that for once
vengeance may be theirs ; but these are acts of individuals, or
of governments ; and this day when our bells are most strangely
ringing a joyful remembrance of the preservation to us of a
profligate, a tyrant, a Catholic, but too well reminds us that no
act of perfidy to sacred rights, no vice however loathsome, is
too bad to be perpetrated by cruel and false governors. But
your States have now acquired a pre-eminence which I trust
they will never lose ; they stand alone in the annals of history,
and I hope will always do so; they have reached a climax of
black wickedness, not of ignorant sin, but of daring and
unblushing defiance of the laws of God, with their eyes open,
with the voice of the civilised world against them, with the
Bible before them. It is the nation that has done this, not the
general government, but the States' Legislature ; not the
rabble, but the free educated people, who hold themselves up
as examples before the world, whose ministers of religion tell
Europe to admire and copy the fair proportions, the glorious
freedom, of their adored Union. When I heard that the Bill
had passed through your Legislature, I thought that this was
the beginning of the end of Slavery ; it revealed no new
wickedness, it only put forth the reality in its true light, so
that men might see it, know it, and detest it. I felt sure that
many would now feel bound to declare themselves for the
oppressed ; that New England, who had spent her heart's
blood, and severed the near ties of mother and daughter for
freedom, would be true to her trust. I had often been assured
by Americans that no slave could be captured in Boston, that
none of her officers could lawfully hold him, or any person
receive him. This trust seemed at first likely to be realised,
yet I discerned in the opposition of the Bostonians to the Bill
more of wounded pride than of genuine devotion to the rights
of man. When your city functionaries refused their court for
a lawful meeting, my mind misgave me, for a municipal body
must really represent the bulk of the people. Sims[1] is to be

---

[1] The first fugitive sent back to slavery from Boston, under the
new Law, April, 1851.

envied rather than one of the judges and officers who enslaved
him. I rejoice that he was able to walk on with a firm and
dignified step, though nature shuddered; and that the faithful
few who were plunged into despair and grief were able to take
refuge with Him who is alone the Rock of Ages, and to support not only their own souls but his with the words of prayer
and the songs of praise. May God's spirit be with him! I
trust that there is still some English blood and spirit in your
nation, and that some of your rulers may be roused to compare
this Bill with the Declaration of Independence, and to prove
to the government that an act has been committed which is
treason to the State. I am just now reading a new and true
Life of William Penn, by W. H. Dixon, and have been much
struck with the similarity of his position under the Con-
venticle Act, and that of the Abolitionists under the Fugitive
Slave Law. The two laws were not very dissimilar in their
intentions: ours, in the dark ages of our history, being
intended to enslave the mind; yours, in an enlightened period,
intending to hold in Egyptian bondage both body and soul.
Penn determined to rest his defence on the illegality of the
Act, as being absolutely opposed to the spirit of the charter,
but he was gagged. The jury were firm to their trust, and
refused to bring him in guilty of disorder; they were famished
two days and imprisoned. They appealed to the Court of
Common Pleas; the Mayor and Recorders were condemned;
they came out of Newgate conquerors. Truly remarks the
historian that ' unjust laws are powerless weapons when used
' against an upright people.' May you, Mr. Garrison, and all
others who are true to their trust, have divine grace to fight
this battle in the spirit of the Lord !

This vigorous letter was among the last that her interest
in the Antislavery cause drew from Mary Carpenter. The
claims of the Ragged School were becoming more and more
absorbing. The home teaching which had been gradually
contracted in range, was finally given up early in 1848 ; and
one of the first fruits of the additional leisure thus secured,
was the preparation of a short Life of her revered friend
Dr. Tuckerman, published by the Christian Tract Society,
and reprinted immediately afterwards in America. Her
object was to depict alike his character and his work, especially among the poor, as one of the purest examples of
Christian philanthropy ; and this review of a career by which
she had been herself so profoundly stimulated, naturally
deepened her own resolves of self-devotion.

The Memoir of Dr. Tuckerman was followed in the year 1849 by a series of papers in *The Inquirer* newspaper on Ragged Schools, in which she developed her views on their proper management, and indicated the place which they ought to hold among existing educational agencies. The papers fell into the hands of Mr. Fletcher, one of H.M. Inspectors of Schools, who declared them to be ' the best ' collection of well-reasoned principles and results of expe- ' rience ' with which he was acquainted. He urged their republication; and the writer was at last induced to issue them in a little book entitled *Ragged Schools: their Prin- ciples and Modes of Operation; by a Worker.* She described the actual condition of destitute children as she knew them, and insisted on the fact that they formed a completely distinct class from those in attendance at the ordinary National and British Schools. A separate organisation was needful for them, and she proceeded to sketch the main lines which her experience had already shown her to be sound. After giving the first place to religious and moral instruc- tion, she passed on to intellectual and industrial training, with the indispensable provisions for the culture of self- respect by personal cleanliness, and the necessity of con- siderate regard for the feelings even of the ignorant and depraved. ' I have always treated my class with courtesy,' she had written in her journal, ' and have always received ' from them respectful courtesy in return. Although some ' of them have been in prison, and I have seen many in the ' lowest condition in the streets, yet there is now little in ' their deportment when in class to remind one that they ' are not intelligent scholars in an ordinary Sunday School. ' I have never but once heard a vulgar word, and then there ' was a cry of " Shame," from the others. My word is suffi- ' cient for them, and I have seldom to repeat an injunction.' She next proceeded to urge the claims of Ragged Schools to Government aid, and concluded by pointing out that for children who had already fallen into confirmed habits of vice, for the regular beggars and the professed thieves, another remedy must be sought, viz. Reformatory Schools.

The fruits of patient toil and long preparation were ripening at last. She had found her work, and happiness was coming with it. ' I have had a peculiar pleasure in ' this book,' she wrote, ' independently of its object; I

'have had a strange and very unusual feeling of satisfac-
'tion in being thus able from my quiet study to tell the
'world (small and unimportant as it may be), what is the
'deep and earnest desire of my soul, and perhaps to stimu-
'late some kindred spirit to the same work.' She was,
indeed, feeling the consciousness of new power. After she
had been engaged in the Ragged School for a year, she
seemed to have reached a truer self-knowledge. The close
contact with others beyond the home-circle had brought
some of the elements of her character into clearer view. 'A
'veil,' she observed, 'has been removed from many of my
'secret thoughts; I see clearer the evil of my own heart; I
'perceive more how much and often it interferes with the
'good, and darkens the brightness of the spiritual life
'within me.' Nevertheless, she knew at the same time that
a fresh interest had been kindled within her, to which her
whole soul responded; and she was ready for any labour or
any trials which might be needful for inward purification.
So on the birthday of 1848, a few days after the final departure of the pupils from Great George Street, she seemed to
stand at the beginning of a new time and thus surveyed her
course :

TO THE REV. R. L. CARPENTER.

Bristol, April 3rd, 1848.

As for me, I look forward with calm hope to the future. I
feel as if I had within me powers which have never yet had
tranquil leisure to expand themselves. I desire to work out
more my own individuality, and to be freer from the shackles
which I have always felt imposed on me in various ways, and
to prepare for this I wish for a period of comparative rest.
Different minds rest differently ; what to some is rest, to me
is exciting mental action, and *vice versa.* Social intercourse
forms a part of my plan of future life, and especially of course
more of real intercourse with my mother, whom I hope to
render happy. I am particularly fond of real society, and feel
that it is very important to have interchange of ideas with
others; and some time must, I know, be sacrificed to what are
called the claims of society; but it is not my intention to con-
form to them in the waste of time and energy usually passing
under that name. There is no reason why one should be
robbed of one's time and thoughts any more than of one's
money.

The new tasks, however, were such as often tried her spirit. She formed plans with ardour, and proceeded to carry them out with immense energy; but failure or disappointment sometimes came upon her with overwhelming force; and those around her were often rendered uneasy at the prostration which frequently followed periods of high enthusiasm. In these hours the cry of a lonely soul poured itself forth for the guidance and sympathy which her father had extended to her in her earlier years. Even the mother's tenderness, as she sought sometimes to soothe the anxious excitement, and restrain the over-eager efforts, seemed to be a check rather than a help : and the first steps on the new way were not without the stings of conflict between filial deference and what seemed the claims of more pressing urgency. Yet these cares were committed, as was her wont, to the Unseen Presence in which she trusted ; and there, by patient waiting, she found a sufficiency of strength. In some verses written on Christmas Day, 1848, amidst the distractions which that anniversary with its numerous school festivals always involved, occur the following lines :

With Thy Holy Spirit, oh do Thou renew me,
  Cleanse me from all that turneth me from Thee,
Guide me and guard me, lead me and subdue me,
  Till I love not aught that centres not in Thee.

Thou hast touched my soul with brightness and with beauty,
  Thou hast made me feel the sweetness of Thy love ;
Purify my heart, devote it to all duty,
  Sanctify me wholly for Thy realms above.

A few months later, and the utterance was even more intense. She was watching by the dying bed of one of her scholars, a lad of fourteen or fifteen years of age, whose refinement and gentleness, in strange contrast with the coarse natures around him, had made a profound impression upon her. He seemed to her like a divine pledge that the utmost purity and delicacy of soul might abide unharmed amid want or squalor and degradation. She too, unknowingly, had been to him a guardian and friend, though their private intercourse had been slight, and she scrupulously avoided ever conferring on him any marks of distinction in the class ;

and it was only in his last hours that she learned from his mother how he had found strength of heart in her. So the two—the matured woman, the dying boy—were drawn to each other by a deep spiritual sympathy, which soon overcame the natural sorrow, and sought a higher dedication. To the verses which follow, written at this time, she recurred again and again in later griefs.

> To Thee, my God, to Thee,
>   Teach me to live ;
> To Thee, my God, to Thee,
>   All would I give.
>
> Whate'er I hold most dear
>   I would resign,
> Sure I have nothing here—
>   All mine is Thine.
>
> What most my soul doth prize
>   The least is mine,
> Naught that is lovely dies,
>   For it is Thine.
>
> The life that came from Thee
>   Can never die,
> Teach me to yield it Thee
>   Without a sigh.
>
> For still my heart doth cling
>   To what is fair,
> Heavenward my spirit wing,
>   And fix it there.
>
> Bear all that most I love
>   To heavenly rest,
> Bear thus my soul above
>   And make it blest.
>
> My all, O God, to Thee
>   I would resign,
> Oh, fix my heart on Thee,
>   I would be Thine.

It was one of the peculiar characteristics of Mary Carpenter's mind, that it united qualities very rarely found in harmonious combination. She had the soul of a mystic, and the insight into affairs and the grasp of detail of a born administrator. So it came to pass that while she was in almost daily attendance at the Ragged School, and was carefully collecting a mass of particulars concerning the condition of destitute children, she was lifted at times into the highest rapture of devotion.

February 10th, 1850.—Blessed Heavenly Father! I thank Thee that Thou dost sometimes permit me to feel Thee very nigh unto me, that it is *in* Thee I live and move and have my being! When I hear others inquiring *how* Thou art and *what* Thou art, I care not to enter into their counsels; it is enough for me that Thou art, and that my spirit is a spark of Thy effulgence, that everything I see around is the beautiful working of Thy spirit. It is but at times that I can *feel* this, but of late I have been able to feel it and to hold thus near communion with Thee, more than I have ever done before; and this has given me a consciousness of power and at the same time of calmness and gentleness which prevents me from being agitated and ruffled, as I used to be, with passing events, whether great or small, as I know they are all from Thee, and that whether Thou permittest me to succeed in my exertions or not, humanly speaking, Thou wilt in Thy own good time bring all about as Thou wilt. So I rest satisfied, whatever is the apparent result, for it is Thy doing, only I *must* work the work Thou hast given me to do, while it is day. And I am not alone, for not only art Thou with me, but blessed witnesses and helpers: my father, ever loved, he who first directed me to this special work, and breathed into me a spirit of divine love, and the pure childlike spirit that loved me and that I loved, which Thou didst disclose to me in his heavenly nature by the touch of the Angel of Death.

The burden of the past was now to a great extent removed. She had been haunted by a feeling that her nature was not lovable, that even her nearest and dearest had not loved her for herself, that there must be something in her which repelled instead of attracting. The somewhat late growth of friendships of unusual tenderness and ardour had in part removed this inner source of self-mortification; and now came the spontaneous affection of her scholars to impart fresh confidence. 'How I prize the love I receive 'there,' she could not help exclaiming; 'I must confess that 'the Ragged School is not so attractive to me from a mere 'sense of duty, for I might find duties elsewhere; but it

'is so delightful to me to gain so much love as I feel I have
'from these young beings, and to help to kindle their souls
'by mine.' In this way the remembrance of her departed
scholar came frequently to her mind with tranquillising
assurance. 'Perhaps at some future time,' his mother had
said, as they stood together in the presence of death, 'he
'may be able to do you good, and what a pleasure it will be
'to him.' 'It was a beautiful and soothing idea,' wrote the
teacher, more than a year afterwards, 'founded on her
'Catholic views, but I have already found it a true one.
'When I have been ruffled and agitated, when the fountains
'of love have been troubled, when the sin and misery around
'me have been most oppressive, then the calm childlike
'innocence, the purity, the loving sweetness of that gentle
'boy have been an inexpressible delight to me, a bright
'heavenly spot to rest my thoughts on. And greatly have I
'been stimulated and encouraged onward in my exertions
'with the poor children of wretchedness around me, by the
'remembrance of the angel spirit I had entertained among
'them.' So the mingled impulses of duty and affection
blended together, and she went on her way with a spirit of
calm resolve. 'I feel as Goffredo did in *Jerusalem Delivered*
'when the Angel committed to him his charge.'

CHAPTER V.

THE WIDENING AIM.
1850—1852.

' Pain and grief
Are transitory things no less than joy,
And though they leave us not the men we were,
Yet they do leave us. You behold me here
A man bereaved, with something of a blight
Upon the early blossoms of his life
And its first verdure, having not the less
A living root, and drawing from the earth
Its vital juices, from the air its powers;
And surely as man's health and strength are whole,
His appetites regerminate, his heart
Re-opens, and his objects and desires
Shoot up renewed.'

Sir Henry Taylor.

CHAPTER V.

MARY CARPENTER had now fairly given herself to the cause of the destitute children, which was never to be abandoned to the last day of her life, whatever other objects might also put in their claims upon her thought and strength. The success of the Ragged School led her to take steps for securing the premises in which it was carried on. This purchase was effected in 1850, and gave an important stimulus to the work. The court in which it was situated came into her hands in August, and she lost no time in improving the dwellings it contained, for occupation by selected tenants. 'I wish you had seen my houses and 'lands,' she wrote in October, 'in their former condition. 'When you come they will be most comfortable little dwell-'ings, with baths and washhouses and waterworks, and all that 'reasonable heart can desire.' Knowing how important a part amusement must occupy in child-life, she turned one portion of the court into a playground, where the scholars might enjoy their games away from the temptations of the street; creepers were planted against the walls, and she watched with interest how the rough lads took pains to avoid injuring them. In the adjoining houses she often arranged lodgings for many a homeless boy, until, twenty years afterwards, she was able to erect a separate building for this purpose; and so the little community was regularly organised under her vigilant and affectionate care.

In the meantime, she was following with earnest attention
the careers of many of the scholars. Some of them, when
they first came to the school, were already notorious as
young thieves. Repeated convictions and imprisonments
failed to effect any reformation; and though she was able
to withdraw some few from their life of crime, and to prevent many more from adopting it, she soon became aware of
the inadequacy of Ragged Schools to cope with the needs of
the vagrant and the lawless class around her, and the lasting
injury produced by the ordinary gaol system forced itself
upon her. Already in her little work on Ragged Schools,
she had drawn attention to the urgent necessity of supple-
menting their efforts by schools of an altogether different
character, in which the young criminal could be kept under
detention, and trained by a mingled discipline of firmness and
love to better ways. This subject acquired more importance
in her eyes with each day's fresh experience. She began
to correspond with those who had already expressed
opinions tending in the same direction, the Revs. T. Carter
and John Clay, the well-known chaplains of the Liverpool and Preston Gaols, the Rev. W. C. Osborn of Bath,
Sheriff Watson of Aberdeen, and many others; by whose
aid she was directed to sources of information, furnished
with valuable suggestions, and copiously supplied with the
records of personal observation. Mr. M. D. Hill, then
Recorder of Birmingham, was naturally an authority of the
first rank,[1] and the grateful recollection which Mrs. Carpenter entertained of the kindness of Mr. Hill's father in her
early days, made the access to him easy. To him Mary
Carpenter now turned, and the foundations of a friendship
were thus laid from which she never ceased to derive help
and support. A careful perusal of the Report of the Select
Committee of the Lords, appointed to inquire into the condition of juvenile offenders in 1847, laid open before her

---

[1] The general history of the movement for the reformation of
juvenile offenders has been so excellently sketched in the *Memoir of
Matthew Davenport-Hill* (1878), by his daughters, Rosamond and
Florence Davenport-Hill, that it is needless to retrace it here;
especially as it is rather the purpose of this work to set forth the
inner springs of thought and feeling which animated the life and
action of its subject, than to write a complete chapter in the history
of modern philanthropy.

what had been said upon the matter; the case seemed to her
so clear that she learnt with amazement that no action had
yet been taken. ' I have been astonished,' she wrote, early
in November, to Mr. Hill, ' on studying the evidence in the
' Blue Book, to find what conclusive and powerful testimony
' to the worse than uselessness of prisons for juvenile offenders
' had been before the Lords for nearly four years without any
' change being made. A Bristol magistrate told me that
' for twenty years he had felt quite unhappy at going on
' committing these young culprits. And yet he had *done*
' nothing !' To see a great evil and to look for no remedy
against it, was not the fashion of Mary Carpenter's nature ;
and she earnestly sought for some method of relief from the
burden which was becoming daily more oppressive to her,
as the young thieves of Lewin's Mead grew before her
thought into a vast band of criminals scattered through the
whole country. There was no way open but to make the
facts known, and trust that a conscience-stricken public
might demand reforms. So the plan of another and larger
work took shape in her mind, which she thus sketched out
in a letter to the Rev. John Clay.

TO THE REV. JOHN CLAY, PRESTON.

Bristol, November 26th, 1850.

It will be my earnest endeavour (the Heavenly Father
giving me, as I trust he will, his aid in the undertaking) to
put forth the subject in the strongest manner possible. I
shall attempt to show first that ' the people perisheth for lack
' of knowledge,' that the appalling increase of juvenile depravity
can *only* be checked by real education—intellectual, moral, and
religious ; that this cannot be given by the parents, and will
not be sought for by them ; that in mere self-defence, if for no
higher motive, we must give it them. I shall then show that
good free schools, such as I have given a practical example of
in my little book, should be extensively provided for those who
will come, and *compulsory* industrial schools on the Aberdeen
plan for those who subject themselves to police interference.
Lastly, and this will perhaps be the most important part of
the book, that since the prison system, even as best conducted,
is proved ineffectual as a preventive and reformatory measure
for children, and such institutions at Mettrai have exceeded
all expectations, they should be tried. . . . It is not the spirit
of fear, but of power and of love and of a sound mind, which

can be powerful enough to subdue these hard hearts; and without touching the inner spirit no external measures will be of much avail. Near intercourse with these poor outcast children for the last four years, has given me a constantly increasing faith in the apostolic precept, ' Overcome evil with good,' and instead of wondering at the wickedness of these poor creatures, I have admired and loved the strength of goodness in them, and their resistance of evil. We find no disposition to steal or to do wilful mischief in the school premises. You have doubtless found the same good feeling excited by an evident desire to do them good.

The book was written in the winter of 1851 upon the lines here laid down, but not without some trepidation and searchings of heart.   ' Few know,' she said to one who possessed most of her secrets, ' what a lamb's heart I have ' under my coat of armour. I used to think I had more a ' masculine than a feminine nature, but I feel more and ' more that my essence is womanly in a peculiar degree. I ' feel so perfectly sure of my principles and the truth of ' all I say in the book, that I am proof against cutting up by ' reviewers ; but here in my own country I do not wish to ' come out as a prophet, knowing well that such have no ' honour, and are rather held in horror by most.' As the spring came round, when the work was nearly finished, the recurrence of her birthday led her to set before herself more clearly the gain and the peril of her new activities.

April 3rd, 1851.—This has been to me more a year of absolute life than any that I have before passed. I feel more a consciousness of my absolute independent life and power to *be* and to *do* what my Heavenly Father sent me into the world for than I have ever had; and this has enabled me to pass through numerous trials, small indeed to outward appearance, but fiery enough to me, and to tread on serpents and noxious things as though I, heeded them but little. . . . I feel that my Heavenly Father has given me a blessed work to do, and a true word to speak, and that nothing but an intimation from Him can hinder me. It is most remarkable to me how He has put hindrances in my way until the fulness of time was come, and then how He removed them and made one and another ready to help me. I believe that I have no self-seeking in anything that I am doing; whenever I find self lurking anywhere, I strive to mortify it. I wish that I could pursue the work I love so much without anyone seeing me, and that I could

speak the word without anyone knowing who says it. It is a
great pain to me to be brought into any degree of notoriety ;
but yet I must speak, for I have to tell a solemn truth which
has not yet been clearly told, and which I trust someone will
hear and *believe* and work on.

A few weeks later, the labour into which the suppressed
passion of years was being fused, is nearly over.

My book is getting on ; I have only the last chapter to
write, and I have had three proof-sheets. I feel myself happy
to have been able to develop my heart and soul's inmost
feelings to some extent, though of course imperfectly.   I
cannot read a proof without feeling my blood boil with indignation and sorrow for the poor children.   I hope that some
of the same feeling will be kindled in others.

At last she was able to announce :

To-day I have finished my book ; it is a comfort to have
completed it ; I have not, of course, said half I wished, but it
is a relief to my mind to have delivered my testimony. . . .
It was only intense conviction on my part that determined me
to write in spite of obstacles and cold water. . . . The book
will doubtless be full of things that might have been improved ;
also everyone, perhaps, will think that I might with advantage
have left out some part of it.   I believe that every part is
necessary to the development of my conception, and that in
matters of this kind it is best for persons not to quench the
spirit, but to speak the truth without fear.

The book was entitled *Reformatory Schools for the
Children of the Perishing and Dangerous Classes, and for
Juvenile Offenders.*[1] A formidable array of facts set forth
the increase of juvenile delinquency and the ignorance of
the offenders.   Their peculiar needs, it was urged, required
special treatment, and three classes of schools were sketched
out for different grades of destitution, vagrancy, and criminality.   These were first, good Free Day Schools ; secondly,

---

[1] A part of this title was suggested by two sermons by Theodore
Parker, with which she had been much impressed.   In forwarding
him a copy of the book, she requested him to send her further
information which would show that the Common Schools of New
England did not reach the ' Perishing and Dangerous Classes.'

Feeding Industrial Schools, aided by rates, at which attendance should be compulsory ; and thirdly, Reformatory Schools in place of the existing prison system. With a sympathy quickened and guided by experience, the writer then described the lot of the children whom she sought to save. She set forth the principles on which all efforts to rescue them must be founded — enumerating among the moral requisites of the teachers an undaunted faith in the divine purpose for each individual soul, a love that should blend with firmness and wisdom, and insight into the laws of child nature and the conflicts of child life; and she especially insisted that no degrading or revengeful punishments should ever be permitted—even chastisement must be penetrated and controlled by affection. These general considerations cleared the way for a review of what had been actually accomplished under each of the three heads. The efforts of the Ragged Schools were first surveyed ; the inevitable limitations imposed upon them through want of adequate means were clearly exposed, and an urgent plea was put forth for Government aid. Next it was shown in detail that the vagrant children already in training for crime could not be reached by Free Day Schools, while the surprising results of the bold action of Sheriff Watson in Aberdeen were invoked to support a scheme of Industrial Feeding Schools, in which daily attendance should be enforced by magisterial authority under the sanction of the legislature. The full weight of argument was reserved for the revelation of the total failure of the gaols to reform juvenile criminals. It was proved with conclusive force that repeated convictions produced no effect, that under the unreformed regulations nothing but utter contamination could be expected, and that under the strictest separate system discipline failed in the case of children ; and severe condemnation was passed on the cruelty and injustice of society in leaving the ' perishing ' child to die, and driving the ' dangerous ' to crime. What remedies were there for these festering sores ? The concluding chapter was devoted to an examination of various institutions designed to grapple with the wants thus nakedly disclosed. The government establishment of Parkhurst Prison in the Isle of Wight, for the reception of boys sentenced to transportation, first claimed attention, the results recorded in the reports of its officials being contrasted with those of the French institution

at Mettrai.   The history and success of the labours of
M. Demetz sufficed to indicate the difference between the
methods of military rule and of Christian love ; and the story
of Dusselthal Abbey on the Rhine, and the moral triumphs
of Wichern in the Rauhe Haus at Hamburg, added ampler
confirmation to principles that scarcely needed further illustration.   The brief experience of the managers of the Philanthropic Farm established at Red Hill, Surrey, early in 1849,
tended in the same direction ; and the institution of Stretton-
on-Dunsmore in Warwickshire had proved, through thirty
years of toil, that it was cheaper to the country to reform
boys than to punish them, and that their reformation was
possible.   Two obstacles, however, curtailed the usefulness of
these institutions—the want of sufficient funds, and the need
of power of detention : private effort and influence required
the permanent support of public aid and authority.   The results thus reached were stated in the following propositions :—

First,—That as a general rule, all children, however apparently vicious and degraded, are capable of being made useful
members of society, and beings acting on a religious principle,
if placed under right influences and subjected to judicious
control and training.   The comparatively few exceptions that
would occur do not invalidate the principle.

Secondly, — That the present system adopted towards
offending children renders them almost certainly members
for life of the criminal class, for it neither deters nor reforms
them ; while, by checking the development of their powers and
branding them with ignominy, it prevents them from gaining
an honest livelihood.

Thirdly,—That good Penal Reformatory Schools, conducted
on Christian principles, where there is a wise union of kindness
and restraint, have produced the desired effect of enabling the
most degraded and corrupt to become useful members of
society ; but that such institutions cannot be efficiently carried
on, or maintained, without a steady income, which cannot be
certainly or justly raised by individual effort alone, and without such legal authority as will impose sufficient restraint over
the scholars as to keep them under the school influence.

Fourthly,—That the parents being in reality the guilty
parties, rather than the children—since juvenile delinquency
usually originates in parental neglect—every parent should
be chargeable for the maintenance of a child thrown by crime
on the care of the State, as much as if the child were at large;
and should be held responsible for the maintenance of a child

in a Reformatory School, or made in some way to suffer for
the non-discharge of this duty.

If these four results are true ones, legislative enactments
will be needed to carry the spirit of them into operation.

A sufficient number of Reformatory Penal Schools must
be established under the guidance of enlightened Christian
benevolence, sanctioned and mainly supported by government
inspection and aid.

Magistrates and judges must be empowered to send all
convicted children to such schools, instead of committing
them to prison; power of detention being vested in the
masters, for such length of time as may seem needful for the
reformation of the child.

The parents, or, if none, the parish of the child, must be
held responsible for such weekly payment as may cover the
cost of his maintenance during his detention.

These suggestions were by no means made for the first
time, nor did Mary Carpenter claim any novelty for them. In
one form or another they had been laid before the Committee
of the Lords in 1847, and the Committee of the Commons in
1850. But no one had as yet brought into one focus the
evidence upon which they were based, or so arrayed the
various groups of facts as to lead without escape to these
conclusions. It was the merit of the treatise on *Reformatory
Schools* that it presented a compact body of carefully reasoned
truths, and pointed out the lines of action to be founded
on them. The principles were laid down; it remained to
give them effect. The case was presented to the public, and
the writer waited to see if the appeal would be heard. She
perceived plainly enough that she was only at the beginning
of her labours; she knew not to what she might be called,
but she steadily pursued her self-imposed duties in the
Ragged School, till new opportunities should arise. ' I do
' not feel as if my work were near its accomplishment,' she
said as the summer went on, ' I only feel as if I had been
' permitted to take an important step in it. My inmost heart,
' my soul, is more and more devoted to it. I am ready to do
' or not to do, as may seem best to my Heavenly Father, and
' shall only watch for openings, and earnestly avail myself of
' them as they occur. I know not whether I shall be able to
' bring anything to pass directly or indirectly ; I do know
' that the devotion of a soul is an acceptable offering, and
' that the seed sown in faith will spring up in good time.'

There were seasons, however, when she was sorely tried, and a heavy strain was put upon her faith, her love, her self-control. Whoever would deal with degraded natures must needs have large reserves of strength and trust; and many disappointments laid their sad burden on her enthusiasm. Moreover her devotion to the Ragged School often placed her in peculiar relations to its regular teachers, from whom she sometimes appeared to expect more than they could give. With a confiding and ardent nature she welcomed each new-comer to the work; but the occasional discovery of aims less lofty than her own, the preference of other plans to hers, the least hint of jealousy at her superior influence, excited her with undue agitation, and renewed within her the conflicts in which she had before suffered so much. She knew well what secret weakness was twined in with her strength, and the longing for deliverance arose again as of old, but now it was tempered with an assurance which brought with it peace. 'I used often to wish for penances, like the Catholics,' she wrote in July, after one of these times of trouble, 'feeling 'as if it would be the greatest pleasure to me to bear them; 'so I take all these as my spiritual penances, feeling only too 'happy to be able to bear them for the sake of the cause to 'which my heart is devoted. I shall hail with joy the '" glorious morn " which shall welcome me to the home of my 'spirit; yet if a wish of mine should bid it dawn on me, I 'would not dare to breathe it; for God's time is best, and I 'am willing and thankful to work as long as He is wishing 'me to stay and has anything for me to do.'

Ere the summer of 1851 was over, Mary Carpenter began to make preparation for a fresh move. She had uttered her message, and had no more resources by herself; further action must be taken in concert with others, and she set forth from home to make the acquaintance of fellow-labourers in the same field, and collect their views on the best method of advance. Her book was already in the hands of some of the acknowledged leaders in the cause, who heartily greeted a new ally. First in London, and then in the North, she sought conference with the advocates of reformatory principles; and as she went from member of Parliament to magistrate, and from magistrate to gaol-chaplain, she saw her way open more clearly before her. At Warrington, in the home of her brother Philip, which he had made the centre of a 'Ministry at

' Large,' in a spirit kindred to her own, she passed a day or
two, and thus summed up the results of her journey.

Warrington, August 15th, 1851.

My various interviews in London, and especially that with
Lord Ashley, passed off very favourably. I was much pleased
to find in all quarters a warm feeling in favour of such plans
as I suggest, together with a feeling that something ought to
be done. The great excuse is that the minds of the people are
not prepared for it, which amounts to nothing more than a
pretext for waiting. So our present work is to prepare the
minds of the public, and excite magistrates and such like to
ask for something. Six newspapers have already taken up the
matter favourably in a review; we must not let them rest.
Since I have been in the North I have had interviews with
fellow workers in Manchester, Liverpool, and Preston, who are
quite preparing to do something. It is a very curious feeling
to me when I think about it, to give out my opinion with a
certain degree of confidence, and to have it received as worthy
of consideration. As I have written a book, it seems to be
supposed that I know something about the matter, and it
seems to be an acknowledged thing that I understand the
subject. All I desire is that this may not in any way minister
to self-seeking, but may I only be truly thankful for it.

It was now evident that there was a large amount of
scattered opinion and endeavour, which only needed organisation to become a really effective power. What better service
could be rendered than to bring together the individual
efforts and unite them in some well-considered scheme? Accordingly the idea of a Conference of workers arose in Mary
Carpenter's mind, as the best means of establishing a distinct
nucleus of energy. The plan was quickly shaped, and communicated without delay to Mr. M. D. Hill, whose settlement
in Bristol as Commissioner of Bankruptcy in the spring of
this year, brought to her the most valuable personal aid of
her life. He responded to the suggestion with alacrity, and
thus expressed his accordance with the basis on which it was
to be carried out.

MR. COMMISSIONER HILL TO MARY CARPENTER.

Ashton Lodge, September 24th, 1851.

MY DEAR MISS CARPENTER,

If I correctly have gathered the principle on which the proposed Conference is intended to meet, I cordially concur in your views, and to prevent mistakes I will set down what I understand to be your object.

You say it is all but universally admitted that prison discipline, however well administered, is not adapted to the wants, either spiritual or physical, of juvenile criminals, and that consequently there must be Reformatory Schools; but that at present Reformatory Schools have their efficiency much diminished by the absence of a legal power for retaining the pupil against his will and that of his parents; and, moreover, that it being necessary that, if detained, he should be fed, clothed, and housed, funds must be found; that these funds ought not to be sought from the benevolent, who are overtaxed already, nor ought the parent to be relieved of his responsibility, or, in other words, to be rewarded for his neglect of duty, or, in many cases, for his positive misconduct towards the child; that failing the *power* of the parent to contribute to the fund, the burden should fall on the parish. And finally I understand you to say that you do not seek for these aids— money and power of coercion—except where the child is already dealt with by the law, or, in short, where the prison would be its lot but for the Reformatory School.

I need not say that all this is considered by me as of the deepest importance, and that I shall most gladly assist in all such steps as may conduce to our attainment of them.

Believe me, my dear Miss Carpenter,

Ever yours,

M. D. HILL.

It was a bold undertaking for a woman, for social conferences were not then the common events which they have since become; but powerful support was at hand. The circular of invitation, drawn up by Mary Carpenter and sanctioned by Mr. Hill, soon bore the well-known names of the Revs. T. Carter, John Clay, W. C. Osborn, Sydney Turner, with those of Messrs. Hubback and Jellinger Symons, Sheriff Watson and Mr. Wigham. The task of distribution fell chiefly upon the originator, who found ready helpers in Lady Byron and the Hon. Amelia Murray, both of whom had long been working in the same direction. But the main

stress of the labour and anxiety still devolved upon Mary
Carpenter, who reported progress from time to time in the
following letters.

Bristol, October 24th, 1851.

We, or rather I, have been trying to get some united
action among the friends of the poor children. Hitherto I
have felt in a small way like Peter the Hermit trying to rouse
a crusade, and like Goffredo to whom the mission was entrusted.
I have always peculiarly sympathised with his humble but
ardent devotion to his work, and the kindling spirit with the
stern abnegation of self which always guided him. I find that
everything that I once loved and sympathised in from my
heart in my early principles was a seed which would spring
up and bear fruit; and so with this. Hitherto I have been
the only nucleus in the matter, adding *lettere a lettere, messi
a messi*, to invite to the Conference, communicating, however,
only with those with whom I had previously come *en rapport*
on the subject. The replies have been most encouraging. I
fortunately was able to draw out a scheme of the objects of
the Conference, which all the people whose opinion I value
approve.

Bristol, November 17th, 1851.

I feel most remarkable comfort in being free from the
earnest attachment to a variety of earthly things that seemed
to me important, that I used to have. All other movements,
or objects of pursuit, scientific, philosophical, or what not,
appear to me so insignificant in comparison with the rescuing
of these poor children, the innocent victims of ignorance and
vice, from their dreadful thraldom, that, while I do not despise
them, and am glad that others possess them, I rejoice that my
heart is fixed, and am inexpressibly grateful to my Heavenly
Father for having given me powers to do the work with, and
to my beloved earthly father for having trained them so wisely.
But after all I feel as you do with your music, that it is not
that I have talents, but that my soul puts itself forth, and I
have no doubt that that is the reason people have been so
much touched with my book.

Being, as you know I am, excessively timid underneath
my armour, I am so very thankful that all my advances have
met with so cordial a response, for I am afraid I should have
been too terrified to speak again, if I had met with a cold

repulse. One thing is, you know, that my instinct guides me
to whom to speak. I have been hitherto a sort of centre of
communication, an unseen spring in this Conference matter,
which has caused me to write multitudes of letters, and so I
must go on till the machinery is fairly at work. Sometimes
I almost ask myself with wonder ' if I be I.'

The arrangements for the Conference were at last completed, through the energy of Mr. Hubback of Liverpool,
who managed all the local details ; and the first meeting
was held in Birmingham on December 9th, for the settlement
of preliminary business, under the presidency of Lord
Lyttelton. The regular proceedings were commenced on the
following morning, the Recorder of Birmingham being in the
chair. Mr. Hill had been in council with Mary Carpenter,[1]
and his address brought the weight of all his experience to
support the gradation of schools which she had already
set forth in her work on *Reformatory Schools*. The resolutions which were subsequently adopted, sanctioned the same
scheme. Three classes of schools were to be established :—first,
Free Day Schools, for those children who had not yet made
themselves amenable to the law, but who by reason of the
vice, neglect, or extreme poverty of their parents, were not
admitted into the existing Day Schools ; secondly, Industrial
Feeding Schools, for those who had subjected themselves to
police interference by vagrancy, mendicancy, or petty infringements of the law, attendance being enforced by the
magistrates, and the cost being in part recovered from the
parents ; thirdly, Correctional and Reformatory Schools, for
those children who had been convicted of felony or such
misdemeanours as involved dishonesty, the magistrates being
empowered to commit juvenile offenders to such schools
instead of to prison.

The attendance at the Conference was not large ; but
those who were present were all actively engaged in social
work, and one spirit of earnestness and goodwill animated
the whole proceedings. To no·one was this more inspiring
than to Mary Carpenter. She took no part in the discus-

---

[1] Among the papers which she preserved relating to this meeting
is a series of notes in her handwriting, endorsed ' Suggestions for the
' arrangement of the Conference, drawn up previously at Mr. Hill's
' desire for his guidance.'

sions ; to have lifted up her voice in an assembly of gentlemen would have been, as she then felt, tantamount to
unsexing herself. Like the Hon. Miss Murray, who had
been labouring for twenty years in the same cause, she sat
silent ; but her silence was penetrated with a profound
thankfulness. As soon as the business sessions were over,
she hastened to communicate her impressions to Lady Byron,
whose sympathy had throughout sustained her, and who had
evinced her interest in the occasion by authorising Mr. Hill
to announce a prize to the value of £200 for an Essay on
the duty of society to destitute children. The reaction after
long effort at first took its jubilance from Mary Carpenter's
tone ; but she nevertheless felt that she had witnessed an
epoch in her cause.

TO LADY BYRON.

December, 1851.

The day is past that we have been working for so long !
I hardly know how to tell you what I feel about it. The real
business and actual conferring which many of us had anticipated, and the hope of which had brought many as deputies
from their respective schools, was *very* imperfectly accomplished from want of time, and still more perhaps from want
of previous arrangement, and knowledge of each other's views.
Yet while in that respect a feeling of regret remains, in other
respects I feel that those hours were worth any previous effort
and labour, and that they will probably give a steady impulse
to the cause which could have been given in no other way.
To myself personally those morning hours of the Conference
were full of deep joy, and if I deserved or could have any
earthly reward for what the world calls exertion, none could be
higher or truer—except the smiles of my ragged children—
than the free sympathy and confidence which I received from
all. Those who have lived all their lives in the midst of
sympathy, can hardly understand the feelings of those everywhere spoken against, when brought into free communion with
their fellow-Christians. I feel able to work better with many
of them from having seen them face to face ; some, one knows
better from correspondence, but most are more revealed by
their looks and words. I did not gather a single new thought
or principle, scarcely a new fact, from the whole proceedings ;
but I derived great stores of knowledge of the human soul. All
seemed, more or less, to feel the same. The 10th of December
will ever be a sacred day to me. The proceedings you will
learn from a newspaper, and I need only say that they were

marked throughout by the most complete unity of purpose—
in reality if not always in appearance—depth of conviction,
high sense of the all-importance of religion, and perfect
freedom from sectarianism. As there was so much that was
necessarily omitted in the Conference as to the basis of future
action, it is thought well to prepare a volume embodying what
was said and *to be* said. I have been asked to prepare the
volume, which I shall devote myself to at once.

Before the Conference separated, a Committee was
appointed to carry out the principles which it had affirmed.
The first step was to bring the resolutions before the
Government, and a deputation for that purpose waited on
Sir George Grey. Slowly, however, as deliberation advanced,
Mary Carpenter became aware of divergences of view which
seemed to her to imperil her most cherished objects. These
differences appeared to her to result from opposing conceptions
of the significance and purposes of punishment. She desired
to lay the whole stress on reformation ; others recognised a
further element of retribution.[1] The two ideas naturally
led to different modes of treatment : the one applied severity
of discipline, the other relied on the power of just but gentle
influence ; and the type of school for which the sanction of
the Legislature was to be sought, varied according to the pre-
dominance of the one or the other method. Into this struggle
Mary Carpenter threw herself with ardour. Early in
January, 1852, she boldly addressed a letter to Mr. Power,
the chairman of the Committee, remonstrating on what she
regarded as a departure from fundamental truths laid down
by the Conference. ' It may seem rather presumptuous
' to do so,' she wrote apologetically to Lady Byron, ' but in a

---

[1] It must be borne in mind in interpreting Mary Carpenter's
position, that the cases which she had throughout in view were those
of children who were not, in her judgment, really responsible agents.
They had not chosen their natures, their parents, or the circumstances
into which they had been forced ; their sense of right and wrong was
not only uncultivated, it was often unawakened ; their misconduct
therefore was not really sin. As such they were not fairly liable to
retribution for violation of a moral law of which they were ignorant.
But it may perhaps be urged, not unfairly, that she confounded the
idea of retribution with that of vengeance in the case of delinquents
who were not acting, in the 'French phrase which she frequently
employed, *sans discernement*.

'matter of principle I often feel rather courageous.' Her own
view was thus stated in a memorandum sent to the Rev.
John Clay, of Preston.

Bristol, February 4th, 1852.

PRINCIPLES OF PUNISHMENT.

In God's moral government of the world, evil invariably
attends violation of His laws, but as a natural consequence, not
by arbitrary punishment.

Revelation teaches us that He is longsuffering and merciful,
sending blessings on the evil and the good, ready to receive the
penitent with fatherly compassion. He commands us to overcome evil with good.

Man's less perfect government requires that punishment
should always follow offence, to mark the sinfulness of violation
of law. But the only ends of punishment are the prevention
of crime, and the reformation of the offender. No *vindictive*
element must have a place in it.

APPLICATION.

By subjecting the child to a lengthened detention in a
correctional school, we punish his offences by subjecting him
to loss of liberty, to privation of his unlawful indulgences,
and the necessity of submission to reformatory discipline.

The human law is thus fulfilled, while the ends are being
kept in view of reformation of the offender and the prevention
of crime.

Crime is a moral disease. The young criminals placed in
the school must be treated as moral patients, for whose cure
we should, as Christians, apply the best remedies in the
wisest way.

The private enforcement of these views absorbed a vast
amount of time and energy. The action advocated by the
Committee would lead, she urged on Mr. Thomson of
Banchory, to 'a multiplication of Parkhursts, instead of
'Mettrais and Red Hills.' The suggestions for a Bill for
dealing with juvenile offenders, circulated by the Rev.
Sydney Turner, filled her with alarm lest the result should
be only to introduce prisons for the young under another
name. 'You can have no idea,' she explained to Lady
Byron, 'how much anxiety and work in letter-writing all
'this has caused me; so that I have not been able to begin to

'write my proposed book, only to meditate on it, and gather
'thoughts and materials.' In the meantime she was wanted
in London, where the Committee were preparing for Parliamentary action. 'Where do you think Mary is now?'
wrote Mrs. Carpenter to her son Philip. 'On her way to
'London. She had been invited up to the meeting of the
'Committee on Tuesday, held to settle the draft of a Bill to
'be submitted to Sir George Grey before the meeting of
'Parliament, but she had declined. She knows how jealous
'the lords of creation are of the interference of women, and
'thought it wisest to be of real use by looking over the rough
'drafts of Bills, all of which had been submitted to her
'inspection, and by corresponding with the leading members
'of the Committee.' Unexpected difficulties, however, arose;
and she hastened up to utter a timely word. Till her
departure 'Mary has been accordingly occupied,' continued
her mother, 'by long conferences with those here who are
'earnestly interested in the object, and by her regular duties:
'they are never omitted. The Ragged School is visited
'daily, and she interests herself thoroughly in the affairs of
'her rescued ones, whom she has located in the court. Not
'one of the Irish lads has turned out steady, but she has
'been more successful than I could have anticipated with
'the English ones.'

The conflict of principles into which Mary Carpenter
was thus plunged, brought her face to face with opposition
of a kind which she had never before experienced. The
children whom she loved seemed to be wounded through her,
and their injuries reacted on her with a double pang. Sometimes she was moved by indignation to language of severe
condemnation, but she knew her own danger and was
anxiously upon her guard. 'I hope that I have not taken
'any wrong steps,' so she uttered her cares to her brother
Russell, 'and feel happy in the friendly confidence shown
'me by many. Some have disclosed themselves in a very
'unpleasing light, while others, while differing, have shown
'a good and candid feeling. The popular theological views,
'giving rise to a vindictive spirit, are at the bottom of the
'mischief. Now, however, there is a truce, in consequence
'of the offer of a Committee in the House of Commons; and
'what we must do now is to enlighten and rouse public
'opinion.' The promise of a Parliamentary Inquiry by Sir

John Pakington led to the suspension of the proceedings of
the Committee appointed by the Conference : but weeks
passed by, and no sign of advance was made.   Under
inaction, Mary Carpenter was always restive, and she turned
to the strong hand that had done such wonders in the
North.

TO SHERIFF WATSON, ABERDEEN.

Bristol, March 30th, 1852.

The more I lament all this, which has been a most painful
blighting of my hopes, the more do I feel that the Conference
was a grand fact, which, preserved in the Report, will have
a great and lasting influence, and the strength of its spirit
will be made manifest through the weakness of the outward
form.

Now what is to be done ?

It appears to me that while there are many who see the
evil and wish it to be remedied, there are but few who carry
this wish in their inmost hearts, determined, by God's help,
to devote themselves to the cause of our poor children, the
'young immortals' so cruelly crushed or neglected by
society; there are few who will 'bate not one jot of heart
'or hope' from disappointment or opposition ; few who will
sacrifice to it worldly interest or approval.   But these few
can, I believe, if strong in faith and wise in action, remove
mountains.   I rejoice in the conviction that you are one of
these few ; unfortunately, perhaps, some of the others are
women, but we must do what we can.

To do what she could was the fixed rule of Mary
Carpenter's life, and her ' could ' had already acquired a considerable scope.   It was now enlarging itself still further.
A month before she wrote to Sheriff Watson, she had confided to Miss Sanford a fresh design.   This was nothing less
than the establishment of a Reformatory School in Bristol,
where the true principles of correction, as distinguished from
retribution, should be developed.   ' This will require cautious
' but persevering exertion.   I have been of late slumbering,
' as it were, but hope soon to be permitted to work with
' renewed vigour.'   No sooner had the plan suggested itself
to her, than she resolved that it should be realised.   With
the swiftness of action that always followed her decisions,

she looked about for suitable premises for the new enterprise.
They seemed just within her reach, but she failed to secure
them.   The disappointment would not yield to the ordinary
consolations.   ' It is easy for those to be philosophic,' she
pleaded, ' who have not these children weighing on their
' hearts.   I have been trying the thing on a small scale, and
' under very disadvantageous circumstances, and know, there-
' fore, what could be done in a better position.   Why delay ?
' But now it is all over.   Sometimes I feel half disheartened
' when I see how very few are to be found who will really
' make a sacrifice for a great cause.   But it is better not to
' think of these things.   Let me only humbly and earnestly
' go on with the work in which I have been abundantly
' blessed.'   The despondency soon passed ; and when, a few
days after, she reviewed her position on her birthday, it was
the same scheme that formed the background to her thoughts ;
that plan she could accomplish in private, with the aid of the
few who trusted her ; and she would be withdrawn from the
arena of combat which had so sorely tried her.

April 3rd, 1852.—With respect to my future course of
action I feel sure that my work is to be done not by attempting
myself any public action, for which my woman's nature quite
unfits me, but by a true, earnest, free, simple, loving action of
my own soul on this great cause, whether in detail or in
general principles ; and then, having spoken the truth in love,
leaving it to have such course as the Heavenly Father sees fit.
It is thus that I have done most good, oftenest most unexpectedly ; thus let me continue, and devote my time and
powers to the further development of the subject.

In the meantime there was another book to be written,
and for this purpose information must be collected.   Her
New England correspondents had already furnished her with
important details on many of the institutions of Massachusetts
and other adjoining States ; and she now turned to Theodore
Parker, with whose general social aims she felt in entire
sympathy, for further illustration of the best modes of applying the principles of punishment to children who did not owe
retribution to Society ' because,' as she afterwards phrased it,
' Society owed retribution to them.'

Bristol, April 29th, 1852.

A great hindrance to the unanimous carrying out of our views has arisen from the vindictive principle of punishment, which is based on the popular theology, and has taken firm possession of the minds of many who should, I think, have arrived at a more true conclusion. I believe that no punishment should be inflicted as a mere vindictive feeling or imagined retribution, but only such punishment awarded as will, however severe it may be, have a reformatory tendency. In many cases those who hold apparently opposite principles will be found to adopt practically the same measures, and one who holds a purely reformatory theory may be practically more severe than one who takes an eye for an eye, or gives a boy a sound flogging, and then yields to the kinder feelings of nature in his after-treatment. But I believe that sound principles are so all-important, and that in this case wrong ones lead to so much evil in the minds of many, and produce such injurious influence on the children, that I am anxious to *demonstrate*, if possible, that the ends of punishment can be fully effected in the case of children without any further punishment than what is the natural effect of their faults, *i.e.* restraint with reformatory discipline. If you can afford me any further light on the principles and practice of your State on this subject I shall be much obliged to you. The ministerial crisis and unstable condition necessarily involve a suspension of efforts to carry out the objects of the Conference; but those who have their hearts in the matter are employing the truce in preparing their forces, and endeavouring to awake the public mind.

The action which had seemed so long delayed, was near, however, at last. On May 6th Mr. Adderley moved for a Committee in the House of Commons. That same day Mr. Hill and Mary Carpenter spent some hours together in conference on the plans to be adopted, and at Mr. Adderley's request sketched out the lines along which an inquiry might be conducted. When the Committee met under the presidency of the Right Hon. M. T. Baines, it naturally resulted that they were among the first witnesses to be summoned. In Mary Carpenter, who had not yet learned how to overcome her reluctance to take any position of publicity, the call awoke a strange shrinking even while it came with a profound satisfaction. But one consideration—the needs of the children— outweighed everything else; and few would have suspected

what a strange blending of deep passion and personal timidity
lay hid beneath the calm self-possession with which she gave
her evidence.   Her remarks were directed especially to the
moral conditions of reform, which were almost entirely absent,
in her judgment, from the existing system.   'A child will
' never behave well in prison from any moral sense : I have
' in point of fact found that those who behave best in prison
' are really more likely to do badly when they come out.
' Those whom I have been most able to act upon have been
' somewhat rebellious in prison.   I would then enlist the will
' of the child in the work, and without this I do not think
' that any true reformation can be effected. . . .   There
' should be that degree of confidence shown to the children
' which will make them feel that they are workers together
' with the teachers.'   The general positions which she maintained were those already developed in her book ; but the
abundant illustrations which she added from her own personal
experience, lent them new force.   To the feelings which
animated her testimony she gave the following utterance :

May 23rd, 1852.—Father of my spirit, I would here record
the overflowing homage of my heart that Thou hast permitted
me in some small degree to bear a testimony to the cause of
those forsaken young immortals whom I love with my heart's
love, and reverence as Thine image, defaced though it be, and
crushed down by the spirit of evil.   I feel my mind greatly
relieved, for though I have not said nearly as much, or that
so powerfully, as I desired, yet I have been enabled to speak
some words of truth, and I trust that the Heavenly Father
will bear them on the wind of His quickening spirit to spring
up in fruitful soil.   Weak and frail is the vessel containing
the treasure.   I have still another day of testimony.   May the
words of my Saviour and the spirit of my Heavenly Father
sustain me.

A week or two later she wrote with much hope to
Mr. Alexander Thomson and to Lady Byron, reporting her
impressions.

TO MR. ALEXANDER THOMSON, OF BANCHORY.

Bristol, June 2nd, 1852.
You will, I am sure, be glad to hear that the Committee of
Inquiry on Juvenile Delinquency seems quite in earnest to do

something. Mr. Turner, Mr. Hill, Mr. Power, and I, have
borne as strong a testimony as we could to the importance of
reformatory action by voluntary agency, supported by government aid and authority, to raise these poor children. If you
have not received a summons to attend as witness, you will
probably have one, and I hope much from the effect of your
evidence, in showing the effect of such instrumentality as you
are exercising in diminishing vagrancy and crime, and the
effect of the Union School system in pauperising children.

TO LADY BYRON.

Bristol, June 9th, 1852.

I should have written before to give you news of the
Committee of Inquiry, which was fixed upon rather suddenly;
but, as Miss Murray was present, I concluded that she would
tell you what was going on. Mr. Hill gave excellent evidence,
and dwelt much on the importance of enlisting voluntary
agency and individual effort in the work. I followed this by
showing that as a necessary consequence the religious instruction must be left to the managers of the schools, the
only concern of the government being to investigate whether
the plans adopted were calculated to 'transform' juvenile
delinquents into good citizens. I was thankful to have the
power of bearing a testimony in such a quarter to many
important principles, and that they will remain inscribed in
the Blue Books, as seed which may one day bear fruit. The
present position of the question, and the warm interest which
it appears to excite in some, at least, whom I met in London,
who are influential persons, make me more earnestly desire
even than before to have a school commenced here on principles
which will, I think, secure results satisfactory to the public. . . .
Mr. Power writes to me by this post that Sergeant A. has
been recommending juvenile prisons, etc., and adds : ' If that
' be the kind of *practical* recommendation which the Committee
' wishes for, I should almost despair. People don't understand
' the first principles of the matter, and having no foundation
' they cannot build to any purpose. These must be dinned
' again and again in every shape and way into their ears.' The
thing must be shown them to be practical, far more practical
than their present system.

This was now Mary Carpenter's great object. It was
inevitable, as she knew, that a long time must elapse before
any scheme founded on the report of the Committee could

secure Parliamentary sanction.[1] Meanwhile she became more and more anxious to prove the correctness of the views and the feasibility of the proposals which she had urged. ' I cannot ' tell how a truth can be more fully demonstrated,' she wrote to Sheriff Watson, 'than it has been in Aberdeen ; and I can ' only say of those who say of such proceedings that they are ' mere theory, that " hearing they hear and will not under-' " stand, and seeing they see and will not perceive." Un-' happily in English towns the experiment cannot be tried, ' because our magistrates are very much afraid of infringing ' the liberty of the subject by letting the police send little ' vagabonds to school, even, as you do, through a committee.' Still, even without authority of detention, much might be done ; at any rate Mary Carpenter was resolved that the experiment should be tried. But the new enterprise was in any case difficult ; it involved a devotion of time, and labour, and means which might well seem beyond her strength and resources ; and those who saw the strain which her previous exertions had involved, were naturally anxious to shield her from further responsibilities. It was a time of sharp conflict between what were urged upon her as the home duties and what she felt to be the larger claims. In brief sentences wrung from her in the struggle she uttered her distress and her cry for help.

May 6th, 1852.—I feel that I have a work which I *must do*, if God gives me strength to do it. Last year I felt I had a word to speak which must be spoken. I was discouraged by those around me who loved me. But it was spoken; it was a true word ; it was listened to. I have now an idea to develop in acts, to be worked out. It can only be proved to be God's holy truth, as I believe it is, by a work difficult to accomplish, and which my friends would dissuade me from. I feel that I must try to do it. Heavenly Father, do thou help me, and by the Spirit of Christ, by meekness and patience, may I overcome them that oppose themselves.

---

[1] The dissolution of Parliament did in fact bring its sittings to a close in the summer of 1852. The evidence so collected was published in a special Blue Book, without any report from the Committee. The proceedings were renewed under a new Committee (of nearly the same composition as the old) after the first meeting of Parliament in November ; but the recommendations of the Committee were not issued till the summer of 1853.

But help came from unexpected quarters. The attention of Mr. Russell Scott, of Bath, had been directed to the subject of juvenile delinquency; and a visit to the Rauhe Haus near Hamburg had awakened a desire to carry out something of the same work. An opportunity now presented itself. Near the village of Kingswood, about four miles from Bristol, stood some vacant premises formerly occupied by a Wesleyan School. The house had been erected by John Wesley himself, and the study and the garden-walk where he was wont to meditate were hallowed by memories of work and prayer. The buildings contained accommodation for upwards of a hundred children, and were surrounded by twelve acres of land. This property was admirably adapted for an agricultural reformatory school, such as Mary Carpenter was desirous to establish.[1] Mr. Scott generously offered to purchase it for this purpose, and to join her in the management. Funds, however, were needed for fitting it up, and for the maintenance of the school, as there was as yet no public source of income in regular allowances for each sentenced inmate, and voluntary contributions from the parents could not be expected with any confidence. The difficulties, the hopes and fears, connected with the scheme, were all communicated to Lady Byron, who wrote in June, offering liberal help, and, further, proposing to hand over to the managers of Kingswood a quantity of furniture and other material no longer needed for a school at Ealing Grove, which she was about to close. To these suggestions Mary Carpenter replied with overflowing heart.

---

[1] 'I quite agree with you,' she had written in 1851 to Lady Byron, 'that all reformatory schools should, if possible, be rural ones. That 'truth is gradually being discovered by experience, the most valuable 'teacher. I believe that rural employments are peculiarly calculated 'for such training in many ways which you will understand. Nor is 'the least valuable element the influence of nature to which it sub-'jects the boy. I shall not forget the feeling with which my boy 'Shaughnessy pointed out to me "the beautiful view from *our* farm" 'at Red Hill.' This principle was also recognised by Mr. Barwick Baker, of Hardwicke Court, and Mr. Bengough, in the reformatory which they established a few months before the Kingswood school was opened.

TO LADY BYRON.

Bristol, June 13th, 1852.

I do not know whether you will understand me when I say that I felt more overcome by your letter showing the will and the power to help me in the dearest object of my heart, than I was when the object seemed thoroughly defeated. I have been more trained to bear disappointment than the prospect of accomplishing my plans. I thank our Heavenly Father! I will not attempt to express how grateful I feel to you ; you will partly imagine it. . . .

I hope that we shall not go on even five years before the public *supports us* or *substitutes better plans*, but I am prepared for patient waiting.

If possible I shall go to Ealing myself before the 24th ; all furniture, etc., which you kindly think proper to transfer to Kingswood, will be *sure* to be useful ; I have learnt from my dear father to adapt things to purposes. Besides, I shall desire to gain as much as possible from seeing the arrangements and plans at Ealing Grove.

In the journal the gladness mingles with prayer.

June 20th, 1852.—What conflicts have I from within and from without! I have had sore ones lately : for some of those whom I was leading on have fallen back, and I have had wearying trials with my fellow workers. Oh fill them and me, Heavenly Father, with Thy Holy Spirit ! And I have had, too, a joy, but such as to make me rejoice with trembling. The heart of one who has this world's goods has been touched to work with me, by buying that place hallowed by the spirit of the holy Wesley, where I have desired that many should be trained to righteousness ; and rich sympathy in the work has already been given by many hearts. O Father ! help me, guide me ; show me the way Thou wouldst have me to take ! Give me that deep stillness in my own soul which will enable me to see clearly the right path !

No time was now lost. As soon as the scheme was made known, subscriptions flowed in, and the promoters were cheered by the unexpected support which they received. ' Mary hopes that she shall now accomplish the great desire ' of her heart,' wrote her mother. ' Above £300 has been ' contributed. . . . It was this day, the day of African ' freedom, that she began her Ragged School, six years

' since ; and it was with a thankful heart that I looked at
' the remembrance of her dear father in the chapel.'

But the joy with which Mary Carpenter prepared to enter on
this new labour, was checked by the death, in the course of
August, of the friend who had for those past six years sustained
her in her first undertaking, Mr. Joseph Fletcher. ' To his
' sympathy and aid in my work,' such was her tribute to
him, ' I owe more than almost to any other. He first made
' me feel that my work was understood and appreciated, and
' from him I have invariably had the kindest encouragement.
' From the first day of his visiting the School, I have felt
' that he understood all I was doing, and saw the bearings
' of everything far better than I did. It was he who
' encouraged me to write, and gave me confidence by his
' approval. He has frequently lately supported our views
' in critical moments ; and at my examination he came to
' let me feel that there was some one who shared my views,
' and gave me an hour's most encouraging conversation before
' I went to the House. No one who has not, as I have,
' laboured on towards a wide and grave object (no one around
' really understanding, and most showing misconstruction)
' can understand the happiness of feeling oneself understood
' and appreciated, and can tell why I feel this a very near
' personal loss, though personally, or in any other way than
' publicly, we scarcely knew him.' Up to the last Mr.
Fletcher had supported her. ' The boldness of your new
' effort,' he said when he heard of Kingswood, ' is quite
' startling.' But now she must learn to do without the help
that was thus withdrawn ; she began to suspect herself of
having depended too much on his sustaining sympathy, and
she passed out of the shadow with fresh stedfastness of resolve.

Early in September all was ready. The master and
mistress were engaged ; the premises were equipped. It was
a golden autumn evening when a cart drove slowly over to
Kingswood with the last load of bedding, on the top of
which there rode triumphantly the first inmate of the
school. ' Kingswood entered,' wrote Mary Carpenter, on
September 11th. ' To-day is too full of thankful yet
' agitating thoughts, mingled with hope and fear, for me to
' do more than to note this utterance, and pray for guidance.'
But hope predominated ; combat was over, at any rate for
the present ; she was secure in the truth of her principles,

and confident in the prospect of carrying them into effect.
Her mother observed with gladness that she was set free
from the long strain which had engaged her energies and
absorbed her thoughts, and could now regain her usual
quickness of participation in the life around her. 'It is
'quite a happiness to see Mary, she is so cheerful, and
'interests herself so much more in her friends. Mary has
'long had a struggling desire to do more and to be more than
'her friends desired for her, fearing the effect upon her
'mental health; but now her desire is gratified, her soul
'finds repose, and her affections expand.'

To these affections the scholars at Kingswood found as
ready access as the children at the Ragged School. 'When
'I last went to Kingswood,' she reported, ere the month was
out, 'a poor little sinner who had been obliged to be locked
'up, a most dreadful punishment to those wild creatures,
'when brought out to me, put his little hand on my shoulder,
'and sobbed out his grievances. The balm of a few kisses
'quite restored him to a sane state; I felt that the poor
'little fellow felt that I loved him, and I was thankful for
'his love.' So the new work brought with it new zest; and
the time that could be saved from the Ragged School, and
was claimed neither by home duties nor by the new book
which was steadily advancing, was cheerfully devoted to the
fresh tie that had been created. No winter's cold could
daunt her enthusiasm; and on the dreariest day she might
be seen patiently making her way on foot—for it was only
by constant personal economies that she could afford to be
generous—to and fro between Bristol and Kingswood. Of
this unwearied activity her mother gives a glimpse to her
son Philip, in mid-December. 'Mary goes on her usual
'course with great zeal and much happiness. Yesterday,
'after writing all the morning, she got her dinner at half-
'past twelve, and set off to walk to Kingswood, four miles,
'busied herself there between three and four hours, and
'then walked back, having Mr. A. as an escort.'

Sometimes she pressed her friends into the cause, as one
of them has thus narrated:[1]

Weather, however hard, was no bar to her journeys. On
one of these, Mary Carpenter was accompanied by two ladies.

---

[1] Miss Davenport-Hill, in the *Sunday Magazine*, July, 1880, p. 454.

Stopping on the way, she bade her companions await her, and disappearing into a police-station hard by, she soon emerged, bringing with her a subdued, half-starved-looking little urchin, whom she called 'Joe.' Placing him under the care of the younger of the two ladies, she resumed her argument with the other, while she led her party onward to the nearest cab-stand. Meanwhile snow had begun to fall heavily. The three boys, unperceived for a time by Mary Carpenter, who was full of her subject, began to pelt Joe with snowballs, not a few of which came in thuds on the umbrella of his young escort, who expected every moment that he would take to his heels, and that she should have to give chase. At length their leader, turning round, became aware of the state of the case, and exhorted the victim to endure the attack with patience, and not to return in kind the balls which were flying about him. The party only reached the cab-stand to learn that no man would drive them, so slippery were the roads. There was nothing for it but to trudge the whole distance on foot. Right glad was the amateur police officer when—the elements and street-boys notwithstanding—she delivered up her charge in safety at the school.

So the end of the year drew on. When Christmas arrived, the circle of festivities was enlarged to gather in the newcomers. It was with unspeakable gladness that Mary Carpenter made the additional preparations. As she looked back upon the time which had passed since the first Birmingham Conference, she could not fail to take courage from the progress which the cause had made. Principles which were then only asserted, were now being triumphantly vindicated; Parliament was awake to the necessity of action; and schools were springing up from the resolute determination of devoted workers to grapple with the evil, even before they were armed with the full authority they sought. There had been sorrow; there had been darkness of spirit; there had been painful contests, even to strivings with tears; but these were past, at any rate for a time, and on Christmas Day Mary Carpenter was able to record: 'A day of deep 'joy and inexpressible thankfulness. I have had a season 'this week too full of deep and soul-stirring happiness for 'me to give utterance to in words.' It was one of the brightest eras of her life.

CHAPTER VI.

REFORMATORY WORK.
1853—1857.

'Witness the women, of His children sweetest,—
  Scarcely earth seeth them but earth shall see,—
Thou in their woe Thine agony completest,
  Christ, and their solitude is nigh to Thee.

What is this psalm from pitiable places
  Glad where the messengers of peace have trod?
Whose are these beautiful and holy faces
  Lit with their loving and aflame with God?

Eager and faint, empassionate and lonely,
  These in their hour shall prophesy again:
This is His will who hath endured, and only
  Sendeth the promise where He sends the pain.

Ay, unto these distributeth the Giver
  Sorrow and sanctity, and loves them well,
Grants them a power and passion to deliver
  Hearts from the prison-house and souls from hell.'

                              Frederic W. H. Myers.

CHAPTER VI.

REFORMATORY WORK.

1853—1857.

AMONG the labours which had occupied Mary Carpenter during the year 1852, was the preparation of a second work in support of the positions adopted by the first Birmingham Conference. As Christmas passed, this task approached its completion, and early in 1853 the new book appeared, under the title of *Juvenile Delinquents: their Condition and Treatment*. The first portion of the volume was devoted to an exposition of the causes of juvenile crime. The condition of young delinquents was set forth with the full knowledge derived from long and careful study of prison reports and police records, illumined by the light of personal experience and touched with the glow of a passionate sympathy. In the analysis of these documents Mary Carpenter felt the advantage of the severe training in accuracy and strictness of reasoning which her scientific pursuits had afforded her; and though history and poetry had to give way to piles of statistics, and the lives of the saints were exchanged for biographies of thieves, she assuredly carried to her work a breadth of view, a quickness of imagination, and a keenness of insight, which owed much to the wider culture that had preceded these special inquiries. The investigation of the circumstances of youthful offenders was of course incomplete without a glimpse at the homes from which the boy and girl criminals issued. Accordingly, the different classes of parents —the professional thieves, the vagabonds, the intemperate—

were all sketched in rapid outline, sufficient to justify the
conclusion that the children's guilt was mainly chargeable on
society and on the parents (who had themselves, it must be
remembered, been children once), so that the young criminal
deserved pity at least as much as reprehension and chastisement. Parental neglect must be repaired by society, yet
even then the parental responsibility of maintenance was not
abrogated, and the burden of supporting their children must
be as far as possible imposed upon them.

What means, the author next inquired, were at hand for
dealing with the problems of delinquency which were thus
complicated by nature and circumstance? The insufficiency
of the best prison schools, in spite of an excellent intellectual
training, seemed amply proved by the large number of
recommittals; the comforts of prison were often attractive
to homeless boys, and abundant opportunities were afforded
for the communication of all kinds of evil knowledge among
the inmates. The results of the Parkhurst prison for boys
were again submitted to rigid scrutiny, and the principles on
which its methods were based received fresh condemnation.
On the other hand, the change of feeling in many of the United
States in which reformatory schools were taking the place
of prisons for juvenile delinquents, was cited in favour of
similar proposals for the United Kingdom. France supplied
materials for an interesting comparison of the Colonies or
reformatory schools with the gaols ; a brief survey was taken
of the farm schools of Wurtemberg, Prussia, and Bavaria, of
Belgium and Switzerland; and more detailed accounts were
offered of Wichern's establishment at the Rauhe Haus, and
of an experiment in the reformation of some London thieves.

The consideration of these various efforts opened the way
to the enunciation of the principles of treatment, having
regard to the physical, moral, and spiritual condition of
children. The essence of the matter was thus stated :

The child must be placed where he will be gradually
restored to the true position of childhood. He must be brought
to a sense of dependence by reawakening in him new and
healthy desires which he cannot himself gratify, and by finding
that there is a power far greater than his own to which he is
indebted for the gratification of these desires. He must perceive, by manifestations which he cannot mistake, that this

power, while controlling him, is guided by wisdom and love;
he must have his affections called forth by the obvious personal interest felt in his own individual well-being by those
around him; he must, in short, be placed in a *family*. Faith
in those around him being once thoroughly established, he will
soon yield his own *will* in ready submission to those who are
working for his good; it will thus be gradually subdued and
trained, and he will work with them in effecting his reformation, trusting where he cannot perceive the reason of the
measures they adopt to correct or eradicate the evil in him. This,
it is apprehended, is the fundamental principle of all true reformatory action with the young; and in every case where striking
success has followed such efforts, it will be traceable to the
greater development of this principle, to a more true and
powerful action on the soul of the child by those who have
assumed towards it the holy duties of a parent.

These words were not written lightly; they were charged
with a deep meaning which the experience of Kingswood was
already confirming; they expressed the conviction which was
to be worked out with unwavering stedfastness through a
quarter of a century of reformatory activity. A brief discussion of the moral effects of productive labour, and especially
agricultural, and of the necessity of proper recreation, then
followed; and a statement of the true nature of punishment
gave an opportunity for a vindication of the theory of correction as distinguished from retribution. The final results, and
the suggestions founded upon them, did not materially differ
from the conclusions set forth in the treatise on *Reformatory
Schools*. Like the earlier work, this second book had no new
story to tell, no fresh plan to urge. It sought only to perform
the same modest function; to collect and group a vast mass
of facts familiar to prison officials, but unknown to any
besides, save the few professional men and philanthropists
who had made them their special study; to proclaim aloud
the wants which they revealed, and to point out the means
of remedying them. Its author felt, as she wrote, that she
was but passing on to others what she had already received
from the revered teacher and friend of her earlier years and
the helper of her maturer enterprise; and as she recorded
the issue of 'this second word on behalf of the forsaken
'ones,' she added: 'This volume I dedicate in love and
'gratitude to my three helpers in Heaven, my dear Father,

' Dr. Tuckerman, and Mr. Fletcher. All three have been
' guiding me through it; the last has uttered many words
' through it which he left as his last legacy to the children.'

The new book put fresh materials into the hands of those
who were urging the establishment of Reformatory Schools.
The battle was indeed fought, it only remained to follow up
the victory. • In June the Committee of Inquiry, which had
been reappointed under the new Parliament in November,
1852, brought its task to a close, and reported in their
favour; and in the following month Mr. Adderley moved
for leave to bring in a Bill for the establishment of
Reformatory Schools in England and Wales. This Bill
reached a second reading, but was withdrawn on a pledge
from the Government that a measure should be introduced
in the next session. In the meanwhile Mr. Adderley
resolved to renew the impulse imparted to the movement
by the Birmingham Conference of 1851, and took steps
to gather a second assembly in the same place. ' There
' is going to be another Conference at Birmingham the
' week before Christmas,' wrote Mrs. Carpenter. ' Mary
' will be there and will be Mr. Adderley's guest. It is
' being organised by Mr. Adderley, who is taking much
' pains to collect together those who are most interested in
' the Reform of Juvenile Delinquents. You will be glad
' to hear that the desired moral tone of feeling in the
' establishment at Kingswood is making much progress. It
' is long since it has been thought necessary to have recourse
' to punishment.'

The second Conference was held under much more
favourable circumstances than the first. The interest which
the subject now excited, drew together large numbers of
persons from all quarters ; and the public meeting in the
evening thronged—not the assembly-room of an hotel—but
the Town Hall itself. Mary Carpenter was, as before, a
silent spectator; but the opportunity of intercourse with so
many fellow-workers refreshed her greatly. A scheme of
resolutions which she drew out, indicated the line which
she desired the deliberations to follow : provision should
be made by law empowering local authorities to enforce
attendance at Industrial Schools on children who had
subjected themselves to police interference by vagrancy,
mendicancy, or petty infringements of the law; and

legislation should sanction the creation of Reformatory Schools, or should support such schools when privately established (due security being taken for their proper management), for the detention of children convicted of crime or of habitual vagrancy. These schools were intended as substitutes for imprisonment, in contrast to what she described as the punishment principle; and they were to be spontaneously initiated, wherever possible, and subsequently conducted, by voluntary action. How far she found sympathy with these views, may be inferred from the following letters.

TO LADY BYRON.

Bristol, December 23rd, 1853.

I have been wishing to write you a long letter, yet I find that I can only send you a few lines, to tell you that the Conference was very satisfactory; the two dangerous questions were started—the 'punishment' principle and the intro-duction of the State religion into these schools, the latter of which would have been fatal to voluntary action;—but I am happy to say that the feeling of the meeting was absolutely against either of these matters being introduced into the resolutions, and the discussions which arose showed how strongly both these principles have taken root. I stayed with Sir J. Pakington at Mr. Adderley's, and am happy to find how zealous both these gentlemen are. The public meeting was everything one could wish, and greatly encouraged our friends. Lord Shaftesbury was admirable;—indeed I feel a greater respect for him than I had even done before. Mr. Milnes seemed to wish to make the *amende honorable* for the heresy he had put forth in the morning, for which he had a severe lashing from Mr. Hill;—the voluntary principle was carried most triumphantly. The next morning ladies were invited to hear your 'suggestions,' and I hope that the result of their meeting will be the forming of a committee of ladies to watch over these poor girls in Birmingham, and immediate efforts to form a Girls' Reformatory School in Birmingham. I cannot take any *active* part in these matters, but have promised advice if needed.

TO LADY BYRON.

Bristol, December 26th, 1853.

Thank you much for your encouraging letter and kind wishes, which I must answer briefly and seriatim, being not a little tired this evening after six or seven hours of work in dining 200 children at the Ragged School, and having to-morrow to prepare the Kingswood Festival, viz. examination, tea, speeches, and singing,—the company,—the children, any parents who are not too ragged or drunken, and *friends*, rich and poor, from the neighbourhood, Bath and Bristol. I per-ceive that persons who positively *work* with the ' dangerous' children, insensibly slip out of their evangelicism, while they think they have it safely embalmed in their inmost spirits. I never undeceive them. Mr. Ellis has done Mr. A. and others incalculable good by *demonstrating* that reformation can be effected without the Church catechisms. I advised the Bir-mingham ladies to form a *small* committee of *real* workers, and to find out their ways and means in their town; only setting out with a strong and devoted purpose, they will, with a general idea set before them, feel their way. I said that if I could be really useful in any such society at any stage of their proceedings, I would go to Birmingham and give them my experience. If such committees could be formed in many towns, and a communication be established among them through the Secretaries, much might be done, for I see that women *may* do more than men, if they will only know their true mission, but everything depends on whether ladies are *judicious*. I fear that such are rare!

When Mary Carpenter returned from Birmingham, she was accompanied by one of the most earnest supporters of the Reformatory cause, the Rev. T. Carter, of Liverpool. Mr. Carter had watched the experiment at Kingswood with great interest ; he had contributed to it some of the worst characters ; and he now came to see what measure of success had been achieved. The result may be told in the words of Mrs. Carpenter : ' Mr. Carter was much pleased with ' Kingswood, and all which he saw there. He hardly knew ' how to believe that the children with fine open countenances ' and affectionate hearts, who so warmly greeted him, were ' the depraved and hardened little wretches whom he had ' sent there. Body and mind appeared filled with new life. ' This was as delightful to Mary as anything which passed ' at the Conference.'

These results, however, were only reached after long and anxious striving. The undertaking was of peculiar difficulty. Plans and methods had to be devised ; the whole scheme of reformatory discipline had to be slowly elaborated in the face of those who were ready to take instant advantage of a single false step. A moment's relaxation of control sufficed to throw into wild confusion all the rude ungoverned elements of character, which only yielded to a force that they recognised not so much as stronger, but as higher than their own. That peculiar and indescribable power, known as the 'tone' of a school, did not yet exist; it could only be evolved by degrees, as the violence of passion was tamed, and self-will learned obedience. Moreover, the School had as yet no legal sanction; most of the inmates were sent by their parents, and the managers had no authority to detain them; and it was occasionally difficult, therefore, to deal with the runaways, when influence and persuasion failed. Parties of the children, led by some more daring spirit, often a girl, would make their way into Bristol, sometimes to revisit their old haunts; sometimes, in the case of young delinquents from a distance, to taste the familiar pleasures of city life in new scenes. In the midst of these embarrassments, it was to the managers, Mr. Scott and Mary Carpenter, that the distracted officials naturally turned. It needed all their urgency to prevent the resort to physical force, which seemed the only means of quelling these appalling outbursts; and when at last, to Mary Carpenter's dismay, the fatal principle was introduced, the very possibility of carrying on the school was in her eyes in imminent jeopardy. One or two extracts from the journal which she kept for some time during the early days of the experiment, will reveal the immense obstacles with which she had to contend. Here is a scene in Bristol :

Saturday, March 12th, 1853.—At eleven A.M. a policeman came to tell me that six girls were then in the Station. I told him that it was owing to the excitement caused by the hair-cutting that they had run away. It appeared afterwards that when they were frustrated in their attempt the evening before, they darted off the next morning as soon as the gates were open, Martha, Ann, and Marianne of Cheltenham being the only ones remaining. Margaret guided them all to her mother's house, who, with a presence of mind and discernment of their true interest which are highly admirable in such a woman, at once locked them together in a room, and sent her younger daughter to the Station, whence two policemen were at once sent to fetch them. In about an hour I went down with Mr. and Miss A. Instead of finding them in a

room waiting for me, as I had expected from what the policemen had said to me, I was told that they were all locked up.
The Superintendent was most indignant with them; he said
he had never seen such girls; they had insulted the officers
and been so outrageous that he had been incited to give two a
slap in the face, and to lock them all in separate cells, whence
they called out, screamed, and sang, in such a manner that
those six were enough to corrupt a hundred. He then led us
to the entrance of the corridor, where I listened to sounds
that indeed shocked me, and that revealed the wicked and
audacious state in which they were. These cells had doors
made of strong iron bars, so that we could see and hear what
passed within. He then accompanied me to the door of each
cell, calling each little girl to the door, as one would call a
wild beast to the front of his den. Had I felt any doubt before
of the useless and injurious effect of physical coercion, and the
force of kindness and moral influence on these poor children,
all doubt would have vanished. As I approached each girl,
and gently but very sorrowfully told her how grieved I was
to see her here in such a condition when I had left her good
and happy the day before, she hung down her head and was
quite softened; one affectionately took my hand. There was
now no fear. I requested that they might be released, which
was done, and said we would walk with them to the Old
Market Stand, and thence take flys. The Superintendent
demurred to this, saying that there were always bad people
about who might misunderstand our motives towards the
children, and insult us, or even try to rescue them. I replied
that I was not afraid of this, for the only time I had been spoken
to was one day when I was taking back three girls, and a very
low-looking woman, as I passed, said 'God bless you!' However, I found that the girls had come without their bonnets
and shawls, so I sent Mr. A. for two flys. While we were
waiting, they told me about Mrs. D.'s proceedings towards
them, but said she had told them that I was a kind lady, and
that she must send them back to me, and that they knew she
did it from kind motives. They had eaten nothing that
morning, and having with me two biscuits, I divided them
among the girls; they ate the few mouthfuls with avidity,
and said to each other 'How kind,' so I sent for two loaves
for them. I asked each if she wished that I should tell
the Superintendent that she was sorry for her conduct to
him, which all quite desired. He seemed pleased and surprised when I told him. At my request Mr. A. asked if we
should give the police anything for their trouble, but he said
that he by no means wished it, for they all sympathised in
our object, and would gladly help us at any time. It was well
we had flys, there was such a crowd of ragamuffins outside; I

told my girls to hide their faces, which they did, and were
very quiet the whole way. Within an hour after our arrival
Catherine had actually run away again; but she was captured
and brought back. I left the rest tranquil, and Mr. Scott
talking very kindly to her. She looked quite subdued.

Three days after another entry gives us a companion
picture at Kingswood.

Tuesday, March 15th.—I received to my dismay a note from
Mr. Scott whom I was expecting in Bristol, stating his desire
of my immediate presence, as he was obliged then to leave
Kingswood, and most of the children were at that moment
divided among the neighbours, confined with their hands tied,
in their respective cellars! I hastened over. Regan afterwards told Mr. A. that he was watching in his cellar for the
sound of my fly, as he was sure I should come. Kingswood
School was nearly deserted; it was long before I could find
any official, as they were all visiting the various culprits. It
appeared that at prayers that morning Rowan and another
were behaving in a very improper manner, and were taken
out of the room. Unfortunately Miss S. did not stay with
them, and they were soon seen through the windows dancing
defiantly about. The infection rapidly spread. The other
children rushed out, and the greater part both of boys and
girls ran into the field beyond the bounds, where they all
danced about in perfect defiance. Mr. Iles and others were
summoned to give their aid; nothing was to be done but to
seize them one by one, tie their hands and even their feet,
and carry them to the houses of the neighbours, who all gave
their ready sympathy and help. The morning's work was
most painful and harassing. I arrived about four, and
Mr. Scott departed soon after. It was arranged that while
Mr. A. stayed with the remaining boys, and Miss S. with the
girls, Mr. Morris should go and bring back the boys by degrees,
while I went to the girls. I found them all much softened
and subdued, and was very glad to unbind them and bring
them home. The evening and the next morning were spent
quietly, and all returned to their duty.

Well might she write after scenes like these: 'As for
'me, it is a blessing that I have an inexhaustible share of
'faith, hope, and love, otherwise I should not be able to bear
'up; but I study every failure to learn how to succeed
'better, and quite see the way opening to a better order
'of things.' One of the chief difficulties arose from the

imperfect grasp by the teachers of what she regarded as fundamental principles. She sometimes felt obliged to sustain them in action of which she seriously disapproved, that their authority might not be weakened; and she was often pained at what seemed to her like misinterpretation and want of confidence. It took her a long time to learn that she must not look for powers or for devotion equal to her own among the fellow-workers whom she gathered round her; and to realise that to pitch her expectations too high was to do them grave injustice. Spring passed into summer, and she was still at her post. Every change in the staff put new responsibilities on her; and again and again the cry went up for help.

TO MISS SANFORD.

Bristol, April 16th, 1853.

On Thursday morning I rose with the half-agonized ejaculation, ' O God, why hast Thou given me a woman's ' heart ? ' The answer was, ' The better to do My will.' And so I went forth from the dejection and weakness of the closet to conquer by the power of love. Never did I more feel the strength of this. My poor girls and I wept together while I told them that their own mother did not love them more than I, and that they had now compelled us in faithfulness to the duty we owed to the Queen who had committed them to our charge, and to themselves, to give them up to the magistrates that they might be controlled, as we could not control them ; that I would visit them in prison if allowed ; or if not, that my thoughts would be with them, and that I begged them as a token of love for me to go off quietly. They remained quite quiet the whole time, till the next day, when they went away as gently with Miss A. to Bristol, as if they were going to a pleasure.

May 23rd, 1853.

I have been gaining immense experience ; I know now what before I believed ; but my faith is not shaken, and all the evil I find out in these poor girls only makes me love them more desperately and gives me a stronger hold on them. As long as I feel that, I am courageous.

June 5th, 1853.—Holy Father, I am *very* weak, but Thou art strong ! Uphold me, strengthen me, shield me, guide me!

I am all insufficient for the work Thou hast given me to do :—
my bodily strength is small, I have a tenderness of spirit
which, if not strengthened by Thee and shielded by Thy love,
is continually torn and wounded by the distrust, by the mis-
conceptions, of those around me; the instruments whom I
have to guide in the work are all inadequate to the undertaking, though most of them are faithful to their powers.
Yet I feel that this is a work which Thou hast given me to
do, and for which Thou hast in many ways and by a peculiar
training fitted me. O Father! I will do it, as long as Thou
permittest me thus to consecrate myself to Thee. Thou *wilt*
support me and give me strength.

A few nights ago I lay in feverish wakefulness:—my friend
and valued fellow-worker —— was struck with sharp illness; I
dared not pray for his recovery, for we know not what we ask.
My Father knows what is best ; I left all to Him—and then it
seemed to me that my spirit reposed in Him with a sort of
intensity of nearness, of satisfied loving union, which words
cannot describe. Those few moments were heaven, which
could be nothing more than this. I desire nothing else. O
Father! I thank Thee above all for such moments which make
me know the holiness of my inmost spirit. Oh fan it with
Thy love into a flame which shall burn steadily and clearly
until it kindles all with Thy brightness, and each immortal
spark burns strongly and purely!

Only with the support of such perception of

> ' Central peace subsisting at the heart
> Of endless agitation,'

could she have made her way through the trials of this
summer. At one time she is nearly broken down: ' I feel
' almost overpowered by difficulties, but still my faith in the
' good and true fails not.' At another time she playfully
compares herself to Kehama, ' whose life was charmed and
' could not be extinguished ; for I feel as if my spirit
' *cannot* be quenched. . . . I have most kind sympathy in
' numerous quarters, and my mother and sisters have been
' most considerate and loving.' Every fresh manifestation of
' the powers of darkness ' in her girls only made her more
resolute to cope with them, and deepened instead of daunting
her determination.

Bristol, June 15th, 1853.

'The *Neglected* Child' gives but a faint and poor idea of the cruel wrong which has been inflicted on the souls of these poor children. If they were all left to die ' neglected,' as some are, the thought of their being laid in a Father's bosom would soothe one's grief for them,—but *now !* I shudder with an indignation and intense compassion which I would not attempt to express, when I look at our young girls and behold the fearful condition to which their passions have been brought by ill-treatment perhaps all their lives. The sufferings of the negroes seem to me of even secondary importance to the wrong done to the immortal souls of these young creatures.

Little by little the results of steady work began to appear. When the school was just reaching the close of its first year she was able to report : ' Our boys are getting into better ' order ; they all drank tea last Friday at our house, after ' being at the Zoological Gardens, and did themselves much ' credit.' Next, an addition to the establishment is announced. ' I left Kingswood in a very pleasing state yesterday. We ' have now rabbits, fowls, and pigs.' As soon as settled order was firmly seated in the place, the turbulent spirits found a new happiness in conforming to it ; and in November Mary Carpenter could write to Lady Byron with fresh testimony to the value of the outdoor labour to which she attached so much importance. ' You will be pleased to hear that our Kings- ' wood boys are improving delightfully ; indeed, a greater ' change has come over them in the last two months than I ' should have thought possible. This I chiefly attribute to ' our gardener, who makes them take delight in their work ; ' indeed, the effect of the agricultural training upon them ' even surpasses my expectations. The girls, too, have made ' much progress, though not nearly so much.' So it came to pass that punishment was needed no more ; the little colony (now containing sixteen boys and thirteen girls) was becoming to many of the inmates a true home ; the boys might be sent on errands to Bristol ; even thievish girls could be trusted in the village with money which they never thought of appropriating ; and no one now ever desired to run away. It was a remarkable transformation ; and Mr. Carter gladly bore witness to the success which had been attained. It was with a thankful heart, therefore, that Mary Carpenter prepared to issue the first report of the School, and invite further aid.

TO LADY BYRON.

Bath, January 7th, 1854.

Here is the first copy of my little report; I shall be happy to learn that it meets with your approbation. Few who read these simple sentences will suspect of what long striving, what rending experiences, what 'striving with tears,' this is the result; nor with what deep gratitude I now feel in a position to make this appeal for help in the work. I feel quite ready to undergo any amount of trial and difficulty which my Heavenly Father gives me strength to bear. Thankful am I that the commencement of the last year did not reveal to me all I should have to go through. But it is now all past.

Time and unremitting effort had thus brought about the justification of the enterprise. Had Mary Carpenter been able to devote herself absolutely to it, this result might have been reached sooner. But the Ragged School could not be abandoned, and the work there went on as usual. That supervision might indeed have been continued, had her centre of operations been transferred from the home in Great George Street to Kingswood. But the dear ties which linked her to her mother could not be thus rudely severed; who but she was free to tend her failing strength and declining years? Another might certainly render the daily services, but no one else could supply the same companionship of high aims and larger interests. 'There is a flood of Christian love ever 'welling up in her heart,' wrote Mrs. Carpenter, 'which 'stimulates my languid affections and keeps me from 'feeling that all is vanity and vexation of spirit.' So the plan of living at Kingswood was relinquished, but Wesley's study was fitted up as a resting-place, that she might avoid the fatigue of journeys to and fro; and there in many an hour of anxious thought by day or night, she realised the force of the words which Wesley had written on a window-pane in his room, 'God is here.'

Soon another scheme arose in her mind. She had observed in the Ragged School that the progress of the girls was much slower than that of the boys. The records of

female convicts showed that they were far harder to reform
than male offenders. And now the experience of Kingswood
tended in the same direction. It was becoming plain that
the union of boys and girls in one school did not afford the
most favourable conditions for the amendment of the girls,
while they were often the ringleaders in mischief. Would it
be possible to separate them, and secure the girls under her
own control? There seemed no way but to take them into
her own home. It was natural that those whom she con-
sulted should dissuade her from such a step; they dreaded
any addition to responsibilities that were heavy enough
already. She chafed against what seemed to her opposition
and want of sympathy, but her judgment yielded; she waited,
and her mother never knew what cherished desires she
abandoned for her sake.

There was in truth enough to occupy her. The oldest
scholars at Kingswood were beginning to leave, and means
must be found for offering them new careers. In April
(1854) she was accordingly waiting at Gravesend with three
boys and two girls for a ship which was to take them among
the emigrants under Mrs. Chisholm's direction. She parted
from them with fear and trembling. 'This is an important
' and critical experiment,' she wrote, ' and I must omit nothing
' which will contribute to its success. I am quite satisfied
' with observing the results of training on these children; the
' doubt is whether they are strong enough to resist future
' temptation. I do not believe in reformations of so short a
' standing, unless they are afterwards carried on by those
' among whom they are placed.' The appointment of a Committee at Kingswood shortly afterwards relieved her of part
of her burden; but she could not lay down the influence she
had acquired, or the experience to which appeal was made in
every difficulty. New troubles arose with changes in the
staff; but from the thick of the conflict she turned to the
Ragged School with a sense of rest. ' My great refreshment
' is to be at St. James's Back, where the tone of the school is
' perfectly satisfactory, and there is an inexhaustible charm
' and agreeable excitement in watching the development of
' the young natural beings around me.'

Meanwhile though she appeared absorbed in these engrossing duties, she welcomed with joy one of the friends
from the United States, with whom she had corresponded

for the past ten years on terms of great intimacy—Mrs. Follen. It was one of the self-denials imposed on her by her voluntary labours, to be unable any longer to pour forth thought and feeling in the unreserved confidences of friendship, except to those engaged in her own tasks. She enjoyed society intensely; and now that her early fear of not being liked had given way before an assured consciousness that she had a work to do, and the power to do it, she entered with gladness into every opportunity which that work afforded her. Such opportunities, however, were necessarily rare; and other pleasures could only be tasted briefly, and then gently put aside. In particular she regretted the cessation of her Anti-slavery activities; these had been handed over to the beloved sister by her side; but this made her the more eager to manifest her sympathy with one so devoted to the cause as Mrs. Follen, whose departure now drew from her the following note.

TO MRS. FOLLEN.

Bristol, July 13th, 1854.

DEAR FRIEND, FAREWELL!

I am thankful to have had the privilege of holding communion with you. I dare not indulge myself in much personal communication with those I love, nor in sorrow at parting with them; all these intercourses must be reserved for the world where time will be no more! This world's time must be devoted to the work I have to do. But not less do I treasure my friends in my inmost heart, where you will retain a sacred place. Nor less do I sympathise in your work, which is holy. I watch it with deep interest, though I cannot work in it; and highly do I honour those who rise above the world's opinions and censures to devote themselves for the forsaken of men. May Heaven's blessing be with you to guide and direct you!

The summer brought with it need of rest, after the long fatigues of the Kingswood work; and Mary Carpenter availed herself of a brief vacation to visit the Isle of Wight and spend a few days at Parkhurst. The unfavourable opinion of this institution which she had originally derived from a careful study of its published reports, and had first expressed in the *Reformatory Schools*, she had repeated in her evidence before the Select Committee, and had again put

forth in the volume on *Juvenile Delinquents.* It was no easy
task to her to do so. She was aware of the irritation which
it might cause, and the opposition which might be created
among the authorities against her own efforts. Her anticipa-
tions were in part verified. Shortly after the publication of
the second book, a long letter reached her from Colonel Jebb,
whose official position gave force to his words, reproaching
her with having impeded the very cause which she and others
professed to be advocating, and warning her that it would
take years of energetic and prudent exertion on the part of
those who had been thus engaged, to regain what they themselves had lost by misdirected attempts. The letter produced
no fresh evidence ; yet it seemed somewhat like a challenge.
At first she met it quite calmly. ' Colonel Jebb, the great
' advocate of Parkhurst, writes with indignation. Mr. Strick-
' land, our firm friend in Parkhurst, says, " Your last work is
' " now causing great excitement in the establishment; it is
' " the occasion of no small stir among us throughout our
' " department." I expect to be severely animadverted on,
' but feel I am on the rock of truth and duty, and that men
' being so bound by position and opinion, no one would have
' spoken out if I had not. So I am glad they are stirred.
' It is wonderful how courageous I am grown.' She was
doubtful what reply ought to be made. Her ever-ready
counsellor, Mr. M. D. Hill, who well knew her love of fun,
wrote to her, *'Delendus est Jebbus,* as we priests of Latinity
' would say,' and advised her to show fight.

MR. M. D. HILL TO MISS CARPENTER.

Ashton Lodge, May 20th, 1853.

MY DEAR MISS CARPENTER,

I send you the suggestions I promised, and the more I
think on the subject, the more it appears to me an imperative
duty not to let an opportunity slip which may never occur
again, of placing the merits or rather the demerits of Parkhurst in their true light. Neither of the Egyptian plagues
is more to be dreaded than a plague of Parkhursts. For my
own private enjoyment I should prefer frogs or lice.

Now this task being to be done by somebody, the question
arises 'by whom?' If you were a man, or if the Women's

Rights Convention[1] had carried its object, and you were all
relieved from the 'crushing slavery' of 'marriage or the
'needle,' it is clear you ought to write it yourself. But in the
present unhappy state of things so justly deplored at Seneca
Falls, I think you have a right to be relieved of such an
enterprise. Now your natural protector is your brother, and
although your family have declared against the use of certain
weapons, the pen, though the most formidable of them all, is
not among the number proscribed. Moreover you all know
how to wield it effectively. . . .

I have sat up till nearly midnight to perform my promise,
and now, until my lectures are over, pray don't ask for anything more, unless you are willing to deserve the character of
the most unreasonable *even* of your sex.

When you write give my affectionate regards to your dear
Mother, and beg her to beware of the severity of a Lancashire
summer, and wrap up accordingly, and above all to recollect
that I shall remain in a state of midday destitution as regards
a cup of good tea until her return,[2] my humble opinion being
that no one born in the present century can make tea as it
ought to be made.

And so farewell.

Ever yours most truly,
M. D. HILL.

P.S. (by the Amanuensis).—Many thanks for the Women's
Rights Report, which, notwithstanding I have been constrained
to write so sarcastically of above, I heartily rejoice in. Could
a more convincing proof of our 'enslaved condition' be afforded
than in my being made an instrument for ridiculing the
struggles of our sex for liberty by one of our 'tyrants?'

FLORENCE HILL.

The more pacific counsels of her family prevailed, and
Mary Carpenter bore her reproach in silence. But when
Captain Hall, the Governor of Parkhurst, forwarded her an

---

[1] Referring to the report of a Convention at Boston, which M. C.
had recently forwarded him with some other American papers.
Among the speakers was a Mrs. Jones from Seneca Falls, who observed that 'she did not *talk* about her rights, she *took them.*' This
saying was afterwards playfully adopted by Mary Carpenter.

[2] When his duties at the Bankruptcy Court permitted him,
Mr. Hill used to adjourn to Mrs. Carpenter's or to the Deanery for
his lunch.

invitation, in the spring of 1854, to spend a few days in the
institution, she resolved to avail herself of the opportunity of
examining it for herself.   The visit was deferred till August.
She went to the Isle of Wight, no longer as the obscure
governess, but as one whose judgment was weighty, for she
now represented an opinion that was rapidly gaining ground.
Some changes had been introduced in the management and
discipline since she first wrote, and the warders with fixed
bayonets had been withdrawn.   These alterations she noted
with satisfaction, and she was led to take a much more
favourable view than she had previously expressed.   ' I
' think that this place,' so she reported to Lady Byron, ' is
' as good as *any* government (not working with individual
' love of the child and knowledge of his nature) and any
' well-disposed officers can make it.   The arrangements are
' admirable, and Captain Hall a man with soul, but in
' chains.'   Before her departure from the island, therefore,
she communicated her impressions to Colonel Jebb.

TO COLONEL JEBB.

Isle of Wight, August 13th, 1854.

I did not reply to a letter I received from you respecting
my work, *Juvenile Delinquents*, because I did not feel that I
could withdraw any of the observations I had there made
respecting the system adopted at Parkhurst; I did, however,
desire to call your attention to the fact that I have nowhere
thrown the slightest blame on any of those who are employed
in the establishment, but, on the contrary, have spoken of the
executive department as being well carried out.

When I wrote I had not visited Parkhurst, conceiving
that a formal visit would not enable me to gain any further
light on the subject than could be obtained from the official
reports presented to the Government, which were before the
country.

Captain Hall having, however, this spring, sent me through
a mutual friend a most courteous invitation to visit the
establishment, offering me every means of freely judging for
myself, I gladly accepted so kind and candid an invitation.
Having spent more than two days at Parkhurst and seen every
part of the establishment in all its workings, I will not delay
to express to you, before leaving the island, my warm appreciation of the earnest and devoted manner in which not only
the excellent Governor, but the officials generally, appeared to
me to be discharging their difficult duties.

I am happy also to find that the introduction of a system of encouragement and rewards, as well as of fear, has proved highly beneficial, and that it is no longer found necessary to employ military sentinels, which was the case when I wrote. These changes I shall make a point of stating whenever opportunity occurs.

In the correspondence which was thus reopened, she maintained, however, many of her former criticisms. She pointed out the evils of massing together hundreds of vicious youths, and thus creating a public opinion more powerful for evil than the instruction of the teachers could produce for good ; she urged the want of proper stimulus for labour, and insisted that the boys were as prisoners in a state of bondage in which their free will was absolutely repressed, while the power of directing the will could only be brought into a healthy condition under the free exercise of it ; she laid stress on the want of any means of bringing the inmates into association with the virtuous portions of society ; and she urged that some provision should be made for the future welfare of boys who were discharged with good characters, by emigration under proper supervision. Friendly relations were thus restored with her opponent, and she pursued her way in peace.

Mary Carpenter could well afford to be magnanimous now, had she needed further inducement ; for there was no longer any danger of that plague of Parkhursts which Mr. Hill had deprecated. While she was under the hospitable roof of Captain Hall, the royal assent was given to a Bill which abolished that peril for ever. On the 10th of August the Youthful Offenders Act became law. This Bill was the fulfilment of the Government pledge of the previous session, when Mr. Adderley's measure was withdrawn. For a long time it had seemed probable that that promise would remain unredeemed ; but the friends of the cause would not let it drop, and by timely inquiries stimulated the flagging zeal of the Ministry. In June, accordingly, a Bill was brought in authorising the establishment of Reformatory Schools by voluntary Managers, which were to be placed under the sanction of the Home Secretary. This Bill gave effect to many suggestions of the two Conferences and the

Select Committee; and though it contained the obnoxious principle of retribution in the proviso that every child must pass fourteen days in prison before he could be transferred to a Reformatory, it was welcomed by all parties as the beginning of a new order of things. Mary Carpenter thus saw one of the objects for which she had been labouring legally recognised; and she joyfully hastened home to take the necessary steps for securing for Kingswood the long-sought stability which the Statute at last conferred.[1] For one at least of the classes of schools which she had described, aid was at hand; similar efforts might yet behold the rest of the programme realised. The following letters give quiet indication of her deep satisfaction.

TO MISS SANFORD.

Bristol, August 31st, 1854.

The school is now placed, with no effort apparent so to place it, in a position in which it commands the endorsement and support of the magistrates. Dear H. may be quite satisfied, or ought to be, with the degree in which I have ' woman's ' rights,' merely in the natural order of things, without asking for them; and would have been amused to see me quietly sitting writing an official letter to H.M. Secretary of State, requesting, on behalf of the Managers, inspection of Kingswood School under the new Act.

A fortnight or three weeks ago I went to the Isle of Wight to visit Parkhurst on invitation from Captain Hall. The visit was one of deep interest to me; you know I like to have people in sympathy, which Captain Hall and the officials now are. My week in the Island was rather painfully interesting, but affording matter for touching remembrance, as well as for deep thought. I made acquaintance with Captain Maconochie in the Island, and saw Lady Byron at Southampton, with whom I had some soul-communion.

TO SIR JOHN BOWRING, HONG KONG.

Bristol, August 31st, 1854.

I must confess to many self-reproaches for never having answered your most kind note, written within sight of Sinai,

---

[1] On the way to Bristol she stopped at Winchester to visit two Kingswood boys, who had ' got into trouble,' and were imprisoned there. One of them, as soon as he saw her, cried, ' Oh Miss Carpenter, ' I knew you would not desert us.'

and am now determined to steal an hour to thank you for your last, just received. That Red Sea letter has given very great pleasure to numerous hearers, both high and low ; indeed, it gave me a more vivid conception than I have ever had before of that most deeply interesting part of the world.

What you say of the present unnamed religious movement in China does not surprise me. It will be a very interesting and curious passage in the history of the human race, and I am glad that one is there who, like yourself, can watch this outbreak from slavery. It is marvellous that, at this period in the history of the human race, a nation has so long been kept in a state of civilised thraldom ; there will doubtless be fearful doings before the end comes. . . .

The public mind and press in England have been so occupied with war hitherto that but little attention has been paid to great reforms. The subject of war is to me so painful if I enter at all into details, and is so utterly opposed to the spirit of Christianity, that I abstain from having anything to do with it. You will, however, perceive that reform is steadily progressing. The Beer Bill, though not all that could be wished, is an important step, especially in connection with the public opinion that brought it about. But to me *the* great move was one that was made so quietly and unostentatiously that the public press scarcely noticed it, viz. the Juvenile Offenders Bill, which we owe mainly to Mr. Adderley. This just recognises all our great principles, it supports voluntary effort, and avails itself of it in the reformation of these young offenders ; it gives to us the power of detention we want, and it enforces parental authority.

This was now the supreme occupation. ' I have sometimes said I live in Kingswood,' wrote Mrs. Carpenter a few days after these letters, ' for I seem now to be cut off ' from the rest of the world, but sometimes the interest which ' these poor boys excite is too much for me. Mary is gone ' over there with a shirtless, shoeless, little vagabond, whom ' she picked up in the Bridewell.' Month after month of labour among them seemed only to intensify her affection, the deep religious ground of which she thus unfolded to Lady Byron.

TO LADY BYRON.

Bristol, September 21st, 1854.

The *oneness* of the human being is an essential principle. In many cases juvenile delinquency is a mere accident arising from particular circumstances ; when these are altered and the

child is so placed that his nature can freely develop, nothing
is wanting but wholesome and natural restraint and ordinary
instruction, and an ordinary teacher with a good system may
suffice.   But when the divine spirit within has been crushed
and stifled from infancy, so that the light of God's dealings is
as much obscured and shut out as was the outer world from
Laura Bridgman, then the action of a *strong* and *loving* spirit
can alone touch the inner springs of thought and action, and
this action must be aided by judicious working on the varied
faculties and powers.   I comprehend better than I did at the
time the wonderful working of my dear father with me, or
rather I perceive that what seemed the natural order of things
was the result of the most profound knowledge of human
nature, combined with a love so tender and true that its daily
action required no extraordinary manifestation to make itself
intensely felt.   Thus I desire to be with my children, and so
to let him still live.   There is sublime truth in the words,
'For their sakes do I sanctify myself.'   The sanctified life
manifesting itself in daily actions has a greater force than any
express or intentional efforts.   I have been struck with this
when hearing our old pupils mention the things which most
influenced them when with us, which were always circumstances
which I had quite forgotten.   Working with these poor
children is intensely interesting to me; their natures are laid
more bare than those who are encased in conventionalisms, and
I generally find that their very sins enable me to get nearer
hold of their spirits.   I fear that I have not half expressed
what I mean, which is too deep for words.   Poetry is, as you
truly say, the best and indeed the only medium for the soul's
working.   But I cannot now *write* poetry; the children are my
poetry.   When I do write, I try, having the whole conception
in my mind in perfect unity, to bring forth the needed parts of
it in such language as the public can comprehend.

The experience of two years at Kingswood had now convinced Mary Carpenter that the union of boys and girls in
one school was not a desirable plan.   She had for some time
been seeking for some means of bringing the girls more
directly under her own supervision, and had even proposed
to receive them in her mother's home.   Lady Byron warmly
entered into her anxiety, and was ready to support her in any
feasible scheme.   On her return to Bristol from Southampton, search was accordingly made for suitable premises;
and her attention was directed to a fine old Elizabethan
building in Park Row, known as the Red Lodge, which was
offered for sale in September.   Lady Byron was at hand

with the promised aid; the purchase was quickly effected,
the house was placed under Mary Carpenter's sole control, a
small sum was collected from friends for the necessary repairs
and furniture, and on the 10th of October the school was
formally opened. The first labours may be best told in the
words of her own retrospect twelve months later.

October 10th, 1854.—I entered the deserted house! Those
stairs I had often in former years trodden with mingled feelings of respect and pleasing anticipation, when going to visit
Dr. Prichard,[1] whose society I always esteemed a high privilege
and an intellectual treat. There I had been present at a grand
soirée of men of high position in the scientific world, assembled
at the meeting of the British Association in 1836. Remembrances crowded thick upon me. But a new era in my life
had for the last few years opened on me. Dr. Prichard had
been summoned from this world; and his house, with the
magnificent oak drawing-room in which he delighted, had been
for many months left desolate. I entered it with the prayer
that this house might be holy to the Lord. I had not the warm
hopes and vivid feelings which animated me when entering
Kingswood on September 11th, 1852. Two years of unwearied
labour, severe disappointment, harassing trials of various kinds,
had quenched the pleasurable excitement at the anticipated
development of principles in which I had perfect confidence;
yet they had not in any way cooled my ardent devotion to the
work, but had given me increased confidence in the principles,
and a degree of experience which could have been gained in
no other way. So I began with a firm faith and trust that He
who had levelled all impediments, and had given me strength
to surmount past obstacles, would still guide, guard, and direct
me; I was also encouraged by the feeling that I was not now,
as formerly, exploring unknown regions, but that I was beginning with the knowledge and experience with which I ended
at Kingswood. Mrs. Phillips, the matron, and Annie Woolham
[the first girl] entered the same day, as we found two rooms
which they could occupy; she was a woman of enterprise and
an energetic spirit calculated for emergencies like this. No
one who sees the house as it is after a year's cleaning and
habitation, can possibly imagine the state of dirt and dilapi-
dation in which it was. Cellars filled with rubbish of every
kind (a human foot was found in an outhouse—we got the
scavenger to take it away privately, lest it should engender
ghosts in the minds of the children), not a window able to be
opened, scarcely a door with a key,—the house-door was

---

[1] The well-known author of the *Physical History of Man*, etc.

believed not to have any key,—the kitchen so dark that it was feared we should have to burn gas at midday, the garden a wilderness, the walls everywhere deadened with dirt and smoke. I at once summoned tradesmen on whom I could rely, settled the work to be done, took their estimates, and stimulated them with the information that several young children in prison were waiting to be admitted there. Fortunately scarcely any alteration was needed, and carpenters, masons, painters, plasterers, etc., soon filled the premises, which in a month were brought into such a state that I could summon H.M. Inspector of Prisons to examine it, as also the School Inspector, though we had as yet only six or seven girls for him.

So the new undertaking was fairly started. The Committee of Kingswood had for some time declined to receive any more girls, and now resolved to transfer those still left under their charge to the school at Red Lodge. The arrangements were soon made, and the number of inmates grew to ten as Christmas drew near. The Red Lodge School was now under the sole management of Mary Carpenter; its operations were directed by her, its officials worked under her, and to the last day of her life she retained her undivided responsibility and control. This supremacy enabled her to carry out her plans without further restraint than was inevitable from the occasional variations among the staff of teachers; and she felt a freedom and scope in this fresh enterprise which renewed the elasticity of a spirit somewhat worn by the anxieties of the past two years. The difficulties which had at first arisen at Kingswood, could not present themselves again in a school where the elements were less conflicting, and where the forces of law could now be immediately invoked. So she set forth upon the task with an ardour chastened rather than eager; no other work was dropped or even relaxed; in the Sunday School, the Ragged School, and Kingswood, she was still punctually in her place at her appointed times; but the Red Lodge was henceforth to be the nearest to her heart. 'You may think of me,' she wrote, in December, to her brother Russell, 'as in a more 'hopeful condition than three months since; Red Lodge 'gives me little anxiety and surpasses expectations; the 'Ragged School going on without storms, and a happy place 'to me; Kingswood somewhat clearing after storms; the

'home peaceful and happy—so may yours ever be.' Christmas approached, and another festivity had to be added to the
cheerful gatherings into which she always threw herself with
so much zest; the preparations were all completed, but the
presence that animated them was suddenly withdrawn. The
energy so long concentrated gave way at last, and she lay
prostrate beneath a severe attack of rheumatic fever.

The disease took a stubborn hold of her powerful frame,
and held her tightly through many weeks of hope and fear.
Improvement and relapse followed each other again and again,
and friends and fellow-workers waited in painful suspense.
Her mother was deeply moved by the inquiries that poured
in from a large circle of sympathy, and not less so by the
effect upon those for whose welfare this fearful struggle
between life and death was the terrible price. 'The interest
'which the children at the different schools take is very
'touching. They seem quite afraid of doing anything wrong
'lest she should hear of it, and it should give her pain.'
Yet even as the poor sufferer lay in tortured helplessness,
the sick-room was no place of gloom :—' I like to look at her
'as she sleeps, there is such an expression of heavenly peace
'on her countenance, and her tones of voice are so sweet
'and gentle that they are quite heavenly music to her
'mother's heart.' It was April before she could take pen
in hand on her sofa, and trace a few trembling lines. The
first utterances were naturally of mingled thankfulness and
regret; but as strength returned the gladness deepened.

TO MISS SANFORD.

Bristol, April 15th, 1855.

Your letter makes me feel ungrateful that notwithstanding
such love, and the strong feeling which I learn has existed of
anxiety for my restoration, I can hardly suppress the frequent
desire that when so near the threshold I had been permitted
to cross it, and join the purified spirits of the blessed beloved
ones, whose life is now hid with Christ in God. Life has been
for me a fearful inward struggle, and it is only in the doing of
my work that I have any happiness I care to live for. All the
enjoyment of the beautiful which was once so entrancing to
me seems gone, and I look at my drawings as the production
of another self, though I confess with very peculiar partiality.

The element which they nurtured in me still exists with increased force, but the actual production of them seems the work of another era, and one separated from my present existence by a great gulf. But little was I conscious at the time of my danger how much you were suffering for me, and many others too. I was in a state of wonderful spiritual clearness and intense repose in the Heavenly Father's will, while in much bodily suffering.

> ' I breathed no prayer, I proffered no request,
>   Rapt into still communion that transcends
>   The imperfect offices of prayer and praise.'

TO THE REV. R. L. CARPENTER.

Bristol, April 22nd, 1855.

I feel much being such a burden to others as it seems I must be for some time. . . . I cannot tell you of the inward joy I have had when all around was suffering, nor how grateful I feel for the love and kindness of my friends. The devoted watching of our Anna has been beyond description. I trust that though not in the same way exactly, I shall still be carrying on the work for which only my life is preserved.

In May she was able to visit her schools for the first time, and was cheered to find the Red Lodge, which had been under the general management of her sister Anna, in as satisfactory a condition as could have been expected. But she was clearly unequal to resuming her former labours, and sought reinvigoration with her mother on the coast of their favourite Devonshire. There news reached her from Lady Byron that her condition of mind during her illness had been made the subject of unfavourable contrast to her own by Miss Harriet Martineau. A visit to Ambleside some time before, on occasion of the marriage of Miss Martineau's valued servant Martha to Mr. Andrews, the master of the Ragged School at St. James's Back, had renewed the friendly intercourse of earlier years, and the sympathy which she had received from Miss Martineau had given to Mary Carpenter especial pleasure. The bare suggestion that Miss Martineau should be led by any misinformation as to her own feelings into further antagonism to the faith which she cherished as part of her life, caused

her acute pain, and she resolved to communicate with her
critic without reserve.

TO LADY BYRON.

Torquay, June 3rd, 1855.

Your letter decided me to write to Miss Martineau, and
yet it made me feel it particularly difficult to do so.   With
respect to herself, I perfectly agree with the sentiment expressed in your lines.   Her character has been formed by
Christianity, of which her own earlier publications give ample
proof; she has been living a truly Christian life, and now I
believe it is with her, as Wordsworth so beautifully expresses
it in the sonnet beginning ' It is a beauteous evening calm
and free '—' God being with thee when thou know'st it not.' [1]
I believe her perfectly sincere, and doubt not that the good,
the true, and the beautiful in her character will live, when
her strange vagaries and inconsistencies—I can call them
nothing else—have been forgotten.   To such I must put down
her having misrepresented me to support her own opinions.
It troubled me a little just at first, but not now.   If I had
been in a state of feverish excitement, instead of the serenity
and trusting peace to which all who were near me can bear
witness, and for which I am truly grateful to the Heavenly
Father, it would have been attributable by any candid person
to the fever attendant on the disease and racking pain.   What
you told me has influenced me only so far as to lead me to
say a little more of myself than I otherwise should.

You are thus again tried, dear friend!   These departures
are not for ever!   I am reading Southey's life to occupy my
too much leisure.   It is beautiful to observe the growth of
religion in him, and its sustaining power when he lost the
child in whom his hopes were centred.   Farewell!   What
a blessing that we can live for, and even *in*, another and
unchangeable world!

TO MISS MARTINEAU.

Torquay, June 3rd, 1855.

Though I hope that words of affectionate sympathy have
reached you from me through some of the friends who have
been in correspondence with you, yet, since I have regained
the use of my pen, it has frequently been in my heart to

---

[1] It need hardly be said that the quotation has received a
different turn of thought.   The line runs,

' God being with thee when we know it not.'

exchange a few words more with one for whom I have felt so much esteem. You would not, I know, wish me to express sorrow to you that your work is well-nigh accomplished, that the Heavenly Father in His wisdom and love has appointed that your time of rest should probably soon come. We who remain cannot but sorrow, when one is withdrawn from us who is a fellow-worker in the Lord's vineyard; but for yourself, I know, you feel such calm satisfaction and happiness in the near prospect of your departure, and you shed so much happiness around you, that I can only express my sympathy in the peace you experience. I pray that He from whom every good and perfect gift proceeds, will still vouchsafe you the fruits of His Holy Spirit, 'joy and peace,' would that I might add 'in believing.' And may those around you still be supported in the discharge of those tender ministrations which to them, if not to you, must often be most affecting.

As kind expressions have reached me from you, I feel sure that you will be glad to hear that there is now a prospect of my being able ere long to resume a portion of the labours which are so dear to me. Before the close of last year I had felt that my strength would not be equal to sustain a continuance of the amount of anxiety and fatigue which the last two years had brought me. I knew not how to escape from it, but was confident that my Heavenly Father would order all aright, and proportion my strength to my work. When this illness attacked me, I knew that it would be very severe, but I saw at once that it would make my way clear. I felt at once relieved from all anxieties, certain that I might cast my burden on the Lord. This gave me an indescribable serenity and repose of mind, which were of the utmost importance to my recovery. I felt a wonderful nearness to the Father of my spirit, and, in the midst of racking pain and wearing disease, could feel

> 'Content, my Father, with Thy will,
> And quiet as a child.'

Though I could not but frequently feel that 'to depart and 'be with Christ' and the beloved departed, is 'far better,' yet as He has restored me again to the world, I trust that it may be to do His will. I know that my poor children want me, and that the work, as yet but in its infancy, requires the earnest efforts of all labourers.

While convalescent, I read your *Life in the Sick Chamber*, and warmly sympathised with many parts, though in others my experience differed from yours. Most truly do you say that pain is but transitory, that the good is lasting, and most truly did I accord with your then ' declared intense convic- 'tions respecting immortality and the Divine life.' That alone did I feel all-supporting, and I was thankful to be able to send my testimony to my school children, that now I *felt* the truth, the reality, of what I had taught them.

I did not intend, dear Miss Martineau, to have been speaking so much of myself; but you were so often in my thoughts during my severe illness, that I was insensibly drawn on.

Miss Martineau's reply somewhat surprised Mary Carpenter by its severe rebuke of her arrogance, and drew from her the following note :

TO MISS MARTINEAU.

Torquay, June 9th, 1855.

DEAR MISS MARTINEAU,

I am truly sorry that my letter failed to convey to you the feeling of my respectful and affectionate sympathy with which it was written, and to assure you that I had no intention of making any strictures on your thoughts and feelings with which I know I am quite unacquainted, still less of comparing them with my own. Of these I regret that I said anything. I am very sorry, dear Miss Martineau, that by writing to you in the circumstances in which both you and I are, I should have poured anything but balm into your spirit. Pray believe this, and that I remain,

Yours truly,
MARY CARPENTER.

The friendship survived this shock, and occasional correspondence on subjects of common work continued for many years.

Other communications from old friends this summer were of a more pleasurable kind, such as the following letter from Sir John Bowring, then on his way back to China from his mission to Siam.

SIR JOHN BOWRING TO MARY CARPENTER.

H.M.S. Rattler, China Seas, May 6th, 1855.

MY DEAR MARY,

I daresay you will have read not without interest how happy I have been in negotiating a Treaty of Peace and Commerce with the Siamese. The splendours of this semi-barbarian semi-civilised court exceed the tales of romance, and the recollections of my visit are rather like the impres-

sions left by the most gorgeous and dreamy scenery of the
Arabian Nights than the veritable history of mundane experience. Though the titles of the king would occupy a page,
among them none is deemed more glorious than that he is
'the Lord of the White Elephant'—this white elephant being
supposed to be the recipient of some divine incarnation, and
entitled to something like regal honours. The elephant has
quite a court of attendants; his ordinary food is the banana
and the sugar cane; his attendants keep him from the annoy-
ance of flies and mosquitoes by ornamented fans and switches.
He has magnificent apartments and a decorated bed for his
repose; he is caparisoned with cloths of gold and jewels; when
his tusks grow they are covered with gold rings, and when he
walks forth he is accompanied by a band of music and a host
of followers, and is the object of universal reverence. In the
apartment he occupies is one of the royal thrones where the
king sometimes sits in state to congratulate himself on one of
the undoubted titles and evidences of legitimate sovereignty.

I received from both Kings—there being two Kings in
Siam—brothers—daily marks of kindness; but perhaps no
honour was done me so great as that of presenting me a few
hairs from the tail of one of the Sacred White Elephants.
Two of these I have sent to the Queen, and I enclose one to
you as a memento of affectionate thoughts of the present and
grateful recollections of the past.

I feel no small amount of happiness in thinking that I have
been able by the instruments of peace and reason to negotiate
a Treaty whose conditions are quite as satisfactory as were
ever extorted at the point of the bayonet, midst the thunders
of artillery, or as the results of glorious and triumphant war.
I am now within less than a week's steaming from Hong
Kong, and after two months' absence on this fortunate mission,
hope to be welcomed with the smiles of my wife and children.
Alas! eyes that would have brightened at the news I have to
record are dull and glazed now, and feelings that might revel
in much that is joyous—too much perhaps—are checked by
melancholy and mournful thoughts about life's sad realities. I
beg very kind regards to all about you.

Believe me, my dear Mary,
Very affectionately yours,
JOHN BOWRING.

Nothing delighted Mary Carpenter more than remembrances
such as these. The merest trifles, as they might seem to
others, became sacred in her eyes; a stone from the shore
of the sea of Galilee, rushes from the banks of the Jordan,
acquired for her an extraordinary sanctity; and the little

gifts which found their way to Bristol across the Indian seas were doubly welcome when they came from the hand of an old and trusted friend. ' All the little Chinese ' curiosities you have sent from time to time,' she wrote to Sir John Bowring, ' are often shown to my children and ' admired by them. Your name is a household word among ' them, and they do not forget you when singing " God ' is love." [1]

As the summer passed by, the former labours were taken up one by one, and the injury done by enforced absence was slowly repaired. The routine of the Red Lodge had only just been established, when the presence which directed it was withdrawn; and the school had been worked without the aid of the experience which specially qualified its manager for the task of superintendence. But now she was at her post once more, and the following letter reveals the deep hold which the history and character of her scholars acquired over her sympathy and affections.

TO LADY BYRON.

Bristol, September 8th, 1855.

Thank you for kindly sending me *Within and Without*; shall I return it to you when we have read it? Having yesterday the excuse of a little extra fatigue, I actually devoured the book at one sitting, not of course reading it as it ought to be read, but taking it as a whole. I agree with you in thinking it a very striking poem. The author is evidently a man of great genius and high imaginings, and yet after reading the two exquisite pieces at the commencement, I felt much disappointed in the development of his great idea. I cannot imagine that the married life of Lilia can be a true one; Julian ought also to have discovered the great secret of union with the Eternal Father while on earth. The father and child, with the influence of each on the other, are exquisitely lovely. I believe, however, that I am not capable of fairly appreciating any poets except Shakespeare, Milton, and Wordsworth, who depict the true life of man, because having so constantly to do with the highest interests, with the human soul in its relation to the eternal, all efforts of the

---

[1] ' God is love, His mercy brightens
All the paths in which we rove.'

A well-known hymn by her correspondent.

intellect or imagination *merely*, however grand or beautiful, seem comparatively insignificant.

Yesterday, after studying Julian, I accompanied to his ship Michael Lynch, with his sister Margaret, an interesting girl of 16, now with me at Red Lodge. They had not seen each other for 5 years, and then Michael, at 13, was condemned to 10 years' transportation beyond the seas. Margaret had already been more than once in prison ; the two older sisters were still more deeply plunged in crime, and even the little Henry was not far behind. Michael's career was thus arrested ; theirs continued until after many imprisonments. Little Henry was sent to Kingswood, and is now with Mrs. Chisholm in Australia; the oldest sister was transported, and the second with Margaret was sentenced to 3 years, after five previous imprisonments in different towns. Anne is at Dalton, Margaret here; a drunken mother still lives in Liverpool. Margaret is very clever ; picking pockets is so much a part of her nature, or rather *was*, a year ago, that when she ran away from Kingswood on occasion of Mrs. Phillips leaving, she picked at least six pockets ! She had then been with us only a short time. *Now* the brother and sister are as earnest to stimulate each other to good as before they were to evil. 'We 'were lost—we are found !' And he was so fearful of himself ! He dared not spend one day in Liverpool, lest he should be lured into evil, so I have had him here. Their pure innocent love to each other will, I am persuaded, be a great stimulus to both, for he hopes to make a home for her and his other sisters in the United States, and he has begged her never to leave the Red Lodge till he can send for her. She had saved 12/-, and was delighted to devote it all to him. Margaret loves me as a mother, I am sure. And I have had happiness too in seeing the great change—'new birth' is not too strong a term—in Tommy Hart, the youngest. The poor boy *feels* he has been 'bought with a price,' a most unwearied labour of love. I have just sent him to Welsboro',[1] and he carries with him a treasured portrait of my dear father, having left for me a beautiful box of his own making. This is the poetry I now delight in, but it cannot be expressed in words.

In the autumn of this year Mr. Barwick Baker, of Hardwicke Court, Gloucestershire, perceiving that Reformatories were springing up all over England, and that it was of great importance to secure the recognition of certain common principles of action, invited the different Managers

---

[1] In Pennsylvania, U.S., where some distant cousins of her family had settled, with whom she liked to keep up friendly connection.

to spend four or five days at his house. Some twenty
persons, all engaged in the actual direction of Reformatory
Schools, accordingly assembled there at the end of October.
It was a memorable time both to host and guests, who were
enabled to confer upon plans and interchange experiences,
and formed by the mutual interests thus generated a compact
and united body, long afterwards known as 'the Reformatory
'Brotherhood.' Mr. Baker had been much interested in the
Kingswood work. Aided by Mr. Bengough, he had himself opened a Reformatory School before the Kingswood
experiment was begun; but he had looked with suspicion
on the attempt to combine boys and girls together, even
with due provision for their separation; and his fears were
justified by results. On one occasion he found a little troop
of delinquents—four boys and four girls, all pickpockets—
near his house, on their way to form a juvenile gang in
Liverpool, and he lost no time in taking them back to
Bristol. He knew well how great were the difficulties
which had to be overcome in dealing with the hardened
class of often convicted children who were at that time the
chief subjects of Reformatory discipline, and his help had
always been generously given to Mary Carpenter and her
fellow-workers. She was naturally, therefore, among the
little band who found so much refreshment of heart in the
midst of Mr. Baker's genial hospitality, and when she left
she placed in his hands a brief record of her past toils. Of
this he wrote to her soon after, in the following terms:

MR. BARWICK BAKER TO MARY CARPENTER.

Hardwicke Court, November 2nd, 1855.

All our friends, alas! are gone except George and Harriet
Bengough. I wonder whether I shall ever enjoy another week
as I have the last!

We read your paper last night and were greatly interested
in the history of the trials you have fought through with such
courage and constancy. The thought how one would oneself
have borne up under such difficulties had one met with them,
makes one feel rather small. Still, however valuable the
experience would be to those few men who really work the
schools and whose energies are up to facing the difficulties—
it was the general feeling of the party on a full consideration
that many might be driven to despair rather than to emulation

by the history; and if it were to get into the hands of any of
the opponents of the system, they might not improbably ask
us the awkward question : ' If the difficulties are such as these,
' where can we find Miss Carpenters to meet them ? '

The success of Kingswood now justified the Committee
in seeking for it a more public recognition than it had yet
attained. The necessary arrangements fell largely upon
Mary Carpenter, who applied herself to them with her usual
zeal. The result was reported in a letter to her son Philip
by Mrs. Carpenter.

MRS. CARPENTER TO THE REV. P. P. CARPENTER.

Bristol, November 16th, 1855.

This has been a most busy week with Mary and with the
Kingswood Committee, preparing for a public meeting, giving
a report of Kingswood with the wish to make it a public
institution under the patronage of the leading men of the
city and the county. A public meeting was held yesterday
at the Institution : the leading men in both counties were
present and many from considerable distances. Mr. Adderley
had friends with him and said that he could not come, but
understanding that his presence was particularly desirable,
he came down yesterday morning, made an excellent speech
and returned home to dinner. There is zeal ! ' Seven years
' ago,' said Mr. Osborn, the chaplain of the Bath Jail to me,
' I obtained permission to lecture at the Institution on the
' subject of Juvenile Reformation. *Seven* came to hear me,
' and almost all looked as though they would rather have been
' away; and now it is the subject which has laid hold of the
' public mind.'

It was easier to gain a hearing for Kingswood than for
Red Lodge, though in Bristol, at any rate, there was no
hostility towards the new school. Early in January, 1856,
a public examination took place at the Red Lodge, of which
a full account appeared in the newspapers. The reporters
excited the mock wrath of Mary Carpenter by serving up a
description of her own appearance : ' It really was too bad
' to enter into details as minute as if I were a murderer
' going to execution, or as H. says, a queen going to
' coronation.' She accordingly amused herself by writing an
ironical paragraph analysing her attire in silk and jewels,
winding up with a reference to what had long since become

a family joke : ' The foregoing particulars will disprove the
' statement of a ragged urchin to a reverend divine, that
' " Miss Carpenter gave away all her money for the naughty
' " boys, and only kept enough to make herself clean and
' " decent ! " ' [1]

The position of Red Lodge, however, was rather peculiar.
By taking on herself the sole management of the Red Lodge,
Mary Carpenter necessarily cut herself off from the co-operation of members of other churches, such as now gathered on
the Committee at Kingswood. Those who have followed
the story of her life thus far, will need no further assurance
of the intensity of her religious nature, or of her power of
quickening the spiritual life of others. But to those who
did not come into close contact with her, she appeared only
as the holder of an unorthodox creed, whose teaching was
distrusted and whose influence must be kept in check.   In
the previous year she had written that her best friends were
' chaplains and other evangelicals,' and had regretted that
the adherents of her own faith took so little part in the work.
She was now to receive an unexpected blow, which inflicted
a wound from which she was slow to recover.   Paragraphs
were circulated about the religion of the foundress and the
manager of the school ; and no evidence of the character
of the religious instruction given there, of the regular
attendance of the inmates at a place of worship, or of the
satisfaction of the Inspector, availed to counteract the
impression they produced. The Somersetshire Magistrates
at the Quarter Session at Wells refused to take cognizance
of the school.

TO MISS SANFORD.

Bristol, March 20th, 1856.

A sign of the times has occurred here. Mr. Miles and
others wishing to make Red Lodge the Girls' Reformatory for
the West, the Diocesan Board took alarm, met in full conclave,
and laid their veto on the Magistrates. W. B. came up to ask

---

[1] One bitterly cold day Mr. Hill met Mrs. Carpenter in College
Green, and when he reproached her with being out in such weather,
she said she was obliged to ' come out to buy clothes for Mary, for
' she never would buy anything for herself, and had really nothing to
' put on.'

me whether I wished him to do anything. I gave him full
information, and armed him with a report of H.M. Inspector,
bearing testimony to the religious and other teaching. He had
the courage, in a full assembly of County Magistrates, to bear
a full testimony, which was listened to attentively, and some
acknowledged afterwards that they quite accorded with him;
but no one dared to say a word, or even to agree that Red Lodge
should be used till they had established a school on their own
favourite principle of 'Gaols and Workhouses.' E. was one of
them, and he could speak in the most flattering way to me in
private, or of me in the public meeting, when it was the fashion
to do so. This is no more than, unhappily, is to be expected.
The true unasked sympathy which I am constantly receiving
from clergymen and people of all denominations, might be in
danger of being too much for me, without drawbacks!

What the real tone of religious feeling was which Mary
Carpenter sought to foster in the school, may be inferred
from the following extract from the journal of the Red
Lodge, during the month preceding the occurrence just
mentioned:

February, 1856.—I have continued to give my lessons as
usual, and have increasing satisfaction in them, perceiving
that they really take root in the girls, who show great capa-
bility of intellectual culture. The Scripture lessons especially
give me most pleasure. At the interval of a week they can
answer accurately every fact of the previous lesson with
evident understanding and recollection of my explanations.
The blank looks of the new girls fully prove to me how much
work has been already done in preparing the soil to receive
the good seed. My regular lesson times are these:
Sunday afternoon, from 2.30 to 4, generally longer. Review
of hymns, with remarks, which have been learnt during the
week. Gospel of Luke, with explanations and comments,
after examination on the last Sunday's lesson. If there is
time, I permit each girl who can read to choose a text for
herself, which much pleases them, and fixes the attention
on particular passages. When there is time, I show them
Scripture pictures.
Monday evening, from 6 o'clock to bedtime, when I visit
them when in bed, which gives an opportunity for private
communication with individuals. Hitherto I have read a
story to the younger ones while the older ones were writing,
and then heard the older ones read. I mean to vary this.
Afterwards I read the Old Testament to them, being now
engaged on the history of Abraham, which rises in grand

antique beauty before me every time I realise it to present to these children. Indeed, the study of these ancient records gives me something of the same feeling that seeing the disinterred Assyrian remains would do. When the girls are in bed I visit each, and find an interchange of affection and occasional private word very useful in strengthening the bond which I wish to exist between my children and me.

The Sunday morning and evening were still, as before, devoted to the Ragged School, and in order to make room for the lesson at the Lodge, something had to be dropped out of the crowded duties of the day. So the Superintendentship of the afternoon Sunday School, which had been steadily maintained for five-and-twenty years, was now laid down, that the vacant hours might be given to those who needed her strength and power more. The teachers who had worked with her, presented her with a statuette of Christ, which was placed among the special treasures of her room in the Red Lodge. As with every other gift, this was immediately brought to bear on her scholars, for the journal continues :

The general conduct of the girls has been improving; petty pilfering of bread, &c., has diminished. C. and K. have at times violent outbursts of the evil spirit, but on the whole show decided improvement in self-control and desire to do right. C. is very sensible of kindness. One evening I took up a play scrap-book I had made for them, and she exclaimed : 'There isn't anything you would not do for us if you could!' B. is often very troublesome, but has, I am sure, great strivings of conscience. One Sunday afternoon she exclaimed : 'Oh, Miss Carpenter, how I *should* like to see our Saviour!' And when I afterwards placed her before my beautiful statuette of Christ blessing little children, she stood without speaking, and the colour rose to her face!

Under influences such as these, the girls rapidly changed in looks, expression, and demeanour, so that even the officers who had known them in their old unregenerate state, could recognise them no more. There were still many difficulties to overcome, many hidden recesses of perversity to explore ; but by degrees she learned to read their most secret natures with ease, and was rarely deceived in the judgments she formed. Another entry in the journal a few weeks later

than that last quoted, reports : 'Evenings as usual; satis-
'factory school.   Some trouble in reconciling feuds rankling
'in the minds of some of the younger ones, but succeeded at
'last.   When harbouring bad feelings they never venture to
'kiss me.   There is a wonderful truth of nature about these
'children, though sadly lying often.'   As her birthday, or
again the Christmas festival, came round, she made them
little presents, which they gradually took pleasure in
reciprocating; and the home-feeling which she so earnestly
sought to cherish, steadily grew.   A Sunday in May was
made memorable by a visit from M. Demetz, the revered
founder of Mettrai, and the acknowledged leader in Reformatory work, who was then the guest of Mr. Commissioner
Hill.   He addressed a few words to the girls ; and the
sympathy with which he expressed to Mary Carpenter his
satisfaction with their appearance, which indicated that they
were at ease with society, gave her fresh strength and
encouragement.

In truth, she needed now every outward support and
stay, for another great sorrow was hanging over her.   Winter
after winter the mother's failing powers had been exhausted
by successive illnesses; and under the long strain of watching
in 1855 they had been well-nigh spent.   For a little while
she still clung to the remains of being that were left to her,
facing every pain with the resolution which had sustained
her through the heavy burdens of earlier years ; but now
the enfeebled frame could bear no more, and as the spring
of 1856 passed into summer, the life that had been so
tenderly cherished by the daughters who remained in the
home, slowly ebbed away.   The death of her surviving
parent, on the 19th of June, brought to Mary Carpenter a
renewal of sorrows, which time had soothed though it had
not lessened them.[1]   Her mother had not only been the

---

[1] From among the letters of affectionate sympathy on the death
of Mrs. Carpenter, the following lines from the Rev. John Kenrick, of
York, may find a place here :
'There can be few who have had more uniform experience of
'her kindness, or better opportunity of knowing how admirably she
'fulfilled all the duties of life.   The recollection of her, too, is
'inseparably united in my mind with that of your excellent father,
'to whom she was such an effective helper in those plans to which his

most closely united to her in the daily life, but she had
shared with her daughter the loving thoughts of that other
parent, who had, ever since his departure, been a 'living
'presence' in the soul of his firstborn, the very centre of
her existence. So the bereavement brought with it a sense
of loneliness at times overpowering. When the first season
of family union was over, and the accustomed ways were
partially renewed, this feeling deepened. 'Now that I
'contrast more the daily life with what it used to be'—she
wrote in July to her brother Russell, 'with my beloved
'mother in the drawing-room, always ready to welcome and
'to sympathise, to be cared for and to care, and feeling that
'I could conduce to her happiness, and was sure of her
'loving kiss and blessing, I have of course felt more painfully
'the desolation and irreparable loss. It is natural and right
'that I should mourn and feel this rending of all my home
'sympathies, but I am sure that the Heavenly Father has
'ordered it wisely and lovingly. I must try to sanctify it
'to the use He intends, and I do feel the love of dear A. and
'you, dear brothers and sisters, most comforting.' By-and-
by the cry goes up out of the depths—yet only to be checked
at once in trust : 'This morning in my deep distress I prayed
'that I soon might be removed ; but I perceived that I
'ought not to have done so. I must have no wish but my
'Heavenly Father's will, and He knows the fit time.' At
first she thought to find relief in an alteration of the
arrangements of the house, by which the wing was given
up, and at the earnest request of her sister Anna and her
husband (Mr. Herbert Thomas), she moved in to her mother's
rooms in the old house. Her brothers and sisters united
in affectionate plans for her comfort ; but the changes they
wrought could not efface the old memories. 'People don't
'like me to tire myself,' she said a little later ; 'but it is
'better to come home ready to drop, and to go to bed and

'life and powers were so earnestly devoted. I reckon the knowledge
'of your father and mother to have been among the beneficial
'influences of my life, and many others, I am sure, have the same
'tribute of gratitude to pay to their memory. Their devotion to
'duty, their entire forgetfulness of self, where any call of duty was
'to be fulfilled, and their warm and affectionate sympathy in the
'joys and sorrows of their friends, were such as we meet with few
'examples of in our progress through life.'

'sleep at once, than 'to have time to feel the dreadful loneli-
'ness of this large house, once so peopled, and all the loved
'ones gone. My room is painfully pretty and nice when
'the last scenes blend with it,[1] as they will constantly do.
'And all my old haunts and places are altered and gone; I
'seem plunged alone into a new life.' The year ran out,
and she felt herself suddenly grown old; that elasticity,
which neither illness, nor labour, nor anxiety, had been able
to depress, collapsed beneath the heaviness of her grief. 'This
'is the great change in my life,' she mourned at Christmas,
to one of her mother's oldest friends; 'before, I was con-
'nected by insensible gradations with childhood; now, I
'seem transported suddenly past middle life to its decline.'
She was weary, and she desired to lie down to rest; the
future had nothing more for her of fear or hope.

A visit to Lady Byron, in January 1857, gave for a
little while the needed change to thought and feeling; and
talk of books and the general movements of philanthropy
brought some freshness of interest, but the jaded mind could
not recover its tone, and with the return to Bristol came a
renewal of sadness, which might be hidden for a time, but
was nevertheless an abiding burden. It resisted the healing
influences of the affection which she gathered up among her
children, and treasured so eagerly. She felt a settled weight
upon her spirits, and longed for the home duties and
interests which had sometimes chafed her by the importunity
of their claims, but had nevertheless formed the ground of
her happiness. The lives of others, she saw, found their
completeness in these tender ties; could she not, also, have
a home of her own? Here is a note of sympathy with
another's struggles.

TO MISS SANFORD.

Bristol, May 28th, 1857.

C. Brontë's *Life* I have finished;—a most instructive
record, a true picture revealing many secrets. Though I
almost regretted to have past scenes of sorrow vividly recalled
by the details of her affecting bereavements, yet, now I know
that she is no longer suffering, I felt it rather soothing to see
her bearing up so bravely while enduring agonies which I

---

[1] It had been her mother's room.

could well comprehend. Her life is a warning. Her novels
now form part of her biography. It was very touching for her
to go as soon as she desired to stay. But I am glad there was
that sunshine at the end.

On her birthday the craving found vent in an almost
heart-broken petition : ' In the most entire submission to
' Thy will, I pray, with trembling indeed, but still I do
' pray, that Thou wilt give me the means of having a
' home of my own, where I may shed around holy loving
' sympathies, and order, beauty, and happiness, after which
' I yearn.' The prayer was not answered; at least, not as
she had sought. But even though hope was delayed, there
came a time of calm. Two months afterwards she uttered
her confession and her trust : ' Heavenly Father ! I have
' been desiring what Thou has not appointed for me ; I have
' felt mournful, as if I could not be happy as I am. This
' morning, O Father, I am inexpressibly thankful that I can
' *feel* that I leave all to Thee with my *heart* and *soul*, and
' that I can rejoice in what Thou givest me, and in the exquisite
' loveliness of this opening spring telling of Thy perfect
' beauty.'
But the desire had taken too strong possession to be
altogether suppressed, even by the severest self-discipline ;
and in the autumn the struggle broke out again. She
seemed to herself cramped and bowed among the memories
of the past ; power was slipping away from her ; energy
was failing ; the continuance of her work, nay, of life
itself, she felt, depended on some change. The foresight of
her mother had anticipated this, and she had counselled her
to form a little home of her own ; and there she longed to
gather a band of workers for the lost ones, who might carry
on her labours when she followed those whom she loved
into the silent land. But the plan on which she had set her
heart, which would have given her her independence, and
yet keep her close to the side of the sister who cherished
her, was frustrated ; in the bitterness of disappointment she
lay prostrate and crushed, but still she found strength
to say—' The Saviour prayed, " Father, if it be possible,
' " remove this cup from me ; " I *can* say, as he did,
' " yet not my will, but Thine be done." I leave all to
' Thee, O Father ! Thou wilt support me where Thou leadest

'me.   Do Thou make known to me Thy will, and *I will
do it.*'

Relief, however, was at hand.   Towards the close of
the year, a house in Park Row, separated only by a narrow
street from the Red Lodge, and commanding an excellent
view of its playground, became vacant.   Why should not
Mary Carpenter take up her abode there ?   The plan
had obviously many advantages, though it involved the
separation from the beloved sister and husband who had
received her into their home.   The house was purchased by
Lady Byron, who had already made other additions to the
Red Lodge property ; and ere the new year set in, the new
arrangements were in train.   The solution of the problem
brought the troubled spirit peace.

December 20*th*, 1857.—It seems as if the Heavenly Father
has now made all clear to me, my duty and devotion to my
work harmonising with what my own nature appears to need.
My *wishes* are not complied with, but what I believe to be a
better way both for the cause and at the present moment for
myself, feeling as I do old memories forming too large a part
of my inner life, is opened before me.   It will be a severe trial
to leave my present home and my loving relatives.   But I
believe that I shall go forth with clear courage and faith, now
seeing that all is arranged.

The conflict of which it has seemed fitting thus to trace
the secret history, because it formed a new departure for
Mary Carpenter's after-life, was not allowed to interfere in
any way with her ordinary labours.   She had quitted the
death-chamber of her mother to bid farewell to one of her
own girls in the last stage of disease.   'The poor girl wiped
'away my tears,' she said, '.and soothed me after her
'fashion.'   Ere long she was busy preparing a paper on 'The
'Reformatory Institutions in and near Bristol,' which was
read at the first provincial meeting of the National Reformatory Union[1] held in Bristol in August, 1856.   A
second paper, 'On the Relation of Reformatory Schools to
'the State, and the General Principles of their Management,
'especially in reference to Female Reformatories,' she read

---

[1] This Association was projected at the gathering convened by
Mr. Barwick Baker at Hardwicke Court, 1855.

herself before the same assembly.[1] Both papers were received
with warm applause. In November she gained a prize for
an Essay offered by the Reformatory and Refuge Union, a
body which represented a somewhat different position from
that which engaged her chief sympathies. The prize went
into her charity purse ; but her success gratified her. 'I am
'pleased,' she wrote to Lady Byron, 'to have my views go
'forth with the endorsement of that party.' A new edition
of her *Meditations* went through the press in the winter.
The following April, 1857, she communicated a paper to the
New York Reformatory Convention, and she sent another to
an Educational Conference held in London in May, under
the presidency of the Prince Consort.

During the spring the purchase of a cottage adjoining
the Red Lodge, by Lady Byron, led to a development of
the plans of the Institution, which proved of the highest
value to the inmates. It was fitted up as a Home for eight
or nine girls under a Matron, and there the older girls who
were qualified by their behaviour in the school, received a
special preparation for domestic service. Slight additional
privileges were allowed them ; they did not mingle with
those whom they had left behind, except on special
occasions and at the Sunday afternoon religious instruction ;
they were sent on errands, and occasionally left alone in the
house, and thus by degrees learned to deserve that confidence
should be reposed in them. The success of this experiment
was watched with great interest and satisfaction by Mary
Carpenter, who superintended its minutest details.

The autumn of this year witnessed the foundation of
the Social Science Association, which held its first meeting
at Birmingham, under the presidency of Lord Brougham.
To no one were the annual Congresses more helpful than
to Mary Carpenter, and few persons contributed a larger
number of valuable papers or more useful information to its
deliberations during the first twenty years of its existence. It
was there that she met her fellow-workers, stimulated friends,
and by degrees convinced opponents. With the determination
to leave no channel of influence unemployed, she secured
the support of its Sections to resolutions in favour of her

---

[1] These papers were published in the Report of the Meeting, and
in *The Law Amendment Journal.*

principles, and inspired its Council to send deputations and present memorials to Government. The long training she had had in reading and teaching in classes where it was essential to retain strong grasp of interest and attention, now enabled her to give forth her papers with clear and easy enunciation; and in the discussions which followed she was always able to bring all her knowledge to bear on some disputed point with unembarrassed distinctness and decision both of thought and utterance. Her contributions on this first occasion dealt with the two subjects at that time prominently engaging her attention, the ' Relation of ' Ragged Schools to the Educational Movement,' and ' Reformatories for Convicted Girls.'

No one who there beheld her calm self-possession or admired her mastery of technical detail, could have surmised through what struggles she was even then passing. But the fresh opportunities which seemed to rise before her mind, as the plan of the new home at Red Lodge House was developed, brought back the hopes of vanished years. The period since her mother's death had led her through greater anguish than any other since her early womanhood ; but it was now past, and as Christmas approached she could enter with something of the old animation into the festivities which she always provided for others, and from which, this time, she herself too derived some gladness.

TO LADY BYRON.

Bristol, December 24th, 1857.

Kingswood is in a very satisfactory and *progressive* state, and I never go over there without a feeling of deep gratitude and happiness. This I feel, too, in being enabled by the sympathising help of friends to provide a good Christmas dinner to about 200 poor children at our Ragged School, beautifully adorned with evergreens by the master.   This year, too, they have their playground delightfully enlarged by the site of four houses which I have removed for the purpose, greatly improving the premises. Kingswood and Red Lodge will also be enjoying their *home* treat ; this evening all the birthdays of the school will be celebrated by the Magic Lantern and a little present for each from me. The thought of young happiness sheds a brightness on a solitary home : I am sure of your sympathy in this, and you will like to know that this season my dear Parents' wedding day, which last

year brought *too* much thought of the past, is this year
brightened by hope,—in which you will always be associated.
May to-morrow bring you an inward joy !

The new year dawned upon her at Kingswood.   As she
retraced the history of her early efforts there, she was filled
with unspeakable thankfulness.   She had sown amidst
storms, and, as it seemed, in sterile land ; but the fruits
were more than she could have dared to hope.   And so, in
the following February, 1858, she left the home of forty
years in Great George Street, and planted herself with fresh
courage in the independence of Red Lodge House.   ' One
' word,' she wrote two days after the removal, ' to say that
' I am comfortably established as " house-mother," and amid
' present external confusion feel beginning a new and happier
' and freer life.'

'So long Thy power hath kept me, sure it still
            Will lead me on
Midst storm and darkness, toil and sorrow, till
            The night is gone,
And with the morn those angel faces smile,
Which I have loved long since, and lost awhile.'

J. H. Newman.

CHAPTER VII.

FROM RAGGED SCHOOLS TO CONVICTS.

1856—1866.

THE Reformatory movement, in which we have now traced Mary Carpenter's share, can hardly be regarded as a detached and isolated phenomenon. On the one hand, in so far as it dealt with children, and the classes from which juvenile delinquents were derived, it was connected with the education of the neglected and destitute; on the other, in so far as it dealt with those who might possibly themselves become criminals, it could not be widely separated from the general principles of the treatment of adult offenders. The first of these subjects had long engaged Mary Carpenter's profoundest study; to the second, her thought and her sympathy were to be afterwards more closely directed.

It will be remembered that the resolutions of the Birmingham Conference of 1851 had sketched out three classes of schools—free day schools, industrial feeding schools, and reformatory schools. For the support of the first of these classes it was proposed that the existing system of Government grants should be extended. This proposal was embodied by Mary Carpenter early in the following year in a memorial, which was adopted by the Conference Committee for presentation to the Committee of the Privy Council. The Memorial set forth the reasons which debarred Ragged Schools from receiving any fair proportion of the Parliamentary grant, and requested that special arrangements might be made for dealing with them. At the same time, Mary

Carpenter herself addressed a letter on the subject to Lord
John Russell, which was forwarded to him in the spring ;
and a subsequent minute recognised the claim, by grants in
aid of industrial training.

The educational condition of the children of the labouring
classes continued from this time to excite great interest, and
plan after plan was laid before Parliament.   First came
Lord John Russell's measure, introduced into the House of
Commons in 1853.   It was of very comprehensive extent,
and contained clauses empowering town councils to impose
rates to be applied in aid of voluntary effort, by committees
appointed for the purpose.   In 1854 a Bill known as the
Manchester and Salford Bill, prepared by a committee of
gentlemen of different denominations, was brought in, but
without success ; while resolutions on the subject were
moved in the House of Lords by Lord Brougham.   The next
Session witnessed the introduction of a measure by Sir John
Pakington.   In a speech of deep earnestness and extensive
knowledge of the subject, he proposed to create education
boards in every town and in every country union, which
should have power to levy a rate for defraying the expense
of maintaining the education of the people in their several
districts ; but this vigorous measure had to be withdrawn.
Lord John Russell next took up the cause again, and early
in 1856 gave notice of a series of resolutions for the revision
and extension of the existing system of education.   His
scheme contemplated likewise the creation of school districts,
with committees of management erected by the ratepayers,
and the imposition of a local rate for the erection and
maintenance of the schools by the Quarter Sessions of the
Peace.   The speech in which those proposals were set forth,
did not appear to recognise the special difficulties of dealing
with the children of careless, vagrant, and criminal parents.
Their noble author expressed great confidence in the general
desire of parents that their children, from ten to fourteen
years of age, when not in employment, should receive
instruction.   He was of opinion that Parliament ought to
aim at nothing less than the complete education of the
people.   He had heard much of the ' dangerous classes,' but
no class could be more dangerous than one, which, acquiring
a little learning, should become discontented with the religion
and the political institutions of the country.   The speech

revealed to Mary Carpenter a want of acquaintance with the
special needs of the class for whom she was labouring, and
she criticised it rather severely in a letter to Sir Stafford
Northcote.

TO SIR STAFFORD NORTHCOTE, M.P.

Bristol, March 10th, 1856.

It is very remarkable that a gentleman who has so long
guided public affairs as Lord J. Russell, should be so profoundly ignorant on this matter. I believe that in the very
divided state of public opinion it will be almost impossible to
introduce any really comprehensive public educational measure. An extension and adaptation of the present system of
the Committee of Council on Education to existing wants
would, I believe, be more generally useful than anything else.
The establishment of *good* evening schools for working boys
and girls would be a great blessing. I have known such learn
more at such opportunities which they have seized for themselves, than is gained in years of forced training. The great
point to be proved is that if society has a right to punish and
check crime and to send children to reformatories, it has an
equal right to check that which necessarily leads to juvenile
crime by a strict education. There should be no limit of age
downwards;—I have known a child of 3 years old rule a house
and refuse to go to school! Surely the liberty of the subject
need not be respected in him.

Sir Stafford Northcote was already pondering on further
legislation in the direction first indicated by the Conference ;
and a few days after her last letter Mary Carpenter wrote
again, expressing her satisfaction at hearing that the Committee
of Council were favourable to helping Ragged Schools, and
hoping that he might be successful in establishing the principle
of compulsory action on the vagabond class. Without delay
she drew up a series of suggestions as to the manner in
which aid could be given to Ragged Schools,[1] some of which

---

[1] These suggestions, dated April 7th, were sent, among her other
correspondents, to Mr. Adderley, then M.P. for North Staffordshire.
Writing in April, 1879, Lord Norton says—' Her earnestness, devotion,
' and practical good sense made her a leader amongst those who were
' interested and engaged in redeeming the debt of society to the most
' neglected children. I went to her for instruction rather than for
' interchange of thought, and even if this little sketch of her ideas

were afterwards realised in the minute issued in June.
When the debate on Lord John Russell's resolutions took
place on April 10th, which ended in their rejection, she
addressed Sir S. Northcote again without disappointment,
inasmuch as experience showed on the whole that, in the
large towns at any rate, the public were able and willing to
provide schools for those children of the labouring classes
who were able and willing to attend. But for those who
were neither able nor willing, Government aid was needed ;
such schools could not be supplied or maintained effectually
by private effort ; and this help might be most beneficially
rendered by some such extension of the action of the Committee of Council as she had suggested. Her hopes were
fulfilled ; a minute was sanctioned in June by which half
the teacher's salary and half the rent of the premises (for
which she had herself asked) were granted to the managers ;
the educational tests imposed on the staff were lessened, and
those on the children were abolished (points on which she
had laid great stress),[1] and other more favourable conditions
were laid down by which a large capitation sum was given
for every child fed at the school.[2] The victory seemed won
only too easily.

The establishment of Industrial Schools followed rapidly.
At the Bristol meeting of the National Reformatory Union
in August, 1856, Mr. Alfred Hill read a paper on the
Industrial Schools of Scotland and the working of Dunlop's
Act in that country, and urged the introduction of a similar
law in England. The Law Amendment Society and the
Birmingham Education Association were preparing to take
action ; and at the request of Sir Stafford Northcote, the
Committee of the Law Amendment Society undertook to
prepare a Bill, which Sir Stafford Northcote brought into the

' on the work in its early days should be all I can find of her writing,
' I shall be pleased to have this little connection of my name with any
' memorial of one so high-minded and beneficent.'

[1] Mr. Lingen, in a letter of the 23rd of June, announcing these
changes, said 'the minute of June 2nd meets in great measure the
' spirit of the suggestions which you have brought under the notice
' of Sir George Grey.'

[2] This grant for feeding by the Education Department was regarded
by Mary Carpenter as an error in principle : it afterwards led to great
abuses, and proved fatal to the whole scheme.

House of Commons in February, 1857. At the same time a Bill was laid before Parliament by Sir George Grey for promoting the establishment of Reformatory Schools, by authorising counties and boroughs to institute and maintain them out of the local rates. The first of these Bills was hailed by Mary Carpenter with deep gladness, as the next instalment of her original design. The second excited her alarm, as it appeared to dispense with what she regarded as a fundamental principle in all Reformatory work, viz. the spontaneous initiative of earnest hearts working in pure love for the children whom they sought to reclaim. Sir George Grey's proposals would create a number of institutions in which official discipline would take the place of that sense of family union which she strove so zealously to infuse into her own establishment at Red Lodge. These criticisms, with some wise remarks about detail which the sequel amply justified, she expressed in a letter to Sir Stafford Northcote.

TO SIR STAFFORD NORTHCOTE, M.P.

Bristol, February 25th, 1857.

I thank you for your Bill, which I think perfectly satisfactory, and an excellent complement to our Reformatory Act. . . . With respect to Sir George Grey's Bill, it is founded entirely on the *prison* idea, the notion urged many years ago by some prison inspectors who had kind and good intentions, but had no conception of the Reformatory principle. My only comfort in the prospect of the Bill passing is that it is a most Quixotic and utterly visionary idea to suppose that magistrates, who have hitherto been our great hindrances in the movement, should suddenly be inspired with Reformatory zeal, incur the odium of a county rate, and take the trouble of managing a race most unmanageable by mere mechanical or magisterial action. And as to their supporting voluntary institutions by a borough or county rate, Kingswood and Red Lodge would have been starved in infancy before any help would have been given in that quarter.

The dissolution of Parliament stopped the progress of these Bills, and when the new Parliament assembled, Sir Stafford Northcote, unfortunately for the cause of social reform, was not returned. The Industrial Schools Bill was entrusted to Mr. Adderley, who carried it through the House of Commons, though the shape in which it was finally

passed differed, and in the opinion of many critics—Mary
Carpenter among the number—by no means for the better,
from its original form.   In particular, the class of children
for whom the schools were intended was inadequately
defined, so that magistrates were at first unwilling to
commit; and further, a special difficulty was imposed on
the managers, by throwing on them the duty of collecting
from the parents of the inmates the weekly payments for
which those parents were held responsible.   The gravity of
these obstacles was shown by the length of time which
elapsed before any steps were taken for carrying out the
provisions of the Act by the establishment of the Industrial
Schools which it was designed to promote.

In the meantime the Ragged Schools were again
imperilled.   The favourable terms offered to them induced
numbers of Schools and Refuges of various kinds to declare
themselves ' Ragged or Reformatory Schools ' in the sense
of the minute, and to claim their share in the grant.   The
rapid increase in the educational expenditure excited alarm;
and within a year it was thought necessary to limit the
range of aid to schools which could show a certificate from
two Justices of the Peace for the district, to the effect that
the young persons received there ' had either been legally
' convicted of crime, or had been accustomed to begging and
' vagrancy.'   For the first of these classes, argued Mary
Carpenter, Reformatories were the proper place ; the second
ought to be received in Union Industrial Schools ; and the
proper Ragged Schools were thus excluded from help.   The
school in St. James's Back lost £100 out of its scanty
income, without any warning.   No time was to be lost.   A
protest was at once addressed by Mary Carpenter to Mr.
Lingen, and this was followed by a letter to Earl Granville,
then President of the Council.   When the Education Conference met in London under the presidency of the Prince
Consort towards the close of June, she concluded her paper
on ' Juvenile Delinquency in its Relation to Ignorance ' with
an earnest appeal for aid for Ragged Schools.   She chose
the same theme for one of her papers at the first Congress
of the Social Science Association at Birmingham in the
following October.   Moreover, she was already at work
behind the scenes.   Communications were opened with the
managers of other schools of the same order, and a memorial

was prepared for presentation to Earl Granville. He did
not give its author much hope of success. 'I am much
' obliged to you,' he wrote in September, ' for your copy of
' the memorial. If all Ragged Schools, both for the present
' and for the future, were to have you and Mr. Hill as
' managers, there would be no difficulty. As this cannot be,
' I am afraid the suggestions in the memorial do not help
' us much in our doubts.' But Mary Carpenter was not to
be daunted. A deputation, of which Sir John Pakington
and Lord Shaftesbury were members, presented the memorial in
December, and urged that ' as there was a large class of children
' not criminal, who were in constant danger of becoming
' criminal, and from various causes were unfit and unable to
' take advantage of the ordinary day-schools, there was no
' reason why they should not share in the advantages offered
' by Parliament in support of education.' These labours were
not wholly in vain. On December 31st a fresh minute was
issued ; the magistrates' certificate was no longer required,
and Ragged Schools were recognised, provided it could be
proved that they were needed in the neighbourhood where
they were placed, and would not injure any adjacent day-
school. But the conditions under which aid was henceforth
to be afforded, were to be far more stringent than heretofore ;
the schools which required help the most would receive it
the least ; and the year 1858 opened to Mary Carpenter with
the weary sense that the battle had to be fought all over
again, and that the goal was farther off now than it had ever
been.

It was well for her that the excitement and interest of
settling into her new home at Red Lodge House gave partial
diversion to her thoughts. She felt a greater freshness of
interest, a larger independence, than she had ever before
possessed. It was characteristic of the peculiar activity of
her nature that she was not afraid to add claim to claim, and
never shrank from fresh responsibility, provided it was self-
imposed ; while restraints far less irksome and burdens much
less onerous, if devolved on her without her spontaneous
adoption of them, proved almost more than she could bear.
The new home, however, with all its freedom, had not the
dear companionship of past years ; and she could not exist
without some one close at hand with whom to interchange

sympathy and reciprocate affection. She thought that she might find a friend who might be willing to share her simple way of living for the sake of studying the principles and methods of her work. For a short time Miss Bathurst joined her, with this object in view ; but her departure again left a void. A succession of difficulties which arose in the summer of 1858 only deepened her loneliness. She reviewed the two years which had passed since her mother's death ; she strove to repress the irritability with which she still had to struggle, even while she felt it needful sometimes to exert all her moral force over her subordinates. ' I ' know that there must be much wrong in me, or I should ' not often be so deeply tried. I would willingly bear all ' things, and yield to all, resisting no evil in others, but I ' am bound to conflict with it, to act with authority, which ' is far from my desire.' But she began to acquiesce in a certain solitude of soul,[1] and to find peace in the general order of her outward life. In her own dwelling, at least, she believed herself secure from the trials inseparable from her work.

TO MISS SANFORD.

Bristol, July 5th, 1858.

Now everything around me is in harmony, and I am gradually getting able to feel my dear Parents working in and with me, though it will be long before the shock and wrench of death are quite gone, and the veil of mortality removed which has been drawn also over my dear Father, since it shrouded my Mother.

But I cannot tell you how thankful I am for this house, and for the sense of freedom which I now have. . . I have lived in so very cramped a condition that in many ways I feel as if—now past fifty,—I were only emerging from childhood. So this rather puts me back at times, but on the whole I feel more 'myself and nobody else,' or rather that I shall soon be so. May that self be wholly subjected to the obedience which is in Christ!

I had a very delightful visit last week but one at Hardwicke Court, meeting with numbers of fellow-workers with

---

[1] About this time she first read the remarkable sermon on the ' Loneliness of Christ,' by F. W. Robertson. She was powerfully moved by his teachings, and never lost her high appreciation of them.

whom I had delightful communion. I had also a hearty
pleasure on Saturday week and since, in seeing a very old
Kingswood scholar, a great plague at the time, who ran away
nine times, now a fine young sailor.[1] He evidently feels that
he was 'bought with a price,' and *looks* as gratefully at me
as even you could wish. He seems quite to love Kingswood
and old times. I showed him an old school photograph which
I keep in my Kingswood relic box; he was much pleased and
went off to get me one stylishly got up of his present self.
To look on this picture and on that, in expression and bearing,
would convert the sceptical.

TO MISS SANFORD.

Red Lodge House, Bristol, July 11th, 1858.

I am now alone on this bright Sunday morning, and
thankful to enjoy my own company; *i.e.* the 'cloud of witnesses' and guardian angels who are ever near me, unless
dispelled by some disturbing element. I am beginning to
realise this kind of existence, and to hope and believe that my
own spirit will become freer and stronger and more beautiful
if left for a time to its own workings. I cannot help throwing
myself into a strange kind of sympathy with those whom I
feel bound to me, and am absolutely *tortured* with diseases of
their spirits, just as we saw in Paris a somnambule over
whose face passed a painful cloud when put 'en rapport' with
a person who had a disease of which we bystanders had no
knowledge.

Yet not even the sanctity of the home was safe from the
invasion of a heavy grief. She had connected her own
domestic arrangements with the scheme of training in the
Red Lodge. The first stage of promotion led to the Cottage,
where the elder girls enjoyed more freedom, and were taught
baking, washing, and other duties of household service. A
second step brought them into the Red Lodge House, for
which two of the most promising were always selected.
There they were under her direct and constant influence,
and shared the home life which she believed to be invested
with such redeeming power. At the end of July one of

---

[1] She had infinite patience with these restless lads. Of one of
them she once said, with a touch of the humour of which she was
fond, that 'he came back resembling the Prodigal in everything
' except his repentance.'

these girls absconded, taking with her some trifling articles
of property. The shock was severe to the loving heart which
was thus wounded in its keenest sensibilities. But she
accepted it as part of her discipline of helpfulness; the
children for whom she was toiling were not in themselves
vicious; rather were they the victims of the vice of others.
She poured out her anguish in secret, and wrestled in a very
agony of prayer for the erring child.

No time, however, could be given to any luxury of
sorrow. Day after day brought with it its appointed duties,
and there were always in the background the multitudinous
ranks of the neglected and untaught for whom help must be
procured. So, ere a week had passed, she wrote, 'I have
'been happy to be able to think again to-day; I must now
'throw my mind into the Ragged School Channel. This is
'the most perplexing and difficult battle I have had to fight.
'I am obliged to write the same things backwards and for-
'wards and crossways and every way possible to try to get
'things, or rather one simple thing, into people's heads.
'Happily, I have the patience of Job and a woman's fertility
'of resource.' The autumn gave her important opportunity
of again enunciating her views. The Social Science Congress
met at Liverpool, under the distinguished presidency of Lord
John Russell : and there she read two papers on the ' Disposal
'of Girls from Reformatory Schools,' and the ' Relation of
'Ragged and Industrial Schools to the Parliamentary Grant.'

In the meantime her home was no longer lonely ; it was
now brightened by a child's presence. In August she had
reiterated her desire to receive some friend who would study
the work ; but still more she longed to ' welcome anyone who
'might be thrown on her to abide as bound to her by natural
'ties.' The occasion soon arose. Natural ties could not,
indeed, be created out of nothing; but it was possible to
cherish affections which might by degrees become almost as
strong. September came, and with it the long-desired charge.
She heard from a Missionary in the south of England, who
had taken a little child into his home. At once she planned
to relieve him of his burden, and the transfer was accomplished
without delay. ' Just think of me with a little girl of *my*
' *own!* about five years old. Ready made to my hand, and
'nicely trained without the trouble of marrying, &c. &c., a
'darling little thing, an orphan. I feel already a *mère de*

'*famille*, and am quite happy in buying little hats and socks
'and a little bed to stand in my own room, out of my own
'money. It is a wonderful feeling.' One want was thus
satisfied; but the child was no fellow-worker. Before
Christmas, however, another inmate brought a genial interest
and sympathy all her own. Miss Frances Power Cobbe had
recently returned from the East; and Lady Byron, who made
her sick chamber the centre of innumerable plans for the
welfare of her friends, contrived to set her in communication
with Mary Carpenter. It was not long before an alliance
was established, and Miss Cobbe took up her abode at Red
Lodge House. Her first impressions she has thus recalled:

My first interview with Miss Carpenter was in the doorway
of my bedroom after my arrival at Red Lodge House. She had
been absent from home on business, and hastened upstairs to
welcome me. It was rather a critical moment, for I had been
asking myself anxiously—'What manner of woman shall I
'behold?' I knew I should see an able and an excellent
person; but it is quite possible for able and excellent women
to be far from constituting agreeable companions for a *tête-à-
tête* of years, and nothing short of this had I in contemplation.
The first glimpse in that doorway set my fears at rest! The
plain and careworn face, the figure which, Mr. Martineau says,
had been columnar in youth, but which at fifty-two was angular
and stooping, were yet all alive with feeling and power. Her
large light blue eyes, with their peculiar trick of showing the
white beneath the iris, had an extraordinary faculty of taking
possession of the person on whom they were fixed. . . . There
was humour also in every line of her face, and a readiness to
catch the first gleam of a joke. But the prevailing characteristic of Mary Carpenter, as I came subsequently more
perfectly to recognise, was a high and strong *Resolution*, which
made her whole path much like that of a plough in a well-
drawn furrow, which goes straight on in its own beneficent
way, and gently pushes aside into little ridges all intervening
people and things.

Long after this first interview, I showed Miss Carpenter's
photograph to the Master of Balliol, without telling him whom
it represented. After looking at it carefully he remarked,
'This is the portrait of a person who *lives under high moral
'excitement*.' There could not be a truer summary of her
habitual state.[1]

---

[1] From 'Personal Recollections of Mary Carpenter' in the *Modern
Review*, April, 1880, p. 281 *sq.*

From Miss Cobbe's memories of the life at Red Lodge House some further insight may be gathered into the methods and spirit of Mary Carpenter's work at this time.

Our days were very much alike, and 'Sunday shone no 'Sabbath day' for us.   Our little household consisted of one honest girl (a certain excellent Marianne, who well deserves commemoration), and two little *professed* thieves from the Red Lodge.   We assembled for prayers very early in the morning, and breakfast was got over, during the winter months, before daylight, Miss Carpenter always remarking brightly as she sat down, 'How cheerful' was the gas!   After this, there were classes at the different schools, endless arrangements and organisations, the looking-up of little truants from the Ragged Schools, and a good deal of business in the way of writing reports, and so on.   Altogether, nearly every hour of the day and week was pretty well mapped out, leaving only space for the brief dinner and tea; and at nine or ten o'clock at night, when we met at last, Miss Carpenter was often so exhausted that I have seen her fall asleep with the spoon half-way between her mouth and the cup of gruel which she ate for supper.   Her habits were all of the simplest and most self-denying kind.   Both by temperament and on principle she was essentially a Stoic.   She had no sympathy at all with *Asceticism*, which is a very different thing, and implies a vivid sense of the attractiveness of luxury; and she strongly condemned fasting and all such practices, on the Zoroastrian principle that they involve a culpable weakening of powers which are entrusted to us for good use.   But she was an ingrained Stoic, to whom all the minor comforts of life are simply indifferent, and who can scarcely even recognise the fact that other people take heed of them. . . . Her special chair was a horsehair one with wooden arms, and on the seat she had placed a small square cushion as hard as a board, likewise covered with horsehair.   I took this up one day, and taunted her with the *Sybaritism* it displayed, but she replied, with infinite simplicity, 'Yes, indeed!   I am 'sorry to say that since my illness I have been obliged to have 'recourse to *these indulgences* (!).   I used to try, like St. Paul, 'to "endure hardness."'

But alongside of this Stoicism there was in Mary Carpenter a strong feeling for Beauty, both of Nature and Art.   So far as her means would allow, she made her Reformatory and her house (the Ragged School was past any æsthetic help!) as pretty as possible; and she frequently expressed horror of the bare and pictureless walls of certain other charitable institutions. She was also a very fair artist in the earlier style of water-colour drawings, and especially showed her fancy and delicate feeling in semi-imaginary landscapes. . . . Speaking of a collection of Miss Carpenter's sketches, I wrote to my friend : 'It is curious ' to know of this real artist mind, and to watch her in a fright-'ful school-room labouring away over some simplest matter ' with those poor little ragamuffins. I have always deemed the ' love of the beautiful to be a fastidious sentiment, but she is ' beyond all that.' . . .

The droll things which daily occurred in the schools, and the wonderful replies received from the scholars to questions testing their information, amused her intensely, and the more unruly were the young scamps, the more, I think, in her secret heart, she liked them, and gloried in taming them. She used to say, ' Only to get them to use the *school comb* is something ! ' Indeed, at all times the events of the day's work, if they bordered on the ludicrous (as was often the case), provoked her laughter till the tears ran down her cheeks. One night she sat grieving over a piece of ingratitude on the part of one of her teachers, and told me she had given him some invitation for the purpose of conciliating him, and ' heaping coals of fire ' on his head.' ' It will take *another scuttle*, my dear friend,' I remarked, and thereupon her tears stopped, and she burst into a hearty fit of laughter. Next evening she said to me dolorously, ' I tried that *other scuttle*, but it was no go ! '

But this innocent mirthfulness was always quenched, if the subject in question trenched on vice or wicked folly of any kind. Miss Carpenter was assuredly not one of the ' fools who ' make a mock of sin.' In another of my letters I find these remarks :—' It is rather an awful thing to live with a person ' whose standard is so exalted, and who never seems to com-' prehend, with all her pity for actual *vice*, the lax moral half-' and-half state wherein most of us habitually muddle. Her ' merry laugh stops spontaneously if my jokes approach to ' stories wherein any sort of wrong-doing is treated as ludi-' crous. . . . At all events, it is a blessed sight to see with ' one's own eyes the state it is possible to reach even in this ' world.'[1]

By this time new schemes were on foot. Years before, Mr. Commissioner Hill had declared of the ardent labourer by his side that she had lost the power of slackening her pace, and had playfully compared her to a boy running down Greenwich Hill, who must go on to the bottom. She had assuredly not abated one whit in her zeal. The last instalment in her programme for which Parliamentary sanction had

---

[1] *Modern Review*, April, 1880, pp. 283-289.

been obtained, was the establishment of Certified Industrial
Schools for vagrant children. But the difficulties attending
the working of the Act were such that only two schools—
and both of those in London—were founded under it, in the
year 1858.[1] These obstacles could not be removed, until
they had been shown to exist, and this task accordingly
Mary Carpenter now resolved to undertake. She might
fairly have pleaded that she had work enough ; the Red
Lodge School depended solely upon her; to the School at
Kingswood she continued to pay the weekly visit which kept
her thoroughly acquainted with every detail of its management ; the Ragged School at St. James's Back could not
dispense with her constant presence ; and the Evening School
still claimed her as of old. Moreover correspondence was
increasing fast ; Parliamentary proceedings needed jealous
vigilance—members must be kept on the alert, inspired
with principles, and convinced by facts ; counsel must be
exchanged with the managers of institutions kindred to her
own at home and abroad ; friends and fellow-workers in the
United States must not be forgotten ; and the ever-growing
band of young men and women in various parts of the world
who owed to her their new careers, must receive timely
remembrance. Nevertheless, the effort should be made ; and
if it failed (and she was prepared for failure), the public
should know that the reason lay not with the principle, which
had been demonstrated to be sound in Scotland, nor with her
management, which had been thrice proved successful, but
with the unwise impediments thrust in the way by legislators
unacquainted with the real conditions. A suitable house and
garden were found in Park Row, but a few minutes distant
from Red Lodge House. The premises were purchased by
Mr. Frederick Chapple of Liverpool ; the gifts of friends
enabled her to furnish them ; a master and matron were
engaged ; and early in April the School was opened. It was
the spring, a season always hallowed to her by solemn and
tender thoughts ; but time often failed her now to give
utterance to the full depth of her feeling, and the record of
her undertaking was brief.

---

[1] A few Industrial Schools, Refuges, and other similar institutions
applied for certificates; but these were not new, and did not afford
a satisfactory test of the principle.

Sunday, April 16th, 1859.—During the last week I have commenced my last work, and entered a new house, which I trust will be holy to the Lord and save some of his children. I have a principle to develop which is less understood than any of the others. I am commencing it single-handed, and knowing that I shall have the greatest difficulty in every way. Yet I begin it, if not with the ardent enthusiasm of twelve years ago, yet with the same hope, with the same love, and with an experience which gives me confidence, and which will save me from many difficulties and disappointments.

The place which she conceived the new Certified Industrial School to hold in her general scheme of operations is set forth in a letter of the same date to Lady Byron.

Bristol, April 16th, 1859.

I am glad to be able to indulge myself with a few words to you this Sunday evening. During the last week I have commenced the completion of my plan of schools to develop the great principle that *society* is bound by every principle, economical, political, moral, and religious, to undertake the care of children who are spiritually orphans—while the parents are still answerable for the supply of their physical wants. (I have perhaps tried to express this too briefly, but you know what I mean.) The principle of Reformatory Schools is established, though the practical development is as yet at a very early stage. The Ragged Schools, giving education to those who are *willing* to receive it, are practically established, but we have still to battle with the State to establish the principle. The class remains who will *not* go to the Ragged Schools, and who are qualifying to become 'children of the 'State' in Reformatories, if not taken hold of. We have been striving to get leave to do by law what Sheriff Watson did without law some 18 years ago—to have a *right* to take hold of these children and give them the needed training. The parents, or, in default, the parish, *ought* to feed them, but will not. Now though numbers feel the necessity of such schools, and the best already established without legal detention prove in working that they cannot touch the class most needing it without legal aid, yet the obstacles imposed by the structure of the Bill and by the Committee of Council are such that no one seems disposed to work the principle out. I have anxiously worked and striven to induce some one to begin, but in vain. I must therefore apply myself to the work, be-

ginning under the most favourable circumstances possible.
Then if, as I expect, the thing *cannot* be done, I shall let the
public know why, and try to get the obstacle removed.   If
it can, others will be encouraged to begin.   I have a capital
house and sufficient garden—into which I have put the least
possible amount of furniture and apparatus.   I have a *certificated* master and his wife, now arrived, and must now wait
till the Committee of Council will send to inspect, before I
can get children sent.   The £200 sent me by Mrs. Evans for
the purpose, and £15 from other distant friends, will make
me independent for the present, for I do not wish to apply to
the public for funds till I can show the work in progress.
So much for this, my last work.   Red Lodge, I am thankful
to say, is now giving me no *extra*-ordinary anxiety.   The
various departments are working satisfactorily.

My inner life is, I hope, opening and strengthening : it
seems as if I were only now beginning to comprehend the
great reality of Death and its meaning; as if the removal of
my dear parents were making me feel, as I have not done
before, my own independent and individual existence.   I feel
a distinct position and work assigned me, and find all marvellously ordered for me.   Yet I seem quite loose to the
world, and I am much happier for feeling free from anxiety,
for I leave all in the hands of Him who cannot err.   This is
in general my present state, which I imagine that you have
enough love for me to make you like to hear.   I was very
glad to hear a little of you and yours in two delightful days
which I spent at Torquay with Miss Bathurst.   I am glad to
send you some rent; perhaps I may have a few lines besides
the acknowledgment.

No sooner was the Certified Industrial School started
than Mary Carpenter resumed her crusade on behalf of the
children whose needs are still unrecognised.   Early in the
year she had published a pamphlet entitled ' The Claims of
' Ragged Schools to Pecuniary Educational Aid from the
' Annual Parliamentary Grant, as an Integral Part of the
' Educational Movement of the Country.'   Her subject
enabled her to review the whole history of the assistance
at various times granted to Ragged Schools.   She again
enumerated the special difficulties which beset the managers,
who were entitled therefore to exceptional help ; criticised
the plea that as there ought not to be a Ragged School class
in the country, no provision need be made for it ; brought
ample evidence to overthrow the opposing contention that
the children of Ragged School classes were in general not the

children of parents who could not pay, but rather of those
who would not pay; exposed the imaginary nature of the
danger that the allotment of permanent educational aid to
Ragged Schools would draw down other schools to them;
and finally declared that Certified Industrial Schools which
were proposed as a substitute for Ragged Schools, both dealt
with a different class of children, and were even worse off
than the Ragged Schools themselves.   The pamphlet was
widely circulated, and in the course of the Session Mary
Carpenter felt justified in again bringing the matter before
Sir Stafford Northcote, now again in Parliament as Member
for Stamford.

TO SIR STAFFORD NORTHCOTE, M.P.

Red Lodge House, July 11th, 1859.

I am glad to perceive that Parliament is sufficiently settled
to be attending to ordinary matters.   I have been waiting for
this to ask for the favour of your attention to the Ragged
School and Industrial School question.   It has now assumed
the position of a matter of principle; it is now a question
whether the educational grant is to be virtually withheld from
those who want it most ; whether it is good for the country
that between one and two millions at least should grow up
without education.   I think I sent you my pamphlet, but if
you have it not by you, I shall be glad to send you another.
Mr. Hill greatly approves of it.   I have not seen any answer
to it, or any attempt to answer it.   The country ought to know
how the funds are spent, and what principles are adopted, and
they should be fairly discussed.   Of course we must look to
you especially, as the original author of the Industrial Schools
Bill, to sustain our principles.   I have just established a
Certified Industrial School just to show what the impediments
to its operations are.   The principle on which we desire that
the Bill should be established will never be carried out with
things as they are.

The autumn gave her further opportunity of developing
her views at the Bradford meeting of the Social Science
Association, where she read papers on both groups of schools
—the Ragged, and the Certified Industrial.   As soon as the
Congress broke up, she went to pay a visit to Mr. Monckton
Milnes (now Lord Houghton), who had been among the first
to move in Parliament for Reformatory legislation.   Among

the guests at Frystone Hall she met Sir J. K. Shuttleworth,
Mr. Chadwick, Mr. G. W. Hastings, and others, and had the
opportunity of privately conferring with them on the
subjects so dear to her heart. It was with profound satisfaction that she found her principles winning at last the
recognition for which she had striven, and she wrote to Lady
Byron with new hope.

TO LADY BYRON.

Frystone Hall, near Knottingley, October, 1859.

I cannot but feel it a subject of deep thankfulness to be
regarded by all with such kind sympathy, after having
struggled through so many long and very dark days. These
privileges are given us always as soon as we are prepared by
long discipline to receive them, and I hope I accept them
from the Father with deep humility. . . . My special objects
have been as successful as possible, *i.e.* both my papers were
received without the slightest opposition, and resolutions
founded on them from each section where I read urging the
Council to action. I am thankful.

In the meantime, *i.e.* till we get justice done by the Committee of Council on Education, I shall want money to carry
on my Certified Industrial School. Not liking to ' beg,' I
have resumed my pencil when I can find time, feeling it a
legitimate object to indulge in this very soothing occupation.

The summer and autumn had brought with it other
pleasures also. Theodore Parker had passed through England
on that sad search for health from which he never returned.
To Mary Carpenter he had long been known as the champion
of the ignorant and the oppressed ; to Miss Cobbe he had
been the prophet of the ' absolute religion ' of love to God
and love to man ; and as soon as he landed at Liverpool, the
two ladies sent an earnest invitation to him to come and stay
at Red Lodge House. But he was too ill to bear the excitement of seeing friends, and he hurried on to Switzerland to
rest beside the Lake of Geneva. From the letters that
passed to and fro, the following passages will serve to mark
the position of the friends who were drawn into strong
sympathy even without the help of personal communion, and
in spite of wide divergences of religious view.

TO THE REV. THEODORE PARKER.

Bristol, June 12th, 1859.

From not seeing your name mentioned as in London,[1] I fear that you are not strong enough to be present at them. Perhaps you feel, however, as I do that the doctrines of religion ought not to be separated from the work of religion in the world. I believe 'Evangelical Unitarianism,' as my revered and beloved father expressed it, to be the 'doctrine of the 'gospel,' *i.e.* simple Christianity, and as such I desire its extension. I value the holy truth, and without it I could not do the work which my Heavenly Father has given me to do. But I should not care much to convert any one to it *intellectually* only, nor do I value it except as a *living reality*, which is to be carried with vivifying warmth to bear on every great social evil. I am grieved to see the tone of many leading Unitarians on this subject both here and in the United States. You, my dear sir, have carried religion into the dark places of the earth, and have shed its light on the great social evils which others pass by or ignore.

THE REV. THEODORE PARKER TO MARY CARPENTER.

Montreux, June 23rd, 1859.

I need not tell you how much interest I take in your noble work at Bristol. Many things are called *Christianity*—a name dear or hateful as you define it one way or another; often it means repeating a liturgy and attending church or chapel; sometimes it means burning men alive; in half the U.S.A. it means kidnapping, enslaving men and women. The Christianity which your admirable father loved, and taught, and lived, was Piety and Morality, Love to God, Love to Man —the keeping of the Natural Laws God writes on Sense and Soul. It is this which I honour and love in you, especially as it takes the form of Humanity, and loves the Unlovely. The greatest heroism of our day spends itself in lanes and alleys, in the haunts of poverty and crime, seeking to bless such as the institutions of the age can only curse. If Jesus of Nazareth were to come back and be the Jesus of London, I think I know what (negative and positive) work he would set about. He would be a new Revolution of Institutions, applying his universal justice to the causes of Ill; but also an Angel of Mercy, palliating the effects of those causes which

---

[1] Among the visitors attending the Unitarian gatherings at Whitsuntide.

could not be at once removed or made null. You are doing this work—the work of humanity. It seems to me you have a genius for it. Accept my hearty thanks for all your kind intentions, and believe me,

Faithfully yours,
THEODORE PARKER.

Red Lodge House, however, received other visitors this summer, whose spirit was not far apart from that of the heroic teacher now slowly dying among the Alps. First came Miss Remond, a coloured lady of high accomplishment, in whose success at a public lecture Mary Carpenter felt something more like a personal triumph than she ever experienced on her own account. The Antislavery ardour which she revived, was further quickened by the Rev. S. J. May of Syracuse, to whose intense earnestness and exquisite simplicity of nature the heart of Mary Carpenter responded at once. He was one of the few Unitarian ministers of America who was able, like Mary Carpenter, to maintain his religious fellowship with Theodore Parker, without abandoning his 'evangelical Unitarianism;' and his long labours on behalf of the slaves enabled him to enter with a completeness of sympathy such as she rarely received, into the various works by which his hostess was seeking to emancipate the ignorant and the depraved from what she regarded as an even more terrible bondage. In the precious hours that could be saved out of the busy days for the intercourse of friendship, Mr. May poured out his rich stores of experience, and spoke of the hopes of freedom which were becoming more and more passionate. When the news of the daring enterprise of John Brown arrived in December, Mary Carpenter was deeply moved; and with the prompt energy which never allowed strong feeling to pass away without some corresponding action, she proceeded at once to collect aid for the forlorn widow. 'I believe,' she wrote to Theodore Parker, 'that December 2nd will prove the beginning of the 'end. Nothing but a separation of the diseased and rotten 'part from the comparatively sound can save the body. I 'am glad that the martyr was one so irreproachable and single-'hearted, though his *means* were to my mind unlawful, . . . 'and that the South are so mad as to be subpœnaing 'Northerners as witnesses in the coming trial. I hope they

' will trample on the North until it is *compelled* to resist. I
' am preparing a little mark of sympathy with Mrs. Brown
' in compliance with the wish expressed by her husband in
' his letter to Mrs. Child, viz. a box of clothing, which I
' hope to send off soon.' At the same time she also forwarded
contributions to a bazaar that was being organised by
Frederick Douglass, whose visit to Bristol some fourteen years
before had done much to stimulate her early enthusiasm.

In spite of these numerous interests, however, the year
passed away rather sadly for her. Her adopted child was
placed at school, and she lost for a time the freshness which
had entered the home with her. Miss Cobbe, whose health
had broken down two or three times in succession, was about
to leave Red Lodge House, and she would be again alone.
Not even this companionship had been able to avert the
dreadful sense of desolation which at times almost overwhelmed her, as she sat among the memorials of the past.
Though amid new order, the familiar objects were all there ;
each with some special association with the beloved whom
she could see no more. She was convinced that she had yet a
work which must be accomplished, and she no longer ventured
to utter even to herself a wish for release. ' I perfectly agree
' with you,' she had written in the summer to Theodore
Parker, ' in your views of life and death, and the peaceful
' way of regarding both which a true belief in Perfect Love
' enables us to take. But Paul felt a tie to life where he saw
' much to be done. We are permitted to desire it, and it is
' too sacred a trust not to watch it with jealous care.' None
the less, however, did she feel alone. ' All true heart-
' experiences,' she recorded on December 31st, ' have their
' unspeakable pain which can be shared with no mortal ;' and
this year had brought her many such. These trials (chiefly
with her fellow-workers in the schools) she interpreted as the
signs that there were yet many faults which must be made
known to her, ' and then put away, or even cut out, or burnt
' away, or washed out with scalding tears.' From her disappointments she strove to learn patience ; patience grew into
hope, and faith was strengthened. Meanwhile, her plans
were prospering more than she could have anticipated ;
sympathy and help were gathering round her ; principles were
emerging into clear light from the obscurity of her small
enterprises ; and she prepared to go her way in lowliness and

self-denial, 'firmly asserting the truth and sustaining the
'cause of the forsaken, irrespective of self.'

The opening of the Session in 1860 was the signal for
new efforts. She was watching and waiting to see whether
any other voice would be raised on behalf of the destitute
children.* No one seemed to stir, and the initiative again lay
with her. A letter to Sir Stafford Northcote entreated his
attention.

TO SIR STAFFORD NORTHCOTE, M.P.

Red Lodge House, March 24th, 1860.

No indication has yet appeared on the part of the Committee of Council on Education of a willingness to do anything
for the education of the portion of the population commonly
called the Ragged School class; but on the contrary, grants
are extended in the contrary direction, viz. to give instruction
in the fine arts to a class that can obtain these luxuries for
themselves. I think that I troubled you with a pamphlet on
the subject a year ago, but there appears no probability of
any acknowledgment of the principle that the grant for
education should in justice, and for the good of the country,
be given at least equally to the classes who most stand in need
of it; that instead of bribing the children of the labouring
classes to come to school with capitation grants on attendance,
they should help others to get education who cannot obtain it
themselves. The public are not fully aware of this state of
things. It appears that the only means left of getting justice
done will be to get the subject discussed in Parliament, on
occasion of the grant for education being proposed. I feel sure
of your support in a matter which is so important to the
country as a preventive measure.

The next step was to lay the case before Mr. Lowe, then
Vice-President of the Committee of Council on Education.
Sheriff Watson from Aberdeen, Dr. Guthrie and Dr. Bell
from Edinburgh, Mr. Adshead of Manchester, and a few
other gentlemen, together with Mary Carpenter, procured an
audience in the middle of April. The regret which Mr.
Lowe then expressed at the recognition of Ragged Schools
by the Minute of 1857 was sufficient proof of his unwillingness to grant them any further aid; there was nothing for it
but for the deputation to go home again and devise some

other line of attack. Mary Carpenter's plan was thus
sketched out in a letter to Dr. Bell.

TO DR. BELL, EDINBURGH.

Bristol, May 9th, 1860.

We are now going to bring a very important question
before Parliament, one which, in its connection and consequences, is of fundamental importance to the whole country.
The question is not whether this or the other school shall be
helped from the Parliamentary grant,—whether Ragged and
Industrial Schools are good or bad,—whether they are subject
to such and such abuses,—whether they are so good and
alluring that they entice children from other schools, or so
bad that they ought not to exist at all,—whether, in fine, any
class of the population actually exists for whom Ragged
Schools are the only means of education. With all these
questions I have been met when I have introduced the
subject, and the objections made have assumed the most
varied Proteus forms, always evading the true question, and
always covering the most insuperable dislike to the whole
movement, or to giving *any* help of an educational kind to
those who cannot help themselves. The philanthropy of the
country may safely be left, they conclude, to take the whole
charge of this class on itself.

We have long enough been discussing these matters. We
have long enough been begging the Lords of Council to give
a small pittance to those who are perishing for lack of knowledge, while they lavishly bestow thousands on those who can
do without help. We have been using every argument to
prove to them the justice and necessity of proper help for
such schools as do really and efficiently grapple with the evil.
It is in vain to reason with those who are determined not to
be persuaded, or who will close their eyes to existing realities.

We are now about to assert to the Parliament of the
country that there is an underlying stratum of the population
which never has been and never will be touched by the
common Day Schools, and which is the seed plot of pauperism
and crime ; that they *are* reached by good schools in which
education is combined with much voluntary benevolent effort
(viz. good Industrial and Ragged Schools), and by these *are*
raised from their degraded condition, and made self-supporting
members of the community; that for the good of society, as
well as a matter of justice, such schools ought to be efficiently
helped by any grant made for the education of the people.

This is the principle which I have laid before Sir John
Pakington as the object of the motion we desire. He saw it

clearly and expressed himself as ready to support it. He said he would confer with Mr. Black on the best mode of bringing it forward in Parliament, and requested me to draw out a kind of brief of the whole case for him. It will now be very important to secure the support of as many members as possible.

The state of public business unfortunately prevented Sir John Pakington from obtaining an earlier day for his resolution than August 14th. It was seconded by Mr. Black, one of the members for Edinburgh, but after a short discussion it was negatived in a thin house; and for that Session, at any rate, all Parliamentary action was at an end.

Meanwhile Mary Carpenter was resolved not to countenance delay by silence. The summer found her at Oxford, where the British Association for the Advancement of Science held its annual meeting in June. There, before the Statistical section, she read a paper on 'Educational Help from the 'Government Grant to the Destitute and Neglected Children 'of Great Britain.' The incident was not without its interest, and was thus described in a letter of her brother Philip to Professor Henry, of the Smithsonian Institute, Washington.

DR. P. P. CARPENTER TO PROFESSOR HENRY, WASHINGTON.

July 4th, 1860.

There was a great gathering of celebrities to hear her. It was in one of the ancient schools or lecture halls, which was crowded, evidently not by the curious, but by those who really wanted to know what she had to say. She stood up and read in her usual clear voice and expressive enunciation. . . . I suppose the first time a woman's voice had read a lecture there before dignitaries of learning and the church; but as there was not the slightest affectation on the one hand, so on the other hand there was neither a scorn nor an etiquettish politeness; but they all listened to her just as they would have listened to Dr. Rae about Franklin, only with the additional feeling (expressed by the President, Mr. Nassau Senior) that it was a matter of heart and duty, as well as head.

Mary was a good deal sought after by Lord This and Professor That, and so forth, and exerted herself according to custom in trying to stick her principles into the dogged brains of John-Bulldom. The pleasantest group was Professor

Sedgwick, Mary, and Madame Mohl sitting together, and
talking over old times.   He well remembered a certain
breakfast at my father's house in '36; so do I.   The said
Madame Mohl is said by some to be the cleverest woman in
Europe; one of the French *savantes* of the first Revolution
type, full of life, fun, witty and sensible conversation, and
grey curls. . . . Mr. Senior shocked my modesty greatly by
coming to take me to the Vice-Chancellor's, and immediately
began to pump me about Unitarianism.   Mary must be a
great puzzle to these people, who think it some horrid form
of infidelity.   Madame Mohl thought my explanation much
what she believed, though she had been brought up in a
convent.

The inauguration of the statue to Dr. Priestley in the
Museum excited Mary Carpenter's highest enthusiasm ; and
the private hospitalities of Prof. Jowett and other friends
further made the visit memorable.   She returned to Bristol
cheered with fresh sympathy, and ready for the continuance
of the fight.   But another branch of the same subject soon
claimed her attention.   A Bill was brought in by Sir G. C.
Lewis to transfer the Certified Industrial Schools from the
control of the Committee of Council to that of the Home
Office.   This change she accepted gladly.   ' It is much more
' correct in principle that the State should take charge of
' these children,' she wrote to Sir Stafford Northcote, ' and I
' am persuaded that it will work better.'   But two evils
remained : one, the provision in the original Act, which
imposed on the managers the duty of recovering the parent's
contributions to the child's maintenance, was met by a clause
proposed by Sir Stafford Northcote ; the other, the limitation
of the class of children to be committed, continued untouched,
and on this subject she thus expressed her views to her
Parliamentary ally.

TO SIR STAFFORD NORTHCOTE, M.P.

Red Lodge House, August 11th, 1860.
The great cause of the magistrates not sending children
here in Bristol is that the ground of commitment is solely
the Vagrant Act, which is here so interpreted as not to
include the known thieves and pilferers, even when caught
in the act of pilfering or petty larceny.   Hence the quay-gangs
and other notorious gangs in Bristol remain untouched, who

are qualifying for the more expensive reformatories, having first received a prison brand. If you could get the words inserted in Clause V. 'or petty larceny,' which I presume would include stealing sugar on quays or other little matters, which indicate a mode of life, but are not called vagrancy, the efficiency of the Act would be greatly promoted. Our Bristol magistrates are the only ones in England who have *tried* to work the Act, and have sent a number of begging children, but the 'Arabs' remain untouched. I trust you may be able to manage this, or to get the Dunlop clause inserted, or your original reading restored.

The Session was over before this request could be carried out, but its author did not allow it to drop. In October she addressed a letter to Sir G. C. Lewis, embodying this and some other suggestions, and she further organised a deputation which enforced the same view in the following month. These proposals were ultimately adopted; and the amended Act of 1861 widened the range within which children under fourteen might be sent to Industrial Schools, so as to include those who had committed offences punishable with imprisonment, as well as vagrants and begging children.

These labours naturally consumed a considerable amount of thought and time. Yet they never deadened either the intensity of her religious feelings or the depth and freshness of her personal affections. These remained undimmed, through whatever struggles she might be passing. In April 1860, after attending the usual commemoration service of the Lord's Supper on the eve of Good Friday (a day additionally solemn as that on which she received the news of her father's death), she wrote: 'It seems as if I increasingly feel our 'Saviour to be our tenderly beloved and revered friend. I 'cannot even now review his sufferings, his deep love, his 'steadfast purpose, his perfect absorption in the Father's will, 'combined with the most acute human feelings, without the 'most deep and tender sympathy and sorrow. It is strange 'that the past is more present to me than the present 'glory.'

It was the tendency of her mind to live much in the scenes, the associations, the characters of those whom she had loved. To these it was that she escaped in thought from the depression following severe moral conflict with the evil

round her, or the weariness of hope deferred. And now
another was to be added to the invisible band whose spiritual
presence she believed to be constantly working with her and
upholding her. On May 16th, Lady Byron passed away.
Mary Carpenter had been expecting the tidings for some
days. She knew that the sufferer was only waiting for the
signal of release, and every time that a few lines faintly
traced found their way to her from the sick-bed, she treasured
them as though they must be the last. The news reached
her in the morning as she was about to begin her usual
occupations. Close engagements in her different schools
detained her all day; she had no moment to pause, to feel,
to weep ; and when the evening came, she could only lay
herself down with a dull sense of unutterable desolation.
But sleep brought rest to the troubled heart ; and when
she awoke early next morning, some lines of verse were
already shaped clearly in her mind. Before the day ran out,
these grew into a little poem. She had for years abandoned
all efforts at composition, but the spontaneous utterance now
brought her relief.

LADY NOEL BYRON, DIED MAY 16TH, 1860.

The veil of death hides thee from mortal sight,
    Friend ever dear;
It opens thine to pure celestial light,
    Eternal, clear.

Long-tried and faithful servant ! Thou did'st run
    A weary race.
The distant goal is reached ! Thy crown is won !
    Thy resting-place.

Thy Lord well knew in weakness thou wast strong,
    And on thee laid
A burden of rich gifts, to use them long,
    E'en as He bade.

How thou did'st strive to spend the treasures well,
    So largely given—
How constant toil—no mortal tongue can tell,
    'Tis known in heaven.

'Midst blighted joys thou trod'st thy path of youth—
    'Midst griefs thy prime—
But thou didst glean from all eternal truth,
    Vanquishing time.

Thence it would seem thou hadst received a dower
 Of strength and love ;
And thy pure soul shed forth a wondrous power
 Drawn from above.

Thy toils of life are o'er, for thou didst hear
 A heavenly voice :
'Thy life on earth is ended, stay not here ! '
 Thou did'st rejoice.

Why should we grieve that the poor suffering clay
 Holds thee no more ?
That from earth's trials thou art borne away
 To Canaan's shore ?

Yet, friend beloved, our tears must warmly flow,
 That thou art gone.
An awful void is nigh us here below ;
 We feel alone.

Be near us yet, because thou art with God ;
 Be with us still ;
And help us on to do, on life's rough road,
 Our Father's will.

Only to herself did Mary Carpenter venture to utter the regret that she had not been able to have more constant intercourse with the friend whom she loved, and show more personal tenderness to her. But the answer arose at once. ' I must not repine that my work has been a barrier here ' to those happy intercourses of friendship. Have I not ' devoted myself to it ? I cannot then withhold my best ' treasures.'—To another, the friend of her mother, she could speak of the hopes which welled up within her as she contemplated the possibilities of the unseen world. 'The loss was ' very deep and irreparable of my beloved Lady Byron. ' Her spirit helped mine much, and she had true sympathy ' in my work. Our friendship steadily grew ; it will be ' perfected, I feel sure, in the Father's house ! What a ' meeting has been hers ! What mysteries have now been ' solved to her ! Have her beloved ones yet been purified, ' and has she seen mine ? Faith answers " Yes ! " ' [1]

---

[1] It may be added that Lady Byron showed her confidence in Mary Carpenter by appointing her one of her three literary executors, to whom all her papers were entrusted. A legacy which she

The autumn brought with it a new and unlooked-for interest, which was destined hereafter to become the absorbing thought of Mary Carpenter's life. A young Brahmin, who had embraced Christianity in the midst of opposition and obloquy, came over to Bristol from the United States, bringing introductions from one of her former correspondents, the Rev. A. A. Livermore. The enthusiasm kindled by the Rajah Rammohun Roy flamed up afresh, and she threw herself with ardour into the intentions and prospects of a convert who seemed to have made a sacrifice which only found its parallel among the early confessors of the faith. To Mr. Livermore she expressed freely the hopes with which she was inspired.

TO REV. A. A. LIVERMORE.

Bristol, September 6th, 1860.

Now I am fully engaged in my life-work, for which all before seems to have been only a preparation. Much has been done, but very much remains to do, and we have to combat against spiritual ignorance in high places. All must be done in the spirit of our Master. Do not imagine that I have lost any of my interest in the subjects which once deeply occupied my mind—the Slavery Question, the Scriptures, Education—I am only obliged to make other things subordinate to the special work to which the Father has called me. I enclose an abstract of a paper recently read by me in support of the great principle for which I am labouring. It is a striking instance of the progress which is made in one important direction, that while the Scientific Association, when it met at Bristol in 1836, did not permit ladies even to be *present* at the meetings of the sections, in 1860 I should myself read a paper before one.

You have doubtless seen in the *Inquirer* or the *Christian Reformer* an account of the very interesting breakfast to commemorate the inauguration of Priestley's statue in the museum. I felt it a great privilege to be present, especially as my beloved father so greatly reverenced him.

I must now speak of Mr. G——'s visit to us, which has been most deeply interesting to all of us. Never before had I *seen* an instance of the wonderful power of Christianity to

bequeathed her enabled her afterwards to purchase the Red Lodge property, under the considerate arrangements made for the purpose by Lady Byron's will.

surmount all old prejudices of gross idolatry, influencing an individual literally to renounce all and follow Christ. His simplicity, unaffected manner, and genuine devotion to the cause of his Master, inspired us all with very warm interest in him and desire to help him. You will have seen a fair account in the *Inquirer*. How would my father have rejoiced to see the day when his pulpit should be occupied by one who reminded us of the early followers of the Saviour. The chapel was more crowded than I ever remember to have seen it, except when my father preached the funeral sermon for the lamented Rajah. It was very interesting at the evening meeting to see this young Brahmin surrounded by the white-headed ministers and fathers of our church.

From the midst of the new thoughts thus awakened, however, she was called away to the Glasgow meeting of the Social Science Association, where she read papers on the ' Principles of Education,' and on the ' Supplementary ' Measures needed for Reformatories for the Diminution of ' Crime.' On her way thither she spent a few days with her brother William at his summer home on Holy Island, Arran ; and after the meeting she· joined a little party for a brief excursion into the scenes of natural beauty which she loved as intensely as ever.

Bristol, November 1st, 1860.

I came back much strengthened and refreshed by my Scotch journey, which left treasures of visions of real mountains and lakes—the actual Loch Katrine, Ben Venue, etc., one has heard and thought of all one's life, and the Trossachs Vale—those glorious places ; three days almost as charming as our Wallenstadt journey ! I seem my old self in those places, and rush to my sketch-book, and am absorbed in my colours and in love with every bit of beauty as much as ever.

In Bristol she took up as usual the various threads of her work without delay; they were becoming more and more intricate, and could be handled by no other. Sometimes indeed she was only the glad spectator of the results she had helped to create; at other times she appears behind the scenes as the moving and directing power. Here is a Kingswood episode :

Red Lodge House, November 21st, 1860.

There was a great celebration at Kingswood Reformatory yesterday, very interesting: a harvest supper for the boys, with a meeting after; clergymen and others present; eighty boys in perfect order, and very good and happy. A wonderful change from eight years ago. Grains of true mustard-seed grow. . . . N.B.—Some people seem addicted to breaking the Ninth Commandment. The report is disseminated, in quarters fit to receive such, that the Bible is not used in Red Lodge.

A letter of the same date to her sister Susan gives a glimpse of the variety and press of her affairs.

TO MRS. ROBERT GASKELL.

Red Lodge House, November 21st, 1860.

So many days have come and gone without my writing to you as I intended! I have so many subjects on hand, each of which requires an entire devotion of thought. First, I must more or less regulate four households—Red Lodge, Red Lodge Cottage, Red Lodge House, and the Industrial. Then there has been a deputation to Sir G. C. Lewis, about Industrial Schools, which has required much time and thought. Next, Mr. Hill and I think we must have another Conference, to develop the principle which is so opposed by the Committee of Council—that children who cannot get Education ought to have Government help. This requires much thought, and will need more as the plot thickens. Then, innumerable miscellaneous businesses, which I keep aloof as much as I can, but must have some of them. Then, St. James's Back and Kingswood; when I am in each, I throw myself entirely into it. Then, Mr. G——'s being here is a new and interesting subject of thought. Then, I am not settled in a head-servant, but mean to persevere till I have a suitable one. Then, I do require a little rest sometimes, and my small child takes up a little time. So you will not wonder that sometimes I get through the day with difficulty, am thoroughly exhausted when I get home at night, get my supper and lie down in my comfortable bed, with thanks to the Heavenly Father for having given me strength for my day and sound sleep at night.

Not even all these occupations, however, wholly engrossed her attention. She had an eye upon Italy, with a look of reverence for its great Liberator. 'Does not that 'glorious Garibaldi take one back to the best of old times 'with the added lustre of Christianity! Just think of that 'fine old Cincinnatus going back to his little island! He is 'my one hero of the whole world!' And her gaze was extending itself further still. The time was coming for the departure of Mr. G——. She was engaged in devising the Christmas festivities of three schools; seventy presents must be bought for her girls; dinners must be provided for her poor families; this was the home view. Beyond that, the arrangements of the Conference on Ragged Schools to be held early in 1861 occupied her thought, as myriads of children—the paupers and criminals to be—arose before her from the courts and alleys of the cities of England. But beyond these again, lay a land of mystery, of which she had heard in her early womanhood, and of which, now nearly thirty years after, she heard again—there was India. The new year opened with visions from which she had once resolutely turned away. Now she might at least contemplate them, even if neither hand nor foot should be stirred to realise them. She had lived so long under the stern pressure of a daily routine, that the bare possibility of release came with an exhilarating pleasure, such as she had rarely experienced. Her whole being was more in harmony with itself, and life now seemed a blessing, containing a promise larger than she had ever dreamed. So she wrote of the young Brahmin to whom she had bidden farewell:

TO MISS SANFORD.

Red Lodge House, Jan. 18th, 1861.

His visit here has been a sort of romance to me in the midst of the great tension of the stronger and less poetic parts of my nature. . . . I find that all my old feelings and enthusiasms are as fresh as ever, only lying dormant or bottled up, as in the Arabian tales, waiting only to come forth in full vigour. And indeed it is well that they are generally imprisoned, for they sadly interrupt me in my work. . . . I have quite a vision of visiting India instead of the Holy Land, when my work is somewhat settled here. I should so delight to carry some help to the 'other sheep,' who are not of this fold, now such an opening has been made. And is it not strange, now that I am growing old, and comprehending the fable of the Sybil's book, and feeling every year now worth a whole decade of former years, I seem to want to have a glimpse of fresh life, without the shadow of death over it, which I am so used to now that it seems only natural. Just now, while in the midst of a very tough condensed address I am writing for this Conference, once for all telling my belief out plainly before the nation, as the spirit compels me to do, I went and opened my Spirit Pictures to see the date of your birthday, and if I had had time, should have melted to tears by the visions of past loveliness they opened to me.

The 'vision' of which Mary Carpenter spoke, had already indeed become a vow.

January 13th, 1861.—I here record the promise which I made to my young brother, that if permitted by the orderings of the Father I shall, as soon as my work here is in such a state that I can with safety leave it, say in about two years, go to India, and do all I can to help him and his wife [1] in their work for the Native women and girls, if possible establishing also the Reformatory principle in Calcutta. When he first came, I thought that I must never leave my children here. But I cannot be always with them; they must be prepared for the time when I shall be called home; it will be well to test my plans and principles while I may still return and correct errors. And the souls of those poor children are as precious to me as any others; 'other lambs I have which are not of 'this fold: and there shall be one fold and one shepherd.'

Such was the purpose which was formed in the opening of the year 1861. It seized upon her mind with remarkable tenacity. Not even the severe disappointment attending the frustration of her hopes concerning Mr. G—— could break it down. It was only that the time was not come yet; let the years go on bringing their appointed work; it might be two, or four, or even longer; if she was wanted, a way would be opened, and for that call she would wait. So she cherished her vow in secret, and turned to the next duty that lay before her. This was not far to seek.

The defeat of Sir John Pakington's motion for additional aid to Ragged Schools, in August, 1860, indicated that

---

[1] Mr. G—— was engaged to be married, but the engagement was afterwards broken off.

public opinion was not yet sufficiently awakened. Letters from Mary Carpenter, published in the *Daily News* and other papers throughout the country in the following autumn, did something to arouse further attention. But it was necessary to collect the scattered strength and organise the forces of the different workers, before any fresh influence could be brought to bear in Parliament. A plan was accordingly concerted with Mr. Hill, and proposals were issued for a third conference at Birmingham, on ' Ragged Schools in Relation to ' the Government Grants for Education.' A statement of principles was drawn up by Mary Carpenter, and widely circulated. Adhesions poured in from the representatives of numerous schools all over the country, members of both Houses of Parliament, magistrates, clergy, professional men, testifying to the wide-spread interest which the movement elicited. The basis was laid down in the following terms :

GENERAL PRINCIPLE.

The Welfare of Society requires that all its Members should be Educated.

Therefore,

It is the duty of the State, both as regards Society in general, and each individual composing it, to provide Education for those who cannot obtain it for themselves.

This duty is recognised by the State since it provides Education for those who are in Gaols and Reformatories, and therefore come compulsorily under its care, and for those who are thrown on Society for support, *i.e.* Paupers.

The same duty exists but has not been discharged by the State towards Children who are not as yet either Criminals or Paupers, but whose Natural Guardians will not, or cannot, provide for their Education.

It is an object of the Conference to lay before the Executive Government and the Legislature, as a consequence of the principle above stated, the imperative Duty of their providing Education for this portion of the community—

The Neglected and Destitute Children of Great Britain.

The Conference met at Birmingham on Jan. 23rd, 1861. At the morning Session, Sir John Pakington, the steadfast friend of Ragged Schools, took the chair. Papers were read by Mr. M. D. Hill and Mary Carpenter. The former dealt with the obligations of the State ' to ensure education for all

' children for whom their parents are through poverty unable,
' or through ignorance unwilling, to provide it.' The latter
was devoted to proof of the existence, in large masses, of the
class for whom Ragged Schools were designed, a demonstration that voluntary benevolence was inadequate to deal with
them, and an appeal for the restoration of the Minute of 1856
without the feeding and industrial grants. The following
words have not yet lost their force :

I believe, and even more strongly than I did when I made
the assertion to the Committee of the House of Commons,
nine years ago, that the children who grow up *untaught* and
uncared-for in our Christian and civilised country, do not
owe restitution to Society when they have infringed its laws,
which they have never been taught, or when they become
dependent on it for physical support, from never having had a
proper training of the powers which the loving Creator has
given them. I believe, as I did then, that Society owes restitution to them for having left them in this condition—passed
by, as it were, on the other side of the world's highway. And
I believe it now with an intensity which I could not then,
because I have for these nine long years been watching the
fearful odds with which these poor children are compelled to
fight the battle of life, who spring into existence in the midst
of the dense ignorance which I strove faintly to portray at the
outset. I have seen them—and many here present have seen
the same, and know it, and can testify it—when presented
with even ordinary advantages, but faintly supplying the bare
family blessings which the Father of all intended for his
children ;—I have seen them rise into an energetic intelligent
youth, and prepare to be worthy members of Society. Why
does Society leave millions of their fellows to perish, regarded
as the dregs of the population, unworthy of the boon of
education, but in reality immortal beings, children of one
Father, and heirs with Christ of eternal life ? Religion and
true political economy are not at variance, for both are founded
on the laws by which the All-wise Ruler governs the universe.
If a great duty is neglected, retribution will always follow.
Such *has* followed, and *will* follow as long as the evil continues; it rests as a blight on our country, and is felt in the
enormous expenditure of public money in our gaols and workhouses; nor will it ever be removed until the underlying
stagnant mass of corruption is cleansed and replaced by the
waters of life.

The racy eloquence of Dr. Guthrie added vivid illustration to this testimony, of which Canon Miller said at the

evening meeting, that it was 'read in a way to touch the
'heart of even the stoutest men, combining the essence of a
'most vigorous mind with the true pathos of a woman's
'tender feeling. That paper,' he continued, 'should be read
'by every man and woman in Birmingham ; and I only hope
'that, as was proposed this morning, when this matter is
'brought before the House of Commons, some one will make
'a motion that every member of that House, before he votes
'upon the subject, shall be compelled to read Miss Carpenter's
'address ; nay, more, that he shall be obliged to lay his hand
'upon his heart, and say upon his honour that he *has* read
'it.' (Cheers.)

The success of the Conference sent Mary Carpenter back
to Bristol with fresh hope, which brightened her lonely
house. 'Sometimes I do long,' she wrote early in February,
'for a little opening, of my deep heart's love ! But it will
'all be in its own time. You will read my paper with other
'feelings than common persons, for you will hear from my
'tones in uttering it that it was wrung out of my heart.' In
March Sir Stafford Northcote moved for a Committee of
Inquiry on the Education of Destitute Children, and Mary
Carpenter was summoned in June to give evidence. She
dwelt earnestly on the importance of recognising that there
was a distinct class of children who could not be sentenced
to Reformatory or Industrial Schools, and who would not go
to National or British Schools. In support of the beneficial
influence which might be exerted by Ragged Schools, she
produced a return from a police-court in the immediate
neighbourhood of the school in St. James's Back, showing a
gradual decline in the apprehensions of juvenile offenders
since the establishment of the school. She urged the
necessity of combining voluntary effort with Government aid
in schools for this particular class, expressed her preference
for free schools, inasmuch as the weekly payment of a
penny led parents to think the education thus purchased of
small value, and again concluded with the same request for
the restoration, under slight modifications, of the Minute
of 1856.

The subject was also brought before the House of Lords
by Lord Shaftesbury, but without immediate result. The
Report of the Committee, dated July 23rd, left the question
of Ragged Schools where it was. It recognised the benefits

they had conferred, but regarded them as chiefly impressed
with a missionary and religious character. It abstained,
therefore, from recommending further interference from the
Government than already existed.

Weary with delay and disappointment, Mary Carpenter
went over to Dublin for the meeting of the Social Science
Association. Before the proceedings began, she spent a week
examining the Prison system and institutions inseparably
connected with the name of Sir Walter Crofton. These had
already been brought under her notice at the Bristol meeting
of the Reformatory Union in August, 1856, by a communication from Captain Crofton, in which the principle
adopted in Dublin was set forth, viz. that ' a very large per-
' centage of criminals can by a system of Reformatory training
' introduced towards the termination of their sentences, be
' restored to the society they have outraged, as industrious
' and useful members.' The methods by which this principle
was carried out, Mary Carpenter now proceeded to study.
She found the general bases of action harmonise entirely
with her own ; and she was deeply impressed with the new
demonstration of their truth under conditions seemingly less
favourable, inasmuch as adults might seem more difficult to
influence than juvenile criminals. Her own experience,
derived from repeated visits to youthful offenders in English
gaols, enabled her at once to comprehend the superiority of
the Irish system ; and her sojourn in Dublin proved of great
advantage to her in leading her thoughts and interests into
a new though an allied branch of Reformatory work, the
results of which appeared in after years. Her papers at the
Congress were on familiar themes : ' The Application of the
' Principles of Education to Schools for the Lower Classes of
' Society,' ' The Connection of Voluntary Effort with Govern-
' ment Aid,' and ' What shall we do with our Pauper
' Children ? ' She had at any rate fresh audiences, even
though she had no fresh message to deliver, except in her
plea for pauper girls ; and she felt quickened by a new
sympathy from friends—among them the Baron von Holtzendorff—whom she now met for the first time. Her brief
holiday ended with a few days at Killarney in the company
of her brother Russell and his wife. There she renewed her
favourite occupation of drawing, and then came back to her

customary works at home, with added food for thought and
many treasured remembrances. ' All my sketches,' she wrote
to her late companion, 'give great satisfaction, and the
' Killarney ones are associated with a pleasing sense of
' gratitude to you for your kindness. My Irish visit
' altogether was the longest and pleasantest I have had for
' many years : I have also gained many new and important
' ideas, but feel more than ever the extreme danger of the
' Catholic hierarchy, tending to involve a nation in the worst
' possible way. The meeting of the Association at Dublin
' saved the Irish Convict system : Captain Crofton is now
' comfortably settled in again.' [1]

It was well for her that this time of refreshing had come,
for the summer had been a laborious one, and its toils were
not even yet over. At the time of the inquiry into the
education of destitute children another Committee was
engaged in investigating questions connected with Poor
Relief. Among the subjects thus opened up, attention was
directed to the condition of Workhouse schools. On the
general principles of their administration Mary Carpenter
had formed strong opinions. In the earlier days of the
Ragged School work she had visited the Union School near
Bristol, and some of her observations had been stated in her
books. She had not continued her visits, but her long
experience among the very poor had brought her into
constant contact with the system of the administration of
relief ; and she had arrived at the conclusion that the
system of pauper education, in particular, contained grave
and indeed ineradicable defects. This conviction she now
stated in evidence before the Parliamentary Committee. ' I
' conceive,' she observed, ' it is in the nature of children to
' be in a home, and to feel around them (as the Creator
' appointed) a family attachment and sympathy. I believe
' that it is especially essential to the nature of girls ; it
' is important for boys ; but it is particularly necessary for
' girls. Now Boards of Guardians have, as their chief aim,
' a desire to keep down the rates, and they are compelled to
' give necessaries to the children. The Committee of the

---

[1] Her observations during this visit were recorded in a series of
papers in *Once a Week*, which Sir Walter Crofton recently described
as ' a most graphic and faithful account of the system.'

' Council of Education undertakes to give education, and
' appoints certain Inspectors who can judge of that education,
' but no Government can give more than these two things,
' maintenance and education. No Government can induce
' that spirit which is necessary to enable instructors to go
' beyond their duty, to strive for the welfare of the child, to
' disregard their own comfort and convenience, and to devote
' themselves for the good of the child; to make the child
' feel the worth of his own soul, and perceive that he is a
' member of society. I conceive that those agencies alone
' will eradicate the pauper spirit from our population.'

It was in this spirit that the simultaneous training of
boys and girls had been commenced in Kingswood, and in
this spirit that the Red Lodge was made a true home for its
inmates. But Mary Carpenter felt that it could rarely exist
in Workhouse schools ; she had herself seen conspicuous
instances of its absence, and she boldly proposed to the
Committee that it should be made unlawful to take children into workhouses ; the management of pauper children
should be placed in the hands of a School Committee, to be
chosen annually by the ratepayers, and all schools intended
for pauper children should be certified as fit and proper by
the Secretary of State. For ' so great an innovation' she
only ' ventured respectfully to beg a hearing ;' but her plan
showed that her object was to avoid the baneful and
depressing influences of pauperism, and to provide a domestic
training instead of the machinery of a large institution. Many
of the remarks by which she supported her suggestions were
of a general nature ; some were founded on incidents in her
own work and the observation of past years. The Bristol
guardians, however, resented her criticisms on the previous
management of the Union, and severe resolutions of
condemnation were passed, with but one dissentient voice.
Rebutting evidence was tendered to the Committee, where
Mary Carpenter also offered to appear again and justify her
statements. This was not required of her; but she published
a pamphlet containing her paper on ' What shall we do with
' our Pauper Children ?' together with a ' Letter on the
' Charges of the Bristol Guardians ;' in which she vindicated
her position. The controversy died away, but not till it
had caused her a keenness of pain which seemed to some
disproportionately intense and long-enduring. She felt as

if the chivalry due to a woman had been outraged; and
her ties to Bristol were for a time loosened by what she
considered the ungenerous treatment of some of her fellow-
citizens.

Red Lodge House, Oct. 27th, 1861.

This year has seemed to me several. Ten years in my
early life were nothing to this one. Each month has seemed
to make me feel so much fuller of experience, and placing me
on a higher and higher standpoint. I have had the privilege
of feeling persecuted for the truth, though like all persecution
it was and is annoying to be dragged forward in the papers,
to be assailed by the whole body of Bristol guardians except
one. However, this very fact will draw attention to the
accompanying pamphlet, in which I have borne testimony to a
grand and solemn truth, which must ultimately prevail. I
believe that it will be of the greatest importance to the nation,
and understand somewhat the feeling of the martyrs in feeling
bound by the truth. The age seems rushing on with railway
speed. . . . In the meantime I have been able to draw a little.
Communion with nature in that way seems enjoyment of
my own personal life. Last week I was at Hardwicke, at
Mr. Baker's. He had assembled for the week a party of
between twenty and thirty managers, chairmen of quarter
sessions, prison directors, &c. It is curious how natural I
feel among them. The work has created a fraternity of
feeling.

The autumn deepened into winter, and the year seemed
to end in gloom. A series of resolutions issuing from the
meeting at Hardwicke Court brought imminent peril in her
eyes on the Reformatory cause, but she rallied others to her
support,—' a few faithful ones strove with me, and prevailed.'
A threatened lawsuit compelled her to purchase large premises
adjoining the Industrial School, and she found her possessions
and her responsibilities increasing against her will. ' It was
' necessary, so I do not repent. I am now making two
' cottages at the top of the Industrial Garden comfortable
' dwellings. I like producing order and beauty out of dis-
' order and chaos.' Across the Atlantic the impending
struggle in the United States excited her keenest interest.
In April she had written, ' The Northern States ought to be
' thankful to be freed from participation in iniquity. Mr.

'Lincoln's address was not true and clear. I hope that the 'Southern States will stand firm to their purposes, and show 'the world whether rebellion against the laws of God can 'prosper.' Now her utterance is sharper: 'How the 'Americans blind themselves! I shall never believe them 'till they proclaim liberty to the slaves.' Then there came upon her, as with a shock of personal sorrow, the death of the Prince Consort. 'Our poor dear Queen! When we 'saw her and the Prince together,[1] how little did we antici- 'pate this awful bereavement. Since we lost our mother I 'have felt nothing so much as this, except dear little M——'s 'death. It seems a deep personal grief, for I have always 'felt a warm sympathy with her beautiful domestic cha- 'racter.'

She poured out her thoughts after the fatal day in prayer for the royal widow : 'Give her still to us to be our ruler and 'the mother of her children.' The Christmas season was brightened by the presence in her home of one of her fellow-workers, who, three years before, had given her 'sore trial.' Now she could say, 'all evil has passed away; the good and 'true have remained, and the real friendship which was 'formed by working together for the lost ones. It was a 'blessed reward!' So with thanksgiving, and entreaty for the far-off 'Hindu brother' and the 'beloved and mourning 'Queen,' did the year whose 'events seemed to belong to 'two,' come to a close.

'I begin the year,' so runs the record of January 1st, 1862, 'without fear, prepared to do in the best way I can all 'I can, and to leave off when the Father sees the time fit.' Not many days went by, before the battle of the Ragged Schools had to be renewed. The Report of the Select Committee of 1861, issued on July 23rd, had left the Ragged Schools where they were. Six days afterwards the first edition of the Revised Code was issued, by which previous minutes were cancelled, including that of December, 1857, and all aid was cut off from schools in which the masters were not certificated, while an educational test was imposed on every child. Both these conditions were in the highest degree unfavourable to Ragged Schools. Few of such schools

---

[1] At Killarney, in the previous autumn.

could afford certificated teachers ; and even in these it was hard to work the wayward scholars up to the requisite standard. The new code, however, shadowed forth a clearly defined policy, and it was evident that it would be the ground of a Parliamentary campaign. In this the fate of the Ragged Schools would be one of the lesser issues; but it could not be neglected, and Mary Carpenter began to make her preparations. She drew up a letter to Lord Granville, in which she reviewed the history of the Government dealings with Ragged Schools, set forth the case of St. James's Back as a typical instance, and made an urgent appeal for the help which was now entirely withdrawn. This was signed by Mr. M. D. Hill and herself. Three days after she wrote to Sir Stafford Northcote : ' We tried not to ' come to open war with the Council, but Mr. Lowe has ' compelled us. Let them give us that Minute of 1856 with- ' out the feeding clause, and let it have a fair trial. . . . ' Truth and justice must prevail, but it is a hard struggle to ' contend with persons who are determined not to allow what ' is just.'

All over the country the provisions of the Revised Code excited eager discussion, and protest after protest was forwarded to Whitehall. Early in the Session certain modifications were announced by Mr. Lowe ; but these concessions appeared inadequate, and a series of resolutions was proposed by Mr. Walpole, which brought the whole subject under debate. Mary Carpenter found ample oppor-tunity for private advocacy of the children whose needs were so heavy on her heart. ' My present grand business,' she wrote, on March 13th, ' is of the unseen order, viz. working ' up an attack on the Council, and supporting the claims of ' the children in Parliament.' Ever and anon she could not help casting a glance on quieter scenes of labour, away from party strife, and in a note of the 23rd she uttered her longing : ' It is a privilege to be able to breathe consolation ' into the dying, and to sympathise with the spiritual nature. ' I often think with regret of the time when such was my ' privilege. Now I have rougher and tougher work. . . . ' My great anxiety now is to get some one to assert a broad ' principle in Parliament, including Ragged Schools.'

Meantime, with the watchfulness for every want which never relaxed, she sent off a box to Garibaldi, ' having heard

'from Mr. Partridge that it would be very acceptable. I feel
' it a privilege to belong to the century of one pure patriot
' such as he.'   A week or two later her interest in the Transatlantic conflict prompts new action. 'I have sent an offering
' to the Antislavery Bazaar, and a nice collection of things
' from the Red Lodge. I sympathise with genuine abolition-
' ists, and with anyone who keeps true to *the* cause, instead
' of worshipping the Union.'   April was passing quickly, and
the meeting of the Social Science Congress in London, during
the International Exhibition, was already in view.   Under
the pressure of work, her correspondence becomes almost
telegraphic in its abruptness. 'My time and thoughts are
' much taken up this week with the Education Minute ; then
' I must be preparing my papers.   I am asked to read one on
' the Education of Destitute Children at the " Bienfaisance "
' meeting.   Tennyson's opening lines are beautiful.   The
' Queen is a noble and lovely woman.'

     The first week in May ended for a time the struggle
which had been pursued with such tenacity.   Further
changes were announced in the Revised Code which were
accepted by Mr. Walpole ; but an attempt was made by
Mr. Walter to secure the benefits of the Government grant
to schools which could comply with the educational test,
whether the teachers were certificated or not.   Mary Carpenter
saw at once that if this restriction were withdrawn, one
obstacle in the way of such schools as that at St. James's
Back would be removed ; and she addressed a letter to
Mr. Walter, pointing out the benefits which his proposal
would confer on Ragged Schools.   The letter was read to
the House, and the very small majority—numbering only
seven—by which the motion was defeated, indicated that
the cause was not hopelessly lost.   No fresh action, indeed,
could be taken for the present ; but success appeared sure,
though it was still deferred.

TO REV. R. L. CARPENTER.

Red Lodge House, May 10th, 1862.

     Last week I got two mental loads off me : one, the *respon-
sibility* of the Industrial, being thrown on a very good committee, who met, ladies and gentlemen, and asked me to
continue my superintendence as heretofore; the other, the

debate in the House on Mr. Walter's motion, which proved
that the sense of the House is decidedly against the exclusion
of all teachers but certificated and pupil teachers from the
grants, which is the cause of the Ragged Schools not receiving proper aid. Now that Parliament sees through the matter,
and determined persons—not any of us—have taken it up, I
have no fears.

The meeting of the Social Science Association in June
brought Mary Carpenter to London, and she plunged for a
brief stay into all the excitements of an unusually busy
season. Papers on the 'Education of Pauper Girls,' and on
the 'Essential Principles of the Reformatory Movement,'
formed her share of the work of the Congress ; but she had
the opportunity of conference with fellow-labourers from all
parts of the country on the new topic of the Treatment of
Adult Prisoners, on which she had been pondering ever since
her visit to Dublin. The sojourn of Sir Walter Crofton at
Clifton in the autumn gave occasion for maturer consideration of the whole subject, and she resolved to devote herself
to the careful study of all its different bearings. A meeting
was summoned at Red Lodge, and plans were discussed.
'My mind,' she wrote in November, 'is now occupied with
'the Convict question, which is of surpassing importance.
'The Committee formed at our Red Lodge Meeting have
'met, and are preparing for action. I shall give myself up
'to this, and strive to keep clear of anything else. This
'and my own work are as much as I can do or bear.
'Anna has been working for Lancashire. I can *do* nothing
'but give a little money.' With this new interest she was
able to overcome in part the constant burden of sorrow which
she had long borne in secret ; painful associations lost their
sting ; bitter remembrances faded ; the sense of loneliness
was touched with a fresh pleasure in the varied intercourse
with high and powerful minds into which she was brought
more and more frequently ; and hope was clear and strong.
'Each month, each day, as it passes, seems richer than the
'last, and I feel life increasingly precious, far more enriched
'with talents to be improved to God's glory. I am Thine,
'O Father ! Do with me as seemeth to Thee best ! In
'prayer, as ever, I close 1862.'
This impulse of gladness carried her forwards through the
opening months of the next year. At the season for the

marriage of the Prince of Wales she followed all the details
of preparation with the most devoted interest. ' I hope you
' will be able to sympathise in the national joy of Tuesday.
' It is beautiful !　What a love that family has given to our
' country ! what a heart !'　The return of her birthday in
the spring brought with it only happy thoughts.　With the
habitual tendency of her inner life to dwell in the past, she
reminded herself that she had now reached the ' six years on
' the sunny side of fifty ' which was the age of Dr. Tuckerman
when she first knew him.　His form had of late been mingling
with that of her father in her nightly visions, which left
behind them a sweet sense of refreshment ; most of the
branches of her work were prospering, and she felt inwardly
at peace.　So the birthday record ran : ' I hardly dare give
' utterance, or even outward expression, to the grateful and
' joyful feeling which this day excites in my soul.　I dare
' not often " stand still and consider," lest I should be un-
' nerved for the work of life which the Heavenly Father
' graciously permits me to carry on.　But there ought to be
' moments when we look at our daily course from another
' standpoint from that in which we move, and the coming of
' such a day as this is one.'

　　Meanwhile she was busily studying the Convict question,
which involved her in constant correspondence ; but this was
laid aside for a time that she might bear witness to her
sympathy with the objects of her brother Philip, then actively
engaged in promoting emigration during the period of the
Lancashire cotton famine.　Her abhorrence of slavery rendered
her impatient of the conduct of those who had gained large
wealth out of the products of slave-labour, and led her to
include all masters in one general condemnation ; while, as
she looked across the Atlantic, she was equally unable to bear
the idea of war for the Union, though war for abolition
would have seemed less horrible.

TO DR. P. P. CARPENTER.

Red Lodge House, April 14th, 1863.

　　Thanks for your very interesting letter.　I am thankful
you are at your present post.

　　There can be no doubt that the present is a most' de-
moralising state of things, the evil becoming so gigantic that

it compels to seek a cure. I read with much interest the
report of the meeting, and viewed it as you do. But I take
people *at their word*, even if they do not mean what they say,
and make them keep it. The public does not yet know the
depth of the cotton lords. I doubt not that they can get
plenty of cotton to work up if they try. There is too much
stock still in their hands. I believe that the only thing anyone can do is to encourage emigration in every possible way,
and the production of cotton in our free colonies. This seems
to me the meaning of Providence. The wickedness of the
North, idolaters of their great idol, will compel us to that,
willing or unwilling. Every drop of oil or Christian love you
can throw in will have its value. But all should work towards
the grand end.

For this purpose money must be raised : and Mary
Carpenter and the sister by her side, who was her partner in
so many toils and anxieties, set themselves to their drawing-
boards, and spent happy hours among woods, and lakes, and
mountains. Contributions were invited from the schools,
where every occasion was seized for ' doing something for
' others. Our Red Lodge girls have subscribed ten shillings
' from their little earnings, and we are going to make up
' articles to put in the box for the emigrants. The Working
' Society has given ten shillings' worth, and the poor little
' Ragged School children made up a shilling in mites.
' Precious offerings ! '

The brightness of the spring, however, was soon overcast.
Troubles had ere this arisen at Kingswood, but she had
resolutely put them aside. Now her visits ceased to give her
satisfaction, and she became aware that she was regarded
with suspicion instead of the confidence which she had a
right to expect. Her share in the establishment of the school
was doubted, and she felt that she was needed there no more.
Distrust by her fellow-workers always caused her the most
acute anguish ; and she resigned her connection with the
place which owed its very existence mostly to her. The
wrench was severe, and all the memories of the past, thronging
in at this season, suddenly turned to gloom. Mental suffering
always reacted on her physical frame, which, with all its
vigour, sometimes lacked the power to sustain the violent
conflicts that went on within. She felt that illness was
hanging over her, but she had a new plan to develop, and
she would not give way. She had been engaged in sending

off to America a number of lads from the Industrial and the
Ragged Schools. The question was suggested, ' Why need
' they go, to secure a chance of getting on in life ? ' It was
the time when Working Men's Clubs were springing up all
over the country. Accordingly, the idea arose within her
mind of an institution which should be a centre of intellectual
interest and social pleasure for the young men who had passed
out of the schools into the activities and temptations of the
world. The scheme rapidly took shape ; she summoned to her aid
two or three gentlemen well known for their participation in
movements for the elevation of the labouring classes, and
invited eight of her old Ragged Scholars, ' most of them
' respectable married men,' to meet them at tea. ' It was
' most delightful to me to see this résumé of my labours in
' the Ragged School, from the first day when Griffiths gloried
' in being present—one of the first few—to a nice little
' fellow of fourteen whom I had as helper. Griffiths stared
' to find that the respectable discreet young man of twenty
' opposite him was the brother of the wild John Shaughnessy,
' and had been dragged into the school as a small creature by
' John. The plan was explained, some money was already
' promised, and the necessary measures were discussed.
' Henley, a regular rough Irishman, was astonished, saying
' he did not know that gentlemen cared for workmen.'

But the weary spirit sank before the next steps could be
taken, and action was deferred. For two months Mary
Carpenter lay prostrate, and strength only returned in September. Recovery advanced sufficiently to enable her to
prepare a paper for the Social Science Congress at Edinburgh ;[1]
and the fresh air of the North, and genial intercourse with
friends fitted her to resume her usual occupations. To these
she added a determination to write a treatise upon Convict
Discipline, but her materials for this were not yet ready, and
the preparation of the book was deferred till the next year. In
the meantime temporary premises were secured, and a little
Workmen's Hall was opened early in December. The year
had brought its deep trials ; much of it had been ' heavy and
' dark ;' but it left her ' in comparative peace and happiness,
' rejoicing in the establishment of yet one more means of use-
' fulness, and seeing as it were the child of her first-born.'

---

[1] On the Treatment of Female Convicts.

She had now laid out for herself two new tasks; and to these she considered herself pledged. Three years had gone by since India had been again brought within her view : it had never faded away, but remained as a background of radiant mystery to all her thoughts. In 1862 the visit of Mr. Rakhal das Haldar had brought fresh testimony to its needs ; and now with the opening of 1864, it seemed to utter to her a far-off call for help. Two gentlemen from Bengal, who were studying in London for the Indian Civil Service Examination (Mr. S. N. Tagore, and Mr. M. Ghose), came down to visit her, with introductions from her early friend Mr. Hodgson Pratt. She welcomed them with ardour ; they went with her to the grave of their great fellow-countryman, Rajah Rammohun Roy ; and out of her converse with them there grew a clearer purpose. They laid open before her the subject of female education, touched in their case with personal interest. At first she thought it might be possible to receive Indian ladies into her house. By-and-by she learned details about the condition of women, which convinced her that there was a vast field of new enterprise awaiting anyone who should go without prejudice or preconceived ideas. The suggestion naturally arose from her Hindu visitors that she should herself lead the way. She saw, indeed, that immediate departure was out of the question, but she was accustomed to waiting and to slow and silent approach to great ends ; and for her, as she once playfully said, as for Napoleon, the impossible did not exist. So she registered her intention in secret, that she might scrutinise it rigidly ere she proclaimed it.

January 12th, 1864.—I here record my solemn resolve that henceforth I devote my heart and soul and strength to the elevation of the women of India. In doing this I shall not suddenly abandon my work here which has long and deep claims on me, nor will I give it up until I have put it so far as in me lies on a firm and settled basis. I believe that it is come to a point at which this can be done. But I shall obey the remarkable call which has been given me so unexpectedly, which is in accordance with former deep feelings and resolves. Without any present and apparent change of plan, I shall watch openings, devote myself to perfecting my present work and bearing my testimony in my purposed book, gain information, and prepare in every way for my great object, going to India to promote the Christian work for the women.

The purpose thus set down, however, might after all be only the dream of a dissatisfied or dejected spirit ; and she would not speak of it till it was strictly tested and confirmed by further reflection, without the stimulus of the personal presence of the young men whose hopes and desires for their country had so profoundly moved her sympathy. A month later, therefore, she once more reviewed her position.

February 14*th*, 1864.—A month has passed since I made the foregoing entry. I have closely questioned myself, suspected myself of enthusiasm, of weariness of work, &c. &c.; but nothing has changed, but only confirmed, my strong and settled conviction that a new field is now about to open to me, one in which I shall seem especially to be working with my beloved Father, and in which the gifts which he gave me of mental culture will be especially useful; one in which my natural powers will have free scope. ' Other sheep I have ' which are not of this fold.' Now that my poor little forsaken ones are cared for here, I may go to the ' others ' and help them. . . . Should I never return, heaven will be as near to me from that region as from here.

From this time India was to be rarely absent from her secret thoughts. It blended in a singular manner to her the past and the future. ' Having them here,' she wrote of her visitors, ' has carried me back thirty years to Rammohun ' Roy and my father. Indeed, my own private life is ' chiefly in the past, with the beloved departed.' She loved to surround herself with outward memorials of the great and good whom she had known and revered. Tablets had been placed in the Red Lodge in remembrance of Lady Byron and her father. A tree had been solemnly planted in the Red Lodge garden, and an adjoining stone testified that it was to keep fresh the memory of the Prince Consort. Yet she never lost her interest in the large events which were passing around her ; and she required the presence of ideal elements to sustain her through the monotony of much weary toil. Free scope was now given to the visions of the future by the thought of India, for which she could privately prepare herself even amid the exacting claims of her institutions and her intended book.

The winter passed away quickly, though not without its

incidents of public gladness, which filled her with a pure personal happiness. 'Are you in spirits,' she wrote after the birth of the first child of the Prince of Wales, 'to share 'in the nation's joy at having their first baby? Dear little 'thing!' And a little while after : 'The Lodge and the 'Industrial had cake and holiday in compliment to "our 'baby." No one else seemed to think of him.' Next came the visit to England of Garibaldi, which raised her enthusiasm to its highest pitch. She desired intensely to see, to speak with him ; but the General's sojourn was abruptly cut short ; the stay at Clifton and at Exeter had to be abandoned ; and he only passed through Bristol, halting at the railway station. There a number of the chief citizens were gathered to give him welcome ; among them Mr. Commissioner Hill and Mary Carpenter. The mob, however, took the matter into their own hands, and swept over the platform, throwing all arrangements into confusion, from which Mr. Hill was with difficulty extricated. His immediate thought was for her ; and seeing her 'pressing towards Garibaldi's carriage, terrified 'lest she should be crushed,' he 'plunged after her into 'the crowd, and bore her off in safety. Unconscious or 'unmindful of her danger, she lamented a rescue by which 'she lost the chance of beholding the hero's face ; but '" when Mr. Hill himself called me back," she added, " I '" could not refuse to come." ' [1]

A letter of this date to her valued correspondent, the Rev. S. J. May, of Syracuse, U.S., gives a rapid survey of her interest in public affairs.

TO THE REV. S. J. MAY.

Red Lodge House, April 16th, 1864.

You have been very kind in sending us newspapers so frequently, and I must have appeared very ungrateful and forgetful of you not to have acknowledged them. The truth is that I have felt a difficulty in writing to my American friends, because I feared that I should hurt their feelings by my expressing to them what I feel about the enormous wickedness of this fratricidal war, this wholesale slaughter of their brethren. Great principles are not truly established by

[1] *Memoir of Matthew Davenport-Hill*, p. 448.

such means. I avoid studying the horrible details, but the
opinion and belief I had at the beginning is only confirmed
by every step that has been taken. I believe with Garrison,
and believe now, that the North *ought* to separate from the
South, and I believe that such separation will be the death-
blow to slavery, which has hitherto been supported by the
complicity of the North. I believe that every month that
this war goes on, is only entailing fresh evils on both States,
and strengthening the worst passions in both.

Now, having delivered this testimony, let me express my
warm sympathy with the blessed work which you are carrying
on, which will bless both those who give and those who
receive. Good seed is thus being sown, which must spring up
silently but surely, and bring forth good fruit.

As for ourselves, I need not speak of public matters, as
the newspapers tell you all. The state of the Continent is
very painful. The wickedness of Austria and Prussia is
perhaps no more than is to be expected from such sovereigns,
but I have great hopes that they will be stopped by the combined efforts of France and England. I have great confidence
in Lords Palmerston and Russell. Just at this moment
Garibaldi's visit absorbs public attention. Such a reception
is unparalleled anywhere, except by what I heard Dr. Tuckerman describe Lafayette as receiving in the United States. I
am proud of my countrymen for so honouring devotion to
country and simple goodness.

The spring was further gladdened by the renewal of her
former labours at Kingswood. 'Last Wednesday,' she wrote
on May 21st, 'I went over to resume my old visits. The
' boys were evidently so glad to see me, and remembered so
' wonderfully my old lessons, that I determined never to stay
' away again, unless compelled by illness.' Arrangements were
at the same time in progress for the erection of a Workmen's
Hall. A site had been procured in St. James's Back, close
to the Ragged School ; and there a commodious stone
building was rising among the crowded houses, to serve as a
centre of instruction for the more thoughtful, and of innocent
comfort and entertainment for all. Moreover, as if to leave
no branch of her work incomplete, she this year appointed a
' Children's Agent.' It was the Agent's duty to visit the
boys and girls who were discharged from the Industrial or
the Red Lodge Schools, and had obtained situations in
Bristol. For those who were homeless he found lodgings ;
for those who were out of work he sought employment ; he

acted often as visitor for the Ragged School, and carefully investigated the condition of special neighbourhoods and reported on them to Mary Carpenter. She was thus kept accurately informed of the proceedings of all the former inmates of the schools who remained within reach ; and this agency proved of the highest value in maintaining a vigilant watch over those who, but for it, might have sunk away into recklessness and vice. Only one part of her scheme was still unrealised. The Ragged Schools were still for the most part deprived of the benefits of the Government grant. A second attempt by Mr. Walter, in 1863, to secure grants to schools without certificated teachers, provided they could comply with the educational tests, was defeated ; and during the session of 1864 no further efforts were made. Mary Carpenter felt that her treatise on Convict Discipline required all her energies, and contented herself with 'bearing her 'testimony' again at York, where the Social Science Associa- tion met in September ; the subjects of her papers being the ' Non-imprisonment of Children,' and the 'Duty of ' Government to aid in the Education of Children of the ' Perishing and Neglected Classes.'

By the close of the year the new book was published, under the title of *Our Convicts*. Public attention had for some time been directed to the subject ; and the progress of legislation, during the very year which witnessed the appearance of the work, anticipated some of the criticisms which it contained upon the English system. Borrowing from the records of prison officials, and the police narratives of the daily papers, the author first described the actual moral condition of the convict class, and then proceeded to inquire what were the influences which produced the fearful moral degradation thus revealed, special stress being laid upon the facilities afforded by imprisonment for corruption and training in crime. The third chapter was devoted to an exposition of the principles of convict treatment, the chief of which was stated to be the necessity that ' the will of ' the individual should be brought into such a condition as ' to wish to reform, and to exert itself to that end, in ' co-operation with the persons who are set over him.' This, it was urged, can never be done by mere force, or by any mechanical appliance. But the possibility of reforming even the most hardened offenders was proved by the remarkable results attained by Colonel Montesinos at Valencia, by Herr von Obermaier at Munich, and by Captain Maconochie in Norfolk Island. How far, then, did the English convict system fulfil the conditions of true Reformatory discipline ? The answer was given in an elaborate inquiry, occupying the rest of the first volume, into the arrangements of various prisons, the disposal of criminals, tickets-of-leave, and, finally, transportation.

From the English convict system the reader was carried to Ireland, where the treatment of prisoners was founded on the same Acts, but had been carried out to very different results. Intermediate establishments were instituted between the prisons and the world. The freedom of agency of the inmates was gradually enlarged as they showed themselves deserving of trust, and strict supervision was exercised over those who went out on license. The details of this method were exhibited with convincing wealth of illustration. The history of the system was set forth ; and to the evidence of personal observation, and the witness of official reports, there was added the testimony of other critics from England, from the Continent, and from Canada, in its support. Was the Irish system applicable to women as well as to men ? The question was discussed in a chapter on Female Convicts, and after a contrast between the prison experiences on both sides of the Channel, it was unhesitatingly answered in the affirmative. In conclusion, various suggestions for improvement were laid down, including strict registration of criminals, greater certainty and uniformity of judicial sentences, cumulative sentences, and changes in the County Gaols in the direction of the principles of the Irish system, such as were already being carried out at Winchester and Wakefield. The next chapter, headed Prevention, afforded opportunity for a survey of the principal agencies available for the diminution of the causes of crime, such as temperance, the diffusion of pure literature, the improvement of the dwellings of the labouring classes. The most important, however, was education; which gave occasion for a review of the progress of Reformatory and Industrial Schools since the Conference of 1851, a plea for the separation of Pauper Children from Workhouse management, and a renewed appeal on behalf of Ragged Schools. Finally, in brief but earnest words, the co-operation of Society was invoked, and different channels for voluntary effort were marked out. 'Thus may all labour together, Government and people, for 'the regeneration of the misguided and neglected in our 'Country, and for the restoration to society of "Our '"Convicts."'

The preparation of this treatise, in the midst of other work, proved a severe strain on Mary Carpenter's strength. She closed the year thankfully, though she saw not any prospect of release from the claims which she had created around her, and the way which she had desired to India was not yet open. But as the months of 1865 one by one passed away, she became aware how much her powers were flagging, and she longed for some variation of scene and thought. It was evident, indeed, that her presence was still needed in Bristol. Early in March the new Workmen's Hall was opened in 'great state.' The arrangements of management soon, however, proved unsatisfactory, and the burden fell upon her and the two gentlemen who had throughout co-operated with her. Still she went on with her usual persistence, and a visit to London in the summer gave a momentary break to her routine. She was actively corresponding about Convict Discipline[2] and destitute children, but had vigour for nothing more. The brief notes of this period are in themselves evidence of her weariness : but fresh interests could still rouse her enthusiasm. 'I am *very* 'pleased,' she wrote to her brother Philip at the end of July, 'that Miss Martineau has written an article for the '*Edinburgh*.[3] I have sent two hundred copies to Mr.

---

[1] The work was received very favourably in England, and drew forth warm commendation from jurists in France, in Germany, and in the United States. An unexpected distinction came from Rome. 'I suppose you have heard of the great honour the Pope has done me 'in putting my books on the Index Expurgatorius! Miss Cobbe says '"The τὸ δέον is satisfied." It ought to be so.'

[2] Sir Walter Crofton writes : 'A very large share of trouble was taken by her in getting Refuges for Female Convicts established 'in England in 1865, by bearing testimony (her very favourite expres-'sion) both on the platform and in her writings to what she had 'witnessed in Ireland.'

[3] The article appeared in October, *Edinburgh Review*, No. 250. It gave Mary Carpenter much satisfaction, and Miss Martineau was in her turn pleased at her correspondent's pleasure.

' Sanborne, in Boston, U.S. He is going to take it up
' thoroughly. Dr. Colenso has sent me his fifth Part in
' return for the *Convicts*, and I am delighted with the preface
' and conclusion. I do not mind about the Creation being
' cut up, and I think in general the light he throws helps one
' out of difficulties and contradictions which I have felt as
' well as the Zulus : but I do not mean to read anything
' against that exquisite narrative of Joseph. I had an hour's
' chat at Miss Cobbe's with the Bishop, and was *much*
' delighted with him and his work, to which I am glad he is
' returning.'

She was busy at the same time in forwarding further help
to her American friends. President Lincoln's address on his
re-election had excited her warm admiration, and the assassina-
tion which followed smote her with horror. She saw very
clearly that the difficulties were not over, and in a letter to
the Rev. S. J. May, on the death of his wife, she thus uttered
her forebodings and her hope.

TO THE REV. S. J. MAY.

Bristol, June 5th, 1865.

The same *Inquirer* which contained the mournful announce-
ment of your loss, brought also the report of the meeting at
which you gave the important vote for the *non*-dissolution of
the Antislavery Society. The work is not done as long as
the equal rights of man, irrespective of colour, are not
acknowledged and protected by the Union. They are not
acknowledged yet, and if this opportunity of establishing
them is lost, the seed will remain of another fratricidal war.
The Constitution is not yet clear of slavery, for the Amendment has not been ratified. Until 'all men are free and
' equal' in the United States, they will not be entitled to the
respect of free nations. No individual State must have power
to rebel against God by scorning his image in man, whether
black or white. The blacks must have suffrage equally with
the whites. I trust that Wendell Phillips will never rest till
this is made a fundamental law of the Union.

We are working zealously in Bristol for the Freedmen.

But these thoughts only rippled the surface of her life.
Its hidden depths were still darkened with the melancholy
feelings which always came over her in bodily weakness.
She had planned a work on ' Our Children,' in which she

would discuss the relation and consequent duties of the State to them, but she felt quite unequal to the attempt to write it.   She believed she had made all the efforts in her power for securing proper legislation, and she thought it would be well for her institutions to learn to do without her guidance. In her enfeebled condition she had relinquished the immediate prospect of a visit to India, and had projected a journey to Italy, where she hoped to interest herself in the schools of Naples, the needs of which had been brought before her. She cared not for a tour of pleasure : she had been so long familiar with great objects that she could not travel without something more than a personal end ; and in the same breath that she declared her work to be 'naturally repugnant' to her, she affirmed her incapacity to go anywhere where she could not carry it on.   'I, too, am beginning to feel a strong ' wish for an entire change, if I am to shake off mournful ' remembrances, and live a fresh life *with* the present genera- ' tion, and *for* the future.'   Such was her desire as the summer passed away.   A Social Science Congress could not deal with this want, and she came back from the Sheffield meeting[1] in October still hungering for the new impulse which she could not impart to herself—it must come from without.

At one time it seemed as though it might come from America.   In the spring she had been busy preparing articles and drawings for the Freedmen's Aid Association.   A visit from Dr. E. S. Gannett and his son W. C. Gannett from Boston, in the autumn, gave further openings for Antislavery work.   'My Antislavery interest is half a century old,' she wrote in November, 'and cannot die out while anything can ' be done.'   The inquiries excited by her book in the United States led her to think that a sojourn in New England and in Canada might enable her to further the principles of reformatory treatment, and 'establish valuable connections ' and points of influence.'   Moreover, the removal of her brother Philip to Montreal diminished the barrier of the ocean, and assured her of a home, and the sympathy for which she craved.

---

[1] Her papers were on ' The Consolidation of the Reformatory and ' Industrial Schools' Acts ; ' and ' Our Neglected and Destitute ' Children—are they to be Educated ? '

But she was not long left in doubt about her way. Her former visitor, Mr. M. Ghose, with two other Hindu gentlemen, came down to Bristol at Christmas, and her conversations with them resulted in the conviction that at last the time was come.[1] It was as though a sacred trust were laid in her hands. Her whole being rose to meet it. Strength began to return ; she looked younger as the flush of new hope passed over her countenance. In solemn words she unfolded the secret of her heart.

January 8th, 1866.—A grand and new life appears opening upon me. Heavenly Father ! by tokens drawn from the marvellous workings of Thy providence, I believe that Thou hast destined for me the unspeakable privilege before leaving this world, of going to our distant India, and there working with the spirits of my beloved father and the noble Rajah for the elevation of woman, and perhaps also for the planting of a pure Christianity. Thou knowest, O Father ! that I have never withheld anything from Thee, since first I offered to Thee and to Thy work unreservedly all my powers and myself. A high reward this will be, if Thou bestowest upon me this privilege ! But if Thou has ordered it otherwise, I shall still know, O Father ! that thou hast accepted the offering.

It was natural that those around her should be at first alarmed at her undertaking. She would be in her sixtieth year ; her constitution, it was feared, had been impaired by severe illnesses ; no relative or friend could accompany her; and the imagination of love easily conjured up a thousand possibilities of harm. Then there were her institutions, for which she had made herself responsible to Government and the public, and to which so long an absence might prove seriously injurious : and the known value of her labours at home seemed far to outweigh the exceeding doubtfulness of success amid conditions so novel.[2] India—with its vast area, its teeming population, its multitude of languages and customs, its diversities of race, of government, and of

---

[1] How readily such a step might suggest itself, was shown by the exclamation of a lady who knew Calcutta well, to whom Mary Carpenter introduced her visitors : ' Oh, that you could go to India— ' you are just the person to help the ladies ! '

[2] In February she was in London on business for ' neglected ' children ;' but all that she heard there only changed her ' visions ' of India into a ' delightful anticipated fact.'

religion,—what could one woman do for more than a hundred million of her sex? It were fruitless now to reckon the objections which arose upon all sides. They tried her sorely, and, in the continuous strain of thought and feeling, were almost more than she could bear. She concentrated herself with passionate desire upon this one thing, till dissuasion seemed to her like personal antagonism. 'Don't write any-'thing but sympathy to me,' she pleaded; 'I have always 'hitherto been led aright, and never did I see such reason for 'my course as now, or such hope. If I neglect such an 'opening for good, I should feel sinning against my conscience 'and inner light.' Her trust was founded where she could show it to few, perhaps to none, as she realised it; others who only saw her position from the outside, could never know why she was impatient of the affectionate counsel which poured in upon her.

Sunday, March 11th, 1866.—O Father! my heart is fixed. In the deep recesses of my heart I feel Thee leading and guiding me. No unbelief of others, no difficulties, no opposition can remove from me the faith, that having used the best powers Thou hast given me to discern what it is that Thou willest, the many remarkable signs and tokens Thou hast given me, and the deep convictions of my spirit, all lead me solemnly and decidedly to resolve to follow what appears to me Thy pointing, and to go to carry Christian sympathy and help to Thy distant children in India, especially those of my own sex.

By way of preparation, and as a signal of the spirit which she desired to infuse, she drew up a narrative of the *Last Days in England of the Rajah Rammohun Roy,* intended especially for his countrymen. By inviting attention to his aims, she hoped the more easily to secure a hearing for her own; she only desired to carry back to his country something of the stimulus which she had received from him more than thirty years before. She was to sail in September, with the escort of Mr. M. Ghose, who was returning to India to practise at the bar. The summer was busily occupied with the necessary arrangements for the conduct of her several institutions. But she found opportunity to criticise the Industrial Schools Act, which gave permanent force to some of the temporary provisions of the Act of 1861; and she

drew up a paper for the Manchester meeting of the Social
Science Association, on the 'Nature of the Educational Aid
'required for the Destitute and Neglected Portion of the
'Community, in connection with Free Industrial Schools;'[1]
while she at the same time responded to the request of Sir
Walter Crofton, who was preparing an address for the same
occasion, on the 'Treatment of Life-Sentenced Convicts,' and
forwarded him a detailed statement of her views on the
subject. One more institution was still to owe its origin to
her. Not boys alone needed the training provided by
Certified Industrial Schools. Accordingly, shortly before
quitting Bristol, she invited to her house a number of ladies,
among whom were some of her fellow-workers in the Ragged
School and other undertakings, and laid before them a plan
for the establishment of a Girls' Industrial School. 'I said
'to them,' she afterwards related, with a touch of the quiet
humour which so often brightened her discourse, 'I said to
'them, "This must be done, and you are to do it." And
'they did it!' A Committee was formed; a house was
taken; the school was opened, and has been successfully
continued ever since.

She could not, however, escape the urgency of friends,
who little understood how much disquiet their apprehensions
caused her ; and so, when any word reached her of sympathy
and encouragement, it was welcomed at once with eager
delight. Among the letters of June came one from the Rev.
Charles Wicksteed, whose sister-in-law, Miss Matilda Lupton,
had been one of Mary Carpenter's pupils in the old days.
This drew from her the following reply.

TO THE REV. CHARLES WICKSTEED.

Bristol, June 8th, 1866.

Matilda was quite right ! On reading the first sentence of
your letter, without seeing the signature, I was going to throw
it aside, anticipating some of those kind expressions of anxiety
which are most dispiriting to me. As I proceeded, however,
I perceived that my correspondent entirely comprehended

---

[1] In this paper she expressed herself as unfavourable to compulsory attendance ; friendly effort must bring the reluctant children,
and she gave some valuable particulars of the success of the
'Children's Agent' in Bristol.

the position, and my motives in going. Before Mr. G——
left us, I had formed the solemn resolve to devote myself to
the elevation of Indian women in any way I could, and to go
out if permitted. The permission has come, it seems to me,
in my restored and remarkably established health, the only
changes being the surmounting of the excitability of my temperament, and the necessity for heat!—in the position of my
work here, every branch here having borne the test of experience, and having been satisfactorily arranged for in my
absence,—and in the fulness of time being come for India. In
Bombay, as you state, the Parsees are awakened, and are
actually establishing good schools in concert with English
ladies. I therefore do not propose staying long there, but
have a promise of welcome from Sir Bartle Frere, the Governor,
and Mr. Cursetjee, who is now returning with his daughter.
In Calcutta many of the Theists, at least all whom I have
seen here, are more than three-quarters Christians, in fact, I
tell them I reckon them Christians, for they hear nothing
they object to in Lewin's Mead. They have, after coming
to England, an intense feeling about the elevation of their
countrywomen. They have an extreme prejudice against
'Christian converts,' and the orthodox missionaries, male or
female in general. I have their full confidence and friendship,
because they see that I have no proselytising objects, and treat
them as friends and equals. I have, therefore, a peculiar
talent granted me; and as I tell them that I go simply to show
my sympathy, and to use my experience in any way that can
help them, they will cordially co-operate with me.

To this may be added another note, three weeks later.

TO THE REV. CHARLES WICKSTEED.

Bristol, June 29th, 1866.

You can hardly tell how much comfort and help your
words of sympathy and *belief* have given me. Friends who
do not comprehend my object, or know my grounds for encouragement and hope, are naturally anxious; but I am happy
to say that those to whom I have been able to explain them
are quite satisfied that I have a 'call' which I am not at
liberty to disregard. I myself am so perfectly convinced that
my going is not only a duty, but a high and crowning privilege of my life, to which every gift that God has given me is
worthily consecrated, that whatever the *apparent* result of my
journey, which will probably be *very* small, I shall feel certain
that results *will* arise, and fruit ripen from the seed sown, even
' after many days.'

The time for her journey was now drawing near. Mary

Carpenter had never been careful about her personal equip-
ment, and it was a new thing to her to be the centre of
affectionate preparations for outfit, and to receive the little
gifts for comfort and convenience which her friends devised.
She had a simple gladness in it which she expressed as frankly
as her conviction that she was but obeying a ' call ' which she
might not disregard.   ' I have plenty of things which gene-
' rally lie dormant,' she wrote to her brother Russell.   ' This
' will be the great event of my life, and I feel some female
' weakness in my pleasure in looking at my things all getting
' ready and looking nice.'   She anticipated with delight all
the associated interests of her journey, as ministering to its
main end.   ' Think of me on the Mediterranean and the Red
' Sea,—Sinai in sight—and sketching at Elephanta.'[1]   August
ran on.   She was to leave home on its last day ; her brother
William was to take her to Paris, and, with her love of anni-
versaries, she noted with peculiar satisfaction that she would
be there on the birthday of the dear father who had escorted
her thither on her previous visit nearly forty years before.
The strain of gratitude rose higher and higher in her heart,
as she beheld the consummation of long desire at last close at
hand.   What she could do might be very little, ' nothing
' visible to the eye of man,' but it would be ' *something* for
' the sisters that sit in darkness in India.'   The spirits of her
beloved seemed as a glorious company around her, cheering
her on ; they would be as near her there as here.   So the
last visits were paid to the schools ; the last farewells were
said to friends and kin ; and in the stillness of the midnight
watch, ere the dawn rose on her departure, Mary Carpenter
solemnly committed herself to God.

August 31*st*, 1 A.M.—Blessed Heavenly Father! I thank
Thee for all Thy blessings, and that thou enablest me to go
forth with a strong and courageous heart to my distant enterprise. I thank Thee that Thou hast made all things so wonderfully to unite and show me that this is the fulness of time.   I
thank Thee for all the affection and loving-kindness of my
friends, and their prayerful sympathy.
     For all I bless Thee, O Father!
     Be ever near me! Amen.

---

[1] One friend had urged her to go or to return by Palestine.   ' I
' told him that all my strength must be for India ; that will henceforth
' be my Holy Land.'

'Is it for human will
To institute such impulses?—still less,
To disregard their promptings!   What should I
Do, kept among you all; your loves, your cares,
Your life—all to be mine?   Be sure that God
Ne'er dooms to waste the strength he deigns impart!
Ask the gier-eagle why she stoops at once
Into the vast and unexplored abyss,
What full-grown power informs her from the first,
Why she not marvels, strenuously beating
The silent boundless regions of the sky!
Be sure they sleep not whom God needs!   Nor fear
Their holding light his charge, when every hour
That finds that charge delayed, is a new death.'

Robert Browning.

CHAPTER VIII.

INDIA.

1866—1870.

On September 1st, 1866, Mary Carpenter left England for Paris, with her eldest brother, Dr. W. B. Carpenter. She was full of gladness that the hour was come, and threw herself into each new experience with almost the zest of youth. Such a holiday she had not had for more than thirty years; for the last season of foreign travel in 1842 had been devised as an escape from a burden of sorrow which she had not then learned to transform into a permanent inspiration; and Paris she had not seen since her father had accompanied her thither in 1829. So she drove along the Boulevards of the French capital with the memories of a previous generation in her heart, and yielded herself to the rush of fresh impressions which blended so strangely with the visions of her girlhood. 'I am filled with wonder and admiration at the place,' she wrote to her sister Anna, 'with the marvellous contrast of 'the old Paris which you and I used to wander in, and the 'magnificence of the new parts. . . . I left London with 'very happy thoughts, remembrances, and hopes for the 'future. . . . Our father's birthday is very happily spent 'by me in the beginning of my work.'

Then came the voyage along the Mediterranean, with still waters and moonlit heavens of exceeding glory, which brought rest after the fatigues of departure, and a sweet sense of peace beneath Divine care. Now it was the splendour above her and around that fascinated her : 'The night

' before, I saw what was a new and wonderful sight to me,
' the Milky Way descending to the horizon and reflected in
' the water. . . . The sunset this evening was glorious.
' The cloudless sky let the sun drop beneath the waves as a
' fiery ball, only leaving a red tint round that part of the
' horizon, when the bright reflection in the water was gone.
' The white pathway on the waters contrasted beautifully
' with it.' Her travelling companions—Mr. Ghose and two
young ladies (one of whom was returning to her home in
Calcutta)—brought her pleasant intercourse ; to one who was
desirous of studying the New Testament in its original language she began to give lessons in Greek, writing out the
Beatitudes one morning from the precious little volume—her
father's gift—which she always carried with her ; while the
presence of several members of the Indian Civil Service gave
her ample occasion for prosecuting inquiries on the subjects
of chief interest to her.

Sunday, September 9th.—Much pleasant conversation with
different gentlemen, Anglo-Indians, about India. I was struck
with the different views they express, according to the position
they hold. One who is Secretary of Public Works at Lahore
speaks very favourably of the better class, and they all seem
to feel that my visit will be useful : of this I am more and
more persuaded from all I hear from Mr. G. and others. The
great thing now is to know the Native families, ascertain their
wants and feelings, and then help them in their own way. Of
this I shall have opportunities which have hardly been possessed by anyone before. Service again in the evening. The
ship's servants all looked so very Sunday-like in their blue
jackets and clean white trowsers. They formed a good band,
and it was very home-like singing ' Glory to Thee ' here on the
Mediterranean.

As the travellers passed from Alexandria to Suez, thoughts
of St. Paul gave way to visions of the march of Israelites ;
and a handful of sand was hastily caught up for the children
at home. The glow that rested on the mountains seemed to
be reflected in Mary Carpenter's very soul, as she found
herself on the Red Sea, and beheld afar off the summits of
the Sinaitic range. Each day that carried her nearer to the
goal brought some fresh strength of conviction, opened some
new path of hope. Yet her high enthusiasm was carefully
tempered by a consciousness that she would be in a strange

land, where preconceived ideas must be laid aside. She was anxious to avoid the semblance of going out with any fixed plan. She desired to see and judge for herself; her first purpose, therefore, was not to teach, but to learn. ' Be sure ' not to let it appear '—so she had written some months before to a Hindu gentleman in England—' that I am going in the ' expectation of accomplishing any great things. I am going ' only as a token of warm sympathy in your work for your ' countrywomen, to gain such comprehension of the position ' as may enable me to be of future use, and to do anything I ' can, and which is desired from me.' Again and again, in letters to her Native correspondents in India, did she reiterate this warning. To testify her deep interest and goodwill was in her eyes sufficient justification for her journey; to visit the land of Rammohun Roy, and perhaps win the confidence of some who spoke his language, that she might inspire them with his aims, would be reward enough.

But this narrower scope was soon enlarged; opportunities which she had not sought were freely given her, and her judgment was invited upon questions which she had had no intention of discussing. She brought with her introductions from Lord Cranborne,[1] Lord Stanley, Sir George Grey, and Miss Nightingale; but her friends in India had already communicated with Sir Bartle Frere, then Governor of the Bombay Presidency, whose kindness at once secured for her more abundant help than she had ever looked for. Sir Bartle Frere was himself at Poona when Mary Carpenter arrived, but he placed his marine bungalow at her disposal on landing; and there, under a shady verandah looking out upon the sea, she received her first impressions of Indian life from the visitors who streamed in upon her. Soon, however, intimation reached her that her attention must be directed to subjects far beyond the range she had marked out for herself. A letter from the Secretary to the Government was placed in her hands, enclosing a copy of instructions which had been forwarded to the heads of various departments for education and prison discipline. ' On questions connected with these ' and other cognate subjects '—so ran the circular—' I am ' desired to state that Miss Carpenter's opinion has, for many ' years past, been sought and listened to by legislators and

---

[1] Marquis of Salisbury, then Secretary for India.

' administrators of all shades of political opinion in England ;
' and his Excellency in Council looks forward to her visit to
' Bombay as likely to be of great public benefit, by aiding in
' the solution of many problems with regard to which much
' has yet to be learnt in India, from the results of late
' European inquiry and discussion.' A vast field of work
was thus at once opened before her, from which it was not in
her nature to draw back. It was with regret that she found
herself involved in fresh responsibilities, but she could not
pass them by ; and she wrote to England at once for copies
of Acts of Parliament, Reports of Schools, and other items
of Reformatory literature, that she might justify her future
recommendations by appeal to facts at home. In the meanwhile she proceeded to carry out the first part of her programme by visiting Mr. Satyendra Nath Tagore, then assistant
Judge at Ahmedabad. To this city she repaired at once,
without further residence in Bombay, and there she plunged
into active investigation of the social needs which she had
come to comprehend.

TO MRS. HERBERT THOMAS.

Ahmedabad, October 12th, 1866.

Last week I obtained most valuable information by the
study of the different Government institutions of this place,—
prisons, hospitals, lunatic asylums, schools, normal training
institutions. As they may be regarded as a favourable type
of the general system adopted, and as I have at the same time
been closely studying Native characters and wants, I have
thus gained an insight into the condition and wants of India
which I could not have got in any other way. I feel that this
fortnight since my arrival has been worth my journey out,
not to speak of the marvellous change and break in my life
which this new world has given me. How often do I wish
that you could peep in on me, as when yesterday we were
fording a river in a bullock-cart, or walking round the tank of
an ancient mausoleum with three bare-footed Indian ladies,
toe-ringed as well as ear-ringed; or when, riding in Mr.
Tagore's stylish carriage (with coachman and footman in red
turbans) through a sandy road bordered with high cactuses,
we came upon a string of camels ; or when, returning from a
visit to some schools, we met three carts, on each of which was
a tiger standing like a lamb held by a cord.

Her rapidity of observation and keen susceptibility to
every new impression—whether of character, of social
circumstance, or the outward surroundings and the scenery
in which they were set—brought her unmingled delight in
the infinite variety of Oriental life. What she had not
time to record in letters or diaries, which became briefer and
briefer as the business of each week increased, was stored in a
memory well trained to accuracy; and the few hours she
could seize here and there from inspection of institutions,
or from conference with English or Native gentlemen, were
given to the sketching which served as an outlet for her
deep joy in the new beauties so much transcending the
visions she had formed. For this, however, there was but
little opportunity; and she felt herself obliged to relinquish
the ordinary enjoyments of travel, that she might devote
herself with the less interruption to the objects which she
had chosen. The history of India, whether ancient or
modern, the successive phases of its religions, the existing
forms of its worship, the ceaseless difference of its races, its
languages, its manners—these she was compelled to ignore;
she could at first think only of its women, and to these were
soon added its prisoners and its youthful criminals.

It was in Ahmedabad that the lines of her future work
were first shaped out. She was aware, in general terms, of
the difficulties which stood in the way of Female Education
in India. Whatever precedent ancient tradition might yield
to justify Hindu women in aiming at a high standard of
culture, it remained unquestionable that they made no
attempt to do so now. Only here and there were there a
few earnest hearts who were beginning to desire it. The
great mass of Natives were unwilling to take any steps
which might involve departure from deeply rooted customs;
and the unique intermingling of social and religious usages
rendered any variation in the one almost equivalent to an
attack upon the other. The universality of the practice of
early marriages had as yet scarcely awakened a protest: and
it appeared to place an almost insuperable bar to further
progress. Education after marriage could only be continued
in the Zenana, where few could afford to pay for the special
instruction which was required, and fewer still would run
the risk of the introduction of religious influences of which
they profoundly disapproved. Before marriage—how far

could the education of a child be carried, who might be
withdrawn from school at the age of ten or twelve? These
considerations had been placed before Mary Carpenter,
whose chief idea was to induce if possible some young Native
ladies to return to England with her, perhaps to reside in
her house, at any rate to be under her general care. Two
or three weeks in India sufficed to dispel this plan. She
found a condition of society entirely unripe for such strong
measures. The visits which she received from Native ladies,
and the visits which she paid to their homes, revealed at
once the impossibility of thus attempting directly to engraft
English culture straight upon Hindu family life.

If help was to be given, then, it must be rendered in
other ways. These were not long in presenting themselves.
She had not been more than a day or two at Ahmedabad,
before she was conducted over a girls' school founded by a
wealthy citizen, and maintained by his widow. Some
eighty children from six to eleven years of age were seated
on the benches. Wealth and rank were indicated by the
abundance and costliness of their ornaments. Some of the
elder classes were examined, their needlework was inspected,
and Mary Carpenter then turned to inquire for the
mistress. There was none. The classes were entirely
conducted by male teachers. It scarcely needed further
reflection to suggest to her what was at any rate one
obstacle in the way of female education. At the top of
the school, girls who arrived at marriageable age had to be
withdrawn; while in the younger ranks the best methods
of engaging the interest, and exciting the nascent powers,
of those who would in England receive their training in
infant schools, were very imperfectly understood. Whatever work, then, was to be done for female education, must
be done, for a time at any rate, in India itself. The special
direction which effort must first take was the awakening of
public opinion to the urgent need of gradually bringing
trained female teachers into the schools. And this led as
a necessary consequence to the consideration of the means
for securing the proper training for such women as might be
found willing to undertake this new labour, in other words,
to the possibility of establishing a Female Normal School.

A brief sojourn at Surat on the way from Ahmedabad
to Bombay afforded her opportunities for further discussion

of this plan with English and Native gentlemen, either
actively engaged or warmly interested in education; and by
the time she returned to Bombay, her objects had become
more and more clearly defined.

Bombay, October 22nd, 1866.

My visit to Ahmedabad gave me an insight into Native
character and wants, and possibilities and impossibilities,
which nothing else could have done. Everything is very
different from what we have an idea of in England. The
experience and knowledge I have already gained is most
important, and will enable me to help them in future. What
I came expecting to do—*i.e.* bring home some young girls—I
find *quite* fallacious. It would not be of the least use as things
are; while the great want is to train female teachers, as there
are none to be had in Guzerat, and probably elsewhere, for
Government girls' schools; and men (!) teach them. To
organise, bring before the Government, and get this carried
out, is my work now for the female schools. In other departments, especially prison discipline, there are very important
matters to be attended to.

These ' important matters' related to the condition of
the gaols which she had already examined, and the facts
which she had learned from published reports and conversation with prison officials. Some of the Indian journalists
who were unaware of the long experience she had had, and
the careful study she had devoted to the treatment of
convicts, expressed from time to time mistrust of conclusions
which appeared to them hastily reached, and too confidently
enunciated. But the labour of twenty years had borne in
upon Mary Carpenter's mind certain principles which she
now regarded as axiomatic. All systems of prison discipline
must be founded on them; they were the tests by which
every existing organisation must be tried; and with the
weight of English, nay, of European opinion behind her,
she did not fear to lay them down as the methods which
must be followed in every attempt of reformation. It was
no new thing for her to visit gaols, and she was trained in
judgment which not all the fresh conditions and unfamiliar
circumstances of India could lead far astray. ' She had

'been so accustomed,' writes Sir Walter Crofton, 'to throw
'her whole mind into the consideration of a subject in which
'she was interested, that I was not surprised to find how
'rapidly she could form her opinion as to the tone of even
'a large prison, before she had exchanged a word either with
'the prisoners, or the official staff,—her examination of
'countenances and manner, which illustrate the tone of an
'establishment, was so minute and thorough.'

Now the essential requisites for a good prison included,
in Mary Carpenter's view, the provision of separate sleeping-
cells, to avoid the corruption which is inevitable when
several prisoners are locked up together for twelve hours;
instruction by a trained and efficient teacher; the adoption
of a progressive system of classification; and the appointment
of female warders to take charge of the women.   Whatever
other conditions might be desirable, these were indispensable;
but they were not to be found in the first prisons which
she visited at Ahmedabad and Surat, nor even could they
be numbered among the improvements effected by the sheriff
at Bombay.   By the side of the need of Female Education,
therefore, there rose the urgency of Prison Reform; and,
after a short stay in Bombay, Mary Carpenter started for
Poona, to confer with Sir Bartle Frere and with the
Director of Public Instruction, Sir Alexander Grant.   It
was her hope that the Government of the Presidency might
be able to carry out the plans which she advocated.   But
she soon learned that the changes which she desired, and
the new institutions for which she pleaded, would require
a higher sanction.   Only the Supreme Government could
grant the needful outlay, and give to the purposes of
benevolence the authority of law.   Once more, therefore,
after a round of visits at Poona, she returned to Bombay, to
set off without delay for Calcutta.

Railway communication across the Indian Peninsula
not having been then established, the route lay through
Calicut, Beypoor, and Madras.   The English traveller was
averse to solitary voyaging, and gladly availed herself of the
companionship of Mr. and Mrs. Tagore, her recent hosts of
Ahmedabad, now on their way, after Mr. Tagore's illness,
to their home in Bengal.   She found rest upon the quiet
seas, and gladly subsided for a time into a condition of simple
receptiveness.

Beypoor, Sunday, November 4th.—We arrived off Calicut at noon to-day, and found that the kind thought of our Bombay friend had telegraphed for boats to take us straight here, instead of our having to be landed at Calicut, and forwarded in bullock-carts. How surprised you would have been, could second sight have revealed us to you in three boats, or rather canoes, rowed by naked black Natives with bamboo paddles; instead of a rudder, another man with a sort of spade beat the water on each side alternately. The coast for many miles was bordered with thick groves of cocoa-nut palms, only separated by a narrow beach of sand from the sea; Indian huts under the trees; beautiful clear water. The Ghauts generally form a background. It is a refreshment to my spirit to see these new scenes.

At Madras she remained for some days as the guest of the Director of Public Instruction, Mr. Eyre Powell. Under his guidance she began the study of the different educational institutions of the city with great vigour, taking especial interest in the work of the missionaries of various Christian Churches. She had already written home with hearty admiration of what she had seen of their labours elsewhere. ' I am very much ashamed and grieved that our body is ' doing nothing to plant Christianity in India. I have been ' very much pleased with the missions I have seen. The ' reports give no idea at all of them. Each is a little centre ' of civilisation and good influence, and is doing an important ' work, though not making many converts.' But she remained convinced that any work which was to go wide and deep in its influence on the condition of Indian women, however obscure its beginning might be, must start from the principle of non-interference with religion ; and she could not hope that the Missionary schools could ever succeed in making provision for the vast needs now revealed to her. Her way therefore lay apart, though she rejoiced whenever the labourers in other fields were willing to co-operate with her.

From Madras she proceeded to Calcutta, where further hospitalities awaited her at the house of Dr. Chuckerbutty. There she was welcomed at once by the well-known leader of the Brahmo Somaj, Keshub Chunder Sen. The connection of the religious movement at the head of which he stood with the early efforts of Rammohun Roy had already awakened her interest and sympathy. She was familiar

with some of his addresses, and was prepared to look to
him for cordial support, on the part of the growing number
of Native gentlemen associated with him. She had attended
the worship of the Veda Somaj in Madras, and was now
glad to avail herself of further opportunities of gaining an
insight into the beliefs and devotion of those who had
abandoned idolatry, and had made the doctrine of the unity
and spirituality of God the basis of an important moral and
religious reform. One or two extracts from letters written
before she had been many days in Calcutta, will suffice to
give evidence of the direction of her activities.

TO MRS. HERBERT THOMAS.

Calcutta, November 25th, 1866.

Numbers of people have called on me, both Natives and
English ; and I have begun in good earnest studying institutions.   One of the first was a Native Free Church of Scotland
Missionary, the editor of a Friday Review, who had written an
abusive bigoted article against me in preparation for my visit.
Dr. Chuckerbutty had shown him his error, and he came in
the most pleasing spirit and took me over their splendid Free
Church College school.   I find that many of the missionaries
look somewhat askance at me at first, but are quite disarmed
when they see how warmly I sympathise in their work, and
tell them with what pleasure I speak of it in England.   The
fact is that they have made an important change in their mode
of operation of late years.   They make less effort about preaching and converts, and devote themselves to good secular
schools, with an hour or two daily of religious instruction.
This is doing great quiet good, disarming prejudice and preparing the way for real conversions.   Most of the converts I
met with were first made by the mission schools.   I am sure
that there is a most important field here and at Madras.
Keshub Chunder Sen came at once to call, and is most friendly.
When I gave Subrayatu, the secretary of the Veda Somaj [at
Madras] a copy of Russell's *Combined Gospels*, he said he should
be very glad of it.   They did not object to Christianity as
Christ taught it, only to the creeds added to it.
    Yesterday evening I went to a most interesting prayer
meeting of Native ladies, which Keshub Chunder Sen leads
every Saturday evening.   He took me on the way to call at a
Native house, and now I quite understand the impossibility of
any English lady living in such an one.   It was one of those
patriarchal establishments of which we hear.   A very large

house surrounds a court, and is occupied by any number of sons with their wives and children, and daughters with their husbands and children, not to speak of other relatives. They occupy different parts of the house, but take their meals together. This house was approached from a miserable lane. Men and children were streaming about everywhere. We mounted a filthily dirty staircase to a large handsome saloon, where I was stared at. The gentleman who took me wished me to call on his excellent widowed mother and his wife. After a time they appeared, and he and most of the male portion of the company withdrew; and the rest of the so-called ladies appeared, but in a state of undress, many of them, which showed that a zenana was the only fit place for them. A lady was with me who spoke Bengali, and could express my thanks for their kind reception and sympathy with the good grand-mother. I was sorry to find that the young ones do not get any schooling in this family. They would not be content without our tasting Indian sweets, and then we departed.

The contrast was very great when we reached the other house. Neatly-dressed young ladies came forward in a pleasing and very affectionate way to greet me, and led me into the well-carpeted little room, where the meeting was to be held. It is wonderful how much they seem touched by my having come so far to see them in the wish to do them good. The husbands of most brought them, and stayed outside. Then they sat round on the floor. Mr. Sen came in at another door and sat on a small platform, with a man who chanted at times between the prayers. There was throughout an appear-ance of deep devotion. The husbands were in an adjoining room, and heard the prayers, in which I was afterwards told I was the subject of supplication. This meeting is a wonderful advance, and the effect on the young ladies is very evident.

November 29th.

On Wednesday evening I went to the Brahmo Somaj service. Being in Bengali, I could not understand anything; but it was very interesting to be in the place of worship of the One God which Rammohun Roy established. They, or rather one man, chanted and sang in Indian fashion, sitting cross-legged, the others listening calmly. Then two, sitting on a platform opposite, read from a book, chanted, or read aloud a manuscript which I was afterwards informed was a sermon composed by Mr. Tagore on the glory of God in creation. I sit serenely during worship in an unknown tongue. When all was ended we went to the room below, which I supposed to be to wait till all the people had gone, so I sat down with Mr. Sen's elder brother and chatted with him. Gradually the

room filled, and a young man rose and said that, as Secretary
of the Brahmo Somaj Church, he would now proceed to read
an address to me on my coming among them. After thanking
them for their kind reception, I made statements to them of
my objects and intentions, and am going to-morrow evening
to have a discussion with them on the subject. Imagine me
sitting there in the midst of all these Hindus receiving an
address in state!

I have been studying the Bethune School this week, and
several others; and next week I am about to meet the Native
gentlemen connected with it who are influential and first-rate,
but opposed to the Brahmos. . . .

To-day I lunched with Sir Cecil Beadon. I explained to
him my three great objects, viz. Female Normal Schools,
Certified Industrial Schools, and Prison Reform, especially in
connection with women. He is quite friendly, and I am to write
a Memorial to him.

Now I must tell you that I am looking forward to beginning
a Free School for the lowest of the low in Calcutta. I am
looking forward to it with as much pleasure—and with greater
certainty of good—as I did twenty years ago to August 1st.[1]
I have from the first been very unhappy that nothing is being
done for those who require to be gathered from the highways
and byways. . . .

There will be the same difficulties here that we had in
England, viz. that Educational Directors cannot bear this kind
of school, and profess to believe that education of the highest
classes will affect the lowest. On the contary, there is a very
deep gulf between the two, here even more than in England.

The plan thus indicated was promptly set on foot. A
master was found in the person of Mr. G——, whose visit
to Bristol six years before had first inspired her with the
far-off hope of Indian travel. The house where the ladies'
prayer meeting was held was vacant, and afforded accommodation both for dwelling-house and school, with a court
which she at first thought might serve for the scholars to
play in, though she sorrowfully observed afterwards that
'Hindu children had no idea how.' In the first week in
December she was in possession, and on Sunday the 9th she
held a service 'in her own house' with a few friends. For
the costs of the first year she made herself responsible,

---

[1] The Ragged School in St. James's Back was opened August 1st,
1846. See p. 80.

hoping that if the school became a centre of Christian missionary work, further aid might be procured from home.

In the meantime the return of the Governor-General, Sir John Lawrence, from Simla to Calcutta, brought Mary Carpenter into immediate intercourse with the highest authorities. An interview with the Viceroy was followed by an invitation from Lady Lawrence, which led to her residence at Government House during the remainder of her stay at Calcutta. The kindness thus extended to her was gratefully accepted as proof of a sincere desire to give her every facility for maturing her plans ; and to the cordial support she thus received she never failed to recur with earnest acknowledgment.

TO MRS. HERBERT THOMAS.

Government House, Calcutta, December 23rd, 1866.

Here I have been located for a fortnight. The Governor-General most kindly sent and appointed an interview with me immediately after his return from Simla, and after introducing me to Lady Lawrence, she wrote and invited me to take up my abode here while in Calcutta. . . . I have beautiful large rooms here in one wing of the Palace, all to myself, where I am perfectly independent, and may receive what visitors I please. At first I felt very like a State prisoner, but soon got to understand the ways of things. A red-liveried man keeps guard in the passage before my door, or rather spends his days in calm repose, lying on the matting, unless I send him on an errand, which I think very good for his health. He cannot, or will not, speak a word of English, except ' Tea ! ' which he gets for me whenever I wish. The household is beautifully ordered, and the servants most attentive. You would be rather frightened at first to meet so many red-liveried soldiers and servants wherever you go, but I get used to it and do not mind it. I have had numerous visitors, and often have been in a constant state of levee when in the house. I have been getting such an insight into Native homes and ways of thinking, as few people have an opportunity of doing. The very bigoted ones keep out of my way. I have no sympathy with them, for it is not from any religious prejudice, but from the selfish wish to keep their wives perfectly in thraldom, that they object to education for them. But there are many good enlightened men who deserve every sympathy. . . . The ladies I visit all receive me with the greatest enthusiasm. They think it so wonderful that I should have taken such a journey on their account. One greeted me with : ' I am very glad you spent your own money to come to see us,' of course in Bengali. The husband of another said that he could hardly make his wife realise that I had come from such a distance to see them, and when he did make her understand, she said that ' I ought to be adored.' The effect of my coming is far greater than I ever anticipated, and I feel inexpressibly thankful to have had such a reward.

You will perceive from the accompanying newspaper extracts that I have had some valuable opportunities of stating principles, and I am glad, in this case, of the disagreeable habit they have of putting everything into the newspapers. I had another opportunity on Friday, at Judge Phear's. He kindly invited me to dinner with Mr. and Mrs. Tagore and Mr. Ghose, and afterwards about a dozen or more of first-rate grand legal Hindus assembled. In the drawing-room, Mr. Phear asked me to say something to them, and I addressed them on the duty of society to criminals, and particularly juveniles. I am glad to find that I can quite trust myself to develop my subject logically and clearly with only a few minutes' thought. To-morrow evening I have promised to join Native Christians at tea at Bwhanipore, and then give an address on Female Education to Hindus in general. On Wednesday I am to go to Howrah, and, at the end of some readings in Tennyson, give an address.

It was a new experience to Mary Carpenter to be called on to speak even at these informal gatherings. She had been accustomed to read her papers at the Social Science Congresses and to take part in the discussions ; she had been examined before Parliamentary Committees ; but she had never been beguiled into continuous extempore address ; and only a strong sense of necessity induced her to quit her usual reserve, and trust herself to the powers of the moment. The regular habits of twenty years, however, especially in the Ragged School, now stood her in good stead ; her faculty of concentration enabled her to pass at once into the midst of a subject for which constant reflection provided the necessary preparation ; and with a calm mastery that never faltered for a word, she announced her principles, or unfolded her plans, in lucid self-possession. If her discourse appeared unadorned, it did not lack the essential requisites of clearness of conception and of language. Entire absence of effort, and complete self-abandonment in pleading a great cause,

gave to her style a charm which no eloquence could have
imparted. She might urge her plans with emphasis and
reiteration; but it was not because they were hers, but
because she honestly believed them to be not only the best,
but the only satisfactory schemes. She was never nervous,
because she never thought of personal criticism; absorption
in high aims lifted her above all fear; and even the sense
of responsibility only stimulated her earnestness, without
agitating the inward springs of thought and utterance.

These qualities were soon subjected to severe tests. Her
presence in Calcutta served to draw out a vast amount of
enthusiasm for social reform both among English and Hindu
gentlemen. To these subjects the Rev. Mr. Long had for
some time past been striving to direct attention. Both in
Calcutta and the Mofussil he had instituted discussion
societies, and had issued lists of questions traversing a
wide range of social phenomena. The time seemed now
ripe for organising these scattered efforts. The difficulties
were considerable, for hard-worked Indian officials had little
leisure for such studies. Nevertheless, it was resolved to
make the attempt. A meeting was held, at which Sir Cecil
Beadon, the Lieutenant-Governor of Bengal, took the chair.
The Viceroy and Lady Lawrence, and several members of
the Government, were present, together with many Native
gentlemen. To this assembly Mary Carpenter delivered an
address, sketching the work of the Social Science Association
in England.[1] A provisional Committee was appointed, which
subsequently conferred with her at her rooms in Government
House; a constitution for the new society was drawn up;
and early in the following year the Bengal Social Science
Association was formally inaugurated.

Christmas was now drawing on, and the thoughts of the
traveller went back to England, to the wedding-day of her
parents, and to the festive gatherings of school children
which would now take place—the first time for twenty
years—without help from her. The Court withdrew to
Barrackpore, but Mary Carpenter remained at Calcutta, and
devised a little celebration in her own school. Already
progress was to be discerned among the boys who had been

---

[1] See *Addresses to the Hindoos*, by Mary Carpenter. London and
Calcutta, 1867.

but a few weeks under instruction. Some Native ladies and gentlemen assembled at the same time, and a short service was held after the scholars were dismissed, the memory of which was long treasured in some faithful hearts, and led to regular weekly worship, aided by books of devotion which she distributed. After a visit to Howrah, where she delivered an address, she found a quiet home at Kishnaghur, in a charming Mission station founded by a German pastor, Dr. Blumhardt. Visits to Native ladies, inspection of the gaol and of various schools, an address at a public meeting of the local Social Science Association, and a variety of other engagements, soon consumed the last days of an eventful year. The religious sympathy which she received from the family of her host, soothed a heart somewhat worn with constant excitement and incessant labour. Hours of peaceful thought were few; but, as New Year's Eve wore on, the utterance of thankfulness could not be repressed. ' In ' deep gratitude do I close the year ever to be remembered ' with holy joy throughout the rest of my life. It is finished; ' but the treasures of love and permission to work will ever ' remain with me.'

The next entry in the diary tells its own brief tale :

January 1st, 1867. Kishnaghur.—Messrs. K. C. Sen, Ghose, and the Doctor cross the river with me to the train. A *very* happy New Year's morning ! Young men meet me at Ranaghât. Calcutta, solitude and work.

The work consisted in the preparation of a letter to Sir Cecil Beadon on her recent examination into the condition of Female Education in Calcutta and several of the suburban towns and villages. She had already presented statements on the general aspects of the same subject to the Viceroy, in response to a suggestion arising out of conference with him.

TO SIR JOHN LAWRENCE, THE RIGHT HONOURABLE THE GOVERNOR-GENERAL OF INDIA IN COUNCIL.

Calcutta, December 12th, 1866.

In compliance with your request to be informed of the result of my observations while in this country, I beg respectfully to offer you the accompanying remarks. I should hesitate to submit them to you after so short a residence in India, had I not previously obtained considerable experience both in female education and in convict treatment, which enabled me more readily to see the bearing of the different subjects to which my attention has been directed. I am happy to be able to state that the views which I am about to lay before you are in full accordance with those of practical and enlightened persons with whom I have been fortunate in coming in contact in every department.

Three topics were embraced in the communication here referred to—Female Education, Reformatory Schools, and the State of the Gaols. With regard to the first, she was well aware that the condition of the three Presidencies—and as she had not visited the North-West Provinces her remarks only applied to these—was by no means uniform ; nevertheless, though some localities were more advanced than others, one general need seemed to pervade them all—the want of female teachers. Here and there training-schools for mistresses had been established on a very modest scale by different inspectors, whether English or Native, with highly satisfactory results. The superior condition of the girls in the Mission Boarding Schools, under the management of female teachers, was further proof of the advantage which would result from their general introduction into schools at present taught by men. Normal schools had been founded by Government for providing male teachers for boys ; why should the same advantage be withheld from the girls? Native gentlemen were already stirring; and although the ignorance of Hindu women, and the difficulty of finding suitable persons, might at first prove serious obstacles, yet even these impediments might be surmounted. The organisation of a Female Normal Training School was sketched out ; and though the plan avoided too much detail, Mary Carpenter was not without an answer for every difficulty.

The memorandum on Reformatory Schools called attention to the chief points of their management in England, and laid stress on the danger of associating boys with adult prisoners, or simply dismissing them, after chastisement, to a roving and predatory life. The Reformatory in Bombay, established many years before by David Sassoon, though not in all respects to be taken as a model, had proved a great

success, even though the managers had no power of legal
detention, and the magistrates had to resort to the expedient
of apprenticing young delinquents to the school to learn
trades.

The remarks on the Gaols were first directed to the want
of separate sleeping cells, in consequence of which numbers
of men, amounting even to forty or fifty, were locked up at
night together ; and to the urgent need of provision for the
instruction of the prisoners by proper teachers and at specified
times. In the erection of central gaols for convicts under long
sentences, it was desirable to make arrangements for adopting
the principles of treatment worked out by Sir Walter Crofton.
Instances were cited from the reports of Indian prisons,
which proved with what advantage efforts already made to
introduce the license system and industrial work might be
carried further, so that discharged prisoners might be absorbed
into society as self-supporting and honest members of it.
Finally the condition of female prisoners was described, and
a series of improvements, including the appointment of
female warders only, the provision of separate cells, of
suitable work, and regular instruction, was proposed.

The period of Mary Carpenter's sojourn in Calcutta was
now drawing to a close. Six weeks had passed rapidly away,
without a pause. 'You will perceive by the newspaper ex-
'tracts,' she wrote after her return to Government House,
' that I have been very busy. Callers take up much of my
' time, but every call is valuable. All the Native gentlemen
' whom I see appear rejoiced for me to say things which they
' had long felt, but had not courage, or did not feel it possible,
' to state. I seem to have dropped a spark on tinder. The
' tone in which I am now spoken of in the papers, is very
' satisfactory, as showing that my motives and objects are now
' generally appreciated. Of course I refer to the Natives, and
' to such official English as I come in contact with. Scarcely
' any ladies have come near me, partly perhaps from fearing
' lest I should meddle with their plans, chiefly probably
' because they were afraid of my heterodoxy. I hear that
' a whole sermon was preached against me in one of the
' churches. I have perceived many symptoms of latent horror,
' but that does not matter, I am used to it.' When the time
of departure came, a little band of Native gentlemen met in
her rooms on the eve of her journey, and resolved to form a

committee for carrying out plans of Female Education. She gave them a letter, copies of which were afterwards distributed among her friends in Calcutta, expressing her gratification in having been assured of their confidence, and urging them never to rest until equal justice was done to both sexes. The education of boys would never have made such great advance, had not the Government taken the initiative, in founding schools and training teachers. Let the enlightened Natives show that the time was come for the same aid to be extended to girls. Not till woman was raised to her true sphere, could India reach the position for which she was destined. ' I am aware of all the difficulties which exist in ' the way of the accomplishment of this great object, but I ' know by past experience,'—and she wrote with a conviction of which none of her readers could know the deep grounds or the full measure—' that strong faith, untiring perseverance, ' and a zeal undaunted by apparent failures, can and will ' surmount them ! '

On the 9th January, 1867, Mary Carpenter bade farewell to her noble hosts at Government House, and the active circle around them, to whose cordial sympathy and help she owed so much ; and amid the good wishes of a crowd of Native friends steamed out of the harbour for Madras. The four days' voyage refreshed her somewhat jaded energies, and it was with quickened interest that she went on shore to be the guest of Lord Napier. There she renewed acquaintances already formed, and rested among the charms of Guindy Park.

TO MRS. HERBERT THOMAS.

Government House, Madras, January 13th, 1867.

I was getting at Calcutta into as busy a state as I am in at home, with constant callers, businesses and notes to answer, and I was getting very tired, and glad even of the rest of the voyage. Here I am at once transported into a kind of Paradise. I have charming rooms looking out into a lovely garden, in which for the first time I have seen native flowers growing luxuriantly, and our hothouse plants standing about as ornaments. Only think of having the flower of the Victoria Regia 'picked for me this evening ! A lovely brilliant white, somewhat reminding me of the night-blowing Cereus. Squirrels run about on the verandah, and birds come in at the window.

Discussions with Lord Napier and interviews with Native
gentlemen enabled her to excite further interest in her chief
scheme. 'My great object of the Female Normal School,'
she wrote a week later, 'is progressing as well as I can expect.
'I have got a sufficient number of enlightened Hindus to
'support the request.' In the meantime, the season of comparative quiet enabled her to communicate with the authorities at home ; and in the following letter to the Secretary
for India, she first laid her views before the British
Government.

TO LORD CRANBORNE.

Government House, Guindy Park,
January 23rd, 1867.

Permit me to thank you for your kind letters of introduction, which have ensured for me every obliging attention in the
education department of each Presidency.   Sir A. Grant,
Mr. Powell, and Mr. Atkinson have not only been ready to
give me information, but have warmly sympathised with my
views on Female Education, and have co-operated with me.

I am quite sure that the bare mention of the want of
Female Teachers, which universally exists in India, will be
sufficient to ensure the co-operation of the Government at
home in supplying the great need.   Without female teachers
it is evident that no reliable or sound progress can be made ;
and enlightened Hindu gentlemen now earnestly desire the
improvement of their wives and daughters.   On my return
home at the end of April I shall hope for an early opportunity
of communicating to your Lordship the actual position of the
work here.

The condition of the Gaols in India is not less a pressing
and *very urgent* matter for consideration, especially as new
Central Gaols or Convict Prisons are being built in various
parts of India.   It would be most important that these should
be so constructed as to develop in them the Irish Convict
System in its entirety; and as this is not at present understood in India, I fear that pecuniary considerations may cause
so great an opportunity of establishing a grand and most
valuable system to be lost.   Prison discipline has not yet been
generally understood or studied here ; and you will have perceived from official reports that one result of this has been
dreadful mortality in Gaols.   All the official gentlemen whom
I have met with are fully sensible of the serious defects I have
pointed out in my letter to Sir John Lawrence, but have not
the means of removing them.

Among the religious communities of Madras which attracted Mary Carpenter's attention, was a little Unitarian Church, which had been built by a Native who had visited England in the service of an English gentleman nearly fifty years before. One of his sons, bearing like his father the adopted name of Roberts, was its minister, and there Mary Carpenter worshipped with peculiar interest. Among the servants of the Governor's household was a member of the congregation; and when the time came for her to take her leave, Lord Napier kindly sent him as her escort to Beypoor. Returning to Bombay by Calicut, she was now on her way home, and though she had yet to visit many of the institutions of Bombay, she could hardly suppress some rising regrets as she beheld the end of her journey approach. She had to give up much that she would willingly have seen and done, for the sake of her work. But she was nevertheless conscious of having received new impulses which would quicken all her remaining years; and she could not contemplate her separation from cherished friends and earnest fellow-workers without an inward pang. The excitements of Bombay society, amid the festivities preceding Sir Bartle Frere's departure, brought her abundant diversion on her arrival there, so that the last weeks were no less busily varied than the preceding months. Conferences with the Governor—who found opportunities amid all his engagements to enter into her plans—and with Sir Alexander Grant; visits to schools, factories, and temples, as well as to Native homes; participation in the establishment of a Bombay Social Science Association; and a brief sojourn, first at Ahmedabad and then at Surat, fast used up the allotted time. The sense of freedom of action seemed to have brought her quite new delights. ' I ' cannot fancy,' she wrote home shortly before she left, ' that ' I am so far from you all ! For I am *myself* always, though ' free from home troubles and painful associations, which I ' suppose will always weigh on me in Bristol. I am inex- ' pressibly thankful to have been able to do so much real ' good as I hope that my plans and efforts will produce ; and ' I certainly could not wish more kind appreciation and grati- ' tude than I have had.' A work seemed open to her from which she could not draw back. One branch of it was thus indicated in a letter to her constant friend and adviser in Bristol, Mr. Commissioner Hill.

Bombay, February 11th, 1867.

I was truly glad to receive your letter. How near India
seems, when twenty-two days bring one into as close communication with one's friends, as if I were at Red Lodge House,
and you at the Court. So I feel in writing now.

The letter from Major Hutchinson is one of the many clear
indications I have had that the fulness of time is come, when
those who believe in grand principles, founded on the moral
laws of Providence, must bring them to bear on India; but
the 'kingdom of God cometh not with observation;' all must
be done very quietly, and just following evident leadings, and
supplying known wants, rather than as proclaiming some new
and important plans or systems. This has been my course
throughout my Indian tour, as it was formerly. . . . I came
to India not knowing that I was to do anything or to be of
any use, but feeling that the end of my coming would be
answered, if only I was a token of sympathy between England
and India. I saw the particular kind of work which was to
be done, in the first fortnight at Ahmedabad, whither I was
led to show sympathy with S. N. Tagore's courageous conduct,
in daring—the first Hindu in the Empire—to take his wife
from the Zenana, and establish for her an English household.
I have ever since steadily pursued the principles and plans
laid down in the official document I sent you ; they have been
accepted by the Government of each Presidency, as well as
by the Central Government, and also by the intelligent Natives
everywhere, as far as I have seen them prepared to propound
them. My strength has been marvellously sustained through
all my journeyings by land and sea. Only think of two
voyages of four days each, and two days' rail to get to Calcutta,
and the same back, all alone ! But I have been sustained, and
have found friends everywhere to give me needful help,
Sir John Lawrence inviting me to Government House, and
showing me every kindness during the whole time of my
being there—a whole month. Lord Napier telegraphed for
me to go to Government House, on my arrival at Madras ; that
was a very important visit, for I believe him to be the one
man in India to carry out these reforms. . . . You will easily
see that I have taken the greatest care of my health, and have
spared myself every fatigue which did not seem necessary for
my work. So I resisted tempting offers to see the glories of
ancient India at Agra, Delhi, and Lahore, while at Calcutta,
and to visit the fascinating Neilgherries on my way from
Madras. I am thankful to say that I have had no illness the
whole time, and that though at times I have had as hard work

as at Bristol, yet I am radically, as well as apparently, better
than when I first came.

Excuse all this about myself. I did not mean to write it
when I commenced. Yet it appeared necessary to enable you
to understand my future course, and counsel and help me as
you have always done. I know, as Major Hutchinson says,
that nothing but a strong pressure from those whose voice
must be heard, will make the Government move. Everyone
in India does his *own* duty very well and conscientiously,
much better than in England; but no one will concern
himself about other people's, or about matters beyond his
sphere. His strength is exhausted, and he is working for
the privilege of going home. Hence there is no public
opinion as in England to urge on and back the Government.
At the same time that every official gentleman whom I have
spoken to sees what is wrong, he remains inactive. What is,
is and must be, because he cannot alter it, though he would
rejoice if it were altered. 1 have told Lord Napier that our
Reformatory party is strong and influential in England, and
that all the principles contained in my paper are so thoroughly
accepted 'at home,' that I should only have to reveal the
existing state of things to enlist the public in the reforms we
ask.

At length the time of departure was near, and Mary
Carpenter yielded to the urgent invitation of friends, and
withdrew from the excitement of Bombay to spend the last
days among the mountains at Matheran. She threw herself
with enthusiasm into the beauties which the morning light
disclosed ; and all her heart went forth in gratitude to the
Unseen Power beneath which she reposed.

Matheran, Sunday, March 17th.—My last Sunday in India !
O blessed Heavenly Father, marvellously hast Thou led me
on ! It seems hardly possible to realise that my heart's
desire should have been so fulfilled. That now I have reached
so advanced an age, in the midst of so many trials and
difficulties and so much illness, I should, as it were, find my
youth renewed, and my strength to do my work greater than
it has ever been before! A new life seems given me; I
have as much power of enjoyment, and my sympathy with
all that is good and beautiful is as vivid as it has ever been,
while my age and experience give me a degree of courage
almost incredible. Utterance has been given me to bear my
testimonies, and my words have been received with candour.
Marvellous riches of memory have been stored up for me in
these six months, in which I seem to have lived years. Each

part of my journey has its own peculiar joys and experiences; each will be treasured; and not least, this last Sunday, which I am permitted to spend with friends, amid the marvellous works of the Father's hand. . . .

And now in prayer I depart. On the ocean the Father will be ever near me, and my guardian angels still surrounding me.

On the following Tuesday she was invited to the Town Hall in Bombay, when an address, signed by a large number of Native gentlemen, was presented to her.[1] The next day, March 10th, she sailed for England.

Mary Carpenter's journey had wrought, so far as she could see, much greater results than she had expected. She had been warned by a Hindu gentleman before she left home that she must not indulge in many hopes. ' You will ' probably find the people loud in talk,' he wrote, ' and ' inclined to do very little !' Keshub Chunder Sen had expressed his fear that ' every desire for good work would ' vanish in the empty air as soon as Miss Carpenter turned ' her back on India.' What amount of truth there was in these representations she had yet to learn ; as the steamer quitted the harbour, with the last greetings of friends still ringing in her ears, she could only look back with joy and forward with confidence. Various causes had contributed to her success. She was a woman, and at once secured courtesy and forbearance upon her side. Her age pleaded in her favour ; and though she used afterwards playfully to describe the shock which she experienced in first seeing herself described in the papers as ' this venerable lady,' yet she was not averse to the sweet title of ' Mother,' which seemed to rise spontaneously on Native lips as the natural utterance of reverence and affection. Her large range of acquirements excited the admiration of those to whom Western culture was only just opened, and was unusual even among the most accomplished members of Anglo-Indian society. The special qualifications arising out of her past

---

[1] At this meeting it was announced that a silver tea-service would be offered her in commemoration of her visit by her Bombay friends. It was afterwards presented to her at a meeting in London, at which Sir Bartle Frere presided.

labours, and the rich experience she had gathered in twenty
(it might almost be said forty) years of constant labour,
could not at once make themselves felt, because only those
who had been intimately associated with her knew their
full measure; and if she herself stated them, as she frequently
did, it was from no vain-glory, but only to inspire confidence, and win a more patient hearing for her appeals.[1]
Moreover, she had gone out alone, simply under the impulse
of an ardent sympathy. She was sent by no public body,
she represented no association. She went without intending
to found any institutions. Her visit was one of inquiry;
and if her counsel was unexpectedly sought, she at least
deserved not the blame of intrusiveness. The Government
not only gave her what aid it could, but invited her
suggestions. She was not, however, pledged by their support
to any official views. She felt herself absolutely independent, and remained free to judge severely, if she thought
it needful, the arrangements which she found in existence.
Lastly, though she never disguised or concealed her own
deep religious convictions, she was scrupulous in her respect
for the convictions of others. She perceived clearly that
all organised efforts for social reform must be kept entirely
apart from direct assaults on the idolatries of which no one
had a greater horror than herself. She cheerfully bore
repeated testimony to the value of the educational work
done by the Missionaries, but she laid down for herself
the strictest rules of non-interference. The gradual spread of
English civilisation would carry with it, she firmly believed,
a knowledge of the simple Christianity which was the
animating spirit of her own life. But she would not imperil
the work of the present, by attempting to force unwilling
hearts into premature adoption of the religion of the future.
What influence she desired to exercise may be inferred from
the record of her attendance at the commemoration service
of the Lord's Supper on the eve of Good Friday, immediately
after her return to Bristol.

---

[1] 'I assured the Bethune Committee when I met them at Calcutta,'
so she afterwards wrote to Sir Stafford Northcote, ' that I had no
' wishes for myself, and that I did not wish to do anything for those
' who do not desire my help. I desired only to forward the views of
' Native gentlemen who earnestly wished help.'

Thursday, April 18*th,* 1867.—At home in my own place, all mercifully preserved whom I love. It would seem hardly credible to me that I have been able to accomplish all that I have, since last at this table. But never will India be now absent from my thoughts. Beloved Saviour! thou hast been especially near me in this feast of love. May thy last prayer be fulfilled! May all be in the end gathered into thy fold, to be one with thee and with the Father! . . . May I bear a testimony with my whole life to the heathen, and draw them with the cords of love!

The necessities of her various institutions in Bristol now claimed Mary Carpenter's first care. She devoted herself with her usual energy to the concerns of the different schools, the Children's Agency, the Workmen's Hall. But none of these could now shut out the vision of larger needs. Communications were at once opened with the Home Government, where Sir Stafford Northcote had succeeded Lord Cranborne at the India Office; and she already expressed to him her hope of going out again in the autumn. But it was evident that public opinion must be awakened in England to the responsibilities attendant upon British rule. Ignorance must be dispelled, the facts calmly set forth, and plans of action carefully considered. The publication of a little pamphlet, containing some of her addresses, led to the preparation of a larger work recording her observations in India. This, however, required several months;[1] but no time was lost in bringing the condition of Indian prisons before the Social Science Association, under whose sanction a memorial was drawn up, and presented in June, by an influential deputation, to Sir Stafford Northcote. To this Mary Carpenter added her private appeals. In the following month she forwarded a report on the subject, from the Inspector-General, Dr. Mouatt, which she described as 'a ' dreadful document.' 'If such a man as Dr. Mouatt can do 'nothing, under the incubus of Indian red-tapeism, it is ' certain that nothing can and will be done without the ' absolute action of the English Government. A commission ' of one or two gentlemen who understand principles 'practically and theoretically, might save millions of lives,

---

[1] It was published early in 1868 under the title of *Six Months in India,* 2 vols.

'and remove from us a dreadful stain. I trust it may.
The autumn brought with it the usual opportunities at the
Congress of the Social Science Association, held this year at
Belfast, where she read a paper on Prison Discipline in India,
and delivered, for the first time at home, an extempore
address on Female Education in India.[1]

Active correspondence had been also maintained on these
subjects with the Governor-General, with Lord Napier, and
with her Hindu friends. It was to the Bombay Presidency
that she looked with the greatest hope. It had become plain
to her that the Home Government would sanction any well-
considered plan adopted by the authorities in India; while
they, in their turn, required assurance that their action would
meet a distinct want, and would receive adequate co-operation
from Native gentlemen. Mary Carpenter strove, therefore, to
procure vigorous expression of the desire in which, under her
commanding influence, so many had been ready to acquiesce.
Let a strong memorial be prepared, and proper support
organised, and success would be assured. The following
passages sufficiently illustrate what was the work of months.

TO DR. ATMARAM PANDURUNG.

Red Lodge House, May 11th, 1867.

Your letter filled me with joy, for I trusted that quietly
and unostentatiously a work was beginning of the greatest

---

[1] At the conclusion of her discourse, Lord Dufferin, who, as
President of the Association, had been in the chair, said: ' It would
' be necessary for me to borrow some of Miss Carpenter's unrivalled
' eloquence and grace to enable me to convey to her in fitting terms
' the feelings which every one present must have experienced in
' listening to her admirable address. Any of those learned and
' distinguished men who have had the honour of addressing you
' during this Congress, might well envy her the power which has
' enabled her to retain during the course of this meeting the attention
' of this large and crowded assembly. During my connection with the
' India Office, it became my duty to acquaint myself with some of
' the subjects in which that great empire is concerned, and more
' especially with the progress made in the education of females in
' India; and in my humble way, I am glad to have this opportunity of
' confirming every word which Miss Carpenter has said. India is a
' great country, and the history of a great country deals only with
' important events; but I am certain that when the history of that
' country is being written during the present century, the visit of
' Miss Carpenter to the shores of India will not remain unrecorded.'

importance to India in the little service which you have
established in your small circle of friends. I hope that your
wife and daughters will not be the only ladies present, and
that the 'middle wall of partition' will thus be broken down,
which hitherto has separated in the most sacred sympathies
those whom God and nature have joined together. You may
be sure that your meetings on Sunday afternoons will be
remembered by me in my prayers, with every hope for their
spiritual success. . . .

My friends are very much delighted with the Addresses
and with all the treasures I have brought home. You will
see that I had a Soirée in the beautiful Oak Drawing-room,[1]
where they were all exhibited, and I have since shown them
to above sixty ladies assembled at our Sewing Circle for the
poor, as well as to our different Schools. I wish that Hindu
girls could laugh as heartily and joyously as ours did, when I
showed them the models I had of a bullock and water-carrier,
and of a palanquin and bearer.

TO DR. ATMARAM PANDURUNG.

Red Lodge House, June 4th, 1867.

I am beginning to be anxious to learn something definite
respecting the proposal to establish a Normal Training School,
and I think it best to communicate with my friends through
you.

When I saw Sir Alexander Grant on the eve of my
departure, he expressed to me his intention to apply to
Government to establish one on the scheme which I had laid
down, probably at Ahmedabad. I recommended this to be
on a small scale, for I have always found that it is best to
begin anything new as quietly as possible, feeling my way,
observing results, and modifying my proceedings accordingly.
So I began at the Red Lodge, with Government sanction and
aid, because the principle was a right one.

Now I am quite satisfied that the plan I drew out for the
Normal School is in its general outline correct. You all who
entered into it, approved it. It is much to be regretted that
there should be any further discussion about it, because no
one would be at all implicated in it, no one need employ it
that does not like, and in fact, some time must elapse under
the most favourable circumstances before any teachers trained
in the school would be fit to go out as instructresses. I have
always considered it very uncertain whether young Hindu
ladies would at first wish to come to be trained. That will

---

[1] In the Red Lodge.

depend on the efforts of Hindu gentlemen; but even if *they* do not come, there is no doubt from what I have heard in various quarters that there will be many glad and ready to come, if only arrangements are made. If these official delays are continued, and if differences of opinion are allowed to hinder the work, the opportunity will be lost, and the cause of female education will be greatly retarded. I may venture to say that the Government here in England have already officially expressed their sanction to the plan, if approved by Sir John Lawrence. The only doubt of his concurrence would arise from his uncertainty whether the Hindus really wish the plan, an uncertainty chiefly caused by the conduct of a few influential but very narrow-minded Native magnates, who greatly hinder the young men who wish to advance, of whom there are many in Calcutta. Surely he will not allow them to hinder the work in Bombay, which is so very greatly in advance.

The representations made from various quarters led the Indian Government to act more promptly than Mary Carpenter had expected. Early in October she addressed two letters to Sir Stafford Northcote, conveying a detailed scheme, with an approximate estimate of its cost. On the very day on which the first of these was written, a despatch was issued from Calcutta, announcing that a sum of £1,500 per annum had been granted for five years for the establishment of Female Normal Schools in Bombay and Ahmedabad, on condition that an equal amount would be provided by the Native community. Mary Carpenter waited for the news that the first steps were being taken. But no signs of action appeared, and she could not brook the delay. ' Begin at once,' she wrote as the New Year came in. ' Only begin without talking ' about it, as I have done every one of my undertakings. ' There are certainly some men in Bombay who can lay down ' money if they choose. Some one might lend a house for a ' year. Others might help in other ways. . . . If only you ' *decide* on beginning at once, I am quite sure I could obtain ' pecuniary help in England. Only you in Bombay must take ' the initiative. We should not have obtained Government ' aid for our Reformatories if we had not begun them our- ' selves, and demonstrated to the sceptical and the Government ' that the thing could be done. I would undertake the work ' myself, but the Government says that the Natives must ' begin.'

Nevertheless it was becoming clear to her that she must

undertake the work herself, even though it should be conducted without Government aid. The energy and the experience requisite for commencing the movement in the
manner which she desired were not to be found in the
Native communities, and the hard-worked English could
not devote to it the time and strength needed for other
duties. She was longing, too, for the freedom from the
peculiar cares and trials of her home-life which had rendered
her six months in India a period of such elastic vigour. Again
and again after her return had her soul been weighed down
with a burden which she could not throw off. The memories
of the departed had been around her, not with help, but with
oppression. The peculiar joy which she had at first had in
personally lifting up the degraded had passed away, for her
affections 'had to be repressed,' she wrote, 'into hard and
' difficult work in developing principles, in coping with crime,
' and doing hard battle for the rights of the poor young im-
' mortals who had been so crushed down.' It had been a
severe struggle to go back with inward contentment from
the excitement, the sympathy, the appreciation of her Indian
journey, to the commonplace life of contest with lower natures,
the rectification of petty abuses, and the daily strain involved
in keeping up the standard of work in her several institutions.
But she had resolutely subdued every longing, and set herself
to her suspended tasks. By the end of the year, however,
all was in order ; the gloom that had hung over her was again
clearing ; she could look back upon the past twelve months
with gratitude, out of which rose strong faith and hope. Still
she yearned to be in India. There her affections had had new
scope, and had been poured forth with fresh intensity. Thus
she wrote to a young Hindu at Barahanagur, near Calcutta,
whose persevering efforts for social improvement had excited
her warm sympathy, in deep grief for the loss of one of her
first Native friends.

TO BABU SASIPADA BANERJEE.

Red Lodge House, August 1st, 1867.

Your letter, received on Saturday, was quite a cordial to
my spirit, for the day before had inflicted a heavy blow on
me. A letter from Madras announced the death of Subroyalu
Chetty, the Secretary of the Veda Somaj, at Madras. The

news came from Rajagopal Charlu, the President. These two
I warmly esteemed. Our departed friend had not only a
gentle loving spirit, alive to all that is good, but a true and
earnest mind. I felt greatly drawn to him in spirit, and
especially from his bringing his sweet young wife to see me
every time he could. . . . I cannot express to you how much
I have felt this sad loss, and especially because, as he had not
emancipated himself as you have, his dear young widow will
be exposed to the cruel usages of Hinduism. Poor dear young
creature! how gladly would I take her to my heart, and let
her be to me as my own R——.

By-and-by came further tidings of sadness. The President of the Veda Somaj did not long survive the loss of his
fellow-worker. 'This morning's post,' wrote Mary Carpenter
on February 12th, 1868, 'brought me another deep sorrow
' from Madras. The broken-hearted friend has gone to join
' his departed one in the world of spirits. . . . Their dear
' forsaken wives and daughters seem very close to my heart,
' and I long to go to be a mother to them.'

There were many circumstances, then, which seemed to
point to a settlement in Madras as her next step. The plan
which had received the sanction of the Bombay authorities
differed in some respects from her own; and she would
prefer freedom of action. At Madras, moreover, she would
have the benefit of the counsel of Lord Napier; and there
she hoped to settle herself into a quiet home, and begin a
voluntary school on a small scale. So the winter passed by
in silent preparation. The long evenings which she rarely
liked to spend alone, were diversified by her various school
engagements; and she formed a class of young men at the
Workmen's Hall for reading Arnott's *Elements of Physics*
with her, two evenings a week. In March she received the
honour of an interview with her Majesty the Queen, whose
interest in her work gave it a new sanction in her eyes.[1] It

---

[1] She was accompanied on this occasion by Sir Stafford Northcote,
Secretary for India. The Queen presented her with her *Leaves from
our Journal in the Highlands,* on the fly-leaf of which was written,
'Mary Carpenter from Victoria R.' The book bearing this precious
autograph was often exhibited in India afterwards, and excited many
a wondering query: 'What! did the Queen really write that for
' you?' The interest which the reports of this interview excited
among her Hindu friends, proved afterwards an important source of
strength to her.

was with characteristic absorption in her object that she
afterwards said of this visit to Windsor, 'People have asked
' me if I did not feel nervous. I was not in the least so.
' I was not going for myself, but for the Women of India.'

Meanwhile, no word of invitation came from the Natives
of Madras; a proposal to the Government of Lord Napier to
establish a Normal School there had been declined; and
without a direct request she would not start. Bombay was
still silent. 'I am ready to work, to collect money,' she
wrote in April to a Native gentleman there, ' and to help you
' in every possible way; but I can do nothing till I am
' asked. I do not wish to force on people what they do not
' desire. I am ready to work with the Government if they
' approve my plan, and wish my help in carrying it out; or
' I am ready to establish a voluntary school with a grant in
' aid, on precisely the same principles as I have proposed for
' the Government school, if the Natives of Bombay, Ahmeda-
' bad, or Madras formally ask me to do so, with a sum from
' the municipal fund or private contribution. . . . In the
' meantime you say and do nothing. . . . I consider this
' continued delay most injurious. The English will be tired
' when they see nothing done. The Natives will suppose
' that there is some mysterious difficulty. I know of none,
' except the want of desire to act.'

But a letter was already upon its way when these words
were written. Ahmedabad, the first Indian city whose
condition Mary Carpenter had studied, had manifested great
interest in the cause of education. The municipality had
given a handsome allowance for a female teacher, but there
was not a single Native woman who could be employed.
An urgent appeal for help was sent from Mr. Gopal Row
Huri Deshmukh, a Native judge, who thus pleaded their
cause to his English friend.

JUDGE GOPAL ROW HURI DESHMUKH TO MARY CARPENTER.

Ahmedabad, March 3rd, 1868.

There are no female teachers in the country. The Schools
in this city have been in existence for the last fifteen years,
but have not produced one girl who is able to teach. The
girls leave as soon as they are of marriageable age (at latest
between ten and eleven), and thus forget what they have

learned. This is the great cause of failure. You have hit on
a right plan. If God will bless your endeavours, the fruits of
them may soon be perceived. There is a vast material in
India. There are thousands of widows under the vow that
they shall never remarry. It is only necessary to utilize
these unfortunate widows, and what is now felt as a curse
will be a blessing. . . . Until there is a Normal School, with
the professed object of sending out competent teachers, no
plan of female education will be successful. We are all on
this side of India looking very anxiously for the success of
your appeal, and *also for your return.*

This was quite sufficient to overcome her unwillingness
to appear to force a new measure upon a reluctant people.
She resolved that she would go to Ahmedabad. Her book
had appeared early in the year, and had excited interest in
the cause. Funds must be collected, but money flowed in
readily on the statement of her wants. She began to prepare
to leave her different organisations for a longer period than
before. She knew not when she might return, and arrangements must be made that would last for some years. Meanwhile she corresponded actively with ladies who were
desirous of going out; gathered together books, pictures,
apparatus, everything which she thought could possibly be
of any use for general purposes of culture, as well as the
specific needs of school education; and made ready to
transfer her home for a time to India.

She had represented to the Government that the absence
of any response to the Minute of the preceding autumn,
which insisted on Native co-operation, did not really show
that enlightened Natives were indifferent to the establishment of a Female Normal School. Many of those who
approved the plan were young men without means; very
few, indeed, were able to make large contributions. It
became plain that, unless Government took the first step,
nothing more could be done than such tentative efforts as
she herself might make. But, as the summer wore on, a
note from Sir John Lawrence brought word that it had been
determined to grant the sum of £1,200 per annum, for five
years, to each of the three Presidency towns—Calcutta,
Madras, and Bombay.

TO SIR STAFFORD NORTHCOTE.

Bristol, July 17th, 1868.

I last night received a kind note from Sir John Lawrence, sending me confidentially the new Education Minute, granting £1,200 per annum to each of the three Presidency capitals, but declining to do anything for the Provinces. The arrangements for the school were in each case left to the local government. Sir John Lawrence kindly said that he hoped this met with my approval. I shall write to thank him by the next mail. I think that this is all that can be reasonably expected from the Supreme Government, and the whole despatch shows entire sympathy with the movement, combined with the necessary caution. I am glad that Sir John Lawrence does not adopt any particular scheme, but leaves it to each district to do what is best.

This grant made no difference, however, to Mary Carpenter's plan. The school in Bombay would naturally be established on the scheme submitted by Sir Alexander Grant, which was by no means identical with her own. The wants of other cities in the provinces received no provision ; and she resolved therefore to abide by her determination to go to Ahmedabad.

TO MRS. WRIGHT.

Lodge House, August 19th, 1868.

I feel inexpressibly thankful to the Heavenly Father for giving me power of body and mind to do this work. My mother used often to be anxious, seeing in me many features of mind like my father, lest I should break down as he did. I now understand from my own experience that contact with ill-conditioned minds and characters wore too painfully on him. I have been feeling the same, and have also a sort of shadow from the past shedding a gloom over my life, when not actively engaged. My powers are overtaxed with calls I *cannot* escape from in Bristol. I have not time or strength to enjoy myself, or to make useful to others the many treasures accumulated in past years, with which I am surrounded without the possibility of availing myself of them. Hence it is a solution of what otherwise seemed inextricable perplexity and cloud, to see a way opened before me where every talent I possess can be well employed and valued by others, and where, beginning with an acknowledged position, I have not to work on for years to obtain a hearing. I expect of course many difficulties, but I have some of the faith which removes

mountains. Besides I can hardly have greater than I had at
Kingswood and Red Lodge. I am accustomed to troubles.
Yet I have had sufficient proof that I shall be rewarded by
the affection and gratitude of a people; this is very dear to
me. So I consider the permission to do this work the crowning
privilege of my life, the reward of long and trying labours.

TO DR. P. P. CARPENTER, MONTREAL.

Bristol, August 26, 1868.

As for me, I have not wavered a moment about returning
to India. Everything has gradually opened so as to make
me feel the duty an imperative one to go and work out
personally the great idea of extending a helping hand to the
women of India, on the grand basis of common humanity,
rising above even the religious, or rather theological relation;
recognising their spiritual nature as children of the same
Father, and helping them to attain some of the developed
nature we have; giving them as far as possible the results,
though they will not accept them if given with the combination of Christianity, which we have been accustomed to think
inseparable. . . . I shall quietly work out on a small scale
what in principle can be developed on a large scale, adapting
it to the habits and wants of the locality.

September was occupied with the final arrangements. A
certificated mistress had been found, and two ladies were to
follow without delay. The meeting of the Social Science
Association at Birmingham gave one more opportunity of
enlisting the interest of English friends; and a paper on 'The
'Gaols of India, from Official Reports,' and an evening
address on 'Female Education,' brought Mary Carpenter's
views again before her fellow-workers at home. Nor was
this all. Some word must be said for the destitute and
neglected children of her own land. 'Is it expedient to make
'Primary Education compulsory?' was one of the questions
propounded for discussion in the Education Section. To this
she replied in a paper on the subject, urging that free education, without compulsion, had not yet been tried. No
proper provision had been made for the lowest class of
children. Let Ragged Schools be recognised, Children's
Agents be employed, and the Industrial Schools Act be
properly enforced, and there would be no need for any
general enforcement of compulsion.

The last farewells were said to friends and helpers at Bristol, and earnest prayers and hopes were poured forth at a gathering of the Lewin's Mead Congregation the night before her departure. On October 13th she started for London with her adopted daughter, accompanied by her sister, Mrs. Herbert Thomas. Four days later she sailed again from Marseilles.

On the 7th November Mary Carpenter arrived a second time in Bombay. She had intended to proceed at once to Ahmedabad; but the removal of friends, the heavy damage caused by recent floods, and other circumstances, had produced a serious depression ; and she therefore relinquished the plan of starting an independent school there, and determined to remain in Bombay. No steps had as yet been taken for the establishment of the Normal School in that city, except the engagement of an English certificated Training Mistress. Within four days of her landing she had reviewed the position and resolved upon her course. She offered her services gratuitously to the Government as Lady Superintendent ; and, when this proposal was gladly accepted, she immediately began to make preparations for the reception of the ladies who were to take part with her in the work. In a fortnight she was writing home from 'her own bungalow;' pictures, books, cabinets, were all unpacked and arranged; and the new housekeeping details afforded her a pleasing excitement by their diversity from her English life.

TO MRS. HERBERT THOMAS.

Bombay, December 11th, 1868.

Now we have got our carriage, holding four, and a fine strong Arab horse—an amusing idea for me. This necessitates a *Garrywalla*, who has not yet learnt the habits of civilised life, and walks about together with his son and heir, in less than undress. This, of course, I shall put a stop to. We have, besides, a *Mally*, or gardener, who does an atom a day towards making the compound look less like a wilderness, and draws the water. He is a persevering and quiet man. I am getting the others to understand that though I speak quietly to them I will have them do their own work, and that they are not to introduce all manner of people on the premises to do it for them. I have also established the use of a bell to call them, and the non-existence of every imaginable untidiness close to our doors and under our windows !

In the meantime, arrangements were made for carrying out the ultimate object of preparing Native teachers for girls' schools; and Mary Carpenter unfolded her plans in an address at the Cowasjee Institute. Visitors poured in from all parts. 'Last Sunday, while at breakfast, we saw two bullocks 'enter our gate, drawing a carriage containing a widow lady 'from Poona, with three male relatives. She showed us the 'greatest affection, and wants to establish a branch Normal 'School at Poona. On Thursday I had a state visit from the 'Chief of Jumkhundi and his lady, and we are constantly 'seeing fresh people.'

TO BABU SASIPADA BANERJEE.

Bombay, December 12th, 1868.

I am now very comfortably situated here. All are friendly to me, and though the timid hold aloof for the present, yet, working on the system I have described in my lecture at the Cowasjee Institute, the ladies are going on very well, and we have as much to do as we can manage, and are progressing very well. Three young Parsee ladies came to visit us at my bungalow this week, and on Wednesday I had a pleasant meeting at Dr. Atmaram's. Five Native teachers came to talk to me yesterday, and to-night we shall have another party. Some of the Natives have been most kind and helpful to me, and the first-class English are very friendly to me. Altogether I am going on better than I could have expected.

TO THE REV. R. L. CARPENTER.

Bombay, December 17th, 1868.

I am truly thankful to be able to tell you that I am feeling taking root here, and finding all my past experience invaluable. One of my greatest rewards and encouragements has been to meet with Native gentlemen whose names and faces I had forgotten, but on whom my views and feelings on my former visit had left an impression which has prepared them for co-operation with me. One of the first with whom I conversed at Ahmedabad called on me to-day, and we had a most delightful conversation. He said, 'We all feel that we may leave our 'wives in your hands with perfect confidence.' They are sure they may trust me.

On Christmas Day her thoughts reverted with more than usual force to the scenes of the past, the cold winter's morn-

ing of her parents' marriage, and the times of union, of
separation, and reunion in the better life, which were never
long absent from her mind. Yet these memories and hopes
were never allowed to interfere with her provision for the
happiness of those around her. ' We could not celebrate the
' day,' she wrote to her brother Philip, ' by giving treats to
' school children. I therefore desired Doola, our cook, to buy
' some fruit, Hindu-cakes, and sugar-candy, which I dis-
' tributed to the four men-servants. The ladies were some-
' what amused to see me giving these things to them as if
' they were children, but they were very pleased.' Next came
tiffin at Government House, where she sat beside Lord Mayo,
then on his way to assume the Viceregal office at Calcutta.
' My visit to the future Viceroy was most satisfactory, and
' will be of permanent benefit to the cause.'

TO BABU SASIPADA BANERJEE.

Bombay, January 1st, 1869.

I received your letter of Christmas Day as the old year was
closing. It gave me much pleasure to find that I was thought
of in remembrance of Christmas Day, 1866. This Christmas
Day was not quite so happy a one to me, for I had no school
and poor children to gratify, and no such friends as then
surrounded me to sympathise with. But it brought its own
pleasures. The sweet young Rani of Jumkhundi sent me
some beautiful boxes of fruit, etc., with a letter nicely written
in English by herself, and has since sent me two scholarships
from herself to train teachers for her schools. The Chief has
presented me with 500 Rs. to use for the two schools where we
have been working. I had also a most important interview,
by his request, with the future Viceroy, Lord Mayo, who is
much interested in my work.

Her methods were by this time organised, and a large field
of work appeared rapidly opening. It was evidently impossible
to form a Training Institution for Native Female Teachers in
India, similar to the English Female Normal Colleges. No
students were to be found in India like those at home, who
had undergone a long course of training as pupil-teachers,
and passed a series of examinations testing the education
which they had received. Years must elapse before such a
class could be created. The future teachers would have to
be carefully selected from untrained Native women. They

would at first be found with difficulty, and would have had
little previous discipline. Their national customs, moreover,
would prevent them from boarding together; the persons
who would train them would for some time be of different
race and language; and other obstacles would surround the
whole scheme. It appeared better, therefore, to begin by
giving some preparation to the Training Mistress, and the
ladies co-operating with her. The Managing Committee of
the Parsi Girls' School Association requested the benefit of
her instructions, and arrangements were made for her
attendance with the ladies at two of their schools. Object
lessons were given for the older classes, the infant system
being introduced, as far as practicable, for the younger ones.
These lessons were reproduced in the vernacular by Native
masters. Mary Carpenter noted with satisfaction the
brightening looks of the scholars, and watched every symp-
tom of interest and success with a zeal that never flagged.
The next step was to prepare for the development of the
English system of Native training in one of the schools of
the Student's Literary and Scientific Society. By this time
the direct instruction of Native teachers in their own schools
could be begun. Scholarships were offered by the Countess
of Mayo, the Rani of Jumkhundi, and other Native ladies
and gentlemen. A class of married ladies was formed for
studying English; and requests for trained teachers came
flowing in from various parts of the Presidency.

It had required no little exertion to carry the enterprise
thus far. Prejudices had to be overcome, opponents con-
ciliated, and the efforts of the little band of workers guided
and harmonised. The task proved too much for Mary Carpenter's strength. In the middle of February an alarming
illness led to the abrupt suspension of her task. She was
nursed with the utmost kindness by English friends, who
removed her into their own home. Convalescence brought
with it hopes of the renewal of her undertaking, and she
thought that a visit to the hills might restore her exhausted
energies. But it became clear that the real remedy lay in
withdrawal from the scene of many anxieties; and after a
sojourn at Bandora, again under English care, she left
Bombay early in April to seek rest among her own people.

In the home of her sister, Mrs. Robert Gaskell, at Weymouth, her powers were restored with a rapidity which took

her by surprise, and awakened her most ardent gratitude. As every day brought her renewed vigour, the determination to return gathered fresh force. She was not daunted by the temporary collapse of her plan. Among the letters of encouragement which the winter had brought her, one from Sir Stafford Northcote, which found her prostrate with illness, uttered sentiments so much in harmony with her own that it may be fitly cited here.

Pynes, Exeter, February 19th, 1869.

I am truly glad to find that you have made so good a beginning, and I heartily hope that you may go on prosperously, though I do not look for very rapid success. After the first flush of novelty is over, the real strain will begin, and you will have much to contend with, both in open opposition and in secret misrepresentation, of which I imagine there is quite as much in India as even in this country, perhaps more. Against this you can only contend by patience and perseverance, and a great deal of prudence. I often think of the saying that ' a grain of wheat, if it fall into the ground, ' except it die, it produces no fruit;' and I apply it to good works such as yours. Not that I mean that the work need really die before it can yield its fruit, but that it must pass through a stage of apparent torpor, and even apparent death, before it can really manifest itself; and the husbandman must for a time be content to wait in faith and not pull it up to see how it is growing, nor be cast down if he is taunted with its failure.

Mary Carpenter was not cast down, but she was aware that she had placed herself in a position for which she was unsuited, and the only course was to relinquish it. She had always had a difficulty in working with others who did not own direct responsibility to her. Not all persons could merge their own individuality beneath her controlling decision ; and any departure from her plans appeared to her like disloyalty to the cause. So she perceived that it would not be well for her again to undertake an official post. There would be an ample field for her in stimulating Native effort, and raising public opinion on behalf of female education. The following letters to Sir Stafford Northcote set forth her desires.

TO SIR STAFFORD NORTHCOTE.

Weymouth, May 14th, 1869.

Before I left Bombay I had a satisfactory interview with the Governor, and explained to him the present position of my work, and what appeared to me best for future action. I have embodied this, at his request, in a letter, a copy of which I propose to send to the Duke of Argyll. As regards the Natives and the anxiety of the enlightened among them for the furtherance of the work, as well as their confidence in myself, I feel *much* encouraged, and shall be glad of an opportunity of conversing with you fully respecting it.

Weymouth, June 6th, 1869.

Many thanks for your kind and sympathising letter, which followed me here from Bombay. I am truly thankful to say that my health is wonderfully restored, indeed, I am in some respects better than usual. I quite feel with you that health is of essential importance, and that we may devote ourselves to our Father's work in every sphere. Still, the climate of India suits me well; and the entire change from nearly half a century's work (for I was taught to be useful when a little child) makes me desire personally to continue at present in that sphere, while all the pointings of Providence which I can understand give me no room to doubt that India is *the* place appointed for me, and where the talents specially entrusted to me can be best employed. I am glad to find that my dear relatives here sympathise in my intention to return to India in October. I should think even a few months worth going for, if I thought it right not to remain longer. What and where my work will be, must depend on circumstances which cannot yet be predicated; but what I have heard from different parts of the country which I have not yet visited, leads me to wish to travel part of my time in the Central Provinces, the North-west and Sind, to which Sir W. Merewether gave me a kind invitation.

London, July 21st, 1869.

After your conversation yesterday, I felt more able to analyse my actual position. My object is to discover and demonstrate the best method of forming Native female teachers —not to establish an Institution. I would gladly have done this in connection with the Government, and from my experience in England during the last fifteen years I believed that this would be possible; but the conditions under which I was in Bombay were such as prevented the possibility of it. Judging in the best way I could, I therefore have come to the conclusion

that I had better not be at all entangled with Government,
but just do what I can quite alone. My mind will be satisfied
if it can be said of me in this, as in other matters, ' She hath
' done what she could.'

Rest at Weymouth and conference with her friends in
London were not Mary Carpenter's only occupations this
summer. A visit to Ireland in June enabled her to take
part in the endeavours of Sir Walter Crofton to introduce
Certified Industrial Schools, by delivering an address at his
residence in Dublin, at which the Lord Chancellor, the
Lord Mayor, and other distinguished persons were present.[1] A sojourn at Exeter in August, during the meeting
of the British Association, revived the recollections of her
early days under her father's care, and some of the tastes of
maturer years which she had long since ceased to pursue,
though her interest in them had never abated. ' It was so
pleasant,' she wrote to one of her oldest friends ; ' a joy
' unmixed with any painful feeling, to see the places familiar
' to us in childhood, the very house where we lived, the dear
' old chapel ! And so delightful also to find his memory
' cherished, and the institutions he planted flourishing. You
' said truly that it was love which had been the guide of my
' faculties. At Exeter I felt that if I had not been bound
' by that, I should have given myself to scientific pursuits.'
Meantime the purpose of revisiting India was growing
more defined. She formally resigned the superintendentship of the Government Normal School, the arrangements
for which she had previously committed to the proper official
hands. The Director of Public Instruction in Bombay,
however, thought her influence with the Native communities
of high value, and encouraged her hopes of accomplishing
further work. One of the ladies who had gone out in the

[1] ' When I was on a Commission in Ireland, in 1869,' writes Sir
Walter Crofton, ' and doing what I could to assist in the establish-
' ment of Industrial Schools in that country, Miss Carpenter remained
' in Dublin at my house for some time, and in addition to addressing
' a meeting there in order to make an exposition of the principles of
' the Industrial School System, she on several occasions stimulated
' those who were likely to be connected with its development. In
' the first report on Irish Industrial Schools, the Inspector gives full
' and deserved credit to Miss Carpenter for her great exertions in
' the cause.'

preceding year, Miss Chamberlain, had been engaged for
some months at Ahmedabad; and Mary Carpenter was
anxious to observe the results of her teaching, to ascertain
how far it was likely to meet the wants of Native Girls'
Schools elsewhere, and what means could be best adopted to
extend and establish the system on a permanent basis. She
also desired to visit other places where female institutions
had been established, in the hope that she might be able to
promote them by further efforts at home.

After the meeting of the Social Science Congress at
Bristol in September,[1] arrangements were again made for a
few months' absence; and in this Third visit to India, the
way which had now become familiar was once more retraced.
The first of her objects was fulfilled by a visit to Ahmedabad. 'This,' she afterwards wrote, 'showed very satis-
'factory results. The superintendence of Miss Chamberlain
'had been so much appreciated by the parents, that the
'attendance had risen from 80 to 130, and the little girls
'remained to a more advanced age. Eleven Native ladies,
'some of them widows, were being trained in the school,
'receiving a small stipend monthly : they took lessons with
'the scholars, and learned to teach the younger ones, and
'there was great improvement in needlework. The progress
'during the nine months appeared satisfactory, both to the
'Inspector of Education and to the Natives.' Visits to
Ratnagiri, Surat, Broach, and Nagpore, enable her to awaken
further zeal both for Female Education and the establishment
of Reformatory Schools.

The feeblest interest was manifested in Bombay, where
the failure of the preceding spring had silenced the voices of
some who had been loudest in her praise. She was at first
deeply disappointed. The week after her arrival she had
been almost bewildered at the apathy which seemed to have
numbed all enthusiasm. But faith and hope were yet
strong; there were a few on whose steadfastness implicit
reliance could be placed ; and with these, fresh measures
were soon concerted. A model Hindu Girls' School should

---

[1] The list of papers contributed by her to this meeting was itself
a sign of restored health : on ' Reformatory and Industrial Schools,'
on 'Female Education,' on ' Children's Agents,' with an evening
address on ' Female Education in India.'

be established, in co-operation with Native gentlemen, and the happy visions which had been overcast the year before, were now permitted to gather round this new plan. All suspicion of coldness and distrust faded away from her mind, as she threw her energies into the organisation of the scheme. She had undertaken to defray the costs for a year, and her offer stimulated a wealthy Native gentleman to place a house at her disposal. The intervals of residence in Bombay between her visits to other cities were chiefly occupied in these preparations.

TO MRS. HERBERT THOMAS.

Bombay, February 25th, 1870.

This has been an eventful week to me. In the first place, Major Frazer, having sent me a note the evening before, called on me on Sunday morning at about 7.30 A.M., in great grandeur, with a white feather and gold-hilted sword, to take me to call on Sir Salar Jung, whom I much wished to see. He has been received at the house of a rich Parsi, and there have been illuminations every night for him. He received me with the greatest politeness, giving me his arm from the bottom of the steps like an English gentleman. I presented to him my *Last Days*, and he read aloud some of the Preface. Some Persian ambassadors arrived, and all sat in state round the room, I sitting by him on the sofa. He impressed me very favourably. His Secretary called on me afterwards.

On Monday I had to work *very* hard to get my little school-house in order. You will easily imagine what a labour it was, all the books having been tossed about indiscriminately in various places, and most of the things never having been unpacked at all, while most of the shells had never been arranged,—the furniture not being in place, and the matting not put down. At length, however, I did get things into order, and on Tuesday we had five very nice little scholars. We have a respectable Hindu pundit to teach them the vernacular, and Miss ——, who will at present be regularly there, takes the sewing. The little things quite take to the idea, and are very pleased to be so occupied. I am fully engaged in getting all my things into order, and you would be quite pleased to see how pretty the little room has been made, with my study-cabinet looking like itself, and a nice bookcase opposite with my books. The room is full of my things, and these I shall leave as a token of my wish to give anything I can. This desire will thus be testified when I am gone. . . . I have faith in the saying, ' She hath done what she could,' and that I shall do.

The winter was now over, and it became necessary for Mary Carpenter to leave Bombay. The experience of this third visit had now convinced her that she would have more opportunity of promoting the cause to which she had devoted herself by general influence at home, than by the actual establishment or conduct of institutions in India itself. She had accomplished what she had sought to do in coming out. Grief over the alienation of some had passed into gladness in the friendship of others before unknown. She had witnessed what she regarded as the complete success of her principles and system through the admirable efforts of Miss Chamberlain, who had laboured amid many difficulties with the utmost patience and courage, and she had found in this a rich reward for all her trials. The love that lay so deep in her heart was still fresh and strong as when she had first left England nearly four years before. No indifference could quench it, no seeming failure weary it, no disappointment exhaust it. 'I know and feel,' she wrote, as she made ready to depart for what she thought the last time, 'that 'while the worldly may scoff and disbelieve, there are many 'spirits here which have felt its power and rejoiced in it; 'and I believe that they will kindle others. The work *will* 'go on. In faith and hope I can say, "India, Farewell."'

'Thrice blest whose lives are faithful prayers,
  Whose loves in higher love endure :
What souls possess themselves so pure,
  Or is there blessedness like theirs ?'

Tennyson.

'Nothing is so appalling as the growing solitude, the void that death creates around us. I have gone through it all; but this state did not last long. There followed quickly another, when I began to *feel* that I was not alone, when I was conscious of something infinitely sweet in the depths of my soul : it was like an assurance that I had not been left alone ; it was a benign, though invisible, neighbourhood; it was as if a cherished soul, passing close by me, touched me with its wings.'—*Frederick Ozanam.*

CHAPTER IX.

PRISON REFORM IN ENGLAND AND AMERICA.

1870—1873.

ONCE more in England, Mary Carpenter returned to her usual home labours. She had come to the conclusion that whatever influence she might exert on the cause with which she had identified herself, must, for a time at least, be employed in the opportunities which the wide circle of her interests might bring within her grasp in Bristol. So she prepared to settle down again amid the old scenes, and make her quiet study the centre of thought that might reach half round the world. A little greenhouse had been built in her garden, and there, as she potted her plants, she loved to think over her great affairs, plan new institutions, prepare the heads of her papers for various congresses, or compose memorials to statesmen.

No time was lost, however, in bringing the results of her third journey to India before the notice of the friends who were interested in her work. The visit of Babu Keshub Chunder Sen, whom she had known in Calcutta in 1866, drew further attention to the subject of female education; and at an address which she delivered in London in May, under the auspices of the East Indian Association, he was able to give emphatic support to her views. Before long he came to be her guest at Red Lodge House, and there a new method of operations gradually grew up in outline before her.

TO BABU SASIPADA BANERJEE.

Bristol, June 24th, 1870.

I cannot tell you what happiness it gave me to receive our much-esteemed friend Keshub Chunder Sen into my own house! After having been away from it nearly three years, it required entire renovation and beautifying, and I had only just completed it before he arrived. It is the first English home he has lived in, and he fully admired it, and seemed quite happy and comfortable here with his friend, especially as I had just the curry and rice prepared for him which I knew he liked. My friends in the country sent me plenty of choice flowers, fruit, vegetables, and Devonshire cream for him; and I got up a splendid soirée for him in the Eliza-bethan drawing-room at the Red Lodge. In fact, I could not have done more than I did for the most distinguished guest. I told him that he had been a great 'lion' in London, but that here he was a valued friend. He was most surprised at finding that servants and all assembled before breakfast for morning prayer and reading, and twice he led our worship. . . . He wished to have an association formed to carry out the work, and I enclose to you a sketch which I have drawn out; but nothing can be effectively done unless he comes again and stays for a little time.

The Association thus contemplated arose out of the obvious need of some means of communication between English and Native fellow-subjects who were interested in promoting social reform in India. Year after year an increasing number of highly educated Hindus and Parsis were coming over to England, often in the face of grave difficulties. In various parts of India important voluntary efforts were manifesting themselves among Native gentlemen who had felt the stimulus of Western civilisation. In the meantime, the social condition of India was little known or understood in this country; where so large an amount of ignorance existed, no intelligent interest could possibly be felt; and no satisfactory co-operation could be brought about, until the ignorance was in part dispelled, and the interest awakened. Mary Carpenter, therefore, proposed to establish an Association for these ends. She wished to enable Native visitors to England to study its institutions, and enter into its society, to the best advantage. She sought to extend a knowledge of India and its special social wants, the education of the masses of the people, the education of women, the improvement of prison discipline, and the establishment of juvenile reformatories. And she desired to find some common ground whereon the scattered endeavours put forth in India itself should be brought into friendly relation, and gather strength by feeling sympathy and support around them, instead of isolation or hostility.

The first draft of the new plan was soon ready, and she looked round for the sympathy of one whose friendly aid had never failed her, though in this fresh enterprise she knew that she must walk without it. In spite of the independence which marked all her judgments, she could hardly repress a sigh that the Indian work could not have the weighty assistance of Mr. M. D. Hill. He, perhaps, like some of her other friends, regretted what seemed like a diversion of her powers to a less fruitful field ; but he cheerfully acceded to her appeal.

TO M. D. HILL, ESQ., Q.C.

Red Lodge House, June 28th, 1870.

It is now nearly twenty years since I drew out the scheme of the Birmingham Reformatory Conference, and felt happy to have one to revise and correct it of such high experience and enlightened judgment as yourself, one also who felt towards me the sympathy and friendship which were the result of hereditary friendship.

I need not say how much I always relied with confidence on the help and counsel which you were so kindly ready to afford. Now I have embarked in a new sphere, in which I can no longer have your aid, but I am sure of your sympathy.

When writing the programme of the enclosed Association, now after twenty years, I had changed places, and, instead of my older counsellor and guide, I was the senior, and gladly received the corrections of my younger friend, from whom I hope much for India, Keshub Chunder Sen, whom I hope to have the pleasure of introducing to you at a future time. He is much pleased that this step has been taken.

I hope that you will sympathise with it, and will allow your name to take a leading place in the list of members. Your daughters, also, I hope, will add theirs.

The Association was inaugurated at Bristol in September, 1870, on occasion of a second visit from Babu K. C. Sen. Its foundress was content with a very modest beginning, and

sought to avoid all unreality or display.   She was ready to
take its whole burden on herself.   Those who joined her in
its management, had constantly to look to her for guidance,
and had many occasions to admire her grasp of details as well
as of principles, her power of applying her knowledge without any hesitation, and the remarkable business capacity
which always kept in control an enthusiasm that never
flagged.   Before any further steps were taken, however, she
went to Southampton to take a last leave of her fellow-worker
and guest.

TO BABU KESHUB CHUNDER SEN.

Bristol, September 15th, 1870.

I believe that your visit to us will have done great good
here by demonstrating the existence of a true Christian spirit
independently of dogmatic theology.   This I am quite sure
no one can deny to exist in you, who is in your company, and
hears you, and *prays* with you.   Dear friend, I thank God for
this.   You as a stranger and a Hindu, coming freshly to
Christianity, have been able to say things which we can only
feel.   You have besides awakened here a feeling of interest in
India, and duty to her, which I trust has prepared the ground
for future action.   I hope also that you have been a great
gainer, and have become strengthened and cheered by the
feeling that you have done some good, and by the possession
of an amount of sympathy you little hoped for.   For this I am
thankful. . . .

I feel sure that you are fully conscious that I love India as
a mother does her child, and that I have a true friendship for
you, her honoured son.   You consider me full of energy and
perseverance; but you do not know that these two last qualities are not natural to me, but are the result of intense devotion of heart and soul and strength to the work which the
Father has given me to do.   It is this which has inspired me
to seek wise means, and so to employ all the natural powers
granted to me, that I have never yet failed in anything I have
undertaken, and that apparent failure has been turned into a
success more abundant than anything I could have anticipated, though it may be of a different kind from what I
sought for.   This I have already been privileged to experience
in the west of India.

The new organisation was now started; but before Mary
Carpenter could take any steps for carrying out its objects,
she was arrested for a time by a sudden grief, in which all

outward purposes were for a brief season laid to rest. Early
on the morning of October 21st, the beloved sister Anna,
Mrs. Herbert Thomas, was taken from her home after a few
hours' illness. 'The very afternoon before,' wrote Mary
Carpenter, two days later, 'we had our pleasant ordinary chat,
'and parted as usual, little imagining that it was the last
'time. A marvellous life and brightness has passed away.
'A life-long, most tender, sisterly love is consecrated; but all
'the loving ministration and self-denying affectionate care
'are withdrawn, and leave us only to mourn in thankfulness
'for having had them so long.' In words that will still speak
to many hearts, she sought the next day to record something
of the exquisite serenity which seemed in death to be the
true emblem of the inner calm of a heart always stayed on
God. 'Self-denying, humble, and loving, her daily life might
'appear to the common eye to be occupied with small concerns,
'little worthy of one so highly educated and superior. But
'it was not so. Every part of her life was occupied with
'tender loving discharge of duty, which hallowed and glorified
'the simplest actions. Thus was her whole being gradually
'adorned with divine beauty, elevated, and strengthened,
'and an inexpressible charm was spread over her whole
'converse with the world. It seems to me as if I did not
'fully know her until I saw the lifeless form impressed with
'the feeling of a satisfied happiness, a completed warfare,
'and a peaceful rest. For me, what inexpressible bereave-
'ment ! We never told each other how much we loved each
'other, for no words would have conveyed a greater certainty
'than existed between us.'

But this fresh sorrow was not allowed to interfere with
any existing duties. It left behind it none of the dreadful
loneliness and depression which followed her mother's death.
Then, the only one to whom she was needful, to whom she
was a daily companion and joy, was parted from her. Her
home was broken up, and the associations of a generation were
destroyed. Now, her own home remained unaltered; and
she had learned to live without any loved one by her side.
She had a large and most interesting sphere of work for
India, quite unconnected with any affecting associations.
She had a pleasure, too, in trying to carry on some of her
sister's plans. As Sunday was already fully occupied, the
class which had always met at Great George Street in the

afternoons, was now invited to Red Lodge House one evening every week. She promised again to preside over the monthly meetings of the Working and Visiting Society, and took a delight in gathering round her the young people of the congregation. In these occupations, in ' the abiding faith ' and habitual resignation to the divine will,' which she constantly cherished, and in the sympathy of which the following letter from Miss Nightingale was one of many touching expressions, she found comfort and support.

MISS NIGHTINGALE TO MARY CARPENTER.

London.

I felt for you and with you so very much about the loss of your dear sister, though I did not like to trouble you with a letter. I know how heavy is the loss of one with whom one has worked as with one heart and mind, and whose useful day on this earth one does not think yet over. Such a loss one feels more and more every day one lives. And time only makes it the more irreparable.

But I must have two hearts, one to rejoice with her who is now in the joy of her Lord, and who we are very sure does not wish to come back, who is not dead but living, and one to grieve with you over this ' insupportable and touching loss.'

God's design, when he deprives us of what is dearest, is no doubt to fill the blank Himself.

And *she* would reproach us if we were to lament too bitterly that, after a life of generous usefulness on earth such as is given to few, she is gone to yet higher and better work in another world, to ' prepare a place ' for us.

God bless you.

Ever yours affectionately,
FLORENCE NIGHTINGALE.

As the year wore away, her thoughts went back, as they so often did, to the past. The anniversary of her parents' wedding-day was at hand, but this time it suggested the remembrance of how her father had been taken ' suddenly, ' silently, and alone.' So on Christmas Eve she wrote to her surviving sister, Mrs. Robert Gaskell : ' This is a gentler ' parting than we had thirty years ago ? And we have fought ' a good fight ! Then we had to begin the battle of life alone. ' Now we have fought it.'

December 31*st*, 1870.—Farewell, O year ! hallowed by many sorrows, all minor ones absorbed in the great grief of the departure of the darling sister who had shared my heart's love from childhood. My greatest sorrow is now passed. No other departure can so take away, as it were, a part of my life. Yet thoughts of my Anna are so hallowed, so lovely, that they will help to sanctify my life, and she will be more a living presence with me than when in the frail mortal covering which divided her spirit from mine. In prayer I close 1870.

The opening of the year 1871 dawned hopefully for Mary Carpenter, as she saw her Indian interests steadily making progress. The Journal of the Association, on which she relied as a medium for the spread 'of information, was successfully started ; and contributions of papers illustrating various phases of social life enabled her to give it an increasing value. Early in January she received from a number of Native gentlemen in Sind a magnificent table-cloth, embroidered in gold and silver. She had never visited the North-West Provinces, and had had no personal communication with any of the donors. ' It is particularly ' gratifying,' she wrote, ' because I have not been there, or ' done anything specially for them. It is only the impression ' produced by the simple facts.'[1]

Quietly and persistently she continued her work, securing for the Association fresh adhesions from both English and Native gentlemen of high rank or official position, and keeping an open eye for every fresh need at home. She had declined to be put in nomination for the newly elected

---

[1] These 'facts' were thus stated in a circular issued in Kurrachi, Sind :

' Is it not a most wonderful spectacle of a lady at an advanced age, ' giving up all the comforts of residence in her own country, and not ' only coming to such a distant part of the world, but sacrificing her ' health, time, and money with no other object than that truly noble ' one of doing good to others ? But our admiration is heightened when ' we reflect that all this Mary Carpenter has done for the sake of those ' who are alien to her in race and religion, and manners and customs, ' and with whom she has no other common tie than that of sex and ' humanity.

' Is it not imperative on us all, when we are indebted to such a ' degree to Miss Mary Carpenter, to show her our gratitude ? We ' have been accused of ingratitude by our enemies, but whether the ' accusation is true or otherwise it is not for us to discuss now. But ' surely we shall deserve the reproach if we let pass such generous ' and disinterested efforts as Miss Mary Carpenter has been making ' on our behalf, without acknowledging them in a fitting manner.'

School Board, as she had already sufficient claims upon her. But she was contemplating a further development of the Ragged School, which had now been in existence a quarter of a century, and seemed no longer to have a distinctive place in the new organisation instituted by the Education Act of 1870. And she had further in view the completion of the group of schools—Ragged, Reformatory, and Industrial —by the erection of a Boys' Home, where lads who found employment in the city, when they were discharged from Kingswood or Park Row, might secure a comfortable lodging beneath friendly supervision. These projects required her presence in Bristol, and she therefore abandoned for a time the idea of again visiting India, which the interest manifested by her friends in Sind had suggested to her.

But her sojourn at home enabled her to carry out another plan, and bring over to England Babu Sasipada Banerjee and his wife. The acquaintance of this gentleman Mary Carpenter had made at Barahanagur, in 1866. She had followed with lively sympathy the earnest efforts he had put forth for the improvement of the working men of his village ; and the completeness of his emancipation from the religious and social restraints of his high caste had won her sincere respect. She hoped that the visit to England of a Brahmin lady for the first time would be a real step towards the elevation of Indian women, by making it easier for others to follow her ; and she gladly undertook to receive her into her own house. There, in the long summer days, Mr. and Mrs. Banerjee took up their abode ; and there, while Mary Carpenter was expounding the progress of Female Education in India to the Social Science Association at Leeds, was born a little son on whom was bestowed the name of Albion. All the deep affections of which there was such a wealth in her heart, flowed forth upon this helpless infant, and on the parents who were so far from their own land. She often lived in a state of repression of her inmost feelings, while she yearned to have some opportunity for action which should give them vent ; and, in spite of the care and responsibility now thrown upon her, she was truly happy in the domestic interests which filled her home. The energies thus called forth, and the response which they in turn elicited from her visitors, helped to dissipate a certain sceptical feeling which had been slowly

creeping over her respecting human nature in India, when
those whom she had tried to serve seemed apathetic or
promised co-operation turned into hostility.   When Mr. and
Mrs. Banerjee, therefore, bade her adieu in January, 1872,
after nearly six months' residence, she felt at first a painful
void, almost as though a son had gone forth from her
home.   But she soon turned from thoughts of loneliness and
desolation to the brightness of memory and the confidence
of hope ; and set forth resolutely on a new crusade for the
neglected and destitute children, whose needs could not be
driven from her heart even by the fascinations and the wants
of India.

The conviction had long been growing in Mary Carpenter's
mind that not even Ragged Schools had succeeded in reaching
the lowest outcasts of the population.   As their teaching
and organisation had slowly improved, they had attracted
scholars of a little higher grade than those for whom 'they
were first intended.   Some of them were scarcely to be
distinguished from ordinary Elementary Schools.   The investigations of the Children's Agent, however, whom she
had appointed in 1864, had clearly revealed the existence
of a class of children in a condition which made it impossible
for them even to attend a Ragged School.   Day after day,
and week after week, he had made his way through narrow
alleys and up broken stairs, in the worst parts of the city, and
had carefully studied the habits of the miserable families with
whom he was thus brought into contact.   What was to be done
for the children whom drunken parents would leave in their
wretched room naked and without food ?   The Education
Act had ' evidently accepted the principle that every child
' in our country should have the power of obtaining
' education, and that it is the duty of parents, or, in case
' of their neglect, of the State, to provide it.'   What means,
then, did the existing system afford for reaching the hapless
offspring of want and degradation ?   None.   They were
unfit for the regular Elementary Schools.   The Ragged, or
simple Free Day Schools, which had been established for
them five-and-twenty years before, had so changed in
character that they, too, could not receive them.   Nay, the
Ragged Schools were now really superfluous, because it was
in the power of School Boards to give free education by
simply paying the fees at existing schools.   Moreover, the

class of children in question wanted something beyond the
common teaching up to the appointed standards of examination. What they required was not so much instruction as
civilisation. For this the usual school hours would not
suffice. The whole day only would give opportunity for the
mingling of industrial with intellectual training, which was
indispensable for the amelioration of their condition. But
if the school was open from morning to evening, the scholars
must be fed; and the scheme, therefore, which alone seemed
adequate to these various needs, called for the establishment
of Feeding Industrial Day Schools, at which attendance
should be compulsory. Schools of this class had been
instituted nearly thirty years before in Aberdeen and elsewhere. They had been included in the programme of the
first Birmingham Conference of 1851. But the failure to
secure Government recognition for Ragged Schools, except
so far as they complied with the conditions of ordinary
Elementary Schools, had of course prevented any further
movement in this direction. At last, however, the occasion
had arrived, and Mary Carpenter seized it with her usual
promptitude. In August, 1871, she addressed a letter to the
Chairman of the Bristol School Board, in which she drew
attention to the work of her Children's Agent, and sketched
out a plan for the organisation of schools of the new type.
A paper read at Leeds in October, reviewed the whole ' Work
' of School Boards for Neglected and Destitute Children,'
and set forth all the needful detail. But this was not
enough. It was her habit, when she had convinced herself
of the necessity of a particular line of action, to seek to
demonstrate it to others by herself leading the way. The
Ragged School, therefore, must be given up. On Christmas
Day it met for the last time, with the customary festivities,
and on New Year's Day, 1872, the premises were reopened
as a Feeding Industrial Day School.

The supervision of the school which had thus been re-
modelled fell at first entirely upon the author of the change,
though in the course of a few months she gathered a committee round her. She was at the same time watching the
erection of the Boys' Home, by the side of the Workmen's
Hall in St. James's Back. This was completed in the spring,
and she dedicated it to the memory of her sister Anna, her
' fellow-worker in the cause of humanity.' She was also

engaged in active correspondence concerning a proposal of
Sir Charles Adderley, to withdraw Reformatory and Industrial Schools from the control of the Home Office, and
place them under the Education Department. And constant communications were kept up with official and Native
gentlemen in India ; besides which the monthly Journal had
to be prepared. To these labours she now added the com-
pilation of a little work on the Crofton system of Convict
Reform, for the use of the members of the International
Prison Congress, which was to assemble in London in July.
The idea of this Congress originated with Dr. Wines, of the
United States. Some years passed before it could be fully
organised, but various Governments had signified their approval of the scheme, and invitations were at last issued.
Mary Carpenter saw that there would here be an opportunity
of great moment for bringing the principles of reformatory
discipline before the representatives of different countries,
and she wrote to Dr. Wines, with the following suggestion.

TO DR. WINES, NEW YORK.

Bristol, January 29th, 1872.

Now that my Hindu friends are gone, I am beginning to
give my mind to the approaching great event, our International Prison Congress, and to think what I am to do to
promote its objects. The first thing that strikes me is that a
clear account of the Irish or Crofton prison system must be
printed in a compact form, yet not too brief to be lucid and
interesting, so as to put a copy into the hands of every foreign
member. I will undertake the labour and exertion of this
gladly.

The proposal was accepted, and she began the work without delay. Further correspondence only made more clear to
her the necessity for such an exposition.

TO DR. WINES.

Red Lodge House, March 10th, 1872.

I have just perused the report of the Meeting at New York
with feelings of the greatest thankfulness that this most
important subject is being taken up with so much power and
earnestness in your country. Our Convicts must always be

' *Our* Convicts' in every country; and until there is felt a personal responsibility about their treatment, the worst results must continually arise. . . .

I am extremely shocked at the proceedings in American prisons as gathered from the various speeches. I trust the States will be ' United' in leading the way to reform.

In speaking of the Louvain prison, you are not a supporter of the cellular system, but speak of Louvain with great admiration. These Belgian prisons may be models of first stage prisons; they may introduce good ideas and feelings into the mind, but cannot rouse to self-action, or fortify against temptation. The essence of the Crofton system is lost in them, the motive for self-action and self-control, without which good aspirations and virtuous intentions are powerless. It is most important to guard against this grand and fundamental error in the Congress, especially as there are many in England who are attracted by the pleasing appearance of a well-ordered prison.

The little work was completed by the end of April, and was inscribed to Mr. Hill. ' I did not like,' she remarked, ' to ask you to permit me to dedicate so small a volume as ' this is to be, to one who deserves so great a tribute; but if ' the occasion and the subject would be considered to make ' the volume of a little importance, I hope that you will kindly ' allow me to dedicate it to yourself.' Alas! the veteran's strength was fast failing, but he was not satisfied without dictating a few lines of acknowledgment.

MR. M. D. HILL TO MARY CARPENTER.

Heath House, Stapleton, Bristol, May 18th, 1872.

My DEAR MISS CARPENTER,

I write from my bed, a fitting place for a worn-out man. I am gratified and grateful for your dedication, the only part of your book as yet read to me, although in no long time I expect to have listened to the whole.

May your most praiseworthy efforts lead to the restoration of that interest in the treatment of juvenile offenders, which for a short time was so warmly felt by many, yourself among the foremost, and employed with deserved success to the best ends!

Farewell, my dear friend!

M. D. HILL.

The value of the book was thus indicated by Baron von Holtzendorff, Professor of Jurisprudence at Berlin, who had long been acquainted with her other writings.

BARON VON HOLTZENDORFF TO MARY CARPENTER.

Charlottenburg, near Berlin, May 29th, 1872.

Let me congratulate you upon the publication of your last book, which may be termed a catechism of prison discipline, adapted to the intellectual power of the general reader. It is the best fountain of information to all those not yet conversant with the Irish system. I am really astonished at your having in so short a time arranged the most important facts bearing on the Irish system. To those that have acquired a full and detailed knowledge of any system of rules, philosophical or practical, it is not easy to throw aside the rubbish of many particular facts. The most elevated minds sometimes are the least successful in instructing the public at large. You command the precious ability of writing for the learned class, and of introducing the general reader to the most important problems of social reform. I have read your account with the greatest pleasure; it would be quite superfluous to mention that I fully agree with your conclusions.

The meeting of the Prison Congress proved full of interest to Mary Carpenter. She took an active share in its proceedings, contributing a paper on the ' Principles and Results of ' English Reformatory and Certified Industrial Schools,' finding occasion also for the advocacy of the new Day Industrial Feeding Schools, and delivering an address at a Ladies' meeting on ' Woman's Work in the Reformation of Women Con- ' victs.' She found herself welcomed by many whom she had known only by correspondence, and was deeply gratified as one gentleman after another from the Continent or the United States came and greeted her as an old friend. New acquaintances, also, were formed, which brought her fresh sympathy. Her heart was open without reserve to all who were workers in the same cause. Some of the members of the Congress afterwards visited her at Bristol, and she cherished the recollection of these days with tender persistence. One of these, Dr. Strasburger, of Warsaw, was especially drawn to her; while she in turn was pleased to enter through him into communication with a country in which from her childhood she had felt deep and mournful

interest. 'I am glad,' she wrote to him after he had been
her guest at Red Lodge House, 'that you had some of the
'same feeling in writing to me as in writing to your mother.
'In India I am regarded as "the old Mother," and I am
'proud of the title.'¹ Another friendship founded at this
time brought her much happiness. Dr. Guillaume, director
of the prison at Neufchatel, had been led to adopt principles
and devise plans similar to those which she advocated ; and
a brief stay at Bristol enabled him to observe her methods,
and study the complete series of her institutions.²

TO DR. GUILLAUME, NEUFCHATEL.

Bristol, July 24th, 1872.

I cannot tell you how very much pleasure your letter
afforded me, with much gratitude to the Father of Spirits
that he has thus added to the number of my friends and
sympathisers in my life-work one from a distant land, of
whose existence even I had never heard before. Though I
endeavour, a follower of Christ, to be independent of human
sympathy, remembering 'I am not alone, for the Father is
'with me,' yet it is a *very* great support, and helps me to 'go
'on my way rejoicing' amidst many trials and difficulties. I
am also thankful that your visit here has afforded you encouragement and pleasure. Remembering how great was the
benefit I derived at various periods of my course from many
now in the world of spirits, I am happy if I can return to
others even a little of what I have received. I am very
pleased that you now know my surroundings in my home,
and do not forget your parting words, that you should leave a
presence still there. This is one of the indirect benefits

---

¹ She always attached a peculiarly holy significance to the relation of motherhood. One of her Reformatory principles was to try
to realise as far as possible the freedom and mutual dependence of
family life; and though in earlier life she had longed for the happiness of being wife and mother, she was content that her affection
could be freely given to those who needed it. 'There is a verse in
'the prophecies,' she once wrote: ' "I have given thee children whom
' "thou hast not borne," and the motherly love of my heart has been
' given to many who have never known before a mother's love, and I
'have thanked God for it.'
² The account which Dr. Guillaume gave of her work, after his
return to Switzerland, led to the establishment of the *Orphelinat
Borel*, and to the gift by M. Lambelet of 600,000 fr. for a similar
purpose.

resulting from the Congress. Nothing draws human beings so much together as being fellow-workers in the same great cause.

TO DR. GUILLAUME.

Bristol, August 3rd, 1872.

Many thanks for your kind letter, announcing your return and happy meeting with your family, and with those others whom the Heavenly Father, as well as the State, has given into your charge, that you may be the blessed means of leading the wanderers back into the fold of the Good Shepherd. I think with the greatest pleasure of the *Home* at Neufchatel, for it can hardly be called a prison. If the spirit of Christ were more widely diffused in the world there would be little need of Prison Congresses! I hope that you noticed the meaning and intention of the few words I uttered at the last meeting, after the reading of the Report. I do not often like to allude to religion in public, or to those whose spirit I do not know, lest it should be misunderstood; but you will gather from each of my books, especially the *Meditations,* that this has been *the* moving spring of my life. The spark was kindled by my beloved father; and he by his life enabled me better to comprehend that of the Saviour whom he so much loved, and to whose work he dedicated himself.

TO MME. OLIVECRONA, STOCKHOLM.

Bristol, August 4th, 1872.

The great interest to me was the *fact* of the Congress. Sitting day after day in that very magnificent Elizabethan Hall,[1] and seeing around gentlemen and ladies from every country of Europe and from most of the United States, and realising what spirit animated them in thus coming together— was deeply interesting. Mrs. Howe came over from Boston to hold a Peace Conference. I was not able to attend it, but when I saw together Russians and Poles and Turks, Austrians and Italians, besides envoys from the more peaceful States, with Americans whom we regarded as brothers, it seemed to me that a bond was being established more enduring than any Peace Congress.

In what light Mary Carpenter's work appeared to her Continental friends, may be gathered from the following

---

[1] In the Middle Temple.

words of Baron von Holtzendorff, who had borne testimony
again and again, in writings both popular and professional,
to the importance of her treatises on reformatory and convict
discipline, and the significance of her Indian labours.

BARON VON HOLTZENDORFF TO PROF. J. E. CARPENTER.

Pegli, near Genoa, January 20th, 1879.

There cannot possibly be two different opinions about the
incomparable value of Miss Mary Carpenter's merits, and the
admirable activity she has displayed in improving education,
reforming criminals, raising the general standard of womanhood in public life, connecting Eastern civilisation with European manners. She appeared to be Argus-eyed in discovering
the manifold moral plagues of our times, and devising practical
means with a tendency to their gradual extirpation. Her
notions about the final ends of popular education were most
complete, and, besides, without that sentimental tincture of
philanthropy which often leads Christian charity into the
direction of barren work. She clearly understood that the
highest aim of individual as well as national education ought
to be placed in attaining the unity of three powers in everyone, by closely connecting clear reasoning with kind feeling
and strong acting, all of these capacities being essential to
human happiness. I have no doubt whatever that she will
occupy a prominent place in the history of modern philanthropy. Of the entirety of her life one could well say : All
her public writing and speaking was action, and all her actions
were preaching the work of Christian charity.

I cannot well express my opinions in your language. But
you will perhaps find out what I am feeling.

Among the subjects which had for some time past engaged
Mary Carpenter's attention was the condition of the Prisons
in the United States. She had carefully studied official
reports, and conversation with some of the Delegates present
at the Congress naturally led to the suggestion that she should
visit America. Invitations flowed in at once, and she began
seriously to contemplate the journey, when a summons to
Darmstadt drew her thither instead. H.R.H. the Princess
Louis of Hesse[1] was then organising a Congress to consider
various questions connected with Woman's work, and the

---

[1] Princess Alice of Great Britain and Ireland.

presence of Mary Carpenter was desired. Together with her friend Miss Florence Davenport-Hill, she was received as a guest in the Palace, where the kindness and consideration of her royal hostess left an ineffaceable impression upon her. The time of her sojourn was largely occupied with attending meetings, visiting schools, and similar engagements ; but hours were found for private conference, to which she looked back as to one of her highest privileges. ' I was as busy at ' Darmstadt after the Congress as before,' she subsequently wrote to her brother Russell, from Neufchatel, 'as we had ' much to think of, and plan, and foresee about the working ' of our Society. The more I saw of the dear Princess, the ' more did I admire and love her. She feels that she owes ' much to her father, of whom she thinks as we do of ours.'

The Princess herself was not slow to acknowledge the stimulus which she had received from her visitor.

H.R.H. THE PRINCESS LOUIS OF HESSE TO MARY CARPENTER.

Darmstadt, October 18th, 1872.

DEAR MISS CARPENTER,

The valuable notice about your life has just reached me, and I thank you many times for having fulfilled my wish in sending it to me, with the permission to make use of it. I would like all to know of and share my admiration for such a benevolent and useful life as yours, which has influence far beyond the limits of its sphere.

To know you has strengthened me and done me good, and made me feel how little I have yet done, and how your example will ever incite me to try and do better.

We missed you very much here, and I am anxious to know whether you are well, not overtired, and really resting. I have not yet received an answer from your friend the Baron. Dr. Becker shall send it you when I receive it.

Believe me ever

Yours most sincerely,

ALICE.

From Darmstadt Mary Carpenter passed on to Neufchatel, where she was deeply interested in closely examining the system of Dr. Guillaume. ' The prison,' she reported enthusiastically, ' is quite unique, and most excellent.' She watched the prisoners at labour in the workshops; heard lessons given in the school ; visited some of them in their cells; and, at the special request of Dr. Guillaume, she even gave a short address in French, on Sunday, in the chapel, choosing for her subject the parable of the Prodigal Son. Of this some of the prisoners took notes, and the 'little sermon' was afterwards lithographed—with a portrait of the preacher —in the prison, and distributed among the inmates.

Some human interest was always dominant in Mary Carpenter's mind whenever she travelled. From Geneva she went, not to Chamouny to stand at the foot of Mont Blanc, but to the Pays de Vaud, to visit a Reformatory. Nevertheless, she had not lost her delight in natural beauty, though the Alps overwhelmed her, and, after one or two efforts, she felt that to attempt to draw them was impossible. She came back from her journey refreshed, with a new store of impressions, some of which were briefly indicated in the notes which found their way home at irregular intervals.

TO THE REV. R. L. CARPENTER.

Neufchatel, October 22nd, 1872.

We crossed the glorious old Rhine in a railway. I confess I felt for the fine old river, after having for so many ages defied the attempts of man to subdue him, to be thus trampled on; and I understood the feelings of the natives at the crossing of the Nerbudda by the railway. . . . To-day we have been taking a most charming excursion to a village, or rather town, on the next lake to Neufchatel—Morat, which has still its ancient walls and fortified towers. It was very curious to be plunged back into the middle of the fifteenth century, and to have to work up an enthusiasm about the natives repulsing Charles of Burgundy. Altogether this is a very interesting country, and I trust that they will be let alone by the neighbouring despots. I do not like republics generally; but here they go on so quietly, and are so domestic, and make such wonderful progress, that it is quite encouraging. It is very curious to see such an old Middle Age town within its high walls, and outside a large new schoolhouse and museum.

Geneva, November 2nd, 1872.

Considering that Neufchatel has become an independent Canton only since 1848, when the Prussians were driven out, it is wonderful how they have organised their government and institutions. They certainly do much more as communes

than we can do, especially if the whole canton unites in anything; but certainly individuality is not nearly as much
developed as in England. I used to say that when lost I
should be found at Ratnagiri, but I now think it will be at
Neufchatel, which is only twenty-six hours from London.

The close of the year brought with it some mournful
thoughts, for she was sorely tried in her own home after her
return. But she recalled with delight the memories of the
summer, and the new friendships which it had brought her;
and whenever a few hours could be saved from the crowd of
daily engagements, she gladly sought to sustain the intimacies
which had thus begun. Correspondence could not, however,
be long continued; letters became notes; and then notes
were given up for copies of the last paper or address to which
she desired to call attention. But during the beginning of
1873 she wrote at greater length than usual to two of the
gentlemen whose acquaintance she had made at the Congress
for the first time. A few passages from these letters will
suffice to indicate some of her moods of thought and feeling.

TO DR. STRASBURGER, WARSAW.

Bristol, January 1st & 10th, 1873.

The commencement of a new year sends the thoughts
round to all friends far and near, new and old, with kindly
greetings and best wishes. The last year has especially
enriched me, through the Prison Congress, and you are one of
those whom it has given me the greatest pleasure to become
acquainted with. Will you accept my best wishes for a happy
and prosperous year to you, and to your country. Last year
completed, I think, a century since that most unprincipled act
by which the three Powers so wickedly divided Poland. She
still preserves her nationality; and I cannot but believe that
in God's good time the rearrangement of Europe, or the
enlightenment of nations, will bring about, quietly and without bloodshed, the restoration of Poland to her rights, as it
has done Venetia. In the meantime you and every good
citizen must strive for progress, and a higher moral tone,
combined with general improvement. . . . To-day we hear of
the death of that remarkable man the French Emperor. I
cannot lament him, and believe it well for Europe that he is
gone. But I am glad that the Exile had a kind reception.

TO DR. STRASBURGER.

Red Lodge House, February 12th, 1873.

I quite understand the religious position which you describe as your own. It is the natural progress of the devout spirit when emancipating itself from the thraldom of creeds and the weight of corruptions with which Christianity has been overburdened. Happily for myself, the pure and rational and loving faith with which my beloved father inspired me from the earliest years, did not give any room in my soul, as it gradually expanded, for those doubts and difficulties about Christ with which so many are troubled. My father devoted his most earnest life-work to the *Harmony of the Gospels*, which he was permitted to complete before he was called from the world. Every event was an intense *reality* to me, and thus the life of Christ was so associated in my mind with my father that I can no more disbelieve one than the other; and communion with the Saviour enables me to understand the real trials and difficulties which he underwent, and to gain strength from him in my own. But I quite understand the feelings of those who have not this kind of belief. They may have the *spirit* of Christ, whether they accept the historical account or not.

TO DR. STRASBURGER.

(After advising him to read a volume of the sermons of Dr. Channing, entitled *The Perfect Life*.)

Red Lodge House, March 22nd, 1873.

I think that, when you become somewhat acquainted with his saint-like character, you will perceive a greater holiness and beauty in his other writings, and will perceive how these spiritual views help us through life. I am sure that those views which in early life I imbibed from him, perfectly in harmony as they were with the spirit of my revered father, helped me marvellously when first encountering the sin and misery which I have striven to grapple with and to overcome. Having naturally an almost intense dislike of everything low and mean, I do not know how I could have lived in such close contact with vice, if I had not been able to recognise the divine nature everywhere, however dimmed.

TO DR. GUILLAUME.

Bristol, January 20th, 1873.

Be assured that your friendship is very greatly treasured by me, and I am happy to feel so remembered in your family.

Living isolated as I am compelled to do, I rejoice to feel that I dwell in the hearts of many, and I assure you that Neufchatel is one of my *very* favourite places.

I hope that I am past spoiling, but we must never be too confident, so I must beg you not to spoil me. . . .

The letter of your poor prisoner is most touching. Assure him of my true sympathy and compassion. Would that I could do anything for him. But one thing I do beg him—to commune with the Heavenly Father, with the help of the Scriptures, and to study the life of the loving Saviour.

TO DR. GUILLAUME.

Bristol, February 12th, 1873.

I have been to-day attending a meeting of the Executive Committee of an International Arbitration Association for South Wales and the West of England, which has just been established here in connection with the Peace Society. You see that the Geneva Arbitration is bearing good fruits. It remains as a *fait accompli.* Whether or not Americans grumble, and Englishmen say they are ashamed of their country, both nations are saved from the *supposed* necessity of making war, and an excuse for unpleasant attacks on each other is withdrawn. An agent from the parent Society is working up our proceedings, and it is very satisfactory. In this we are better off than you in your separate Cantons, for we have no line of demarcation round our counties, and all work together to get up a public opinion which will support any member who brings on a subject. There were about as many ladies present as gentlemen, and I was asked to take the chair. This of course I declined, as I always keep within my own womanly sphere. But I had no cause to complain of any want of respect and attention to my opinions, nor had any of the ladies. It is quite striking to observe how much the useful power and influence of woman has developed of late years. Unattached ladies, such as widows and unmarried women, have quite ample work to do in the world for the good of others, to absorb all their powers. Wives and mothers have a *very* noble work given them by God, and want no more. I was much struck with a remark made by Mr. Deshmukh, a very superior young Hindu, who is just now returned to his own country. He said that it was most important for society to have some unmarried women to give a tone to it. You know that they have none in India.

I think much of the letter of that poor prisoner. It indicates a most wretched state of mind. His punishment is not making him penitent, or bringing him nearer to God. I do

not believe in any reformation without religion. I am sure
that unless the soul can be brought to prostrate itself humbly
before the Eternal One, and, when humble and penitent, to
commune with the Father of Spirits, there can be no peace.
I think it very sad that in Switzerland the sinner is not
helped to this by the daily ministrations of religion, and true
devotional Sunday services; but surely *you* cannot be prevented from quiet talk with them, and striving to touch their
consciences. When I can, I shall write a few lines to the poor
man for you to give him if you approve.

February 16th.—Through an oversight of mine this letter
has not reached you, which enables me to thank you for your
very interesting letter and Prison Journal since received.
The prisoners' letters seem to me touching and genuine.
Their inner spirits have been reached by your true sympathy
with them. How little society can understand the condition
of those who have heard of Christmas presents but have
never received one, till the gaol brought them into contact
with a loving heart!

TO DR. GUILLAUME.

Bristol, March 16th, 1873.

A part of my Sunday evening I consecrate to commune
with those distant friends whom I feel very near to me in
common sympathy with humanity. I feel it a privilege to
have a couple of hours to call my own for so delightful an
occupation. I used to go up to the Industrial School to teach
the older boys, and thus establish a connection with them of
the best possible kind. But I have been finding it of late too
much for my strength, after spending the afternoon at the
Red Lodge. I have therefore most unwillingly given it up for
the present; and it is a great refreshment to me to be alone
for a time in my study, where every single object recalls the
memory of some one much beloved, or very noble, or very holy.
You remember it?

I have been just reading some of Dr. Channing's new
volume, *The Perfect Life*. It is, indeed, a true breathing of
the spirit, a most elevating call from the world of spirits,
where he is now in near communion with the holiest and the
best whom I have had the privilege of knowing during their
sojourn on earth—those who, like himself, incited me onward
in the course to which I have devoted myself. I think that it
was his writings which especially gave me that unquenchable
faith in the human soul, and that near sense of the absolute
Fatherhood of God, which, aided by the living presence of
Dr. Tuckerman, and the life of my ever-loved father, have
carried me on unswervingly in work for humanity, under what-

ever form it presented itself to me. Robertson of Brighton has given me some encouragement and help by his views expressed in his sermons, especially respecting Christ's treatment of sinners; and Law's *Letters* inspired me in earlier times with a deep sense of devotion. My father *led* me to our Saviour, and made me comprehend his holy and loving life.

I did not mean, when I began, to speak so much of myself. You have kindly encouraged me to do so by telling me that my letters give you much pleasure. Be assured that I reciprocate that feeling.

The customary occupations of the winter—the supervision of her schools, the work of the Children's Agent, the Workmen's Hall, and the Boys' Home, together with her Indian correspondence and the preparation of the Journal of the Association, had not driven the condition of American prisons from Mary Carpenter's mind. In January she transmitted to Dr. Wines a paper for a Congress at Baltimore, on the treatment of long-sentenced and life-sentenced prisoners. This was followed by a short series of suggestions for Prison Reform, addressed to Dr. Harris of New York. But, as usual, she longed for action. ' Society ought to realise,' she wrote in January, ' that when it takes away liberty from ' a fellow-being, it is responsible for the way in which that ' being is treated. Society suffers if it misuses the prisoner.' A week later the tone is more decided : ' I perceive that no ' writing, or printing, or talking, can induce people to take ' up the subject ; it is only determined action.' So it was gradually settled that the plan of the preceding autumn should be no longer postponed. She could not indeed undertake any organisation in the United States, but she might at least succeed in drawing attention to principles which were imperfectly understood. A Prison Reform Association had been established, and she might stimulate its labours. She felt in much need of change, for she had been harassed by anxieties which were no longer lightened by the sympathy of the sister who had hitherto shared every trouble with her. But she went without enthusiasm, feeling jaded and worn ; and, as the time for departure came, she seemed to have little strength or heart for the graver labours of pleading for the prisoners. ' I cannot fancy I am going,' she wrote to her brother Philip in Montreal, ' but I tell

'every one I am, to make myself believe it. I do not feel
'a call, as I did to India. The only little business I wish
'to do is to excite a little interest in female education, which
'gives great encouragement to the natives and to myself.
'Last week I received from Darmstadt a box of beautiful
'presents for Hindu ladies, and photographs of the family,
'from the Crown Princess of Prussia and the Princess Alice.
'Was not this most gratifying?' So her affairs were once
more put into order; a parting appeal was addressed to
the Right Hon. W. E. Forster, then Vice-President of the
Committee of Council on Education, in behalf of the Feeding Industrial Day Schools; six large boxes of books,
educational apparatus, contributions of needlework, and
other gifts, were despatched to Calcutta, Madras, Bombay,
Ratnagiri, Nagpore, and Ahmedabad; and by the third
week in April the way was clear for her to go.

On landing at Boston, Mary Carpenter was received by
Mr. and Miss Ware, who belonged to a family for whom she
had early learned to entertain warm feelings of respect and
regard, and who were eager to return the hospitalities which
different members of it had enjoyed in Bristol at various
intervals reaching back for forty years. The cessation of
active duty on the voyage had revealed her weariness, and
she seemed at first too feeble for any exertion. But the rest
and quiet of a few days' sojourn at Milton partially restored
her. There she could talk of the loved ones who were gone,
confident of sympathy and affectionate remembrance; and
this was itself a balm to a much-tried spirit. 'It is very
'interesting,' she wrote to her brother Russell, 'to come to
'this house, where the dear Anna and I have been known by
'our pictures for more than thirty years,[1] and where the
'memories of our respective parents are so closely and
'sacredly linked.' Among the friends who greeted her at
once in this country seclusion, was Mr. W. C. Gannett, who
had visited her at Red Lodge House, and with whose late
father (Dr. E. S. Gannett) she had long entertained respectful
friendship. Knowing her love for relics, and objects of
sacred or interesting association, Mr. Gannett brought her
some 'Mayflowers' from Plymouth. Specimens of the
treasure were soon on their way to England, Switzerland,

---

[1] The drawings were actually dated 1829.

and Australia; and some rushes recently brought her from the Jordan were offered in return.

Then came three exciting weeks at Boston, where she was the guest of Mrs. Gannett Wells. In spite of long-continued hoarseness, and the nervous excitability resulting from a close succession of engagements, she visited schools and prisons, gave addresses on India, on Education, on Reformatories, expounded to 'experts' the principles of prison discipline, attended the meetings of the Social Science Association and the Unitarian festival, and was still ready to devote every available hour to private society. Old friends in the Antislavery cause, with Mr. W. L. Garrison at their head, and new friends—of whom the remembrance of Mr. Longfellow was specially cherished—gathered round her with hearty interest and affection; and sometimes some long forgotten act of kindness served for introduction. 'Dr. 'Buckminster Brown,' she noted, 'asked me if I remembered 'sending a lithograph of a fossil elk some thirty years ago by 'Mrs. Lee, the authoress, to a lame boy in Boston. It was 'he. "Thou shalt find it again after many days."'[1]

At the end of May she left Boston for New York, breaking her journey at Hartford, to stay with some family connections, Mr. and Miss Wells. It pleased her thus to feel that she was welcomed by kindred in the New World. There, as in Boston, an invitation was at once forwarded bearing the signatures of the chief citizens, with the earnest request that she would deliver an address on Prison Reform. She had only one day at her disposal; it was a Sunday. The pulpit of the largest church in Hartford was immediately offered her. She was unwilling to lose a valuable opportunity; she was also unwilling to depart from the customs of her education and her country. But her reluctance to seem to assume a function not belonging

---

[1] Most people who do acts of kindness by the way, forget them afterwards, and Mary Carpenter certainly never thought of taking count of hers. On one of her homeward voyages through the Red Sea, the child of a passenger in the fore-part of the ship was dangerously ill. She persuaded the ladies in the cabin to forego their share of milk, which was administered to the sick child, who gradually recovered. Some years afterwards, her brother Russell was conversing with a fellow-traveller in a railway carriage about India, and mentioned his sister's name. His companion related this incident, and added that he was the child's father. But when it was reported to Mary Carpenter, she had wholly lost remembrance of it.

to her, yielded before the trust that she was acting as befitted a disciple of him who came 'to seek and to save that which 'was lost,' and she consented to speak in the evening. In the morning she worshipped quietly with the Baptist congregation to which her friends belonged. In the evening all the churches but one were closed, and a vast assembly filled the Center Church. 'Her eloquence,' it was said in one of the papers the next morning, 'was the eloquence of a con-'secrated conviction, and of that perfect familiarity with her 'theme, which gave to all she said the highest interest.'

New York, with all its wealth and magnificence, failed to stir her enthusiasm. ' Gigantic city,' so ran her memorandum, 'rich and immense, but without soul or poetry.' The same programme of soirées, addresses (this time in two churches—though not on Sundays), and visits to institutions, was repeated. Both Sing Sing and the Tombs[1] filled her with horror. The chief novelty was the Bible House, ' where ' whole Bibles are printed in two minutes. Women were ' employed in almost every department. The institution very ' large and wonderful.' Then followed a day or two of quiet on the Hudson, first in one home and then in another, while she rested her soul in the glory of beauty round her, and took pleasure in finding herself ' in the classical scenes of the War ' of Independence.' She would willingly have lingered among friends and sympathisers, but she was obliged to hasten on, under the guidance of her host of New York, the Rev. Dr. Bellows, to Virginia, to be present at the celebration of ' Commencement,' at the Hampton College for coloured people. Of this a brief notice came in a letter from the next resting place.

TO MR. HERBERT THOMAS.

Philadelphia, June 17th, 1873.

I had a poor voyage to Virginia, there being a head wind, but we had very pleasant people on board, and it was happy to land on that shore, the scene of such awful struggles (Monitor, etc.), and think that the slaves were free. Dr. Bellows and I, with a lady from the Sandwich Islands, were at the house of General Marshall, who had been also there. In the

---

[1] Two of the prisons. Sing Sing is thirty miles distant from New York, on the Hudson river.

evening (Wednesday), there was a baptism and Lord's Supper for the students and others. Dr. Bellows and I joined them. It was a most affecting occasion. Close by was a cemetery for the soldiers, with a fine granite column, erected by Miss Dix, very affecting in the moonlight. The proceedings of the next day's 'Commencement' you will see in a paper which I shall send. We were all deeply touched at seeing these young men and women so well ordered and intelligent, who had been in the very lowest condition. General Armstrong is a very noble young man who deserves help. We proceeded by night boat to Baltimore, and thence by rail to Washington, where my time was well occupied in seeing the fine public buildings. In the evening I took a ride with the Hon. C. Sumner. It was very interesting.

At Washington she enjoyed the escort of General Eaton over the great buildings devoted to the various departments of public business, while General Howard conducted her over the Howard University, and her old friend Mr. Frederick Douglass uttered a few words of introduction before she rose to give an address 'in sympathy with the coloured people.' It was nearly midsummer, but she was not to be deterred by heat or fatigue, and resolutely went on to Philadelphia to fulfil a request from the Board of State Charities, and expound the principles of ' Reformatories for the Young, and Prison ' Discipline.'

Philadelphia, June 19th. —Thursday morning. Felt it prudent to remain at home in the lovely country house, resting quietly, and thinking of my evening lecture. Many friends called on me at the town house as arranged, whom I thus missed.—Afternoon. Drove through the extensive and beautiful park, which is very varied, and overhangs the river. It is preserved for the public, and will, when finished, unite the charms of nature and art. Tea in town. Dr. Wines arrived, and informed me that I was advertised to lecture at Newark, New Jersey, the next evening. It had been arranged by him without my knowledge. Telegraphed to Mr. Page my regret that this was simply impossible. Very full attendance at the lecture notwithstanding the great heat.[1] Had felt it difficult to arrange the lecture, on account of the different principles held in Philadelphia, but I got through pretty well.

---

[1] One of the reports next morning described it as 'absolutely ' sweltering.'

The friends at Newark, however, were not to be disappointed, and the traveller found an opportunity two or three days later for pleading her cause. At last she was free to make her way to Montreal, where she met her brother Philip for the first time for eight years—eight years in which so much had happened. But there was not much time for the private intercourses of family life ; excursions on the St. Lawrence, inspection of Gaols, addresses in Sunday Schools and Churches, followed in quick alternation. The state of the City Prison excited her into something like anguish ; ' the very worst I have ever seen,' she observed in her memorandum-book. Two days after, the Mayor and the City Council assembled to hear the result of her investigations, and she did not shrink from laying her opinion before them in the frankest terms. The evil was so grave that it demanded earnest efforts for its amelioration, and before she quitted America she forwarded the following letter to the Governor of Canada.

TO HIS EXCELLENCY LORD DUFFERIN, ETC. ETC.

Boston, Mass., July 28th, 1873.

MY LORD,
          It is a source of much regret to me that I have not had the opportunity I had hoped for of having an interview with your Lordship during my stay in Canada, as I was anxious to confer with you on various subjects in which you know I am deeply interested.
          I have been exceedingly shocked by the condition of the gaol at Montreal. It is the very worst I have ever visited. I had a conference with the Mayor and the City Council about it ; and my statements were fully endorsed by gentlemen who were well acquainted with the facts. I also regretted to find that there was no Protestant Reformatory in the Province. The English Acts have been introduced, and there seems a willingness to carry them out, but as yet no practical steps have been taken. I also visited the Kingston Penitentiary,[1] which is under the management of an excellent warden. There is, however, serious evil to the prisoners, and inconvenience in the management, arising from the small size of

---

[1] Here she gave an address to the prisoners in the Dining Hall. Her eldest nephew, W. L. Carpenter, when going over the same Penitentiary in June, 1879, found that her visit was still remembered by the warden, and also by many of the prisoners. The cells which she criticised are now only used for sleeping.

the cells, which are less than three feet wide—such as would not be tolerated in any gaol in England.

I have sent a full report on these subjects to the Minister of Justice. I fear that there is great ignorance existing in Canada as to the principles of Prison Discipline; and that consequently many of the gaols may be in bad condition. I trust that you will soon feel at liberty to enter into this most important subject. I have devoted a large proportion of my visit to the United States to the subject of Prison Discipline, which is now attracting the attention of many influential and enlightened men; and I shall take the liberty of sending to your Lordship anything I may print on the subject.

It has given me great pleasure to hear how highly your Lordship and Lady Dufferin are appreciated in Canada. With my best wishes for your continued success, I beg to remain,

Yours respectfully,
MARY CARPENTER.

LORD DUFFERIN TO MARY CARPENTER.

Government House, Ottawa,
December 18th, 1873.

MY DEAR MISS CARPENTER,

I am very sorry that I have not sooner been able to reply at length to your letter of last July which reached me while I was travelling, but I need not assure you that I have given the subject of it my very gravest consideration, and have taken every opportunity of impressing upon my Government the reprehensible state of affairs it discloses. Indeed, my Minister of Justice acknowledged to me that the Gaol at Montreal was in a condition that could not be defended, and I trust that ere long you will find that very great improvements have been effected.

I cannot conclude without expressing my admiration of your courage and devotion in facing with such energy on behalf of our prisoners the difficulties which so few would encounter. I was sorry to miss you, but I hope on your next visit I may be more fortunate, and it will give me great pleasure to welcome you, and to talk over freely the subjects you have so much at heart, and in which you have already done so much good.

Yours sincerely,
DUFFERIN.

The condition of the prisons was not the only subject which awakened Mary Carpenter's interest in Canada. In a discussion at the meeting of the Social Science Association in Liverpool, 1876, on a paper by Mr. F. W. Chesson, Secretary to the Aborigines Protection Society, she gave the following account of an Indian community.

Three years ago I was on a visit to Montreal, and was desirous of learning something respecting the North American Indians. I learnt that there were few or none of the aborigines in that part of Canada, as the natives had intermarried with the soldiers, and they were, therefore, a mixed race. Most of them were Roman Catholics, and lived in small villages along the river St. Lawrence. But I was informed that at Brantford, near Lake Ontario, there was a school connected with the Reservation of the Six Nations, and I visited it. These Six Nations had originally a large hunting-ground assigned to them by the British Government; but their enlightened leader, thinking that the possession of so large a territory would encourage their wild and roving propensity, and prevent their civilisation, induced them to sell a large part of it to the British. As there was a difficulty about the investment of the money, they were made, as it were, wards of the Government, the interest being divided among them half-yearly, a political agent residing near them to watch over their interests. They hold a solemn assembly, or pow-wow, at certain times, when they vote the expenditure of this money for making roads, erecting useful buildings, schools, etc. They are gradually improving; all but about 600 are Christians of different denominations, and these are Theists, believers in one Great Spirit. Intoxicating drinks are, as much as possible, kept from them; and, so far from showing any tendency towards extinction, they are gradually increasing in number. The New England Company, which was established about 200 years ago, is directing its efforts towards improving this interesting settlement. It was a boarding-school, established and supported by them, which I visited. The Indians are indisposed to exertion and to industrial work. This last was, therefore, made a special object with the young people, and an experienced master had just been obtained from England. The youths and girls looked intelligent, and were making fair progress when they had mastered English, and the scene was a very interesting one. The quality of the instruction is proved by the fact that one of the masters is an Indian who had been educated in the school. Near the schoolhouse is a church, the first that was built in Canada. Queen Anne presented to it a silver communion service, which was buried during the wars. They are very proud of it. The Ten Commandments had recently been freshly painted in the Mohawk language; one of the scholars, who was our guide,

was unable to read it, being more familiar with English. The
master regretted that this school was very seldom visited by
strangers, or received any recognition. A few books or
presents would be an encouragement to the pupils and
gratifying to the teachers. This was a very interesting visit,
and I hope that this brief mention of it may lead others to
visit the settlement.[1]

After her labours in the States and in Montreal, Mary
Carpenter spent a few days with her brother Philip and his
wife at Niagara, and in other excursions ; and then turned
southwards once more to prepare for her return to England.
Visits at Newport and Boston rapidly exhausted the
remaining days. Her journey had been one of considerable
fatigue, and she had never felt in complete possession of her
usual strength. Nevertheless she looked back upon it with
increasing satisfaction. At every fresh place she had been
received with the warmest hospitality, and the attention
paid to her opinion had been a means of help and strength
to her. 'This is my last Sunday in the United States,' she
wrote on July 27th, 'and I am thankful to believe that my
' coming here has been of far greater use than I expected.
' I have not done much for India, but I have awakened
' attention to the dreadful state of the Prisons, and enlisted
' different persons to take the matter decidedly in hand.'[2] A

---

[1] Writing to the Rev. R. L. Carpenter in October, 1877, Mr. Chesson
said : ' I have too long delayed sending you the enclosed resolution
' expressing the deep regret of the Committee of the Aborigines
' Protection Society at the lamented death of Miss Carpenter. We
' shall never forget or cease to feel grateful for the practical interest
' she took in the Indians of Canada and the United States. If I
' mistake not, one of her last speeches was delivered in the discussion
' which took place on a Paper on the Education of Native Races
' which I read at the Liverpool Social Science Congress. I am sure
' that those who were privileged to listen to her remarks on that
' occasion, will long retain a lively recollection of her clear and
' forcible exposition of the Indian question in Canada. The labourers
' in this good work are so few, that it may with perfect truth be said
' that in this case her loss is irreparable.

[2] The results of her observations and her suggestions for reform
were embodied in a Report addressed to Dr. Harris, Corresponding
Secretary of the Prison Association of New York, and in a Paper
entitled ' Suggestions on Reformatory Schools and Prison Discipline
' founded on Observations made during a Visit to the United States,'
communicated to the Prison Congress held at St. Louis in 1874.

few notes of the impressions left upon her friends may serve
to supplement the actual record of her travel.

Boston, September 17th, 1877.

I am very glad she is to me a personal memory. How
well do I remember her great grey eyes, so slow and wise, yet
so kind sometimes, settling down on me, in two or three
evening talks in her own house; and a strange childlikeness
that came round her lips in certain smiles. She quite surprised
me by her kindness of invitation and of writing after I came
home; but that I always took for a kind of family faithfulness
to American friends, and I supposed I came in vicariously for
a share of her old gratitude to Joseph Tuckerman and Henry
Ware, and men whom her father knew and loved. Old as she
was to me, she used to give the feeling that I was talking
with *some one's daughter*, her words had so much filial reference
in them. Shall I tell you that when she came to America, I
was a little disappointed that she seemed so much more the
missionary than the guest; but doubtless I was expecting
her to be *not Mary Carpenter*, and her errand-earnestness
showed that we really had *her* with us. It was a part of her
life's faithfulness, and that which made her life's fruitfulness.

New York, October 27th, 1877.

I recall your sister's visit in my own house very freshly.
Her union of enthusiasm for all that was good and holy with
patience of labour and persistent hope was a rare combination.
She had, too, a great deal of humour under her solemn earnestness, which relieved it of its otherwise oppressive weight. I
have seldom known so lofty a soul, so steadily sustained, or a
fire that burnt so fiercely, yet so long, and with such benignity
in its heat. It will ever be a grateful recollection to us that
we knew her thus domestically. Such visitants leave something heavenly and holy behind them. The love she showed
the memory of her sister, Mrs. Thomas, must be very grateful
to all who knew that beloved and precious woman. I recall
her with continued gratitude and admiration. When I parted
with her the tabernacle was already bright with excess of
light, and looked ready to be consumed as she escaped from it.

MR. W. R. WARE TO THE REV. R. L. CARPENTER.

Milton, July 20th, 1877.

She deserved everything that personal kindness could do for her, and needed it, I am sure, more than she would admit, or than many people would have suspected. The day before she sailed for home she seemed quite nervous and depressed, almost unstrung; and it has been the greatest pleasure and satisfaction to me ever since, that I was able, by taking her out to Cambridge, and showing her a number of things which she cared to see, to dispel the clouds, and give her what she again and again declared was one of the pleasantest and most interesting days she had had since her arrival. It was this helplessness and dependence, so curiously in contrast with her courage and self-reliance in affairs, that endeared her greatly to those of us who saw her most intimately; this and her gaiety and love of fun and nonsense, in which she seemed to me younger and younger every time I saw her; and I feel quite sure that she grew more free and unconstrained in these respects as her fine quality grew riper and more mellowed.

MR. W. R. WARE TO PROF. J. ESTLIN CARPENTER.

She was suffering greatly from nervous sensibility, the consequence, perhaps, of the fatigue and excitement of travel in a more stimulating climate than that to which she was accustomed. I was more than ever impressed by the delicacy of her physical organisation, by the singular combination she presented of a firmness and almost hardness of purpose with a feminine lightness of touch and a shrinking from the rough encounters of ordinary life, which, though seemingly quite out of character, gave her a grace and charm which those who experienced it can never forget.

MRS. GANNETT WELLS IN THE 'CHRISTIAN REGISTER.'

She had a wonderful faculty of separating the various parts of her work; and both in this country and abroad, each one with whom she held a conference felt that the particular business under consideration was her only one.

She formed a National Indian Association to promote her cherished objects; and whilst in Boston established a branch society, for her broad spirit made charity international. Some of us may remember her address on India; it was more than an hour and a half long, yet given without any notes. Was

this an indication of approaching age? Pleasant welcomes
were given her here by specialists in various departments;
but the elder Unitarian ministers and the prison reformers
received her warmest greetings. Men came from many States
to consult her.

She quickly saw excellences in our institutions, and reluc-
tantly pointed out our deficiencies. Severely simple herself,
she deprecated the lavish expenditure in some of our charitable buildings, as the same amount otherwise expended would
have benefited a larger number. Luxuries are not needed, she
argued, to help the self-respect of the criminal or the recovery
of the sick.

Her English loyalty was conspicuous. Her photograph
album of the royal family with some of their autographs; her
letters from the children of her beloved Princess Alice; the
recollection of the hamper that the Princess had put up for
her on her departure from Hesse-Darmstadt; the interview
with her Queen, and two or three slight gifts from Her Majesty—one a Scotch pebble bracelet [1]—were to our American
eyes oddly valuable. When in Boston, she never but once
trusted that album out of her own hands, and then on an
emergency, to a most careful friend.

She was very simple in her tastes and habits, and yet
most precise in the hours and frequency of her meals, that
thereby her physical vigor might be maintained. When here,
she would see friends all the morning, address a meeting in
the afternoon, and go out to dinner in the evening; but twice
between times must come the fifteen minutes' rest and the
beef tea. One evening, when two or three gentlemen had
each an appointment with her, she said to the first, after the
business part of his visit was ended, 'I think that is all you
'need of me, sir;' and, bowing to the puzzled man, went to
obtain a few minutes' rest, before the arrival of her next
visitor. Afterwards speaking of it apologetically, she said,
'I must do so, or I should accomplish nothing.'

She wanted all to be interested in Reformatories, yet
appreciated the intellectual and æsthetic work of others. Few
knew how strong and able were her own capacities for such
work, nor how keenly she loved science and nature, whilst
her religiousness shone over all she did. She was practical
and keen in all matters of business and domestic economy,
and observant of people's ways. After a dinner-party given
her by Mrs. Howe, the first word she uttered on her return
was not one of enjoyment of the noble men and women she
had met, but the exclamation : 'How elegant was Mrs. ——'s

---

[1] This had been a gift from the Queen to the Princess Alice, who
took it off her own arm to clasp it on Mary Carpenter's.

lace!' She had the aristocratic fondness for real old lace.
Another time, Lucretia Mott and Mary Carpenter were to
meet each other. Mrs. Sargent's parlors were filled with
guests talking to one another or to Miss Carpenter, when a
soft hush fell on the company, an opening was gently made,
and Lucretia Mott glided in. Mary Carpenter felt the movement and broke from her circle, bowing low before our
Quakeress, who in turn seized the offered hand and bent over
it; whilst no word of introduction broke the reverent silence
that fell on our hearts.

Many emulate Miss Carpenter's sympathy, patience, and
hope, and laboriousness; but not all her intelligence and comprehension of philanthropy. It was her *knowledge* that gave
her power, and her gentle tact that held as friends those who
were forced to believe in her principles.

The home life during the autumn of 1873 brought back
again the cares which Mary Carpenter had left behind, and
she found little opportunity of relief. The meeting of the
Social Science Congress at Norwich gave occasion for a paper
on the 'Treatment of Life-sentenced Prisoners;' and, in
reply to the question, ' How can Education be brought to
' bear upon the hitherto untouched portions of the popula-
' tion?' she again urged her plan of Feeding Industrial Day
Schools, in which every month's experience gave her
increasing confidence. Visits from Dr. Guillaume and a
native gentleman from Madras, Mr. C. Sabapathi Iyah, gave
variety from anxious thoughts; and she wrote resolutely to
her sister Susan on December 28th : ' I fear that I have been
' getting into a morbid dwelling on painful things; but I
' buried all my troubles under Christmas holly, and am free
' from them. But since I lost my Anna, I have felt a sort
' of unmooring of heart, except when absolutely engaged in
' definite objects.' As the last hours of the year ran out,
it was to this dear memory that her heart turned with
unspeakable yearning : with all its experiences this was
inseparably connected.

December 31st, 1873.—'The year has passed away!' Its
trials, its efforts to do the Father's work, its griefs, its pain,
its desolation, its struggles, its weakness. I wonder at times
how I have been borne through it. Yet it has had its joys,
its consciousness of greater power and talents than I previously knew that I possessed, to do the work assigned; its

treasures of work and of sympathy ; some *very* glorious scenes
of nature which are a treasure for ever to me, the Hudson, the
St. Lawrence, and Niagara.   Still more, the certainty that I
have been permitted to sow some seed which may bear fruit.
I receive an increasing amount of confidence in my experience
and wisdom.   I have made many valuable friendships.   My
Father, may I consecrate all to Thee !   I thank Thee for all
Thou permittest me to do and be.   Touch my spirit with Thy
grace.   May all pride and self-esteem be fused in the love of
Christ, my Lord !.   May the spirits of the blessed ones, last
and tenderest memory, my darling Anna,—art thou near me,
my Anna ?

O Father, strengthen, soften, and guide me !   In prayer for
all I close the year 1873.

CHAPTER X.

THE WORK CROWNED.
1874—1877.

'Thoughts of Fate, and of Life,
And the end of it all,
Of the struggle and strife
Where few rise, many fall:
Thoughts of Country and Empire
Of Future and Past;
And the centuries gliding
So slow, yet so fast;
Old fancies, yet strange,
Thoughts sad and yet sweet,
Of lives come to harvest,
And lives incomplete;
Of the lingering march,
Of the Infinite plan,
Bringing slowly, yet surely,
The glory of man;
Of our failures and losses,
Our victory and gain;
Of our treasure of hope
And our Present of pain.
And, higher than all,
That these young voices teach
A glowing conviction
Too precious for speech;
That somewhere down deep
In each natural soul
Sacred verities sleep,
Holy waterfloods roll;
That to young lives untaught,
Without friend, without home,
Some gleams of a light
That is heavenlier come.'

Songs of Two Worlds.

CHAPTER X.

THE WORK CROWNED.

1874—1877.

THE opening of the year 1874 found Mary Carpenter again at home in the midst of her customary occupations. A new object, however, was now added to thoughts that seemed already to have range enough, as the condition of the prisons in the United States and in Canada was drawn within the scope of her purposes. In the States, indeed, she could do no more than make her voice heard, and enforce the truths which she had expounded by constant correspondence, and by paper after paper addressed to Congresses held from time to time in different cities. But Canada was a possession of the British Crown, and influence might be brought to bear upon the Home Government ; so the memorandum of matters of public concern which took her to London in April includes 'Day Industrial Schools,' '*India*, Prisons, and National ' Indian Association,' ' *Canada*, Prisons, and Indians.'

Nevertheless, these larger interests could not fill the place of the personal affection for which, since the death of her sister Anna, she had never ceased to yearn. No change of scene could obliterate memories wrought into her very being; no fresh exertions could bring any equivalent for the sound of the voice that was still. She found occasional relief in the rare opening of the heart which she permitted herself to the sympathy of friends with whom she had been drawn into close relations by their common work.

TO MME. OLIVECRONA, STOCKHOLM.

Bristol, May 5th, 1874.

My American journey brought many sources of interest. I was quite astonished at myself in my power of public speaking on the great principles and objects which constitute my life. I am very glad to have been, and hope I sowed some seed which may spring up some day. But I have no idea of going again. It was, however, something to have made personal acquaintance with Sumner and Agassiz, and to have sketched Niagara at a respectful distance. But that journey did nothing towards filling the void caused by the departure of my sister Anna, my loved companion for sixty-two years. I shared all my thoughts and pleasures with her. She was so proud of all the kindness shown me, and every success that attended my efforts! There is no one who cares for me as she did. You can imagine the loss! Excuse this personality. But you know that I am *essentially* a woman. I have, however, many blessings, and I am most grateful for the affection shown and felt towards me by many.

Mary Carpenter had, indeed, enjoyed for years a respect and admiration which passed into a deeper and warmer feeling among those to whom the secrets of her inner life were made known. She had sacrificed much that she might have *been*, in order to accomplish a work which she felt it was given her to *do*. Of this the outer world knew nothing, and she was too often regarded only as the living embodiment of principles to be reiterated with unceasing urgency. Even as such, however, she was a power; and so beyond the limits even of her own labours—and these were broad enough—the support of her name was widely sought for many kindred movements of philanthropy. The progress of the Higher Education of Women she watched with a constant interest; she felt that her own training had been directed by a mind of rare wisdom, and not one element in it could have been spared. The systematic study of language, of literature, of science, of philosophy, had given her a variety of culture which had proved of the utmost value to her in unexpected ways; and every effort to supply a loftier guidance to capacities which had too long remained undeveloped, seemed to put in a positive claim upon her aid. Seldom could she be induced to speak on any subject in which she was not an active worker. But on this topic she possessed a large store

of observation and experience ; and these were always at the
service of the leaders who were striving to carry out through
a wider range principles of education with which she had
been familiar since her earliest years.

The great social aims of temperance, purity, peace—
everything which affected personal character—likewise com-
manded her earnest help. The Temperance cause had from
the first enlisted her ardent sympathy ; and her advocacy of
it, especially when she realised its importance for India, never
ceased. To the movement for the repeal of the Contagious
Diseases Acts she early gave emphatic countenance. She
was in India when the Ladies' Protest appeared, which
roused attention to the subject throughout the kingdom ;
but the opprobrium which was cast by a portion of the
Press on the women who dared to agitate the question,
did not deter her from joining with Mrs. Butler, Mrs.
Harriet Martineau, Miss Nightingale, and other ladies, in
signing an appeal for the formation of the Ladies' National
Association, the object of which, they said 'involved
' not only the personal rights of our sex, but the morality
' of the nation.' She subsequently became a Vice-President of the National Association (for persons of both sexes),
and bore her testimony by attending meetings of these
societies. The efforts of those who were working for repeal
engaged her heartiest interest. 'A gigantic insult to the
' female sex,' she wrote to her sister-in-law, Mrs. R. L. Carpenter, in September, 1872, ' is being offered by legislators
' to us, and *legislators must remove it.* Immense progress
' has been made in this short time in educating the public
' mind, and we have every reason to be thankful that so
' much has been done. The noble true-hearted men and
' women who are standing up for the degraded and oppressed,
' *must prevail* in the end ; and the true position of women
' be asserted. You know I sympathise with them and with
' you most warmly.'—Another time her view thus was con-
cisely stated. 'The question is whether the two sexes are entitled
' to equal rights, or whether one is created for the use of the
' other. This once settled, the rest follows easily. Granting
' medical necessity for stamping out a disease, then *any law*
' *to effect this must affect both sexes equally.*' When a Committee was formed in Bristol for securing the repeal of the
Acts, she so far departed from her usual reserve in reference

to social objects not directly connected with her own work, as to become a member of it. Near the end of her life she presided over a meeting in the oak drawing-room at the Red Lodge, when an address was delivered by Mrs. Steward, of Ongar. At its close, Mary Carpenter spoke of Mrs. Butler with deep respect, dwelt on her courage and devotion, and urged all present to aid her in the cause, saying that ' it was ' one that every woman of mature age ought to feel bound to ' assist.'

Her peculiar sense of womanliness rendered her at first unfavourable to the claim for Women's Suffrage. It was somewhat remarkable that she who so well knew the importance of legislation, who had herself done so much to direct it in certain channels, should be indifferent to the power of a vote. She felt, however, that her influence had been of far greater effect than if she had been merged in the crowd of Bristol citizens. Sometimes she would playfully evade the difficulty by saying 'I don't talk about my rights, I take ' them;'[1] or she would declare that she had all the rights which she wanted, given to her. But her attitude on this matter gradually changed. As early as 1867 her attention had been forcibly called by Mr. J. S. Mill to the importance of the duty of voting;[2] and the subsequent course of legislation as it affected women, deepened the impression which his words produced upon her. She could not, indeed, be at first induced to give more public advocacy than was involved in signing a petition for the suffrage; as one invitation followed another to take part in, or preside over, meetings for this and other social objects, she felt compelled to reserve her time and strength for the special purposes to which her life was dedicated; but in her last years she frequently expressed her belief that legislation would not be established on its true basis, until women had the power of voting on the same terms as men; and only a short time before her death she made a brief speech at the annual meeting of the Bristol and West of England Society for the Promotion of Women's Suffrage, expressing hearty sympathy with its principles.

[1] This was a reminiscence of Mrs. Jones, of Seneca Falls. See p. 159.
[2] See Appendix.

The time which was saved from the discussions of general
philanthropy, was only devoted all the more earnestly to
the special objects concerning which Mary Carpenter felt
that there must be no delay. Among these the most pressing
was the recognition of the Feeding Industrial Day School. In
April, 1874, she was urging it upon the Duke of Richmond;
and the next month she was again in London, at a Conference on the working of the Industrial Schools Act of 1866,
where an afternoon session was devoted to the consideration
of her scheme. Her persistence was, as usual, winning
converts by degrees, and each fresh adhesion inspired her with
new hope. Once more in Bristol, she began to lay her plans
for Parliamentary action, and wrote to the venerable Sheriff
Watson, who had carried out a similar scheme in Aberdeen
thirty years before, with a fresh note of encouragement. ' I
' have conferred with many M.P.'s and Lords in London,
' chiefly Tories (they are best in *this* work), and we think
' there must be a short Act for certifying the Feeding Indus-
' trial Day Schools by the School Boards. It is too late to
' try this session; but I am preparing the way, and there
' will be a regular campaign at Glasgow, when I hope we
' shall get the Social Science Association to take it up.'

The campaign was fought and won. The subject of her
paper was, ' How far is it desirable that the Industrial
' Schools Act should be extended to Feeding Industrial Day
' Schools ?' ' I did not go to the opening meeting,' she
' reported afterwards, ' as I arrived late, was rather tired,
' and had my field day on Thursday. That was a most
' satisfactory one. In the Repression of Crime Section, of
' course, the question could be understood better than in the
' Education Section.' Three days later came the triumphant
exclamation, ' The Day Industrial Paper has converted
' all.'

Her success at Glasgow brought her further confidence,
which was amply justified by the increasing importance of the
School in St. James's Back. Changes in the neighbouring
streets, however, had long been threatening it, and now she
received notice that the City authorities would require for
their improvements the whole of the playground and part of
the yard. New premises had therefore to be found, and
early in 1875 the school was transferred to the lower part
of the Workmen's Hall close by. It was not without regret

that Mary Carpenter quitted the place consecrated by so many happy memories : but the expression of feeling was checked by the necessities of action ; and within a week or two she was again in London, seeking the co-operation of former fellow-workers like Lord Shaftesbury and Sir Charles Adderley, and laying her case anew before the Duke of Richmond. With the aid of the Rev. Sydney Turner[1] proposals for a ' Bill to provide for the proper Education by ' School Boards of Neglected Children ' were drawn up, and these were afterwards embodied in the draft of a ' Bill to ' enable School Boards to establish Feeding Industrial Day ' Schools.' Copies of these were widely circulated, and the plan was slowly gaining a hearing from the leaders of educational opinion. ' I have read attentively your draft ' Bill,' wrote the Right Hon. W. E. Forster. ' The evil is ' clear enough, and I do not doubt that for it your plan will ' be to a great extent a remedy. In fact your experience ' proves this. The question remains, could any publicly ' elected body work your plan without encouraging parents ' to get their children fed out of the rates ? I must confess ' my fear on this point is not removed, but I should like to ' see your Bill brought before Parliament, and well discussed.' No Parliamentary champion had, indeed, yet been found ; but Mary Carpenter's tenacity was not to be baffled. She was well accustomed to waiting, and though years were precious now, she would not lose heart. To Sheriff Watson she still turned, sure of his sympathy. ' I am glad Glasgow ' is stirring. I went to London in February, and saw the ' Government, and have great hopes of getting an Act. If ' the Government will not take it up, they still are not ' opposed, and I have hopes. . . . I have no one to rely ' on, and am single-handed. But I shall go on fighting the ' battle of the Children.'

Parallel with these efforts ran the vigilant activity for India. The want of any attempt to introduce what she believed to be a simple and true Christianity, had for a long time caused her real pain. She was profoundly convinced that India would ' some day acknowledge Christ, the well ' beloved, as *her* beloved Lord and Master, and also that ' she would never free herself from the cruel bondage of

---

[1] H.M. Inspector of Reformatory and Industrial Schools.

'caste and superstition until she had learnt from Christ
'that we are *all* children of the same Father, and fellow-
'heirs of immortality.' She looked with deep regret on the
tendency to undervalue Christianity, which she thought she
discerned in those of her own country, who, 'perhaps with-
'out knowing it, owed everything good in them to its
'influence.' But she felt the position to be very different in
India. There she thankfully hailed anything which loosened
the hold of idolatry, and was ready to accept what she could
get. Wherever she could, she had worshipped with the
members of the Brahmo Somaj ; and it was characteristic of
her modes of religious thought that she was not anxious to
weaken the trust of the Native mind in what they regarded
as their ancient Revelation. Nevertheless, she longed to
establish a church of the faith which had been her perpetual
inspiration and support ; and in the autumn of 1874 she was
ready with a plan for a Unitarian Mission, to be fixed in the
Presidency of Madras. It met, however, with little response,
and was at length set aside, but not before her failure to
awaken an enthusiasm like her own had caused her deep
disappointment. Something, however, she must do, and she
reverted to the teachings which had been her earliest guide.
Her father's faith, her father's example—these she would
offer to the young enquirers of whom she had met so many
in India. It mattered not to her that a generation had
passed away even in her own country, that new questions
had arisen, that none else could share her filial reverence. A
little volume of *Sermons* was prepared,[1] and with it an
abridged edition of the *Memoir of Dr. Carpenter*, originally
drawn up by her brother Russell. ' My object in publishing
' this Memoir,' she wrote to him, 'is to present to the reader
' a devoted Christian life, showing how it was formed, the
' influence it had, the results it left ; and I especially desire
' to show that pure Christianity, not dogmatic theology, was
' its moving spring.' To these she added a reprint of her
Last Days of Rammohun Roy. The three books were
intended to express her idea of the manner in which
Christianity might be presented to, and accepted by, the
educated Hindu mind.

---

[1] These were selected from a larger volume, published after
Dr. Carpenter's death, and entitled *Sermons on Practical Subjects*.

This, however, was but one of the occupations of the winter of 1875. Her house was always open to her friends, and especial welcome was given to any visitor from India. She delighted in hospitality, and one traveller after another came to share the 'plain living and high thinking' which made her home so remarkable. Even the friendless and unknown found immediate access to her. The following narrative of Mr. K. M. Shroff, of Bombay, who had heard one of her addresses as a student in the Elphinstone College, relates his reception on landing in Bristol in January, after a journey through the United States.

MR. K. M. SHROFF, TO PROF. J. ESTLIN CARPENTER.

Bombay, January, 1879.

Friday being the day for the despatch of the Indian Mail, she was busy as usual with a lot of letters to different friends in India. However, she despatched the work by afternoon, gave me a warm reception, inquired about my visit to the Western Hemisphere, gave out her experiences of a visit to the same country, dined with me, and, though she was not in very good health at the time, went with me to the Red Lodge and to the Industrial School in the neighbourhood, with great effort, and even took me over to the Museum and the Library personally, introducing me to various friends. I marked with pleasure that wherever she went she was welcomed and loved heartily by people, and particularly by children. During my week's stay in Bristol she gave me opportunity of delivering a lecture on India, and to say my say. Every day of my stay she asked me to dine ànd sup with her, and had long conversations with me till ten and eleven p.m. It was at this time that she drew my attention first to the National Indian Association for our country. Then the Association had been in existence five years. She spoke to me despondingly, that her benevolent efforts were not responded to by the people of Bombay; and she said she was sorry nobody could work to get a few subscribers to the Journal in my city, and that the few friends she had written to answered that nothing could be done in that line. She then appealed to me whether I would undertake the work on my return to Bombay; she furnished me with letters of introduction to some principal citizens in this city, promised that she would keep up an active correspondence with me, and give me hints, provided soon after my return I worked for it in Bombay. I at once took up the idea, and promised her to carry out her wishes by my humble efforts; and I thought that though others had failed, I should do something in the matter, when such a person was taking an unusual interest. I am glad to say my endeavours met with success, and then I wrote to her, that although I had secured some subscribers to the Journal, nothing could be done towards forming a Branch unless she came out to India, and influenced some European residents to take up the matter. She agreed with me, and came out to India in October of the same year. We had several conferences in Bombay after her arrival, and, with the assistance of those whom I had impressed with the importance of her work, we opened a Branch; and although I should not take to myself all the credit, I must honestly say that the Bombay Branch of the Association, which is in such a flourishing condition, and has the largest number of subscribers and members, owes to a great extent its origin to my efforts, and is the result of my visit to Bristol.

I cannot close this subject before I have mentioned one more point. On the morning of my departure from Bristol, after a week's stay, when I went up to her to bid her good-bye, I found to my great astonishment and delight, that she had a box ready for me, which she insisted upon my accepting. She said that it contained toys, children's books, and other fancy articles, which I should present to my sisters and brothers on my arriving in Bombay. Not only this. She had ready for me, wrapped up in a piece of paper, a piece of Christmas cake, which she said would be of use to me in my few hours' journey by the train; and under no consideration would she allow me to refuse these articles. These little facts are in themselves nothing, and I would not think them worth mentioning; but what struck me most was that in the preparation of all this, as I marked, there was a sort of motherly affection in that heart that was universally tender to all who came in contact with her; and she especially felt for the men, and more particularly for the uneducated women, of our country.

The appeal of Mr. Shroff for the personal aid of Mary Carpenter in India in carrying out the objects of the National Indian Association, found the purpose already formed. Five years had passed since her last visit. During this time she had been steadily endeavouring, by means of the Association, to make the wants of India known, and to create public opinion in favour of social reform among the Natives themselves as well as in this country. She had gained the support of H.R.H. the Princess Louis of Hesse, who had become the President of the Association; the Native Princes, anxious for the spread of Western civilisation in their dominions, gave in their adhesion to its objects, by the side of the late Governor of Madras, and the former Lieut.-Governor of Bengal. The time was now come when another tour might enable her to secure a hearing such as even she had never received before.

The movement for Female Education had been slowly making progress, in spite of apparent failure here and there. Of the three Female Normal Schools established in the Presidency capitals, that at Calcutta had been given up after nearly a year's trial, in consequence of want of adequate support; but a small Girls' Boarding School had been established by private effort. The School at Madras had proved successful, and was in active operation. The Bombay Normal School had been discontinued after the death of the mistress; but another had been established at Poona under an experienced teacher. At Ahmedabad the Government had established a Female Normal School; and a Native gentleman had erected premises for it, including a residence for the Lady Superintendent, and a boarding-house for Students. The Nagpore Normal School had been discontinued on account of serious evils, but another had been commenced at Jubbulpore. At Hyderabad (Sind) a lady had been appointed Superintendent of several small Day Schools, and the success of this had led the Government to establish a Normal School under her direction. These efforts were all directed to the training of Teachers, and were independent of the ordinary Girls' Schools which were springing up in increasing numbers. There was much to be done in studying them, as well as in examining the general progress of the whole movement, and noting its influence on the elevation of women.

Prison Discipline had also engaged the attention of the Indian Government from time to time since Mary Carpenter's last visit. The practice of the different local governments, however, was by no means uniform; no attempts had yet been made to reduce to a minimum the variations arising from diversities of climate, of the habits of the people, the character of the criminal classes, and other causes; and the question which Mary Carpenter had always propounded, viz., how far the general features of English gaol discipline were applicable to the circumstances of India, had never been seriously considered. The field was yet open here, therefore, for further work.

Two other subjects had also been prominent in her mind ever since her first journey : she had never ceased to urge the necessity of establishing Reformatory Schools in India ;[1] further, the condition of children employed in the Factories which were now rising in various parts of India had been strongly brought before her, and a Factory Act appeared necessary for their protection. ' Think much of ' those poor oppressed children in the cotton factories,' she wrote to Mr. Shroff in January ; ' keep them in your heart, ' as I did the poor delinquent children a quarter of a ' century ago, and never rested till an Act was passed to ' place them in a proper position.' Their case, too, must be laid before the authorities at home. ' I have been twice in ' London,' she reported to Dr. Strasburger, at Warsaw, in July, ' each time endeavouring to move Government about ' Indian Reformatories, and a half-time Factory Act for ' India, in both of which I have been successful.[2] In the ' matter of the Day Industrial Schools, the Government— ' Committee of Council on Education—seemed to listen ' favourably, but do nothing as yet.' Legislation was, in fact, already in preparation for the establishment of Reformatory Schools in India, and a Factory Commission was appointed at Bombay. But there was still abundant room for her energy, in expounding the best method of developing Reformatory principles in India, and in collecting information on the employment of children in different parts of the continent.

How the time passed in these London visits may be gathered from one of the notes in which she enumerated a day's diversions.

---

[1] One of her latest public utterances had been a Paper at the Glasgow Congress of the Social Science Association, October, 1874, on ' Reformatory and Industrial Schools for India.'

[2] Lord Shaftesbury also called attention, in the House of Lords, to the employment of women and children in the Bombay Presidency.

TO MR. HERBERT THOMAS.

London, June 6th, 1875.

I had a most successful day yesterday, and one to be remembered. First I drove to Marlborough House, where I found the Princess [of Hesse] still looking quite altered since her sorrow, and rather worn with excessive engagements. She was most kind and affectionate, and begged me to come and see them again. The Prince of Hesse came in and was very cordial. She gave me portraits of herself and the children, just taken. Then I went to Aunt M——, and told her all particulars; and then drove to Sir Walter Crofton's for early dinner at half-past one, where I stayed in full talk till half-past six ; returned to dinner at William's,[1] and then went to Dr. Leitner's, where I met many interesting persons, among them an Indian official who had had charge of a Thug establishment. He gave me most curious particulars of the religious feelings which they have in entering on their horrid work. They now take to poisoning instead of strangling. Dr. Leitner showed me some wonderful sculpture which he had himself dug up in India; quite of a Greek type, of the age of Alexander the Great !

There were many reasons, then, connected with the progress of social reform in India, which combined to make it desirable for Mary Carpenter to visit it once more. But besides these she felt again that some change was necessary. The loneliness of her home had become insupportable to her. Her absorption in her work had obliged her for many years to avoid ordinary society, and her friends feared to intrude upon her busy hours. There was no sister now to pay the daily visit of affectionate care ; so it often happened that she passed whole days in solitude, broken only by intercourse with her different school officials. And even among these, in spite of the strong attachment by which she often bound them to her, she could not help feeling herself still alone. ' Persons who have such powers of organising and administer- ' ing on a large scale as she had,' wrote an American friend, who had seen all her operations in Bristol—' and women ' more than men—cannot easily adapt themselves to the ' wants and wishes and ideas of others. The very clearness ' of perception and decisiveness of conviction which make

---

[1] Her eldest brother, Dr. W. B. Carpenter.

' them a power in their own sphere, isolate them also from
' their immediate friends, so that they live apart from them,
' amid separate interests and indeed in a different world. No
' daughter or sister could have been more loving or beloved
' than Mary Carpenter. And few persons have ever found in
' their own family so warm and intelligent a sympathy and
' readiness to help as she found in hers. But she was a
' person who, in what was most important, could not be
' helped very much. She must tread her wine-press alone.'[1]
This had been the necessity of her work for years ; and
successive bereavements had made the inevitable solitariness
still more solitary. No one was by her side on whom she
might pour out the treasures of personal affection which she
constantly longed to lavish. It was not enough to work for
India ; it could only be reached through the post. Destitute
children might feel the thrill of her deep love, but it was
afar off, for they could not gather by her own fireside. The
wide correspondence which linked so many social movements
to her quiet study, brought to her desk a load of needs and
sorrows from both hemispheres, which was sometimes more
than she could bear. The perplexities and the griefs of her
friends frequently awoke a sympathy keen even to anguish,
and keener for the impotence forced on her by the distance
that arrested her helping hand, or dulled her voice of counsel
and cheer. Many a night was passed in sleeplessness during
the winter of 1875 ; and a temporary pause in occupation
often surprised her into tears. There seemed to be but one
remedy for her complaint of desolation : ' I cannot go on as
' I am, alone ; it is wasting my life-power.' Some young life
she must have near her to cherish, that in these dear cares
she might forget the strain of her anxieties. But she could
not frame such a scheme for the simple gratification of her
own wishes ; it must promise help to some one else. So her
thoughts turned to India, and the family at Barahanagur, of
which one child already bore her father's name, and another
had come into the world in her own house. The two eldest
of the group she now proposed to bring back with her ; and
the parents, who had had good reason to know how Mary
Carpenter fulfilled her promises, gladly consented.

---

[1] The Rev. J. H. Morison, D.D., in the *Unitarian Review* (Boston,.
U.S.), March, 1880.

This happy vision carried her through the summer months. Amid the activities of approaching departure she took a full share in the proceedings of the British Association for the Advancement of Science, which met at Bristol in August, and then prepared for her journey. On September 16th she sailed for Bombay. ' I go with hope and thankfulness,' such was her utterance three days before leaving home, ' for I can ' feel that much progress has been made since I was there ' first, and that the way is prepared.'

The progress of her journey may be best related, as far as possible, in her own words, drawn partly from her diary and letters home, partly from her Report on Female Education to Lord Salisbury, and partly from other memoranda found among her papers.

TO PROF. J. E. CARPENTER.

Mediterranean, September 23rd, 1875.

I am thankful to say that I never set off on a voyage with more comfort and better hopes. The weather is beautifully fine and calm; we have every possible comfort, and the exquisite sky and sea are soothing and elevating objects of contemplation. Of course it is not very congenial to my nature to have so long a period of absolute inaction ; but being compelled to it, for it is rather a painful effort to me to write at all, I accept it thankfully, after a long period of great mental strain, as a preparation for future work. I give myself up to reading Walter Scott, whom I admire more than ever. Some agreeable travelling companions I have also found to talk to between times. Among them is a Countess G——. All her property having been absorbed in paying her husband's debts, she went to India and engaged in education in the Punjaub. She showed me a book which she said had entirely changed her life and character, as well as that of another friend who was worldly and dissatisfied. It was Mrs. Follen's *Extracts from Fénélon*, with remarks by Dr. Channing; it was a well-worn volume. She had never heard of Mrs. Follen or Dr. Channing, but the spirit of Fénélon brought the Father near to hers, and influenced her life. How would those departed ones rejoice in such results following their labours ! I am glad to renew my acquaintance with the volume, which I have not seen for many years.

TO MR. HERBERT THOMAS.

Red Sea, October 3rd, 1875.

We are in the midst of the Red Sea, out of sight of land. It is of course warm, but not overpowering; and we glide on charmingly in our glorious ship, with no motion but that of the screw, as you will judge from my steady writing. Indeed, this is the first voyage I have taken in which I have been able to write without positive discomfort. When I wrote last, we were entering the Canal. I consider that transit through the desert the one event of the voyage; and I think it worth the voyage to any one who has time and money, simply to go through it. Having heard of it as a narrow canal with mud banks, I was agreeably surprised, on entering from Port Said, to find a beautiful shallow lake on each side of us, and many objects of interest as we passed, e.g., the gigantic dredging-machines, which cost £25,000, to take up buckets of mud and throw them on the bank, also the huge masses of concrete formed of the sand of the desert and lime, etc., which are as strong and hard as stone, and much cheaper, to make the pier. At sunset there was an exquisite glow on these lakes, which we watched till dark, when the ship was moored till morning. The greatest care is needed to prevent these great ships from stranding in the mud, and a special pilot is always on deck. We pay a toll of £1300! It was a wonderful idea that we had Asia on one side and Africa on the other! The next morning the bright sunlight on the blue waters of the Canal, and the winding sandy shores, produced exquisite effects, and I seated myself at the prow and made four sketches during the day, which, with some photographs I bought, will give some idea of this Canal. As Ismailia there is a large expanse of water, and we saw at a distance the palace surrounded by trees. The opening must have been a magnificent spectacle. Afterwards we came to a large lake, twelve miles long, which the Captain had crossed as a desert. It was a depression, and the water rushed in and filled it when the Canal opened on it. I was full of admiration of the genius of Lesseps and this wonderful work, which is *the* work of the century, unless indeed Sahara should be made an inland sea.

She landed at Bombay on October 14th, and, after only a few days' pause, proceeded to Kurrachi, where she was most kindly welcomed by Sir William Merewether. Visits to schools and gaols, public meetings and receptions, occupied nearly a week, and then she hastened on to Hyderabad, to be the guest of Mr. S. N. Tagore. There she arrived on the

morning of the 27th, and her friends lost no time in testifying
their respect.

Between Kurrachi and Bombay,
November 6th, 1875.

That afternoon I was surprised by a triumphant public
reception, when a beautifully illuminated address was presented to me; and a large table was covered with presents of
silk embroidery, and other Sind manufactures, porcelain,
wood-work, etc.   Hyderabad is a very curious old Mahomedan
capital; it is built entirely of mud, the thick walls being a
protection against heat and cold.   The old Mahomedan fort
commanding the whole city is too much in ruins to be more
used, while the wonderful tombs of the Ameers are a memorial
of a passed dynasty, and a contrast to all the new Schools,
Kutcheries, and other official buildings, which tell of English
civilisation and rule during the past thirty years. . . . I was
worked very hard in Hyderabad, having to give the prizes to
numbers of schools. A Sind play had been prepared in honour
of my visit, the actors being students of the Male Normal
School; and at the end all the Dramatis Personæ appeared,
and sang a piece of poetry, each *line* of which ended with
' Miss Mary Carpenter.'   The Collector, Colonel Wallace,
presided on each occasion, and was very kind. I also paid a
visit to the ladies of the Ameer, who were adorned with
splendid pearls.

Hyderabad, Sunday, October 31st.—9 A.M. Service at the
Gaol, conducted by two Brahmo gentlemen.   About six
hundred, all sitting on mats in a large courtyard. Very
attentive to the address, and all joined quietly in the concluding prayer. My name having been mentioned, the men
thought that I could do something, and about a dozen rose,
begging to be allowed to wear their hair, to have more food,
and to be allowed to pray five times a day. It was explained
to them that they had incurred discipline through their own
fault, and that I could do nothing. A Sunday air pervaded
the place. These services were begun by V. A. Abaji, and
have done much good. A missionary wished a Mahomedan
convert to address them, but they would not listen to him.

From Hyderabad the way of return lay through Kurrachi
to Bombay; but there was no time to tarry; from the steamer
the unwearied traveller hurried to the train, and on the
evening of the day of arrival she left again for Poona.

TO THE MOST NOBLE THE MARQUIS OF SALISBURY.

In Poona my great object was to study the Normal School
which had been carried on for some years previously by Mrs.
Mitchell, a lady of long experience among the Natives, and
who had previously conducted the Alexandra Girls' School at
Bombay for many years. This school has developed the
objects intended very successfully, as far as circumstances
have permitted. On entering, I was surprised at being
warmly greeted in English by one of the young women. I
asked her if she knew me. ' Do I not know my benefactor ? '
she exclaimed. ' Nine years ago you came with Sir A. Grant
' to visit a little school which I was teaching. You encouraged
' me. I was so vexed at not being able to understand you that
' I determined that I would learn English.' I learnt that she
had attended the Normal School at Bombay, and then came
here ; that she had married, but the conduct of her husband
obliged her to live separate ; that she was now receiving a
salary as teacher in the Normal School ; that her two sisters
had followed her example, but had declined marriage ; that one
was a teacher in the employ of a Native chief, and that the
other was a teacher here. During my visit, an English lady,
governess of the Rani of Kolapur, came to the school to obtain
a Native female teacher for the Girls' School at Kolapur.
Beechebai, my young friend, was selected. Mrs. Mitchell had
assembled as many as were acceptable of the students who had
already become teachers,[1] with the children under their care
—some two hundred. This was a gratifying spectacle, and a
striking contrast to the state of female education nine years
ago, when Beechebai's little school, in a small room painted
over with idols, was the grain of mustard-seed from which
this promising work had sprung. There were about twenty
students, all Native women.[2] I heard lessons given to them,
and to the practising School, by their Native Teachers, in a
superior style. An English lady was employed as an Assistant,
but there were no teachers in the School acquainted with the
English system. At Poona I not only became acquainted with
the ladies of some Native families, and received a visit from a
widow lady who has long taken active interest in female education, but on the eve of my departure from the city I met a
large number of Native ladies, who desired thus to indicate to
me their sympathy with my object. About sixty were assembled
in one of the ancient palaces of that remarkable city, under the
presidency of a Sirdar lady of much influence, and who ex-

---

[1] There were twelve altogether.
[2] Among other signs of progress manifest at this visit, she noted
that ' few of the students wore nose-rings ! '

pressed a warm interest in my work. Mrs. Mitchell from the
Normal School attended as interpreter, accompanied by the two
sisters who were working with her. These young Native
ladies were not only able to translate my remarks to the ladies
present, but spoke fluently in English. The meeting was a
very interesting and encouraging one, and indicated great
progress.

Further advance was palpable at Madras, on which she
afterwards made the following notes :

I left Poona for Madras on Monday evening, November
22nd, and reached that city on Wednesday afternoon.

When I visited India nine years before, there was no direct
railway communication between these two important cities,
nor, indeed, between Bombay and the other chief cities of the
mpire. I was therefore obliged to return to Bombay. I proceeded then by coasting steamer to Calicut, passing a coast
thickly wooded with cocoa-nut trees, and then went on from
Beypore, a railway journey of about thirty hours, to Madras.
The country we then traversed was lovely. The first part of
it was rich in tropical productions, the verdant rice-fields just
in full beauty, and cocoa-nuts abounding everywhere. The
general aspect of the inhabitants was also very different from
what I had seen in the other parts I had visited. On account
of the extreme heat they were generally nude, carrying in one
hand a large palm-leaf umbrella, fixed on a long pole, and in
the other, or fixed in a belt, a knife to open cocoa-nuts, which
form an important item in their food. The notices along the
road were now in Tamil and Telugu, with English, instead of
the Marathi and Gujerati, with characters perfectly different.
As we proceeded, our view was bounded by the out-crops of
the mountain-ranges forming the Deccan, and the range of the
Neilgherries, until we approached the more level and cultivated
districts in the vicinity of Madras.

This railway journey[1] to Madras, passing through part of
the Nizam's territory, presents a striking contrast to the other.
A very large portion of the route was barren, and indicated a
rocky table-land thinly inhabited, the scattered cottages indi-
cating extreme poverty ; yet where pains had been bestowed
on cultivation, it was evident that Nature lavishly rewarded
well-directed efforts.

On my first visit to Madras, I had the honour of being the
guest first of the Director of Public Instruction, and then at
Government House. In Madras the Missionaries have long

---

[1] From Poona.

taken a large share in the education. The late Rev. Mr.
Anderson, of the Scotch Presbyterian Church, began the work
in 1837 with a devotion and energy which ensured success, and
won the gratitude of the Natives, who still value Anderson's
Schools. Six years later he commenced Girls' Schools, and
now a large part of the Native female education is in schools
which are under the management of the Missionaries. Mrs.
Anderson established a boarding school for girls of high caste,
a very rare institution, thus preparing them for future usefulness as wives. The Wesleyan Methodists have several schools
here both for boys and girls. They are well attended, the
scholars being evidently attracted by the real kindness and
moral sympathy they receive. In the Girls' Boarding School
excellent needlework is taught, as well as the ordinary branches
of education. Some years after, when visiting the Gaol at
Nagpore, I was surprised to find in the female department
that the convict women were well taught, and instructed in
needlework. On inquiring with astonishment where so good a
mistress had been obtained, I learnt that she had been one of
the pupils of this very school. The Government Schools and
the Presidency College I also visited with very great pleasure,
regretting only that the instruction given was too purely intellectual, without the introduction of science or practical studies.
There were large boarding schools for the civil orphans, and
the military orphans, both for boys and for girls; a large proportion of the inmates were Eurasians, and a painful apathy
appeared to pervade them as to the means of gaining their
future livelihood; the introduction of industrial work into
these schools would have solved many future difficulties. A
visit to the Hospital presented the painful spectacle of patients
unattended by any means to soothe their sufferings. Among
other institutions which I then visited, was a large Native
poor-house for indigent Hindus, established at the cost
of a benevolent Native, and under European management,
called the Monegar Choultry. Everything was admirably
clean and well organised, and everything possible was done
to promote the comfort of the poor inmates. The children's
department only was very unsatisfactory, nothing being done
either for instruction, or to prepare them to earn their
living.

On my present visit I had the pleasure of conveying to
the Normal School a copy of the Queen's *Journal in the Highlands* from her Majesty, with her own autograph, as a token
of her sympathy with this work for the women of India.[1]

---

[1] Copies were also sent to the Female Normal Schools at Ahmedabad and at Hyderabad (Sind).

About sixteen students, Native Christians and Eurasians chiefly, had passed a Government examination. Many Native gentlemen were present, and on another occasion the young Jaghirdar of Arnee accompanied me there, to endeavour to obtain a teacher for the Girls' School which he was about to establish in his State. It was quite evident to me that a great work of improvement had been going on among Hindu women during the last ten years. This had been greatly fostered by Lady Napier and Ettrick during her residence in Madras. She made personal acquaintance with many Hindu ladies; and for one, at her husband's request, she obtained an accomplished English governess, who resides in a bungalow in the garden of their beautiful suburban villa. This lady invited me to be her guest during my stay in Madras, a wonderful mark of progress. Other arrangements had been made for me, but I frequently saw her and her accomplished stepdaughter, and met them in society. Another family received lessons on alternate days from a Missionary lady, and the beautiful hand-writing of these as well as the other ladies shows how well Hindu ladies repay good instruction. I did not see another (in consequence of her illness) connected with the same family, who had actually been in England, and had written in the vernacular an account of her travels. These are striking signs of progress. I was deeply grieved to find that two other Native ladies, who on my first visit were the happy wives of two very superior young Native barristers, and who had led a movement for the training of female teachers and also for Theistic worship, were now widows, and experiencing many of those painful trials which are still the lot of such unhappy women. Even though Suttee is abolished in British territory, we know well, from a recent painful event, that it is not yet abolished in the dominions of Native Princes. The Mission schools were also prospering, and many young ladies were being trained in them to be teachers.—I did not attempt in my short stay to visit all the schools and other institutions which I had seen in my former visit. I was struck, however, with seeing the splendid and well-arranged College, which had been erected near the sea. I was particularly glad to learn that instruction in physical science was to form a part of the curriculum, and that a large grant had been awarded for the purchase of apparatus. Near this was a handsome new Hospital and Medical School. Ladies had been admitted to this, and I was present at an examination of male students with four ladies, who did themselves credit by their ready and accurate answers. But the most interesting feature of the Hospital was the introduction of a system of training skilled nurses, under the direction of a highly experienced lady and her assistant, both of whom had filled similar positions in a large hospital in London. Many nurses of superior position in society are here engaged in actual work, and preparing to train others, to the great comfort of the patients. Another institution is regarded as even superior to this, the Monegar Choultry. To the institution I had formerly seen was now added a hospital, in which young Eurasian women were receiving an excellent training as nurses under the Superintendent Medical Officer. After six months they may obtain a certificate, and then receive further training in the Midwifery and in the Children's Hospital, when they receive a certificate as professional nurses. This is quite a new feature, and Madras is leading the way admirably in an important department of female employment. It is a particularly important movement in a city with a large population of Eurasians, and shows that with proper training these may become valuable members of society. Another important improvement had been made in the Monegar Choultry since my last visit. Industrial training had been introduced into the juvenile department, both for boys and for girls. The boys were taught many branches of manual labour, and were readily engaged in good situations as soon as their age permitted; the girls were taught domestic work, and quickly obtained places in families. Very few children, and those quite young, of either sex were in the Institution; the success of the plan was complete. There are large numbers of Eurasians in Madras, who are a considerable burden to the city. An effort has lately been made which promises to be very successful, and to lead the way to a movement of a more extended nature. This is an Institution to receive by day destitute Eurasian youths, who have no means of gaining a livelihood, and to teach them some skilled industry, supplying them at the same time with two sufficient meals of substantial food. I visited this Trades' School; the young men were evidently greatly improved by the regular food and training they had received, and were learning carpentering, shoemaking, bookbinding, and other manual exercises, with an earnestness which would soon enable them to earn a living. The development of a system of industrial employment both in schools for orphans and destitute children of whatever race, and in industrial Trades' Schools for older youths, would not fail to be of immense advantage in Madras, and generally in large Indian cities.

The next place of sojourn was Calcutta, where business and hospitality were as usual actively mingled.

TO MR. HERBERT THOMAS.

Dacca, December 23rd.

I wrote last on December 17th, and can hardly fancy that it is only six days since, so varied have been the scenes through which I have passed. That evening I dined at Government House. A Mr. Mathews was requested to take me in to dinner, and I felt puzzled what to say to him. He was the next gentleman to the Viceroy, and I was glad to find Captain Baring, Private Secretary, on the other side of me. What was my amusement to find, after a time, that my neighbour was the celebrated Charles Mathews, come out to act, on occasion of the Prince's visit. Next morning I breakfasted with Sir R. Temple. His sketches are first-rate. In the afternoon I gave an address at the Town Hall, Sir R. Temple presiding, on Prison Discipline and Reformatories. At eight I started by train for Goalunda, whence the next morning I proceeded by steamer to Dacca. I had an enthusiastic reception that evening, the Hall being decorated, and an address read to me.

In Calcutta the cause of Female Education appeared to Mary Carpenter to have made little progress since her first journey.

The Mission Schools and the Zenana visiting were in operation as before, but the Bethune School exhibited the same miserable paucity of attendance ; a Normal School had been established by the Government, but had been closed from want of support, and the ladies of the higher classes were even more secluded than before. Not even the Prince's visit could, as elsewhere, open the doors of the Zenana. At one house only was he admitted to the ladies' apartments, and his visit called forth very severe criticisms in the Native papers. Among the Brahmos, however, remarkable progress has been made. A boarding school had been established through the efforts of Miss Akroyd, who had devoted herself to the work with the warm co-operation of Hon. Mrs. Phear, and the help of some English and Native gentlemen. The school was discontinued shortly after my visit in consequence of the departure from India both of Miss Akroyd and of Mrs. Phear ; but it had done a good work ; it had prepared some of the pupils to be intelligent companions to their husbands on their return from England, and some to engage in education.[1]

---

[1] This school was afterwards re-established by Mr. Ananda M. Bose and other Bengali gentlemen, and the Bethune School

Though the Female Normal School established by Government had been abandoned, Babu Keshub Chunder Sen had commenced one in connection with a small Girls' School under his care. I visited it, and found three Native ladies, two of them the wives of Native gentlemen connected with his work, pursuing the higher branches of English studies. Those whom I had seen on my first visit had been making progress in many ways, and had formed a small society among themselves; I had the pleasure of meeting them and conversing with them in English.

Besides these I had the pleasure of visiting three Hindu families where the lady of the house received me in English style, each having become educated in consequence of her husband having been in England. It is quite remarkable how easily these ladies adapt themselves to a new style of living, and learn to speak and even to write our language correctly. I also went to a party at the house of a conservative Hindu family, where we were invited to meet his Honour the Lieut.-Governor, Sir Richard Temple. Everything was arranged in distinguished style for the comfort and recreation of the guests, the quadrangle within the house being temporarily converted into a splendid drawing-room. There were professional singers and performers on the piano; the refreshments were in first-rate style, though our enjoyment of them was greatly diminished by our host's declining to partake of them with us. I hoped that the ladies of the house might at least be observing the gay scene from an upper window, or through a lattice. Some of the English ladies were at last invited to visit them, and after going through many winding passages we found three in a remote room, where they could not see or hear anything of the festivities.

Before leaving for Dacca, I visited the large Central Gaol and the Presidency Gaol. The Industrial work is admirably developed in both of these Gaols, and the prisoners are taught various kinds of skilled labour. But there is no systematic instruction given, and all good results which might have been hoped for are more than neutralised by the system of association at night. When fifty or sixty prisoners of different degrees of criminality are locked up together for twelve hours every night, nothing can be anticipated but the most contaminating influences. In a separate department I saw 150 young men employed separately from the adults, who are necessarily preparing to be adult criminals; while in another compartment were a number of very young boys, some of whom had been

---

Committee ultimately took it into their hands as a boarding department of the Bethune School.

several times in prison, and who were evidently preparing for a life of crime. In Madras Gaol, I saw a boy of ten who was a life convict and in irons! In England a child under twelve may be sent to an Industrial School without the prison brand, whatever offence he may have committed. Sir Richard Temple is very anxious to see a Reformatory established. He presided at an address which I delivered in the Town Hall, on Prison Discipline and Reformatory Schools, thus lending his influence to this important subject.

On my former visit to Calcutta, ten years ago, it would have taken me about a fortnight to reach Dacca, to which city I had received a very cordial invitation. Now, however, one night's railway travelling brought me to Goalunda, which is at the confluence of the two majestic rivers, the Brahmaputra and the Ganges. Viewing them in their ordinary calm state, it is difficult to realise the tremendous force of these great rivers, when swollen by the snows of the Himalaya, and the torrents from the rains. A large railway station, erected at a cost of 30,000 Rs., had been completely swept away by their combined fury.

Dacca was formerly a place of considerable importance as the capital of East Bengal, but it is now in a state of decay. The manufactures of jewellery, muslins, and other articles for which it was formerly celebrated, are declining, and the general aspect of the city inspires one with a sense of departed greatness. There is a grand Mahomedan fort now in ruins, but exhibiting traces of exquisite beauty of architecture, and surrounded with parapet walks commanding a lovely view. Some princesses lie within the walls in magnificent tombs which are allowed to go to ruins, and the very building containing them is not protected from the cattle, which roam undisturbed by any sentries. The Armenian merchants have been very rich and powerful here, but although infusing a good element into the city, their ancient church and tombs rather tell of what has been, than what is. The Native city has not yet been disturbed by attempts to introduce a more sanitary condition, for it rivals some of the worst towns I have visited in unhealthy odours ; but with this condition the Natives are so well contented, that a proposal by the municipal authorities to introduce reform was met by remonstrance and petition from the inhabitants. The moist unhealthy climate appears to deaden their energies, and the rich virgin soil and the forests which border the Ganges for perhaps a hundred miles, remain, I was told, uncultivated and unutilised; nor do the young men of the district who have developed their talents by foreign travel, here find any scope for their powers. The British Government has here, as everywhere, established

schools and a college, built a hospital as well as a gaol, and
established so good a system of municipal government that
when all the English officials, and most of the influential
Natives, were absent on leave, in honour of the Prince's visit
to Calcutta, one young Assistant-Magistrate had the sole
charge of the public order. With all this apparent stagna-
tion, a spirit of enlightenment had been kindled even here,
and for some time a few earnest Native gentlemen had been
endeavouring to raise the standard of public opinion. A
Philanthropic Society had been established six years before
with a view to the promotion of improvement in Social Science,
especially of everything connected with the female sex. An
adult school had been established for Native ladies, and about
a dozen were in attendance, some widows, some married ladies
at the wish of their husbands, and others unmarried ladies
who had passed the ordinary period when Hindu customs
require a young girl to be married. A girls' school with about
forty scholars was connected with this. The simple existence
of such an institution indicates a considerable advance in this
locality; the ladies were allowed much more freedom than is
usual in Bengal, and, as is generally the case, this liberality is
connected with the abandonment of idolatry on the part of
the Native gentlemen who are conducting the movement. A
building has been erected for the worship of the Brahmo
Somaj by an Armenian gentleman of the city, and in it I
heard an excellent sermon delivered by the minister, on the
text ' We walk by faith, and not by sight.'

Christmas Day was spent at Dacca. Amid the memories
which it always revived, the thought of her parents and her
poor were usually uppermost. The year before, she had been
obliged to content herself with sending money for Christmas
dinners : ' I cannot send baskets as my mother did. I also
' make plum-pudding for a few poor people. So I am not
' like Mr. Scrooge ! I rather mourn over the Christmas
' dinners of old, but do my best.' But this time she had
not even this limited opportunity of good-will. ' I felt at
' first rather sorrowful this morning,' she wrote to her sister
Susan, from Dacca, ' that I cannot this time spend our dear
' parents' wedding-day in making many poor people happy ;
' but as my whole journey is intended to do so, I must be
' contented.'

Before the end of the year she was again on her way
back to Calcutta.

TO MR. HERBERT THOMAS.

Calcutta, January 6th, 1876.

I was three days and three nights on a tiresome river steamer, but was glad to get a little quiet, and enjoyed the sight of the grand broad river, pursuing its course just as it likes, encroaching often but fertilising in its course. I made three sketches. After a wearisome night journey on a very poor railway, I arrived two hours late at Calcutta, actually forgetting that it was New Year's Day until reminded. I was fortunately just in time to dress hastily, and go to the wonderful Durbar of the Chapter of the Star of India, of which you will have seen an account in the papers. The quiet grandeur of the British throne was striking, compared with the massive and gorgeous adornings of the Native Princes. One wore on his head poor Eugénie's diamonds. He paid £60,000 for them. I saw and heard the Prince very well. He sustained his position. The whole was splendid and admirably arranged.

The next day, Sunday, was deeply interesting. I went with Mr. Mookerjee to Barahanagur to help Mr. Banerjee to decorate his Hall which was completed for the occasion, a very well built convenient nice building for his workmen. We had a quiet service in it at 12, to open the year, each taking part. I read my father's sermon 'Hope in God.' Judge Phear opened the Hall with prize-giving to the Girls' School. . . .

I have been at a grand soirée at the Bishop's, and an afternoon ball on a man-of-war—*very* gay! I was interested in seeing over the wonderful arrangements of the ship.

Calcutta, January 14th, 1876.

We had a capital meeting of the National Indian Association. We established a Bengal Branch, which met at Belvidere on Monday, Sir R. Temple President, the Bishop (!) Vice-President. I have accomplished all I wanted, set things going, and constantly thought ' In *due* time ye shall reap, *if* ' ye faint not.'

From Calcutta Mary Carpenter travelled rapidly through Benares to Allahabad.

TO MR. HERBERT THOMAS.

Benares, January 20th, 1876.

I left Calcutta with the feeling that I had done very satisfactory work there, and I hope that things are in a train to go

on. I had a pleasant excursion to the Botanical Gardens
before I left. I started at 11 p.m., and my fellow-passenger,
Mr. Wagstaff, who is officially engaged on the line, gave me a
most comfortable reserved carriage. The Begum of Bhopal
was in the train, and her political Agent, Col. Osborne, to
whom Mr. Wagstaff introduced me. This enabled me to have
an interview with the Begum at Benares. She was much
puzzled by my not being a Government Agent, or connected
with any Society, but seems to have had a glimpse of the idea,
and will be a Vice-President of our Association.

I stayed the first day at the Missionary's house, and went
to his Chapel. A high Calvinistic sermon such as I had heard
at Dacca, quite obscuring the paternal character of God, and
giving a claim from the blood of Christ. Quite unscriptural.
This is the Christianity of India, which the people will never
accept. *We* offer them nothing better, to my grief. A young
Deputy-Magistrate told me he had read the Testament several
times, but had found nothing in it like the teachings of the
Missionaries.—I have also seen the Maharajah of Vizianagram,
a noble and excellent man, but still bound by caste. This
town is wholly given to idolatry, and is in a very dead state.
I am now staying at Dr. Macgregor's, the Superintendent of
the Gaol here, which is a very good one, except the sleeping
in association. I give a lecture to-day, and go on Saturday to
Allahabad, when I shall be at Judge Lushington's.

It is very striking to observe the difference between the
North-West and Bengal, even when passing along by rail.
Here all I see is cultivated. The trees are rarely any kind of
palm, but Mangoes, Teaks, Bamboos (very lovely), Tamarinds,
Peopul trees, Banians, etc. Grass eight feet and more high,
useful to tigers for concealment in the jungle, to man for
making fine matting.

TO THE MOST NOBLE THE MARQUIS OF SALISBURY.

Benares exhibited some very interesting and instructive
features. This being considered a sacred city, it would consequently be a very conservative one in the matter of Female
Education. Fortunately, however, the Maharajah of Vizianagram commenced the movement soon after my first visit to
India. This nobleman is deservedly celebrated for his enlightened benevolence, and spends a large proportion of his
income in works of charity. At first the children were paid
for attending school, and a great number came; they discontinued attendance when the payments were no longer made.
His Highness then engaged an English lady of experience and
energy to carry on the schools at his sole expense, which she

has now done for some years. On occasion of my visit I
found that she had four schools in houses of easy access to
the scholars, and in secluded localities, and she had succeeded
in gradually obtaining female teachers only for the scholars.
These were Eurasians, Native Christians, and Hindu women.
These latter were not very efficient, and there was considerable
want of trained teaching in the schools, Mrs. Etherington not
being able to give more than general superintendence. The
simple fact, however, of no males being on the premises was
of very great importance. Not only were there about 500
Brahmin children in attendance, but many widows and
marriageable girls were obtaining so advanced an education
as to prepare them to gain their living by skilled industry.
A remarkable proof of this came before me. The Native
Doctor of the Hospital had a class of about ten women from
the School, chiefly widows, who were undergoing regular
training and instruction for the medical profession. I was
present at one of his lessons, and was much struck with the
readiness and accuracy of their answers. The Doctor found
them quite equal to the male students in aptitude and intelligence in the preparation of their lessons. They were still in
regular attendance at the School.

At Allahabad no Girls' School existed, even among the
Missionaries, which was deemed worthy of a visit. Here
and there a few girls were drawn together by the payment of
a few small coins. Nevertheless, the city was not without
its interests. The note in the diary observes with admiration,
' No smell !   Neat streets !   Good roads everywhere ! '

TO MR. HERBERT THOMAS.

Allahabad, January 27th, 1876.

I have been this morning to see the great Hindu festival
of the Mala, at the Junction of the Jumna and the Ganges.
Hundreds of thousands of pilgrims from great distances flock
here to bathe in the sacred river and make offerings to the
priests. I could not in any way have had an idea of their
idolatry so well as by visiting the Golden Temple at Benares,
and this feast.

Allahabad, Wednesday, February 2nd.—Visited the Fort
and Arsenal, the original building three hundred years old.
A Frenchman carried it out. Akbar's Palace. The Jumna
and Ganges overflow the whole plain below : places in the
walls for mooring boats. Last year the river rose to within

four feet of the bridge. Muddy Ganges flows on calmly and
clearly after receiving the beautiful clear Jumna. A wonderful place. Subterranean passages full of snakes 'jostling
'each other' for room in the rainy season. Enormous depot
of rum for the army. Old guns, etc., to be kept bright. The
Shrine, a long subterranean passage parallel with the Jumna
and under the Fort, with no entrance but through the Fort,
filled with various gods ; at this festival neary 20,000 visited
the Shrine in one day, carrying in offerings, and throwing
flowers on the images ; the Maharajah Scindia, Holkar, and
others, throw in gold coins. Private persons claim a right to
proceeds. One woman complained that she had been de-
frauded of her right to three days, each worth many hundred
rupees.

From Allahabad Mary Carpenter returned to Bombay,
where she felt more at home than in any other city, except
perhaps in Ahmedabad.

Bombay, Sunday, February 6th.—Afternoon, Brahmo Somaj.
New capacious building, capable of seating fifteen hundred.
The members raised £1,000, each giving a month's salary.
This being done, a good piece of land bought and plans made,
they appealed to the public. Native princes helped, the Rao
of Cutch, Holkar, etc., to build a temple to one true God!
They began with five members and soon had seventy : others
attend. The ladies have the galleries, *not screened.* It is
managed by a Committee who choose preachers. The service
is entirely Marathi, some members and ladies not understanding English. They chant, with the leading of a sort of
hurdy-gurdy or bagpipe, the same Marathi chants I heard at
Poona, from the Vedas. There is evidently heart in the thing,
and I expressed my sympathy. M. W. drove me home. He
returned from Baroda, and is now a barrister. He has to
support a widowed mother, to put forward in life two brothers,
fifteen and nineteen, a wife and three children, the former still
clinging to idolatry, and a sister and husband not well off board
with him. He does not complain. Good !
Monday, February 7th.—The Mohurrum. Sacred play of
the death of the Prophet's son and family ; about two thousand
Mahomedans of the Shiah party present, apparently absorbed
in deep grief, many beating their breasts. The aged Ali
Shah is the head of the community,[1] a lineal descendant from

---

[1] The real head of the Shiah community called the Khojas was
[and still is, 1879] His Highness Agha Khan. But in consequence
of his age his eldest son Ali Shah acts for him.

Mahomet, and from the Old Man of the Mountain, 'Assassin.' [1]
He receives a large pension from the Government for his
services. General effect favourable to good feeling, but a
striking contrast to the death of Christ. The other party
carry about ornamental shrines, some on mock elephants,
which they afterwards throw into the sea.

In Bombay, Mary Carpenter observed great advance in
female emancipation during the period since her first visit in
1866. The Parsis had taken the lead in the movement, but
it was still too much under the influence of a conservative
spirit, which confined the education of girls to the Vernacular,
and prohibited English, in all but one of the schools under
their control. On the other hand, the Hindu schools seemed
even to have declined. The model school which she herself
had established in 1870 had been discontinued after four
years, 'as it did not develop a principle.' Nevertheless,
education was spreading among women of a lower class.
Dr. Hunter had opened two classes for the training of Native
Midwives. None were eligible for these who could not read
and write the vernacular; but a number had already taken
out certificates after regular scientific instruction, and due
practice in the hospital.

A fortnight passed away rapidly at Bombay, and it was
time to proceed to Ahmedabad, of which the traveller
afterwards reported in the following terms.

Since I last went there, six years ago, there had been a
great flood, which caused much destruction. Swollen by
heavy rains, the river, which is very shallow, rose to an
immense height, and, overflowing its banks, the water rushed
with frightful force into the city, destroying multitudes of

---

[1] On this name Mr. F. Pincott kindly contributes the following note:
'The word is not English, but is a corruption of the Arabic name
'Hâsan, or Hâsan-es-Sabbâh, a fanatic, who founded a sect in A.D.
'1090, based upon the principle of extending its influence by secret
'murder. The emissaries became a terror to both East and West, for
'no distance seemed too great to shelter a marked victim. Hence
'the crime took the name of the originator of the design, Hâsan or
'Assassin. In the year 1090 he made himself master of the fortress
'of Alamût, on a high hill to the south of the Caspian; and brought
'the neighbouring territory under his sway. He was then called
'Shaikh-al-Jabal, i.e. Mountain Chief, a term easily corrupted by the
'Crusaders into the Old Man of the Mountain.'

houses, and devastating whole districts. Notwithstanding
this disaster, they are going on well in the work of social
progress. A Native gentleman has erected a temple for the
worship of the One God; another has compiled a collection of
hymns in Gujerati from different sources, and it was most
striking to hear how fervently the Native gentlemen joined
in the services when they assembled for worship. A Male
Normal School has long been established; the gentleman
who conducts it has been to England and mastered our system,
and his pupils are being trained on the same principle. A
Female Normal School has been lately erected by a Native
gentleman. In Ahmedabad there is much advance in female
emancipation. A Native lady with her husband met me at the
station on my arrival; and I found that the ladies generally
were permitted to walk about attended only by a servant, a
custom which has not yet been allowed in any other part of
India with which I am acquainted. A short time before my
visit, the daughters of a Native Judge actually delivered an
address on the worship of the One True God to their countrywomen. On seeing the account of this in the newspapers, I
could hardly believe it; but the judge assured me it was
perfectly true, though he had wished the fact to remain
private.

The journey was now extended to Baroda.

Baroda, February 27th.

I find Baroda extremely interesting. It is emerging from
barbarism, and is most fortunate in having so very remarkable
and admirable a man as Sir T. Madava Rao to guide it. I
never saw anything so primitive as the Mint!—They feel my
visit very useful in stating principles and explaining their
working in England. Yesterday I saw a Native procession of
one of those dreadful deified Maharajahs [1] who happened to be
in the city. First a number of men with flags and musical
instruments, then four elephants grandly caparisoned, on the
last of which was mounted the Maharajah in great state; then
a large body of women, looking very happy to be let out on
such an occasion; then five camels carrying his luggage.

Bandora, March 5th, 1876.

I wrote last from Baroda, where I had the constant escort
and kind attention of Mr. Kazi Shahabudîn, whom you must

---

[1] High-priests of a very immoral sect, the Vallabhācāryas. Great
efforts were made some years ago to expose their practices.—Comp.
Monier Williams, *Indian Wisdom*, pp. xlvii. 327.

remember. He has a most responsible situation as Finance
Minister, and has shown wonderful skill, ability, and good
feeling in getting the State finances into some order. He
and the Dewan, Sir T. Madava Rao, work together in the
most friendly manner. There has been the most frightful
and lavish expenditure, and in some cases it is impossible at
present to make alterations, which would interfere with old
charities. The Kazi took me to see the daily distribution of
food. In a large enclosure, in which are temples, shrines, and
large shady trees, anyone who chooses to come may have daily
a quantity of rice and curry, uncooked, to carry away. As
many as 7,500 men, women, and children, come every morning, and are seen carrying away their share. Even persons in
decent circumstances come, and if they have more rice and
curry than they require for their families, they exchange it for
other food, vegetables, etc., with persons who sit selling. It
is said that Kunderao was at heart a Mahomedan, and that he
was daily visited by a priest. He instituted another charity
for the Mussulmans, and built a large commodious place
where cooked food is given out every day to those who like to
come and have a good meal. The better classes of them have
more self-respect, and do not come ; about 2,000 assemble
every day, and eat enough for the twenty-four hours ! They
chiefly live in the 'most low miserable way in hovels, in this
part of the city, which is called the beggars' quarter. On
two days in the month, however, an extra meal is given in the
evening, together with sixpence each, and to have this about
8,000 come under cover of darkness, and they say that £20,000
are thus spent annually, while £10,000 go to the Hindus. I
visited the offices and courts of justice, and was astonished to
find how completely the British system has been already
introduced, though formerly there was nothing regular, and
all the justice was dispensed at the Palace. The prison is in
the most horrible state, the prisoners—murderers and all—
being huddled together in one large yard doing nothing. Sir
T. Madava Rao is doing all he can to bring things into order,
and it is wonderful how much is done. In fact we all think
him the first Hindu of the age.

I gave a lecture there on ' Voluntary Benevolent Work in
' England,' and another on the ' Various Marks of Progress I
' have seen in my Travels in India,' both of which he said were
very suggestive, and would bear fruit in time. The evening
before I left, Mr. Melville invited a party of English and
Natives, and an address was read to me signed by all the
leading gentlemen. Sir T. Madava presented me with 2,000
Rupees, on behalf of the Government, as a mark of esteem, to
employ in benevolent work in India. I was much gratified by
this, but I have since returned it with thanks, not liking to

receive any State money. The Maharani and Maharajah also sent me their portraits. The next morning between thirty and forty Native gentlemen assembled at the station with the Dewan to bid me farewell!

At Surat I had a very warm reception, the good old Juggeevandass having assembled at his house to welcome me between forty and fifty Native gentlemen, and ladies in another room. I was very busy during my short stay in visiting institutions, etc. The city is wonderfully improved since I saw it last, and will probably be more so, for there are constantly fires among the old wood houses. Last night, the Judge, Mr. Birdwood, gave a large party in my honour, of Natives and Europeans. Illuminations outside! I had to go off to the train, and arrived here this morning.

Before quitting India, Mary Carpenter spent a week among the wood-crowned heights of Mahableshwar. There a new subject was brought under her notice, the cultivation of silk.

Dr. Mackenzie, when Superintendent of Dharwar Gaol, had devoted much attention to the rearing there of silkworms, and he showed me a beautiful dress, which had been made from the produce in the gaol. Unfortunately, after he left the place, the thing was dropped, but he had done enough to prove that the culture of silk would be most important to India. Silk can be reared in many places where cotton would not grow; and, from inquiries which I made on the subject, I found that experiments had been made in various directions, which showed that the cultivation of silk could be carried on with great advantage. The gaols are excellent places for making these experiments, the men being under control.

The time had now come for departure, and on March 27th Mary Carpenter sailed from Bombay, bringing with her the two eldest boys of Babu Sasipada Banerjee for education in England under her own care. The results of her journey she afterwards summed up in letters addressed to Lord Salisbury on Female Education, and the Condition of the Prisons, which were laid before Parliament in the next Session.

Four subjects had specially engaged her attention, the Education of Women, Prison Discipline, Reformatory and Industrial Schools, and the hours of labour and the employment of women and children in Factories.

Under the first head she recorded her observations in the following terms :

The general impression I have formed from my present visit to India on the subject of Female Education is a very hopeful one. The idea of education seems increasingly to permeate the masses from high to low. Native chiefs are thinking of the education of their ladies, and a single instance in which they carry this into effect, is more valuable than any mere professions of interest. Native gentlemen of position are in many cases anxious to obtain for their ladies instruction from English ladies. The class of women requiring to obtain a maintenance, find that they can do so better by being educated. I have formed a much higher idea than before of the capabilities of Native ladies, both in acquiring knowledge and in becoming Teachers. There is not the great dread of female education which formerly existed, and altogether the way appears open to rapid progress, if only the conditions necessary to this are provided. These conditions are, in the first place, a good teaching power, with suitable premises and appliances. These cannot be supplied by the Natives, and without them the schools for girls will continue as they have done, without any sensible improvement.

The remedies which Mary Carpenter proposed, were analogous to the methods already employed by the Government in promoting male education. Trained and efficient Teachers must be chosen in England and sent over to India. These might superintend small groups of schools, in which Native assistants could be gradually instructed in the art of teaching. Further, the material already in the country ought to be utilised. There were numbers of educated young women—English, Eurasians, or Native Christians—who would be much better prepared than most strangers, by their knowledge of the vernacular, for entering on the work. Let a proper Normal School be established for them, to which they might be admitted on producing suitable testimonials, and passing the appointed examinations. Lastly, it was in the highest degree desirable that Native women of experience and culture should enjoy the advantage of residence in England, where they would have opportunities of thoroughly studying the English system. Mary Carpenter had herself seen such persons in Poona and Madras, and had informed

the Directors of Public Instruction in Bombay and Madras
that she would undertake, with her friends, to superintend
the arrangements for such students in England. So strong,
indeed, was her conviction of the usefulness of this step,
that she afterwards invited a young Native Christian whom
she had known in Madras, to come and reside for a year
in her own house. But before this could be carried out, she
had herself passed away.

On the subject of Prison Discipline she had kept a
vigilant eye. Visits to the gaols had formed an important
part in the programme at each place of sojourn. She
observed with satisfaction that on one of the points to
which she had directed the attention of the Government on
her first visit, the condition of female prisoners, great
improvements had taken place. They were now almost
universally under the charge of female warders. Sometimes
regular discipline was carried out; in one gaol separate
sleeping cells were provided for them, with immense benefit;
and instruction was given daily. Other evils, however, were
still in existence, on which she collected during her journey
a large quantity of evidence. In Calcutta she had conferred
with the highest authorities on the chief necessities of reform.
At the request of the Secretary to the Indian Government,
before she left the capital, she drew up a paper, in which
she stated the principles adopted by the British Government
in all prison discipline, which ought also, in her opinion, to
be universal in India.

I. That all prisoners should sleep in separation during the
whole term of their imprisonment.

II. That education should be given daily by competent
Native teachers, with moral instruction.

III. That a first stage in all imprisonment should be
passed in separation from other prisoners, day and night, with
unskilled labour, penal dietary, and instruction.

IV. That there should be a system of marks for conduct,
labour, and education, with gratuities for extra work, enabling
the prisoner by his own exertion to rise to greater privileges,
and to obtain remission of sentence.

Suggestions were also made for the adaptation of these
principles to the conditions of climate and character in India,

and for the distinct separation of long- and short-sentenced prisoners.

The best mode of carrying out these and other reforms was early taken into consideration. In the following July a despatch was issued by order of the Governor-General in Council inviting the attention of Local Governments and Administrations to them; and in the spring of 1877 Major Burne wrote from Simla, 'You are, I daresay, aware that a 'Prison Conference has been recently sitting at Calcutta, 'having under its consideration, amongst other matters, some 'of the questions raised by yourself on Prison Discipline.'

At Calcutta, it will be remembered, Mary Carpenter had given an address on Prison Discipline and Juvenile Reformatories. A Bill for the establishment of Reformatory Industrial Schools was then before the Supreme Government; and the Lieutenant-Governor of Bengal had prepared a similar measure for the Provinces over which he presided. Concerning these proposals, she thus drew the outlines of the institutions which she desired to see founded throughout the country.

I will now just briefly sketch the general principles upon which Reformatory Schools are established, because I observe in this Bill it is assumed that such schools are known and understood in India, and yet I still find that some juvenile departments of prisons are called Reformatories. It is very necessary that we should clearly ascertain what are Reformatories. In the first place, there should be nothing of the gaol element in Reformatory Schools, except the element of detention; and that is to be effected, not by walls, bolts, and bars, but by moral discipline. There must, therefore, be free, open houses, where these boys can feel themselves in a home. There must be always a considerable portion of land, for it is found that agricultural work has a reforming influence on young persons. They should learn trades, which would give a development to the muscles. But this labour must not be for the sake of gaining funds, but for the good of the boys. That principle must be generally laid down. We desire that every boy should be also able to make his own clothes. He is then fit for any position in life. I need not say that moral instruction should be given them. These schools should not be large. It has been universally accepted in England that it is better not to have more than fifty or sixty boys in one school—that is as many as can be properly influenced by one head; it is therefore much better to have a number of small

schools in different parts of the country, than one large one.
There is one large school in England, which contains some
hundreds of boys, but in that school there are a number of
separate houses independent of each other though under one
general management, and all working together. Then there
should be as much friendly influence as possible exerted from
outside. Gentlemen and ladies should take an interest in
these schools. It is natural for the female sex to look after
the young, and their influence upon young boys particularly
is very good. Besides this, care should be taken to watch
over them when put out in the world. We put them out on
licence, but we look carefully after them, and if they are not
happy, or doing well, we take them back. If they do well, we
obtain for them a discharge. But at the end of their time,
when they are sent into the world, we still are required by the
Government to give a report of them, to keep an eye upon
them, to correspond with them, and to learn how they are
getting on. These schools are under a separate Inspector,
who has charge of all the Reformatories in Great Britain.
This Inspector requires the managers to give a report every
year : we can thus test the success of the different institutions. I have now given you a general sketch of the subject.

The hopes which Mary Carpenter expressed in Calcutta,
were soon realised. The Bill which she had supported in
her Address was passed by the Indian Council, and became
Act V. of 1876. Two of her objects were thus fulfilled :
children were no more to be sent to prison, and voluntary
effort was to be enlisted in their reform.

On one other question she had never failed to make
constant inquiries, and she had formed decided opinions.
Six years before, she had visited some recently established
cotton-mills in Bombay, and had then pointed out that there
ought to be half-time schooling for the children.   Her
attention was again attracted to the matter by a report of the
evidence given before a Commission appointed in Bombay to
inquire into the management of the Factories.   The employment of children of five years of age and upwards, and the
long hours of labour for the workmen, appeared to her to
involve the most serious evils.   Wherever she went she took
care to ascertain the number of hours of labour, whether in
prisons or in factories ; and she came to the definite conclusion that the protection of adults, both men and women,
and the education of the children, could never be secured

without the enforcement of rules similar to those in operation in England. On this matter she communicated with Lord Shaftesbury before her return home ; and her views were afterwards laid before the Secretary of State for India.[1]

When Mary Carpenter took up her abode again in Bristol in the spring of 1876, she had entered on her seventieth year. Yet few would have suspected that she was verging on three score years and ten, for there seemed little diminution in her physical and mental energy. She was still capable of the same enthusiasm ; the springs of affection were fresh and clear as ever ; and the tenacity with which a principle once grasped was actively carried out, had not a whit relaxed. The home was now brightened with the young faces of her Hindu boys ; her adopted daughter returned from abroad and resided with her ; and the desolation of loneliness came over her no more. Visits to London followed as a matter of course ; Ministers must be seen, and the results of her tour placed before them. The extent of her journey had brought her in to relation with so many new friends that her correspondence greatly increased. The Native Princes who were favouring the spread of female education in their dominions must be assisted with information and encouragement ; and the labours of the Secretaries of the different branches of the Indian Association must be guided and sustained. In the midst of these occupations she found amusement in adorning her house with the memorials which she delighted to associate with the places and the friends whom she might see no more, but never could forget.

TO S. N. TAGORE, ESQ.

Bristol, June 15th, 1876.

I shall quite be with you all in spirit, for I seem more at home in Ahmedabad than elsewhere. Please tell my friends that I much treasure the beautiful little box, etc., that they kindly gave me. I had so many presents in India that I was obliged to have a pretty little cabinet with a glass door made for these precious things, and the door taken off the china closet in my drawing-room to exhibit my larger treasures, chiefly those from Hyderabad. How very many they gave me ! I am quite astonished now I look them over. Do you

---

[1] The agitation thus begun has been since carried to a successful issue. As these sheets pass through the press, it is announced that a Factory Act has been passed by the Indian Government.

remember my picking up the fallen pieces from the Ameer's
tomb? I have had them fastened together so as to make a
complete pinnacle. I have not been able to enjoy as I wished
these recollections of my Indian journey, because Lord Sandon
has been bringing in a Bill on Education which we consider
extremely useless and injurious; and I have been very busy
writing, getting up memorials—in fact, giving my whole mind
to get the Government to understand that neglected children
ought to be educated in a way adapted to their needs.

The Bill introduced by Lord Sandon contained provisions for dealing with children ' found habitually wander-
' ing, and either not under any control, or in the company of
' rogues, vagabonds, disorderly persons, or reputed criminals.'
These it was proposed should be detained for a month in
Certified Industrial Schools, and should then be released
from residence there, but compelled to attend by day.

Mary Carpenter saw at once that the children grouped
together in the Bill constituted two distinct classes. Those
who were found associating with criminals were already in
the magistrate's power, and could be committed to Certified
Industrial Schools.[1] These institutions were arranged for
inmates who could be kept there during long terms. The
whole system of training—physical, industrial, intellectual,
and moral—depended on the perfect regularity and control
ensured by uninterrupted detention. The introduction into
them of a number of day scholars of irregular habits and
from indifferent homes, would seriously disturb the conditions essential to success. Of the other class of children,
who were simply not under control, or whose parents were
neglectful, many might be drawn into the Public Elementary
Schools. There were, however, some, and in the large cities
they amounted to multitudes, who were in so wild and
miserable a state that no ordinary school would be willing
to receive them. For these, Mary Carpenter urged, Industrial Day Schools, with a regular allowance of food, would
ensure the most efficient and the least costly training. Such
schools could be provided at one-fourth, or less, of the

---

[1] The effect of these schools had been such that Mary Carpenter
was able to assert, ' Juvenile crime, as it was twenty-five years ago,
' does not now exist.' The Government Inspector, when visiting the
Red Lodge in 1877, observed : ' We shall not want any more
Reformatories ; the Industrial Schools are stopping the supply.'

expense of Boarding Schools ; the family tie was not broken
by them ; the children could go freely, and were spared the
brand of a magisterial sentence.

This was the substance of a plea which she hastened to
circulate among the managers of Certified Industrial Schools.
She had long been in correspondence with some of the chief
School Boards in the country, and was now able to rally a
large amount of support to her cause.   Her own draft Bill
was laid before the Vice-President of the Committee of
Council on Education, with a letter which showed clearly, as
the Permanent Secretary of the Department remarked,
'what she wanted, and why she wanted it.'   By-and-by
came a friendly note of encouragement : 'Your case and
'views are in good and sympathising hands, and I trust that
'to a great extent *you* will be satisfied.'   At last the victory
was won.   On July 18th Lord Sandon proposed a clause
authorising School Boards to establish Feeding Industrial
Day Schools.   In doing so he observed that 'he did not
'wish to take to himself, or the Government, the credit of
'the scheme itself.   The real credit of it belonged to many
'benevolent people outside the House, and amongst them he
'must mention the honoured name of Miss Carpenter, who
'had tried Industrial Day Schools under disadvantageous
'circumstances, and with marked success.'

So the work of thirty years, since the Ragged School
had been opened on August 1st, 1846, was crowned at last.
Whatever other interests had gathered round her, whatever
new openings had presented themselves for her energy, the
needs of the 'perishing and dangerous classes,' to whom she
had first devoted herself, had never been allowed to fade
from her view.   If the intensity of personal affection for
individual scholars had been exchanged for the wider vision
of the consequences, to the community at large, of neglecting
the wants of a whole class, this had not diminished her
earnestness or dulled her sympathy.   As she looked back
upon her course, she felt that she had traversed unknown
paths under the leading of a light that only revealed one
step at a time ; and she was thankful that she had had no
foresight of distant difficulty, which might have turned the
ever fresh springs of hope into despair.   The words in which
on Christmas Day she reverted as usual to her parents' marriage, are most fitly applicable to herself.

December 25th, 1876.—Marvellous are the ways of the Heavenly Father, guiding His children with an unseen and imperceptible hand, while to their own perceptions they seem to be guiding themselves. If in so doing, they are following with hearts devoted to Him their own best judgment, and the suggestions of the powers and affections which He has implanted in them, all will redound to His glory, in the advancement of the human race, and the coming of the Kingdom of Heaven on earth.

The share which Mary Carpenter took in securing the national recognition of the three classes of schools for which she had pleaded from the first, was thus described by one of her fellow-workers, Mr. G. W. Hastings, President of the Council of the Social Science Association, in an address delivered at the annual Congress in 1877.

I remember well when, some twenty-five years ago, she mainly originated the movement for dealing effectually with the criminal and vagrant classes. It was she who, in conjunction with the late Recorder of Birmingham, Mr. Matthew Davenport Hill, organised the Conferences which laid down the lines of future action on that subject. There were others, like Mr. Baker of Hardwicke and Mr. Sydney Turner, in England, and in Scotland Sheriff Watson and the late Mr. Dunlop, who had much to do with obtaining Reformatory legislation and establishing the first Reformatory Schools. But what was most remarkable in Mary Carpenter was the prevision which she showed on the whole subject. She maintained from the first, and kept steadily in view, the sound opinion that there were three classes to be dealt with—a class of habitual young criminals, who could be treated only by long sentences in Reformatory Schools; a class of lesser criminals and vagrants for whom Certified Industrial Schools were required; and beneath these, and feeding their ranks by a constant influx, a third class of truant and neglected children, infesting the streets of every considerable town, who formed a hotbed in which juvenile crime and vagrancy were hatched. For these last, she recommended from the first a separate class of schools, not so much of a penal as of an educational character; and she always maintained that the war against crime and vagrancy would never be successful, until the whole of this programme had been carried out. Reformatory Schools were established, Certified Industrial Schools followed, the necessary legislation was enacted on their behalf, and Miss Carpenter took no small share in showing how the work could be practically carried on by her admirable Girls' Reformatory at

Red Lodge, with its Cottage for intermediate treatment attached thereto; but it was not till after many years of effort, and not till last summer, that she succeeded in obtaining a Parliamentary enactment for the provision of those Feeding Industrial Day Schools which she believed to afford the ultimate solution of the whole question. I had the honour of acting as Chairman of the Committee which assisted Miss Carpenter in obtaining the insertion in Lord Sandon's Bill of a series of clauses providing for such schools; and it will ever be to me the satisfaction of my life that I was able to assist her last and successful effort towards the object for which she had so long striven. She thus lived to see the completion of her hopes. It remains for others to carry out in practice the last beneficial work she planned; and I have been rejoiced to hear at this meeting such valuable testimony as has been given in favour of Industrial Day Schools, and to find that they are established, or are in process of establishment, in many of the large towns of the kingdom.

To this sketch of the place of Mary Carpenter's efforts in the national movement for dealing with neglected and destitute children, may be added the appreciative words of Sir Stafford Northcote, M.P., in a speech at the Anniversary Festival of the Home for Little Boys (Farningham, Kent), on March 19th, 1881.

There is no one to whom I have felt more indebted for instruction and advice in the great questions of the last twenty-five years in regard to the improvement and education of the young than to Mary Carpenter. No one was so single-hearted, so shrewd an observer, or so indefatigable a worker as she was in whatever she took in hand, and with regard to the particular kind of work done in your institution she took especial interest. She had her share, as every one of us has had, in the promotion of general education, but she was particularly anxious to see education applied to the classes which have need of it in the way that would be most suitable to them, and in the way which would address not only their heads but their hearts. I remember—for we worked together for several years—how anxious she was to impress upon our rulers, who were zealous for the ordinary system of head education, that if they wished to get at all classes, and especially at the classes in whom she felt especial interest, it was necessary that the routine of the Education Department should be somewhat relaxed and somewhat enlarged in order to bring in those who could only be properly got at by industrial training.

The series of institutions in Bristol owing their existence to Mary Carpenter's efforts, was now complete. The Boys' Reformatory School at Kingswood was satisfactorily accomplishing its work under the direction of a Committee. The Girls' Reformatory in the Red Lodge, with the adjoining Cottage, remained under the sole supervision of the foundress. In the management of the Certified Industrial School for Boys in Park Row, which she had established and conducted for two years by herself, and of which her eldest nephew, W. Lant Carpenter, had long been the efficient Secretary, she continued to take an active part. The Girls' Certified Industrial School, located in the Fort, which took its origin at a meeting summoned at her house before her first journey to India, claimed from her no more than a friendly interest ; but she was always ready for counsel and co-operation with its promoters. In St. James's Back, the Ragged School had been merged in the Feeding Industrial Day School, which was now receiving the little wanderers of the class whom she had first sought to draw within the range of her labour and affection. This School was also the centre of the Children's Agency, whose officer was instructed to keep a friendly oversight on the discharged inmates of the other schools, helping them to find work or situations, and visiting them from time to time ; while it was also his duty to seek out the young vagrants, who might be gathered in for regular training and instruction. The upper part of the Workmen's Hall, containing a Lecture Room and Library, still fulfilled the original purpose of providing a place of simple entertainment and innocent recreation. By its side there had arisen the Boys' Home, which offered excellent lodging to between twenty and thirty boys, under due supervision, and was always well filled. Each one of these had been devised to meet a felt want. They were, as her American friend Dr. Morison well said, ' the ' working models of an inventor, which, comparatively in- ' significant in appearance, are yet evolving and testing ' principles and methods which may at last revolutionise the ' conduct of Governments and individuals towards the criminal ' classes, and particularly towards the still larger numbers ' who are in danger of becoming criminals. They were the ' laboratory in which she prepared plans for universal appli- ' cation.' Their success was due to the clear thought which had determined the relative place which each was to fill, and sketched out the modes of operation; to the invincible patience which had presided over their minutest concerns; and to the dauntless determination which had sustained the sometimes drooping energies of fellow-workers, or had resolutely borne the whole burden alone.

Many a visitor came to inspect the group of institutions which Mary Carpenter's long labours had now rendered so well known. None was more competent to understand their bearings than Professor Sheldon Amos, who thus spoke of them in a letter written just after her decease to her eldest brother.

PROFESSOR SHELDON AMOS TO DR. W. B. CARPENTER.

London, June 16th, 1877.

It is a gratification to my wife and myself to remember that only a few weeks ago we had the privilege of spending a good part of two days in a minute examination of every part of your Sister's work at Bristol. We came away with the impression that no description we had met with, even from herself, had done justice to the patient and conscientious elaboration of every detail; and we felt it to be a rare advantage and delight to hear her own logical and exhaustive explanation of the problems which had lain before her, and of their solution. The void her departure makes can never be completely filled, though her example will bear rich fruit. I rejoice to have been permitted to know her with something of the affectionate reverence which belongs to a circle nearer than that of the broad public which will lament her.

The year 1877 opened peacefully on Mary Carpenter's home. Her various lines of work were kept in steady control, for the mind showed no trace of waning powers; and the heart was as warm, and the will as firm, as they had ever been. But a sunny glow seemed to spread all around her. The sense of conflict was over. She could enjoy her labours; the anxieties of earlier days had all passed away; and a mellow sweetness inspired those around her with an indefinable sense of charm which they had scarcely 'felt before, in the midst of the reverence, and sometimes the awe, with which they had followed her. She delighted to devote herself to old friends; she set her house in order; even the shabby books must be repaired; and frequent intercourse with the group of cultivated men and women of Clifton

society brought her many a happy evening hour, when the
engagements of the day were all discharged. A few notes,
spreading through the winter and the spring, show how
thought and feeling played round subjects old and new.

TO MRS. RICKARDS.

(After the completion of her eightieth year.)

Red Lodge House, January 3rd, 1877.

MY DEAR FRIEND,

I was very happy to see you so bright and serene, at
the age which in the olden time before our blessed Lord came
was 'labour and sorrow!' I too am able to 'rejoice evermore.'
The enclosed [1] will give you a little idea of my work last year.
Now I am settling down quietly to work upon it.

I am truly thankful that though I cannot do much walking,
I can get through really as much as ever, in *intensity* if not in
quantity, often in the latter. I am also very happy to have
enough money to do everything I want! Few people can say
that. I am not obliged to stint myself; and I can indulge
myself in making my places and things very nice, and binding
books and making presents, and subscribing to good objects,
and taking journeys! I am only stingy in things which I do
not *like* spending money about! So I am rich. And I have
after thirty years got the Government to attend to the miserable
children!

And so we both thank God!

Your affectionate friend,
MARY C.

TO MISS WANSEY, BRIDPORT.

Bristol, January 14th, 1877.

Let me offer you my affectionate congratulations on having
completed your threescore and ten years, which my brother
tells me is the case to-morrow. We used to think that a very
great age, and look at those who had attained to it as quite
old people, and yet now that I have nearly attained to it, I
feel as young in all powers of true enjoyment and power of
work as I ever did; and had not my darling Anna's departure,
between six and seven years ago, given me a strong warning
of the nearness of the invisible world, I should have had
difficulty in believing myself so advanced in the journey of

---

[1] Papers relating to the National Indian Association.

life.[1] . . . You have, I hope, found out the secret of pre-
serving health which keeps me well, viz. to ascertain the
measure of your strength and not to attempt to go beyond it,
but to accept all the little indulgences which we did not allow
ourselves in younger life, but which are now lawfully our due.

TO AN INSPECTOR OF THE WESTERN PENITENTIARY, NEW YORK.

Red Lodge House, Bristol, February 14th, 1877.

DEAR SIR,
    I have read your report with very great pleasure, and
send some papers of mine which will interest you. I am
surprised and pleased to hear of the new intermediate prison
in New York. Sing-Sing was creating criminals—a fearful
place; and also the Tombs and Randall Island. Day Industrial
Schools should be established in every large city in the States.
Save the children.   Yours truly,
                                  MARY CARPENTER.

    'I send you herewith,' wrote Miss Cobbe, after Mary
Carpenter's decease, 'a copy of her last very characteristic
'letter to me, written only a few weeks before her death. The
'paper she enclosed with it was one in which, if I remember
'rightly, both she and I had been preached at by some
'stupid man in America, for denying the eternity of future
'punishment.'

TO MISS FRANCES POWER COBBE.

Red Lodge House, Bristol, March 27th, 1877.

DEAR MISS COBBE,
    There are some things of which the most clear and
unanswerable reasoning could not convince me!
    One of these is that a wise, all powerful, and *loving* Father
can create an immortal spirit for eternal misery. Perhaps
you are wiser than I, and more accessible to argument
(though I doubt this). I send you the enclosed, which I do not
wish back. Joguth's answer to such people is the best I ever
heard. 'If *you* are child of devil, *good!* But *I* am child of God.'
    I was very glad to get a glimpse of you. I do not trouble
you with my doings, knowing that you have enough of your
own. You may like to see an abstract of my experiences.
                Yours affectionately,
                                    M. C.

---

[1] 'One forgot her age,' wrote Miss Nightingale six months afterwards, 'in the eternal freshness of her youthful activity.'

TO MR. A. W. BENNETT, M.A.

Red Lodge House, Bristol, May 9th, 1877.

DEAR SIR,

I most gladly sign this Memorial.[1] I have long felt that denying a Medical degree to women on the same terms as to men was an act of injustice, and I have regretted that our country should be, in this respect, behind others. My opinion of the great importance to the community of women obtaining this act of justice has been greatly strengthened by my four visits to India, where the fact of the medical profession being confined to the male sex in many cases precludes the other sex from receiving the benefits to be derived from the healing art.

Yours truly,

MARY CARPENTER.

TO PROF. J. E. CARPENTER.

Red Lodge House, May 13th, 1877.

To-day I sat as usual with my girls at the Anniversary service,[2] with ever new interest, and looking down was pleased to see F. with his wife and sister-in-law. At the top of his seat were a gentleman and lady, with a small darling standing on the seat between them, encircled by his father's arm. To this day, after all these long years, such a sight vividly recalls the feeling of my father's arm around me, either at chapel, or when saying a lesson. The gentleman turned round; it was W. L. with his dear little Bertie. It quite drew tears from my eyes when I looked through the vista of years, and remembered the present happy proud father a darling little thing.

---

[1] Addressed to the Senate of the University of London in favour of the admission of Women to Medical degrees. All degrees in this University have since been thrown open to women.

[2] On the second Sunday in May it had long been the custom for all the schools connected with the Lewin's Mead Congregation, the Sunday Schools, the Day Schools, and the Stoke's Croft School, to assemble in the chapel at a special Service. The gathering was further increased by the attendance of the girls of the Red Lodge and the boys from the Certified Industrial School in Park Row; and it was Mary Carpenter's habit on this occasion to quit her place in the family seat, and join her girls in the gallery reserved for them upstairs.

TO MME. OLIVECRONA, STOCKHOLM.

Bristol, May 27th, 1877.

You have indeed with a loving hand traced out the general
history of my work[1] which may encourage and incite others,
and show what any one may do with a devoted and loving
heart, dedicating all its powers to the service of the Heavenly
Father. I am sure that numbers have as much and more
talent than myself, if only they will steadily devote it to the
Father. You will find my poems as they proceed form a little
autobiography, and the spirit pictures which will follow.[2] I
cannot now write any poetry or anything purely literary, but
can only express my experiences or principles in simple language. I am glad to be able to do this orally, and have
just finished a course of six lectures on my last tour, at the
Museum Theatre of the Philosophical Institution, when persons were surprised to hear me speak fluently without notes
for an hour and a quarter.

The lectures mentioned in the last extract were delivered
in behalf of the Philosophical Institution, which had recently
been transferred to a new building. During the fifty years
which had passed since it was established, she had felt a
constant interest in its welfare, an interest largely owing to
the share which her father had taken in its foundation ; and
she rejoiced in the opportunity, now secured by comparative
leisure, of thus adding her testimony to its usefulness.
Moreover, speech about her travels and her work was always
a pleasure to her. ' My lecture went off well last night,' she
wrote. ' My India being so shut up in me, I am glad to
' give out a little.' She was at the same time in active
correspondence with Dr. Wines, Sir Walter Crofton, Mr.
T. Ll. Barwick Baker, and Baron von Holtzendorff, con-

---

[1] In a short biography designed for publication in Sweden and in
Switzerland, and submitted to Mary Carpenter for revision.

[2] Referring to a little volume then in the press for circulation
among her friends, entitled *Voices of the Spirit and Spirit Pictures.*
It contained a collection of her poetical and prose pieces, utterances
of the thoughts which had filled her soul in earlier life which could
not otherwise find expression, and pencillings of the scenes through
which she had passed. She characteristically dated the few words of
preface on the birthday completing her seventieth year.

cerning a second International Prison Congress. She had also entered into communication with the Unitarians of Transylvania, through a Hungarian Student who had shortly before been in England, and she had despatched a box of books as a token of sympathy to the English Conversation Club in Koloszvár.

Among the friends who saw her in her home this spring was Miss Cobbe, who took with her a young niece. ' I ' found Miss Carpenter at Red Lodge,' says Miss Cobbe, re-calling the visit, ' and she insisted on my going with her ' over all our old haunts, and noting what changes and im-' provements she had made. I was tenderly touched by her ' great kindness to my young companion and myself, and by ' the added softness and gentleness which years had brought ' to her. She expressed herself as very happy in every way; ' and in truth, she seemed to me like one who had reached ' the Land of Beulah, and for whom there would be henceforth ' only peace within and around.' [1]

The 3rd of April, 1877, brought Mary Carpenter to the completion of her seventieth year. Greetings flowed in upon her from her kindred and her friends, and gifts and flowers crowned with the observance which she loved, an anniversary that meant so much to her. In brief notes to different members of her family she disclosed the feelings of gladness which rose out of her retrospect of the past, and her hopes for the future.

TO PROF. J. E. CARPENTER.

Red Lodge House, April 3rd, 1877.

This day seems to mark a distinct era in my life, when the great battles are over and I have only to carry on the work to its completion, always, however, watching and working quietly to amend and perfect where required.

I do not look back with sorrow on the past. There have been many painful woundings, and sad bereavements, and great struggles, and dark perplexities, but they have all blended together to make a calm whole of the past, very wonderfully calm when I think of parts alone. As you say, there has been

---

[1] *Modern Review*, April, 1880, p. 300.

one deep moving spirit running through all.   I used often to
desire to have

> 'A soul by force of sorrows high
> Uplifted to the purest sky
> Of undisturbed humanity.'

Now, I do not seek that, or anything, but thankfully take
whatever is given. 'She hath done what she could,' I can
truly say of myself, whatever errors I have fallen into; so I
look very serenely back from this boundary, and hopefully to
what remains of life, the brightest and best of all, and most
full of blessings.

To the united utterance of her nearest kindred she replied
as follows:

Red Lodge House, Bristol, April 3rd, 1877.

My Dear Brothers and Sisters,
    I am indeed greatly enriched this day by the love of
you all, and of your children, expressed so beautifully in the
joint letter from you.   . . .
    I thank you all very much!
    Happiness and gratitude to the Heavenly Father, for
carrying me through so long a life and so wonderfully pre-
serving me, fill my thoughts to-day. I am very grateful also
that we are so united a family, both the beloved ones gone
before, and those that remain. May we ever remain so to
the end!

The end was nearer than she knew. A few weeks later,
on May 24th, came tidings by telegraph of the death of her
youngest brother, Dr. Philip P. Carpenter, at Montreal.[1] To
her surviving sister she turned to give and receive comfort.
'This is a great blow to me, but there is no bitterness; it
'comes from the Father's hand.' 'My heart is very heavy,'
she mourned a day or two later, to Mme. Olivecrona. 'This
'was a love of fifty-seven years, since I nursed my brother
'as an infant. You know what heart sorrows are.' Her
thoughts, however, passed at once from her own grief to

---

[1] Dr. P. P. Carpenter in a different sphere of usefulness had given
his life, not less devotedly than she did, to the service of God and
man. See *Memoirs of the Life and Work of Philip Pearsall Carpenter,
B.A., Ph.D., chiefly derived from his Letters.* Edited by his brother,
Russell Lant Carpenter, B.A.

the venerable aunt now approaching the completion of her
ninetieth year, to whom she was tenderly attached.

TO MISS CARPENTER, LONDON.

Bristol, May 25th, 1877.

You will indeed feel with us all, and with me who am
alone, in this heavy blow. We knew that our dear Philip was
ill, but had no reason to think that he wanted more than the
rest and care which he was getting. I had written to him
begging him to give up his school, and telling him with what
pleasure I should help to make up his income.

Dear Philip! You know I nursed him in childhood, and I
am so thankful that I went over and saw him, and that he
came here in 1874 to see you, and had so happy a time with
us all.

What a happy glorious meeting in the spirit world will he
have had with our dear Father and Mother and Sister, after all
his battle of life! We ought not to grieve for him. But I
know that you will feel this very much, dear Aunt.

She needed now a riper sympathy than the young life
around her could afford. A visit from her brother Russell,
during the first week in June, cheered her with the home
intercourse which she most loved. The talk ranged over
family history, the incidents of work, the failure and success
of different undertakings, of all which she spoke with the
gentleness of one recently stricken and tenderly chastened,
yet with a surprising freshness of life and hope. One day
they visited the Workmen's Hall, where, with her love for
family memorials, she had hung a likeness of her brother
Philip as a youth. At the entrance of the Day Industrial
School, they found two little ragged children, who were
excluded from the midday meal as they had not come in
time. She went to the master and interceded for them.
On June 6th, she gave an address in a little chapel at
Kingswood, on the Religious Aspects of India. Her brother-
in-law, Mr. Herbert Thomas, who was always ready to
support her in her smallest, as in her most serious undertakings, occupied the chair; and her brother Russell closed
the meeting with prayer. The place was crowded, chiefly
with working people. She spoke for an hour, and then
stopped, but her hearers eagerly asked her to continue.
After a pause she resumed her discourse for a short time,

and then consented to give another lecture a week or two later. It was a matter of deep interest to her thus to turn to the scene of her first Reformatory labours ; and her thoughts went back through nearly a quarter of a century to the days when she had regularly visited the Kingswood School, and had traversed the four miles of road, and back again, sometimes in a dirty omnibus, but more frequently on foot. The next day the Committee of the National Indian Association met at her house. Correspondence on its business, impending changes in the staff at Red Lodge, and arrangements for the reception as her guest, at the beginning of July, of the veteran Antislavery advocate, William Lloyd Garrison, were at the same time occupying her thoughts, which constantly tended to dwell on the sad accounts of the illness preceding her brother's death, now received by the post. Many an hour of the night-watch was passed in silent weeping ; and the touch of a friendly hand by day would bring forth anew the flow of grief.

On Thursday, June 14th, she wrote proposing to visit her brother, Dr. W. B. Carpenter, in London, for the furtherance of her Indian work. The day's occupations included the revision of the last sheet of her *Spirit Voices*, now completed. In the evening she chanced to meet in the street near her house one of the Parliamentary friends who warmly aided her in her philanthropic labours, in spite of wide divergence of view in politics and religion. They parted after conversation on public topics, in which she had stated her opinions with unabated clearness of thought and earnestness of feeling. She went into her quiet study, and wrote till a later hour than usual. The nightly greetings were exchanged with her adopted daughter, and when she was last seen it was with a smile upon her face. She lay down to rest and slept ; before the dawn she had passed quietly away.

Four days later, on Tuesday, June 19th, the remains of Mary Carpenter were laid beside those of her mother and her sister Anna, in the beautiful cemetery of Arno's Vale. The surviving sister and the brothers who followed, remembered that it was the anniversary of their mother's death. A large multitude of friends, rich and poor, of all religious denominations, gathered round the open grave, where the flowers

which she had loved in life lay heaped in rich profusion.
The long procession, as it passed through the grounds,
included the girls of the Red Lodge Reformatory, the boys
of the Park Row Certified Industrial School, a detachment
of boys and girls from the Day Industrial, whose tattered
clothes and shoeless feet betrayed too well the vagrant habit
and the home of neglect, and a body of strong and active
youths who had marched over from the Reformatory at Kingswood. Nor were these all. As the mourners filed past the
stately tomb of the Rajah Rammohun Roy, it was noted
that two little Hindu boys walked among them, hand-in-
hand weeping. They were the last self-imposed charge
which Mary Carpenter had undertaken in her work for the
social elevation of the people of India. Side by side they stood
with the scholars who represented her long labours for the
' children of the perishing and dangerous classes ; ' together,
the different groups bore witness to a devotion to the cause
of humanity which knew no restriction of creed or race ;
which rested on the deep trust that ' there is one God and
' Father of all, who is above all, and through all, and in all ; '
and which sought to lift the least developed—nay, even the
most degraded—natures to that new manhood ' where there
' is neither Greek nor Jew, circumcision nor uncircumcision,
' barbarian, Scythian, bond nor free ; but Christ is all and
' in all.'

Four months afterwards, a public meeting was held in
the Guildhall, Bristol, under the presidency of the Mayor,
at which it was resolved to perpetuate the memory of the
late Mary Carpenter by the promotion and extension of some
branch of philanthropic work in which she took especial
interest. With this object an association was formed for the
establishment and support of homes for working boys and
working girls, which should bear her name. The Committee
included the Dean of Bristol and Canon Girdlestone ; Mr.
W. K. Wait, M.P. for Gloucester, and Mr. Lewis Fry,
subsequently Member for Bristol ; with other gentlemen and
ladies of different denominations. Two dwellings were
opened in the course of the next year ; one for Working
Boys, to be conducted on the same method as the Home
built by Mary Carpenter in St. James's Back ; and another
for Working Women and Girls. At the invitation of the
Dean, who had long been her warm friend, a monument was

placed in the west wall of the north transept of Bristol
Cathedral. The tablet is surmounted by a medallion profile,
and bears the following inscription written by the Rev
Dr. Martineau :

SACRED TO THE MEMORY OF

MARY CARPENTER,

FOREMOST AMONG THE FOUNDERS
OF REFORMATORY AND INDUSTRIAL SCHOOLS
IN THIS CITY AND REALM.

NEITHER THE CLAIMS OF PRIVATE DUTY
NOR THE TASTES OF A CULTURED MIND
COULD WITHDRAW HER COMPASSIONATE EYE
FROM THE UNCARED-FOR CHILDREN OF THE STREETS.

LOVING THEM WHILE YET UNLOVELY,
SHE SO FORMED THEM TO THE FAIR AND GOOD
AS TO INSPIRE OTHERS WITH HER FAITH AND HOPE,
AND THUS LED THE WAY TO A NATIONAL SYSTEM
OF MORAL RESCUE AND PREVENTIVE DISCIPLINE.

TAKING ALSO TO HEART THE GRIEVOUS LOT
OF ORIENTAL WOMEN,
IN THE LAST DECADE OF HER LIFE
SHE FOUR TIMES WENT TO INDIA,
AND AWAKENED AN ACTIVE INTEREST
IN THEIR EDUCATION AND TRAINING FOR SERIOUS DUTIES.

NO HUMAN ILL ESCAPED HER PITY, OR CAST DOWN HER TRUST :
WITH TRUE SELF-SACRIFICE SHE FOLLOWED IN THE TRAIN OF CHRIST,
TO SEEK AND TO SAVE THAT WHICH WAS LOST
AND BRING IT HOME TO THE FATHER IN HEAVEN.

DESIRING TO EXTEND HER WORK OF PIETY AND LOVE,
MANY WHO HONOURED HER HAVE INSTITUTED IN HER NAME
SOME HOMES FOR THE HOUSELESS YOUNG,
AND NOW COMPLETE THEIR TRIBUTE OF AFFECTION
BY ERECTING THIS MEMORIAL.

BORN AT EXETER, APRIL 3RD, 1807,
DIED AT BRISTOL, JUNE 15TH, 1877.

With these words, from one who knew the beginning
and the end of her labours, and truly interpreted their spirit
this record of the Life and Work of Mary Carpenter is
brought to a close.

APPENDIX.

Avignon, December 29th, 1867.

DEAR MADAM,

I have to thank you for your letter of August 11th, which a journey of some length on the Continent, and much occupation ever since, have prevented me from answering before now.

If you think that to give your name in aid of the movement for the political enfranchisement of women might be in any degree injurious to the work you have chosen, I cordially agree that those who are working in another department than your own for the public good, have no claim upon you. Whether giving your name to our Society would have any such mischievous effect, you are far better qualified to judge than I am, and I will not therefore venture an opinion. I will content myself with thanking you for the pleasure with which I learn from your letter that you are with us in principle, and with expressing the hope that the time may not be very far distant when the progress of events and of public opinion may remove the obstacles which prevent you from joining us. There are, however, one or two points in your letter in which I cannot agree with you. To take the most important first—most important, because it is a point of moral obligation. You say you do not desire a vote for yourself. I have too great a respect for you not to venture to say, that in my opinion this is a dereliction of the duty you owe to your fellow-creatures. If your vote could affect only yourself, that is to say, if you only could be the sufferer, materially

---

[1] See p. 338.

speaking, from allowing yourself to be governed by others, it would still be a question whether, unless those others govern you with perfect justice, you are morally entitled to forego the right and power which a vote would give you to force them to do justice, and thereby themselves become better moral creatures. But it is not the fact that the possession of a vote would enable you only to protect yourself. Every citizen possessed of a vote is possessed of a means of protecting those who cannot vote, such as infants, the sick, idiots, &c., as well as of a means of helping others who can vote to do good in every conceivable way in which just and provident legislation can affect human happiness. I am deeply persuaded that nothing but a most regrettable absence of thought on this subject can account for, or even partially excuse—for wholly excuse it cannot—the very common neglect of the power of voting which prevails among gentlemen and educated persons. I am certain that a time will come when it will be felt that a man, and I need not add a woman too, because any rational creature, is committing a most gross dereliction of duty when he habitually neglects to make use of this power, conscientiously, and at any cost of labour to himself. He owes it as a return to the civilisation to which he owes not only all the security and peace, all the highest enjoyments of his life, but also the possibility of attaining refinement and moral elevation. He owes it, therefore, by the deepest debt that man can owe to his fellow-creatures. Nor is it less imperative that he should pay it, because if the duty of voting is not fulfilled from virtuous and public motives, the power of voting will be left to people who are induced to exercise it by the spur of selfish interest or ambition. Thus I can conceive no duty, not even the most primary duties of private and personal morality, that it is more absolutely essential to the happiness of mankind that every virtuous and rational citizen should fulfil steadily and carefully. The right of voting is, in my opinion, not only a power to be coveted (although it is a legitimate power, which may be honestly coveted by an honourable ambition), but it is still more essentially an obligation to be dutifully fulfilled.

You will see from this that I cannot agree in the wish you express that the right should rather be '*given* to women by 'those who deprived her of it, than from her own *demand*.' Because, even if any sentiment of generosity should make one feel that it is a more beautiful thing to receive a legitimate power unasked than asked, there can be no generosity and nothing noble or beautiful in waiting to have a duty thrust upon one, instead of asking to be allowed to take it upon oneself for the good of everybody concerned.

In regard to the third point on which you express yourself

uncertain whether the time has yet come for agitation, there are several reasons which concur to make me think it has. In the first place, to agitate for the change in the law is not to obtain it; and therefore, even if any of us think that women are not yet prepared to exercise the suffrage, that will still not be a reason against agitating for it, because much smaller changes than this can never be obtained until after the agitation for them has lasted some time, and the agitation itself will be the most effectual means of preparing people for the change whenever it comes. The great change now taking place in the right of voting among men is, however, the main reason for bringing forward this question at this particular time. The subject of the right of voting is under discussion, and people's minds are comparatively open to receiving new ideas on the subject. If it is true that women ought to vote, it is wrong to lose the present opportunity of spreading the truth as far and wide as possible. By doing so we are only sowing seed to bear fruit in due time, suited to the soil and the climate. We do not dream of reaping the harvest directly.

I have troubled you, dear madam, with a very long letter, but I agree too much with you not to wish to agree still further. I am, dear madam,

Very truly yours,
J. S. MILL.

THE END.

INDEX.

INDEX.

Birmingham Conference on Reform-
atory Schools, *cont.*
1861, 220, 222-4
Birmingham Education Association,
192
Blumhardt, Dr., 266
Borel Orphanage (Neuchatel), 310-11
Bose, Ananda M., 356
Bowring, Sir John, 162-3, 171-3
Boys' Home (in St. James Back,
Bristol), 304, 306, 319, 377
British Association for the Advance-
ment of Science, 48, 165, 212,
217, 348
Brougham and Vaux, Henry Lord,
185, 190
Brown, Dr. Buckminster, 321
Brown, John (abolitionist), 208-9
Brown, Mrs. John (née Mary Anne
Day), 208-9
Brown, W. W. (escaped slave), 102
Buckland, Prof. William, 48
Burne, Maj., 370
Burritt, Elihu, 82, 99
Butler, Josephine, 337, 338
Buxton, Sir Thomas Fowell, 100
Byron, Lady (née Anne Isabella
Milbanke)
death of, 215-16
friendship of with M.C., 67, 162,
182, 199, 237
support of reformatory schools by,
123, 136-7, 164-5, 184-5
See also under letters of Mary
Carpenter

Canada
Indian community (Brantford,
Ontario), 326-7
prison visits of M.C. in, 324-5, 335
Carpenter, Anna (née Anna Penn,
mother)
death of, 180-1
home life of, 1-6, 8, 14
illness of, 39, 46, 155
letters of, 82, 129, 139, 146, 176-7

superintendence of girls' school by,
17, 18, 38, 43
Carpenter, Anna (Mrs. Herbert
Thomas, sister)
childhood of, 2, 3, 6, 11
death of, 301
as instructor in girls' school, 17, 18,
38
as manager of Red Lodge, 168
mentioned, 60, 65, 68, 70, 181,
232, 234, 251, 286, 306, 319,
328, 336
See also under letters of Mary
Carpenter
Carpenter, Joseph Estlin (nephew),
letters to, 312, 329, 342, 348,
381, 383-4
Carpenter, Lant (father)
foreign visitors to, 30-1, 34, 39
Harmony of the Gospels, 316
home life of, 1-5, 341
illnesses and death of, 13, 51-2
memoir of, 341
as teacher and minister, 6-7, 9, 12,
17, 47, 70, 72, 95, 341
Carpenter, Mary
criticism of Parkhurst Reformatory
by, 157-61
death of, 386-8
defense of views on treatment of
juvenile offenders by, 127-35,
224-7
drawing interest of, 50, 67, 74, 314
early education of, 5-6
and early work among the poor, 36,
38, 39
on education of women, 336
effect of father's death on, 57
geological interest of, 19, 48-9
illnesses of, 10, 12, 167, 235, 289
institutions in Bristol founded by,
377
letters of. *See main entry*
literary interests of, 5-6, 8, 9, 14-20
passim, 29, 48-9, 62-73 *passim,*
81, 91-7 *passim,* 101, 104, 169,

* new material added   † new edition, revised or enlarged

PATTERSON SMITH SERIES IN
CRIMINOLOGY, LAW ENFORCEMENT, AND SOCIAL PROBLEMS

* new material added   † new edition, revised or enlarged

PATTERSON SMITH SERIES IN
CRIMINOLOGY, LAW ENFORCEMENT, AND SOCIAL PROBLEMS

* new material added   † new edition, revised or enlarged